# The American Heritage®
# Book of English Usage

*Packaged by Cader Books*

Houghton Mifflin Company
Boston    New York

*Library of Congress Cataloging-in-Publication Data*
The American Heritage book of English usage.
    p.  cm.
  Includes indexes.
  ISBN 0-395-76786-5.  —ISBN 0-395-76785-7 (pbk.)
  1. English language—Usage.
PE1460.A57 1996
428′.003—dc20                 96–6802
                              CIP

DESIGN BY CHARLES KRELOFF

For information about this and other Houghton Mifflin trade and reference books and multimedia products, visit The Bookstore at Houghton Mifflin on the World Wide Web at http://www.hmco.com/trade/.

Manufactured in the United States of America

QUM 10 9 8 7 6 5 4 3 2

# Contents

# Editorial and Production Staff

## Editorial Staff

**Vice President, Director of Lexical Publishing, Production, and Manufacturing Services**
Margery S. Berube

**Senior Lexicographer**
Joseph P. Pickett, *Project Director*

**Managing Editor**
Marion Severynse

**Senior Editor**
David Pritchard, *Social Groups*

**Assistant Editors**
Beth Anderson
Susan S. Chicoski

**Editors**
Ann-Marie Imbornoni, *Pronunciation*
Ann Marie Menting, *Science Terms*

**Contributing Editors**
Joseph M. Patwell
Martha F. Phelps, *Gender*

**Associate Editor**
James J. Boyle, *Science Terms*

**Linguistic Consultant**
Geoffrey Nunberg,
Stanford University

**Citations Clerk**
Lily Moy

**Administrative Assistance**
Crystal Stillman

## Production Staff

**Production and Manufacturing Manager**
Christopher Leonesio

**Production Supervisor**
Beth Rubè

**Database Production Supervisor**
Tom Endyke

**Senior Art and
Production Coordinator**
Margaret Anne Miles

**Manufacturing Coordinator**
Elizabeth McMullen

# The American Heritage Dictionary Usage Panel

**Geoffrey Nunberg, Ph.D.**
*Chair*
Department of Linguistics,
Stanford University

**Edwin Newman**
*Chair Emeritus*
Journalist; lecturer; author

**Elie Abel**
Author; journalist

**Shana Alexander**
Writer

**Cleveland Amory**
Humorist

**Roger Angell**
Writer; editor

**Natalie Angier**
Science journalist; recipient,
Pulitzer Prize

**\*Isaac Asimov**
Writer; Professor of
Biochemistry

**James Atlas**
Writer; editor

**Margaret Atwood**
Writer

**Kathryn H. Au**
Professor of Education

**Louis Auchincloss**
Writer

**\*Ralph Backlund**
Editor; television news
producer

**\*John Bainbridge**
Writer; columnist

**Sheridan Baker**
Formerly, Professor of English

**Letitia Baldrige**
Author; lecturer

**Jacques Barzun**
Writer; literary consultant;
educator

**John Baugh**
Professor of Linguistics

**Carolyn Wilkerson Bell**
Professor of English

**Daniel Bell**
Scholar; Professor of Social
Sciences Emeritus

**Pierre Berton**
Author; historian

**Alton Blakeslee**
Science writer; newspaper
editor

**Harold Bloom**
Professor of Humanities;
Professor of English;
MacArthur Fellow

**Roy Blount, Jr.**
Writer

**Kallia H. Bokser**
Housing consultant

**\*Dwight Bolinger**
Professor of Romance
Languages and Literatures and
Professor of Linguistics

**The Hon. Julian Bond**
Formerly Georgia state legislator; professor

**The Hon. Daniel J. Boorstin**
Historian; recipient, Pulitzer
Prize and National Book Award
Medal

**Charles P. Boren**
Newspaper editor

**Barbara Taylor Bradford**
Writer

**The Hon. William W. Bradley**
U.S. Senator from New Jersey

**Leo Braudy**
Professor of English

**Paul Brooks**
Writer; editor

**Heywood Hale Broun**
Writer; actor; television
newsperson

**Rachel M. Brownstein**
Professor of English

**William F. Buckley, Jr.**
Writer; broadcaster; publisher

**Gabrielle Burton**
Writer

**\*Gerald Carson**
Social historian; writer; advertising agency executive

**Claudia Cassidy**
Writer; critic

**Walter C. Clemens, Jr.**
Writer; Professor of Political
Science

**Pat Conroy**
Novelist

**Claire Kehrwald Cook**
Editor; author of works on
editing

**Robin Cook, M.D.**
Physician; writer

**Alistair Cooke**
Journalist; broadcaster

**\*Roy H. Copperud**
Professor of Journalism; colum-
nist; author of works on
English usage

**\*Norman Cousins**
Writer; editor

**\*Malcolm Cowley**
Writer; editor

Robert W. Creamer
Writer; biographer; editor

Gene D. Dahmen
Attorney

*Marshall B. Davidson
Writer; editor

*Robertson Davies
Novelist; Professor of English
and Drama

Lois DeBakey
Writer; Professor of Scientific
Communication

Vine Deloria, Jr.
Professor of Law, Religious
Studies, Political Science, and
History

Joan Didion
Author

Annie Dillard
Writer; recipient, Pulitzer Prize

William K. Durr
Professor of Education
Emeritus

Andrea Dworkin
Writer

Freeman J. Dyson
Writer; Professor of Physics

Anne Edwards
Biographer; novelist

Gretel Ehrlich
Writer

Louise Erdrich
Author

Carolly Erickson
Historian; writer

Howard Fast
Writer

Frances FitzGerald
Writer; recipient, Pulitzer Prize

Elizabeth Frank
Writer; Professor of Modern
Languages and Literature;
recipient, Pulitzer Prize

Reuven Frank
Author; columnist; formerly
President, NBC News

John Kenneth Galbraith
Economist; writer; formerly
U.S. Ambassador to India

Sara Garnes
Linguist; Associate Professor of
English

Michael G. Gartner
Language columnist; newspa-
per editor; formerly President,
NBC News

Henry Louis Gates, Jr.
Professor of Humanities

J. Edward Gates
Lexicographer; Professor of
English Emeritus

*A. Bartlett Giamatti
Sports executive; educator;
Commissioner of Baseball;
President, National Baseball
League; President,
Yale University

Francine du Plessix Gray
Writer

Linda Gregerson
Associate Professor of English

Patricia Hampl
Writer; Professor of English

The Hon. Mark O. Hatfield
U.S. Senator from Oregon

*The Hon. S.I. Hayakawa
Writer; educator; University
President; U.S. Senator from
California

Mark Helprin
Writer; editor

Oscar Hijuelos
Author; recipient, Pulitzer
Prize, Rome Prize

Douglas R. Hofstadter
Professor of Cognitive Science
and Computer Science; recipient, Pulitzer Prize

Gloria Hom
Educator; consultant; Professor
of Economics

*Paul Horgan
Novelist; biographer; historian;
recipient, Pulitzer Prize

The Hon. Shirley M.
Hufstedler
Attorney; formerly U.S.
Secretary of Education; for-
merly Judge, U.S. Court of
Appeals for the Ninth Circuit

*John K. Hutchens
Literary and drama reviewer

Molly Ivins
Journalist; syndicated
columnist; author

Jennifer James
Cultural anthropologist; writer

Joyce Johnson
Writer; recipient, National
Book Critics Circle Award

*William F. Johnston
Associate Professor of
Communication

Erica Mann Jong
Poet; novelist; essayist

*The Hon. Barbara Jordan
Educator; attorney; writer;
Professor in National Policy;
formerly U.S. Representative
from Texas

June M. Jordan
Poet; Professor of African
American Studies

Alfred E. Kahn
Professor of Economics
Emeritus; formerly Economic
Adviser to the President of the
United States

Roger Kahn
Author; journalist

Justin Kaplan
Writer; recipient, Pulitzer Prize
and National Book Award

**Stanley Kauffmann**
Film critic

**Alfred Kazin**
Writer; Professor of English
Emeritus

**Trudy Kehret-Ward**
Educator; writer

**Garrison Keillor**
Author; radio host

**Elizabeth T. Kennan, Ph.D.**
Formerly President, Mount
Holyoke College

**Walter Kerr**
Formerly drama critic; recipient, Pulitzer Prize

**Jamaica Kincaid**
Author

**Florence King**
Writer; critic

**Maxine Hong Kingston**
Writer; recipient, National
Book Award, National Book
Critics Circle Award, and PEN
USA West Award in Fiction

**Galway Kinnell**
Poet; Professor of Creative
Writing; recipient, Pulitzer
Prize, National Book Award

**Ambassador Jeremy K.B.
Kinsman**
Canadian Ambassador to
Russia

**The Hon. Jeane J. Kirkpatrick**
Diplomat; writer; educator;
formerly U.S. Ambassador to
the United Nations

**Maxine Kumin**
Writer; recipient, Pulitzer Prize

**Charles Kuralt**
Author; former CBS News
correspondent

**\*J.J. Lamberts**
Professor of English; author of
works on English usage

**\*Milton I. Levine, M.D.**
Professor of Clinical Pediatrics;
radio commentator; columnist

**Flora Lewis**
Columnist

**Robert E. Lewis**
Lexicographer; Professor of
English

**Sara Lawrence Lightfoot**
Professor of Education; author;
recipient, MacArthur Prize

**J. Anthony Lukas**
Author; journalist; recipient,
Pulitzer Prize

**\*Russell Lynes**
Writer; managing editor

**Claudine B. Malone**
Management consultant;
formerly Professor of Business

**William Manchester**
Writer; Professor of History
Emeritus

**Robert Manning**
Writer; editor

**Richard Curry Marius**
Novelist; biographer

**Suzanne R. Massie**
Writer; lecturer on Russian
history and culture

**Armistead Maupin**
Author

**Alice E. Mayhew**
Editor

**The Hon. Eugene McCarthy**
Writer; poet; lecturer; formerly
U.S. Senator from Minnesota

**David McCord**
Poet; essayist

**Kenneth McCormick**
Editor

**Mary McGrory**
Journalist; columnist; recipient,
Pulitzer Prize

**Leonard Michaels**
Professor of English

**James A. Michener**
Writer; recipient, Pulitzer Prize
and Presidential Medal of
Freedom

**Hassan Minor, Jr.**
Vice President for Government
Affairs, Howard University

**\*Richard Scott Mitchell**
Mineralogist; educator; writer;
Professor of Environmental
Science

**Jessica Mitford**
Writer

**Lance Morrow**
Essayist; writer; recipient,
National Magazine Award

**The Hon. Daniel Patrick
Moynihan**
U.S. Senator from New York;
formerly Professor of Political
Science

**Cullen Murphy**
Managing editor

**Hon. Maurine Neuberger**
Formerly U.S. Senator from
Oregon; formerly Oregon
state legislator

**Ambassador Thomas M.T.
Niles**
U.S. Ambassador to Greece;
U.S. Representative to the
European Community

**David Ogilvy, C.B.E.**
Advertising copywriter

**Cynthia Ozick**
Novelist; essayist

**Robert S. Pirie**
President and Chief Executive
Officer, Rothschild Inc.

**Alvin F. Poussaint, M.D.**
Clinical Professor of Psychiatry

**Ellen F. Prince**
Professor of Linguistics

Jane Bryant Quinn
Author; journalist; financial columnist

Tony Randall
Actor

William James Raspberry
Urban affairs columnist; Professor of Journalism; recipient, Pulitzer Prize

Edward W. Rosenheim
Editor; writer; Professor of English Emeritus

Judith Rossner
Novelist

Leo Rosten
Writer; social scientist; editor

*Berton Roueché
Writer

Vermont Royster
Writer; educator; Professor of Journalism and Mass Communication; formerly newspaper editor; recipient, Pulitzer Prize

Carl Sagan
Professor of Astronomy and Space Sciences; writer; recipient, Pulitzer Prize

Robert Saudek
Television producer; former Division Chief, Library of Congress; founding President, Museum of Broadcasting

Antonin Scalia
Supreme Court Justice

Arthur M. Schlesinger, Jr.
Writer; historian; educator; recipient, Pulitzer Prize

Glenn T. Seaborg
Professor of Chemistry; formerly Chair, U.S. Atomic Energy Commission; recipient, Nobel Prize

*Art Seidenbaum
Journalist; newspaper editor

Harvey Shapiro
Poet; editor

Elaine Showalter
Professor of English

John Simon
Drama and film critic

Carlota S. Smith
Professor of Linguistics

*Jack Smith
Columnist

Susan Sontag
Writer

Theodore C. Sorensen
Attorney; writer

Susan Stamberg
Radio correspondent

*Wallace Stegner
Writer; recipient, Pulitzer Prize and National Book Award

Shane Templeton
Professor of Curriculum and Instruction

Paul Theroux
Novelist; travel writer

Elizabeth Marshall Thomas
Writer

Nina Totenberg
Radio and television correspondent

Elizabeth C. Traugott
Professor of Linguistics and English

Calvin Trillin
Writer; columnist

Anne Tyler
Novelist; recipient, Pulitzer Prize

The Hon. Stewart L. Udall
Writer; formerly U.S. Secretary of the Interior and U.S. Representative from Arizona

Helen H. Vendler
Professor of English

Douglas Turner Ward
Actor; playwright; recipient, Vernon Rice Award and Obie Award

Calvert Watkins
Professor of Linguistics and Classics

Fay Weldon
Writer

Eudora Welty
Writer

Jacqueline Grennan Wexler
Writer; formerly college President

Tom Wicker
Author; journalist; newspaper editor

Alden S. Wood
Lecturer on Editorial Procedures; columnist on language and English usage

Richard A. Young
Writer; editor; lecturer; publisher; engineer

William Zinsser
Writer; editor; teacher

*We regret that these members of the Usage Panel have died.

# Introduction

This book is designed to inform you about current problems in English usage so you can make intelligent decisions when communicating. When confronted with a choice about a usage, you may ask yourself a number of questions: Has this usage been criticized for some reason in the past? If so, are these criticisms substantial? What are the linguistic and social issues involved? Have people frequently applied this usage in the past, and for how long? What do well-respected writers think of the usage today? You will find answers to these and many other questions in this book.

We have organized the book by subject—instead of presenting a single alphabetical list of entries—so you can explore issues that interest you in some depth. At the same time we have organized individual chapters alphabetically in an effort to make it easy to find what you are looking for.

## The Usage Panel and Usage Ballots

For many of these problems, it is hard to know what to think. People sometimes do one thing, sometimes another. What should you do? To help you decide we present the opinions of the American Heritage Usage Panel, a group of successful people whose work involves writing or speaking effectively. The Usage Panel has been in existence since 1964. The current panel consists of 158 members, of whom 93 (59 percent) are men and 59 (41 percent) are women.

We periodically send the panel members ballots containing usage questions. While the ballots are not scientific surveys in that they are not conducted under controlled circumstances with stringent questioning criteria, they are nonetheless very carefully worded to get useful responses. The examples we use in the questions are actual citations from our files or are sentences that we have adapted from actual citations. For most issues we present a number of examples, giving a specific usage in a variety of different linguistic environments. Many usage issues have a number of faces, and experience has shown us that the panel's opinions about a usage can vary considerably.

Once the ballots have been returned, we tabulate the results and present the findings in the usage notes we write. Over the years we have amassed a valuable collection of information on many usage issues, and we present this information whenever we feel it can help in adjudicating an issue. In fact, with ballot responses going back to the 1960s, we are confronted with the problem of historical perspective. In this book, when we refer to the panel's current opinions, we are using results from surveys done in 1987 and later. The phrase *in an earlier survey* refers to one of the surveys done before 1987.

# Acceptability

In most of our ballot questions we ask the panelists whether they find a particular word or construction to be acceptable or not in formal Standard English. By this we mean not whether the panelists would use a particular usage in their own writing but whether the panelists find that the usage violates some notion of propriety that they consider inherent to formal Standard English. We realize that there are many shades of acceptability. What one panelist approves enthusiastically, another may accept only grudgingly. But in surveys of this kind, it is not practical to differentiate degrees of approval or disapproval. For certain controversial usages we add to the question the option of indicating acceptability in informal contexts. Sometimes we ask panelists to indicate their own preferences or to provide alternative ways of saying something.

Acceptability is thus not really a matter of grammaticality but rather a broader notion of appropriateness. It can entail a sense of aesthetics, as when a panelist rejects a grammatical sentence for faulty parallelism. It may involve a concern about pretentiousness, as when a panelist rejects a term that has been borrowed from the technical vocabulary of a particular field of science. In some cases, the notion of appropriateness involves issues of social justice, as when panelists allow the pronoun *their* to refer to a singular noun in order to avoid using the masculine *his* to stand for both men and women. In such instances, these panelists choose to supersede the dictums of traditional grammar with what they feel is the overriding need to avoid an injustice.

# The Power of Precedent

When unsure of the status of a given expression, you might find yourself wondering whether—or for how long—the expression has been used by other writers, particularly by respected writers. The fact that a word has a lengthy history of use by many of our finest writers provides a compelling argument for its continued use today. If it was good enough for Milton, Swift, Austen, and Wharton, you might think, then it ought to be good enough for me. But sometimes historical precedent clashes with contemporary attitudes. On occasion, the Usage Panel frowns on usages that have appeared in the works of our most esteemed writers. In these cases, we present both sides of the controversy, and we sometimes suggest that historical precedent should outweigh the judgments of the majority of our panelists. On the other hand, some expressions have become so stigmatized and elicit such a resounding chorus of disapproval from the panel that even the weight of history may not save them from provoking a negative response in a good portion of your readers. In these cases, we provide you with fair warning about the consequences of using a stigmatized usage.

# Levels of Usage

In this book we use a number of terms to indicate different levels of usage to give you an idea under what circumstances a given usage will be appropriate.

*Standard English* Standard English is the language we use for public discourse. It is the working language of our social institutions. The news media, the government, the legal profession, and the teachers in our schools and universities all aim at Standard English as a norm of communication, primarily in expository and argumentative writing, but also in public speaking. Standard English is thus different from what we normally think of as speech in that Standard English must be taught, whereas children learn to speak naturally without being taught. Of course, Standard English shares with spoken English certain features common to all forms of language. It has rules for making grammatical sentences, and it changes over time. The issues of pronunciation discussed in this book mainly involve how to pronounce specific written words or written letters, such as *ch* or *g*, in different words. The guidance to pronunciation is not meant to standardize or correct anyone's naturally acquired form of spoken English.

The name Standard English is perhaps not the best, since it implies a standard against which various kinds of spoken English are to be measured, and this is hardly a fair comparison. A better name might be Institutional English, Conventional English, Commercial English, or Standardized English for Writing and Public Speaking, but these names all have their own negative connotations and shortcomings. So, since Standard is what this brand of English has been called for generations, we use the name here.

*Nonstandard English* There are many expressions and grammatical constructions that are not normally used in Standard English. These include regional expressions, such as *might could,* and other usages, such as *ain't* and *it don't,* that are typically associated with dialects used by people belonging to less prestigious social groups. These nonstandard varieties of English are no less logical or systematic than Standard English. In this book an expression labeled *nonstandard* is not wrong; it is merely inappropriate for ordinary usage in Standard English.

*Formal English* On some occasions it is important to adhere to the conventions that characterize serious public discourse and to avoid expressions that we might use in more casual situations. Formal writing and speaking are characterized by the tendency to give full treatment to all the elements that are required for grammatical sentences. Thus in formal English you might hear *May I suggest that we reexamine the problem?* where both clauses have a subject and verb and the subordinate clause is introduced by the conjunction *that.* Of course, formal English has many other features. Among these are the careful explanation of background information, complexity in sentence structure, explicit transitions between thoughts, and the use of certain words such as *may* that are reserved chiefly for creating a formal tone. Situations that normally require formal usage would include an article discussing a serious matter submitted to a respected journal, an official report by a group of researchers to a government body, a talk presented to a professional organization, and a letter of job application.

*Informal English* This is a broad category applied to situations in which it is not necessary, and in many cases not even desirable, to use the conventions of formal discourse. Informal language incorporates many of the familiar features of spoken English, especially the tendency to use contractions and to abbreviate sentences by omitting certain elements. Where formal English has *May I suggest that we reexamine the manuscript?* in informal English you might get *Want to look this over again?* Informal English tends to assume that the audience shares basic assumptions and background knowledge with the writer or speaker, who therefore alludes to or even omits reference to this information, rather than carefully explaining it as formal discourse requires. Typical informal situations would include a casual conversation with classmates, a letter to a close friend, or an article on a light topic written for a newspaper or magazine whose readership shares certain interests of the writer.

Of course, these functional categories are not hard and fast divisions of language; rather they are general tendencies of usage. People use language over a spectrum that shifts from intimate situations to public discourse, and a given piece of writing may have a mixture of formal and informal elements. We use the labels *formal* and *informal* in this book as guideposts to give you a clearer notion about when it is appropriate to use a particular usage.

It is important to remember that *formal* and *informal* refer to styles of expression, not standards of correctness. Informal English has its own rules of grammar and is just as logical as formal English. You can be serious using informal English, just as you can be comical using formal English. The two styles are simply used for different occasions.

In this book, we offer advice that we hope will seem reasonable and worth serious consideration. But as any experienced writer knows, there are occasions when even the best advice may not apply. The demands of writing for different audiences, with different purposes, on different subjects, at different levels of formality are so varied that they cannot begin to be anticipated in a book like this, and we recognize that what is appropriate for one piece of writing may not be appropriate for another. In most cases, you will want to avoid ambiguity at all costs so as not to leave your words open to misinterpretation. But if you are interested in making a joke, ambiguity may be just what you need. In these and similar situations, you will be better off being aware of the effects that certain usages can have on a reader. And it is here that this book can help.

# Grammar

## *Traditional Rules, Word Order, Agreement, and Case*

This chapter treats traditional problems of grammar and problems involving word order, grammatical agreement, parts of speech, conjunctions, pronouns, and verbs. Problems that are inherent to individual words or entail a choice between words are generally treated under *Word Choice*. If you cannot find the word or subject you are looking for, check the indexes at the end of the book.

**?**

**absolute constructions** Absolute constructions consist of a noun and some kind of modifier, the most common being a participle. Because they often come at the beginning of a sentence, they are easily confused with dangling participles. But an absolute construction modifies the rest of the sentence, not the subject of the sentence (as a participial phrase does). You can use absolute constructions to compress two sentences into one and to vary sentence structure as a means of holding a reader's interest. Here are some examples:

> *No other business arising,* the meeting was adjourned.
> *The paint now dry,* we brought the furniture out on the deck.
> *The truck finally loaded,* they said goodbye to their neighbors and drove off.
> The horse loped across the yard, *her foal trailing behind her.*

Constructions like these are used more often in writing than in speaking, where it is more common to use a full clause: *When the paint was dry, we brought the furniture out on the deck.* There are, however, many fixed absolute constructions that occur frequently in speech:

> The picnic is scheduled for Saturday, *weather permitting.*
> *Barring bad weather,* we plan to go to the beach tomorrow.
> *All things considered,* it's not a bad idea.

**absolute terms** Absolute terms are words that supposedly cannot be compared, as by *more* and *most,* or used with an intensive modifier, such as *very* or *so.* The terms identified in many handbooks as absolute include *absolute* itself and others such as *chief, complete, perfect, prime,* and *unique.* Language commentators also like to list terms from mathematics as absolutes: *circular, equal, parallel, perpendicular,* and so on.

Of course, many adjectives in English cannot normally be compared or intensified. Adjectives from technical fields or with very narrow meanings often fall in this group. Think of *biological, catabolic, macroeconomic, millenial, on-line, retroactive, ultraviolet.* You just do not encounter statements like *These cells are more somatic* or *Our database is so on-line.* But you do come across remarks such as *He wanted to make his record collection more complete* and *You can improve the sketch by making the lines more perpendicular.*

People object to these constructions because they seem to violate the categories of logic. Something is either complete or it isn't. Lines are either perpendicular or they aren't. There can be no in-between. The mistake here is to confuse pure logic or a mathematical ideal with the working approximations that distinguish the ordinary use of language. Certainly, we all have occasion to use words according to strict logic. It would be impossible to teach mathematics if we did not. But we also think in terms of a scale or spectrum, rather than in distinct, either/or categories. Thus, we may think of a statement as either true or false according to rigorous tests of logic, but we all know that there are degrees of truthfulness and falsehood. Similarly, there may be degrees of completeness to a record collection, and some lines may be more perpendicular—that is, they may more nearly approximate mathematical perpendicularity—than other lines: *Is that picture frame more horizontal now, or have I made it even less? She has some of the most unique credentials I have ever seen on a resume.* Such examples are not less logical than their stricter counterparts. They simply represent a different way of using language to discuss a subject.

Certain absolute terms, such as *parallel, perfect,* and *unique,* have become enshrined in the lore of writing handbooks and may provoke a negative response when modified by degree. These words are treated in more detail at their entries under *Word Choice.*

## adjectives

**comparison of adjectives** We often use adjectives—words that modify nouns—to make comparisons. We say *That building is bigger than this one, She is the most intelligent student in the class,* and so on. Some adjectives add *-er* and *-est* to form the comparative and superlative degrees. Others cannot do this, but must be preceded by *more* and *most.* How can you know which is which? Fortunately, there are some simple rules you can follow. Adjectives that have one syllable usually take *-er* and *-est.* Adjectives that have two syllables and end in *y* (*early*), *ow* (*narrow*), and *le* (*gentle*), can also take *-er* and *-est.* Almost all other adjectives with two or more syllables require the use of *more* and *most.* The rules are indicated in the chart below:

| Number of Syllables | Unchanged | Comparative | Superlative |
|---|---|---|---|
| 1 | fast | faster | fastest |
| 2 | happy | happier | happiest |
|  | complex | more complex | most complex |
| 3 or more | beautiful | more beautiful | most beautiful |

The rules for spelling changes of compared adjectives are treated under *Word Formation.*

English also has a few adjectives whose comparative and superlative forms are irregular:

| Positive | Comparative | Superlative |
|---|---|---|
| good | better | best |
| bad | worse | worst |
| little | littler, less | littlest, least |
| far | farther, further | farthest, furthest |

You can also compare adjectives in a decreasing way by using *less* and *least: Jack is less skillful at carpentry than Bill is. Roberta is the least likely employee to have complained about working conditions.*

There are also some adjectives, like *acoustic, biological,* and *reverse,* that cannot be compared and others, like *unique, parallel,* and *perfect,* whose comparison is controversial.

More at **absolute terms.**

## adverbs, comparison of

Adverbs modify verbs, adjectives, other adverbs, and sometimes entire clauses or sentences. Many adjectives can be made into adverbs by adding the suffix *-ly:*

We made a *conservative* estimate of the costs.
We estimated the costs *conservatively.*

The monosyllabic adjectives *fast, hard,* and *long* do not change to form adverbs:

He is a *fast* runner. He runs *fast.*
She is a *hard* worker. She works *hard.*
We waited for a *long* time. Have you been waiting *long?*

Some adjectives, like *close* and *high,* have two adverbial forms: one that is unchanged and one that ends in *-ly.*

We are *close* friends. Stay *close* to me. Look *closely* at the first chapter.
The platform is *high.* The bird flew *high.* The artist was *highly* praised.

It is best to check a dictionary to be confirm the forms used by a specific adverb.

Similar rules to those for comparing adjectives apply to adverbs and are shown in the chart below:

| Number of Syllables | Unchanged | Comparative | Superlative |
|---|---|---|---|
| 1 | soon | sooner | soonest |
| 2 or more | early | earlier | earliest |
| | frequent | more frequent | most frequent |
| | comfortably | more comfortably | most comfortably |

English also has some adverbs with irregular comparative and superlative forms:

| Positive | Comparative | Superlative |
|---|---|---|
| badly | worse | worst |
| well | better | best |
| little | less | least |
| far | farther, further | farthest, furthest |
| much | more | most |

To compare adverbs to a lower degree, use *less* and *least: We rehearsed less often than the other actors. We rehearsed least often of all the actors.*

**adverbs, position of** Adverbs can modify verbs, participles, adjectives, other adverbs, and even whole sentences. Because they have so many functions and they tend to modify the words they are closest to, it can sometimes be tricky positioning them to convey the exact meaning you want. This is especially true of certain adverbs like *also, just,* and *only.* Sentences with more than one verb also can pose difficulty. Which verb does *rapidly* modify in this sentence: *His insistence that the new sales plan should be implemented rapidly increased the company's profits?* It is important to make sure that the sentences that precede one like this establish a context that leaves no room for ambiguity. It may be easier to rewrite the sentence to avoid ambiguity. Here are two possibilities for the previous example: *His insistence on implementing the new sales plan caused the company's profits to increase rapidly. Because he insisted on rapid implementation of the new sales plan, the company's profits increased.*

In initial position the adverb is usually followed by a comma: *Suddenly, the train started moving.* Many adverbs in initial position modify the entire sentence rather than the verb: *Fortunately, Higgins survived the ordeal. Admittedly, the city could use a new library. Frankly, the Bruins don't stand a chance in the playoffs.* Strangely enough, a few of these sentence modifiers, especially *hopefully,* have been criticized by usage commentators for decades as grievous faults, while others like *thankfully* and *mercifully* have gone relatively unnoticed. For more on this, see **hopefully** under *Word Choice.*
More at **also, however, not, only,** and **split infinitive.**

**agreement** See **pronouns, agreement of** and **subject and verb agreement.**

**ain't** *Ain't* is a word that ain't had it easy. It first appeared in English in 1778, evolving from an earlier form *an't,* which arose almost a century earlier as a contraction of *are not* and *am not.* In fact, *ain't* seems to have arisen at the tail end of an era that saw the introduction of a number of our most common contractions, including *don't* and *won't. Ain't* and some of these other contractions came under criticism in the 1700s for being inelegant and low-class, even though they had actually been used by upper-class speakers. But while *don't* and *won't* eventually became perfectly acceptable at all levels of speech and writing, *ain't* was to receive a barrage of criticism in the 19th century for having no set sequence of words from which it can be contracted and for being "a vulgarism," that is, a term used by the lower classes. At the same time *ain't*'s uses were multiplying to include *is not, has not,* and *have not.* It may be that these extended uses helped provoke the negative reaction. Whatever the case, the criticism of *ain't* by usage commentators and teachers has not subsided, and the use of *ain't* has come to be regarded as a mark of ignorance. Use it at your peril.

But despite all the attempts to ban it, *ain't* continues to appear in the speech of ordinary folks. Even educated and upper-class speakers see that *ain't* has no substitute in fixed expressions like *Say it ain't so, You ain't just whistlin' Dixie,* and *You ain't seen nothin' yet.*

**ain't I?** The stigmatization of *ain't* leaves us with no happy alternative for use in first-person questions. The widely used *aren't I?*, though illogical, was found acceptable for use in speech by a majority of the Usage Panel in an early survey, but in writing there is no alternative to saying *am I not?*

## also

***also* beginning a sentence** Some people maintain that it is wrong to begin a sentence with *also.* They are probably in the minority, since there seems no reason to condemn *also* and not another conjunctive adverb like *nevertheless.* In an earlier survey, 63 percent of the Usage Panel found the usage acceptable in this example: *The warranty covers all power-train components. Also, participating dealers back their work with a free lifetime service guarantee.*

***also* used ambiguously** *Also* shares with *only* the virtue of modifying the parts of the sentence to which it is closest, but this can sometimes lead to ambiguity. In the following examples, the sentence containing *also* is exactly the same, but in each example it modifies a different part and creates a different meaning:

> I read in the paper that their band was coming to town. I also heard that the band would play here.
> Mary heard that their band is coming to town. I also heard that the band would play here.
> The band has been playing out on the West Coast for weeks. I also heard that the band would play here.

It's a good policy to check that the context is sufficiently clear to limit the meaning of *also* so you won't be misunderstood. If you're in doubt, try moving *also* to another position and see if the meaning is less ambiguous: *I heard that the band would also play here.*

More at **adverbs, position of** and **only.**

**and** "*And now, here's Groucho,*" said George Fenniman, introducing the host of the game show *You Bet Your Life* in the manner of all game show moderators. But this time at least Groucho would not be so introduced. "*What do you mean, Fenniman? You can't begin a sentence with* and. *What kind of show do you think this is?*" Groucho's mock indignation only points out the difficulty of grammatical rules like the one asserting that sentences beginning with *and* or *but* express incomplete thoughts and are therefore incorrect. But it is Fenniman and not Groucho who has history on his side, for writers from Shakespeare to Joyce Carol Oates have used *and* and *but* to start sentences. When members of the Usage Panel were asked whether they paid attention to the rule in their own writing, 24 percent answered "always or usually," 36 percent answered "sometimes," and 40 percent answered "rarely or never."

More at **both, but,** and **try.**

## any

**any as a pronoun** When used as a pronoun, *any* can take either a singular or plural verb depending on how it is construed: *Any of these books is suitable* (that is, *any one*). *But are any* (that is, *some*) *of them available?*

**of any** The construction *of any* is often used in informal contexts to mean "of all," as in *He is the best known of any living playwright.* Although this construction has been around for centuries, you may want to use *of all* with a plural noun for formal writing. In an earlier survey, 67 percent of the Usage Panel found the "playwright" example to be unacceptable.

**any as an adverb** *Any* is also used as an adverb to mean "at all" before a comparative adjective or adverb in questions and negative sentences: *Is she any better? Is he doing any better? He is not any friendlier than before.* This usage is entirely acceptable. The related use of *any* to modify a verb is also acceptable but usually considered informal: *It didn't hurt any. If the child cries any, give her the bottle.*

**any with he** *Any carpenter worth his salt would have done a better job.* Is it all right to use masculine pronouns to refer back to an *any*-construction? For an answer to this question, see **he** under *Gender.*

**any with plural pronouns** For a discussion of whether plural pronouns can refer to noun phrases using *any,* see **every.**

## anyone

**anyone is always singular** *Anyone* and *anybody* are singular terms and always take a singular verb.

**anyone or any one** The one-word form *anyone* means "any person." The two-word form *any one* means "whatever one (person or thing) of a group." Thus, *Anyone may join* means that admission is open to everybody. *Any one may join* means that admission is open to one person only. When followed by *of,* only *any one* can be used: *Any one* (not *anyone*) *of the boys could carry it by himself.*

**anyone instead of everyone** *Anyone* is often used in place of *everyone* in sentences like *She is the most thrifty person of anyone I know.* While this construction has been used for centuries, 64 percent of the Usage Panel in an earlier survey found this sentence unacceptable in writing.

**anyone with he** *Anyone worth his salt would have done a better job.* Is it all right to use masculine pronouns to refer back to an *any*-construction? For an answer to this question, see **he** under *Gender.*

**anyone with plural pronouns** *Anyone who wants to go must bring their canteens.* Can *anyone* be referred to by a plural pronoun? For a discussion of this issue, see **every.**

## as

***as . . . as* versus *so . . . as*** A traditional usage rule draws a distinction between comparisons using *as . . . as* and comparisons using *so . . . as.* The rule states that the *so . . . as* construction is required in negative sentences (as in Shakespeare's *"'tis not so deep as a well"*), in questions (as in *Is it so bad as she says?*), and in certain *if-* clauses (as in *If it is so bad as you say, you ought to leave*). But this *so . . . as* construction is becoming increasingly rare in American English, and the use of *as . . . as* is now entirely acceptable in all contexts.

***as . . . as* and *than*** When making comparisons involving both *as . . . as* and *than,* remember to keep the second *as* in formal style. Write *He is as smart as, or smarter than, his brother,* not *He is as smart or smarter than his brother,* which is considered unacceptable in formal style.

***as* instead of *that*** In many dialects, people use *as* in place of *that* in sentences like *We are not sure as we want to go* or *It's not certain as he left.* But this use of *as* is limited mostly to speaking. You should therefore avoid it in formal writing.

***as* instead of *that* or *who*** Some nonstandard varieties of American English differ from the standard language in the form and usage of relative pronouns. Where Standard English has three relative pronouns—*who, which,* and *that*—regional dialects, particularly those of the South and midland, allow *as* and *what* as relative pronouns: *"They like nothing better than the job of leading off a young feller like you, as ain't never been away from home"* (Stephen Crane). *The car what hit him never stopped.*

***as* meaning "because" or "when"** When *as* expresses a causal relation, it should be preceded by a comma, as in *She won't be coming, as we didn't invite her.* When *as* expresses a time relation, it is not preceded by a comma: *She was finishing the painting as I walked into the room.* When you begin a sentence with a clause that starts with *as,* make sure that it is clear whether *as* is used to mean "because" or "at the same time that." The sentence *As they were leaving, I walked to the door* may mean either "I walked to the door because they were leaving" or "I walked to the door at the same time that they were leaving."

***as* used redundantly** *As* is sometimes used superfluously with verbs like *consider* and *deem.* For more on this issue, see **redundancy** under *Style.*

***as* in parallel constructions** Constructions of the *as . . . as . . .* form are sometimes difficult to keep parallel. For an explanation of this problem, see **parallelism** under *Style.*

More at **like; pronouns, personal; so;** and **than.**

**as far as** As far as the Usage Panel is concerned, *as far as* had better be followed by both a subject and a verb. *As far as* is sometimes used as a preposition meaning "as for" or "regarding," especially in speech. But a large majority of the panel frowns upon this usage. Eighty percent find the *as far as* construction in this sentence unacceptable: *As far as something to do on the weekend, we didn't even have miniature golf.* Eighty-four percent reject the sentence *The Yankees are still very much alive, as far as the divisional race.* And 89 percent object to *as far as* when followed by a noun clause as in *As far as how Koresh got shot, we don't know yet.*

**auxiliary and primary verbs** *Auxiliary verbs,* sometimes called *helping verbs,* help complete the form and meaning of main verbs. The auxiliary verbs include the *modal verbs,* the *primary verbs,* and a few special verbs like *dare* and *need.* The *modal verbs* are *can, could, may, might, must, shall, should, will,* and *would.* They are called *modal* because they express the *mood* of verbs (for more on this, see **verbs, mood of** and **subjunctive**). The *primary verbs* are *be, do,* and *have.* The *primary verbs* have the distinction of being able to function either as main verbs or as auxiliaries.

The auxiliary verbs differ from main verbs in the following ways:

1. They do not take word endings to form participles or agree with their subject. Thus, we say *She may go to the store,* but never *She mays go to the store.*

2. They come before *not* in negative clauses, and they do not use *do* to form the negative: *You might not like that.* A main verb uses *do* to form the negative and follows *not: You do not like that.*

3. They come before the subject in a question: *Can I have another apple? Would you like to go to the movies?* Main verbs must use *do* and follow the subject to form questions: *Do you want to go to the movies?*

4. They take the infinitive without *to: I will call you tomorrow.* A main verb that takes an infinitive always uses *to: I promise to call you tomorrow.*

When functioning as auxiliary verbs, the primary verbs serve the following functions. *Be* shows continuing action (*We are working on a new plan*) and forms the passive voice (*The shed was destroyed in the storm*). *Have* is used to make perfect tenses—tenses that show completed action (*She has finally finished her book. Have you ever gone windsurfing? We had planned to go out tonight*). *Do* is used to form negatives (*I do not wish to offend you*), to ask questions (*Do you ever write to her?*), to show emphasis (*I do want you to come to the party*), and to stand for a full verb in certain other constructions (*She likes jazz more than he does*).

In their capacity as auxiliaries, the primary verbs retain some features of main verbs. All the primary verbs can change form to agree in number with their subject. We say *I am going, He has eaten,* and *She does not travel much. Have* and *be* can form participles and still play an auxiliary role in a verb phrase: *Having finished in the garage, he went home. They did not give up even when being badly outplayed. Have* and *be* are used with participles and cannot take an infinitive without *to.*

As main verbs, *have* and *be* present certain exceptions to the criteria stated in rules two and four above. They can come before *not* in negative sentences (*We haven't any pickles. He is not there*). They can also appear before the subject in questions (*Is anybody home? Have you no shame?*). It just goes to show that even the most basic words can turn out to be quite complex once you examine how they are used.

More at **can, dare, have to, may, must, need, ought, shall / will, should,** and **used to.**

## because

**because beginning a sentence** "*Because I could not stop for Death—/He kindly stopped for me.*" So begins one of Emily Dickinson's most well-known poems, and so falls another of the more arbitrary rules of usage, which states that you should not begin a sentence with *because*. As Dickinson's poem attests, there are occasions when *because* is perfectly appropriate as the opening word of a sentence. In fact, sentences beginning with *because* are quite common in written English.

**because in clauses that are the subject** A related rule states that you cannot use a clause beginning with *because* as the subject of a sentence, as in *Just because he thinks it's a good idea doesn't mean it's a good idea.* This construction is perfectly acceptable, but it carries a colloquial flavor and you may want to save it for informal situations.

**because after negated verbs** When *because* follows a negated verb phrase, it must be preceded by a comma when the *because* clause explains why the event did not occur. *They didn't want her on the committee, because she was so outspoken* means roughly "Her outspokenness was their reason for not wanting her on the committee." When there is no comma, the *because* clause is included in what is being negated. Thus *They didn't want her on the committee because she was so outspoken* implies that they may in fact have wanted her on the committee but for some reason other than her outspokenness.

**the reason is because** For a discussion of this frequently condemned phrase, see **redundancy** under *Style*.

**better / best** A traditional rule of grammar states that you can only use the comparative degree when comparing two things. Thus you must say *She is the older* (not *the oldest*) *of the two cousins.* And you had better use *better* in similar comparisons: *Which house of Congress has the better* (not *best*) *attendance record?* Native speakers will recognize the natural sound of *best* in this sentence (and of *oldest* in the previous example) and will conclude that this traditional rule is often ignored in practice. In fact, many of our most celebrated writers use *oldest, best,* and other superlatives to compare two things. But don't be surprised if someone objects when you follow suit. The traditional rules have many devoted adherents.

Keep in mind, however, that there are certain fixed expressions, such as *Put your best foot forward* and *May the best team win!*, where you can't go wrong using *best*.
More at **had better.**

## but

**but beginning a sentence** "*In his youth Dostoevsky had been attracted to utopian socialism of the Fourierist variety. But four years in a prison camp in Siberia shook his faith.*" As this quotation from J.M. Coetzee shows, the conjunction *but* can be highly effective as a sentence opener. You may still hear the injunction against beginning a sentence with a conjunction. The idea is that these sentences express "incomplete" thoughts. But a glance through any magazine or newspaper will show you that beginning with *but* has become common practice, and initial *but* must be considered acceptable at all levels of style.

**but not followed by a comma** *But* is generally not followed by a comma. Correct written style requires *Kim wanted to go, but we stayed,* not *Kim wanted to go, but, we stayed.*

**but however** For a discussion of this word combination, see **redundancy** under *Style.*

More at **and, cannot, however,** and **pronouns, personal.**

## can

**can and may** *Can I go to the bathroom?* Nearly every child has asked this question only to be corrected with *You mean, May I go to the bathroom?* Generations of teachers have insisted that *can* should be used only to express the capacity to do something and that *may* must be used to express permission. But let's face it, children don't use *can* to ask permission out of a desire to be stubbornly perverse. They have learned it as an idiomatic expression from adults: *If you finish your spaghetti, you can have dessert. After you clean your room, you can go outside and play.* In these and similar spoken uses, *can* is perfectly acceptable. This is especially true for negative questions such as *Can't I have the car tonight?* probably because using *mayn't* instead of *can't* sounds unnatural. Nevertheless, in more formal usage the distinction between *can* and *may* still has many adherents. Only 21 percent of the Usage Panel accepts *can* instead of *may* in the sentence *Can I take another week to submit the application? May* is common in official announcements: *Students may pick up the application forms tomorrow.* The increased formality of *may* sometimes highlights the role of the speaker in giving permission. *You may leave the room when you're finished* implies that permission is given by the speaker. *You can leave the room when you're finished* implies that permission is part of a rule or policy rather than a decision on the part of the speaker.

**can showing possibility** Like *may, can* can also be used to indicate what is possible: *It may rain this afternoon. Bone spurs can be very painful.* In this use, both *can* and *may* often have personal subjects: *You may be right. You may see him at the concert. From the mountaintop you can see the ocean on a clear day. Even an experienced driver can get lost in this town.*

More at **auxiliary and primary verbs** and **may.**

## cannot

**cannot but** "*I cannot but be gratified by the assurance,*" Thomas Jefferson once wrote. He might have said *I can but be gratified by the assurance* and meant the same thing! How is this possible? The *but* of *cannot but* indicates an exception, as it does in sentences such as *No one but Jefferson could have written such a document.* But the *but* of *can but* means "only," as it does in the sentence *We had but a single bullet left.* So the two phrases *cannot but* and *can but* mean essentially the same thing: "cannot do otherwise than." Both *cannot but* and *can but* are standard expressions that have been in use for hundreds of years.

**cannot help** The construction *cannot help* is used with a present participle to roughly the same effect as *cannot but* in a sentence such as *We cannot help ad-*

*miring his courage.* This construction usually bears the implication that a person is unable to affect an outcome normally under his or her control. Thus if you say *We could not help laughing at such a remark,* you imply that you could not suppress your laughter.

**cannot help but** The construction *cannot help but* probably arose as a blend of *cannot help* and *cannot but;* it has the meaning of the first and the syntax of the second: *We cannot help but admire his courage.* The construction has sometimes been criticized as a redundancy, but it has been around for more than a century and appears in the writing of many distinguished authors.

**cannot seem** The expression *cannot* (or *can't*) *seem to* has occasionally been criticized as illogical, and so it is. *Brian can't seem to get angry* does not mean "Brian is incapable of appearing to get angry," as its syntax would seem to require; rather, it means "Brian appears to be unable to get angry." But the idiom serves a useful purpose, since the syntax of English does not allow us to say *Brian seems to cannot get angry.* We use similar "illogical" constructions all the time, such as *I don't think it will rain* instead of *I think it will not rain.* In this case, being illogical is just speaking plain English.

**collective noun** Some nouns, like *committee, clergy, enemy, group, family,* and *team,* refer to a group but are singular in form. These nouns are called *collective nouns.* In American usage, a collective noun takes a singular verb when it refers to the collection considered as a whole, as in *The family was united on this question* or *The enemy is suing for peace.* It takes a plural verb when it refers to the members of the group considered as individuals, as in *My family are always fighting among themselves* or *The enemy were showing up in groups of three or four to turn in their weapons.* In British usage, collective nouns are more often treated as plurals: *The government have not announced a new policy. The team are playing in the test matches next week.*

Be careful not to treat a collective noun as both singular and plural in the same construction. Thus you should say *The family is determined to press its* (not *their*) *claim.*

Collective nouns always refer to living creatures. Similar inanimate nouns, such as *furniture* and *luggage,* differ in that they cannot be counted individually. That is why you cannot buy *a furniture* or *a luggage.* These nouns are usually called *mass nouns* or *noncount nouns.* They always take a singular verb: *The bedroom furniture was on sale.*

More at **subject and verb agreement.**

**dangling modifiers** *A modifier must never dangle unless you want your sentence to mangle.* This rule of botched syntax should remind you always to be on the lookout for dangling modifiers—participles, infinitive phrases, clauses, and prepositional phrases that grammatically modify the noun or noun phrase next to them but logically refer to a noun or noun phrase that has been displaced to another part of the sentence or is absent altogether. These constructions are common in speech, where they often go without comment, and they can be found occasionally in writing. But they are distracting to the reader, and they can sometimes lead to unintended absurdities. Consider this example, penned by a well-respected writer and published by the *New York Times:*

> *After wading through a long, quasi-academic examination of the statistical links between intelligence, character, race and poverty,* the reader's reward is a hoary lecture on the evils of the welfare state.

This sentence begins with a prepositional phrase that has a gerund for its object. As a verb form, the gerund cries out for a subject, and we must supply it mentally. The sense requires *reader,* but the the subject of the main clause is *reward.* We want the reader, not the reward, to do the wading. We can easily solve this conflict by keeping the modifying phrase as it stands and giving the main clause the proper subject:

> After wading through a long, quasi-academic examination of the statistical links between intelligence, character, race and poverty, the reader is rewarded with a hoary lecture on the evils of the welfare state.

Here is another example, also taken from a famous writer in the *New York Times.* Describing the perils of being a newspaper columnist, the writer imagines interviewing his spouse as the first in a series of increasingly desperate measures to come up with material:

> *Once hooked on interviewing his wife,* degradation proceeds swiftly.

Again we are asked to connect the modifying portion of the sentence with the grammatical subject of the main clause. But we can't. We want a person—in this case the husband—to be hooked, not an abstraction like degradation. Here the solution is to turn the phrase into a full clause with the subject specified:

> Once the newspaper columnist is hooked on interviewing his wife, degradation proceeds swiftly.

Now we can witness the degradation with peace of mind.

A third example, also from the *New York Times,* puts the modifying element at the end of the sentence:

> Mr. Clinton acknowledged the role played by the men who subdued the gunman *when he spoke at a dinner on Saturday night.*

In this case, the modifier is a full clause that can't be made fuller. (The clause would be elliptical if it read *when speaking at a dinner on Saturday night.*) It is clearly Mr. Clinton who spoke, not the gunman (who missed dinner, as he was in jail at the time). The grammatical ambiguity caused by the misplaced modifier makes the sentence sound absurd. Here the answer is to reposition the clause so that it is closer to the noun it modifies:

> When he spoke at a dinner on Saturday night, Mr. Clinton acknowledged the role played by the men who subdued the gunman.

Modifiers often dangle because the agent of the action is not the subject of the verb in the main clause. The chief culprit here is the passive voice, which banishes the agent of the action from being the subject. Consider these examples, one using an infinitive phrase and another using a prepositional phrase with a gerund:

> *To improve company morale*, three things were recommended by the consultant.
> *In reviewing the company's policy*, three areas of improvement were identified by the committee.

These sentences can easily be fixed by making the consultant and the committee the subjects:

> To improve company morale, the consultant recommended . . .
> In reviewing the company's policy, the board identified . . .

For more on the passive voice, see **verbs, voice of** in this chapter and **passive voice** under *Style*.

Sometimes, of course, what the opening phrase refers to is not an agent, as this sentence attests: *Baked, boiled, or fried, you can make potatoes a part of almost any meal.* Better to put the non-agents like potatoes where they belong: *Baked, boiled, or fried, potatoes make a welcome addition to almost any meal.*

You should also bear in mind that, while most danglers occur at the beginning of a sentence, a modifier can dangle just about anywhere. In fact, as we saw with Mr. Clinton, delayed danglers can be treacherously ambiguous. Remember too that when you end a sentence with a modifying phrase that follows a comma, the phrase always refers to the subject of the sentence, not the closest noun. Thus, the sentence *A few guests lingered near her, mumbling pleasantries* can only mean that the guests mumbled the pleasantries. She may have well been silent.

Some participles, such as *concerning, considering, failing*, and *granting*, function as prepositions, and you can use them to introduce a sentence without fear of dangling. A few participial phrases, such as *speaking of* and *judging by*, also work this way:

> Concerning the proposal, there was little debate among the board members.
> Considering his reputation for honesty, his arrest came as a shock.
> Speaking of exceptional performances, did you see her latest movie?

More at **participles** and **prepositions.**

**dare** Depending on its sense, the verb *dare* sometimes behaves like an auxiliary verb (such as *can* or *may*) and sometimes like a main verb (such as *want* or *try*). When used as an auxiliary verb, *dare* does not change to agree with its subject: *He dare not do that again.* It also does not combine with *do* in questions, negations, or certain other constructions: *Dare we tell her the truth? I dare not mention their names.* Finally, it does not take *to* before the verb that follows it: *If you dare breathe a word about it, I'll never speak to you again.* When used as a main verb, *dare* does agree with its subject (*If he dares to show up at her house I'll be* *surprised*), and it does combine with *to* (*Did anyone dare to admit it?*). It may optionally take *to* before the verb following it: *No one dares* (or *dares to*) *speak freely about the political situation.* The auxiliary forms differ subtly in meaning from the main verb forms in that they emphasize the attitude or involvement of the speaker while the main verb forms present a more objective situation. Thus *How dare she take the exam without ever once coming to class?* expresses indignation at the student's action, whereas *How did she dare to take the exam without ever once coming to class?* is a genuine request for information. When *dare* is used as a transitive verb meaning "challenge," only main verb forms are possible and *to* is required: *Anyone who dares* (not *dare*) *him to attempt* (not just *attempt*) *it will be sorry.*

More at **auxiliary and primary verbs** and **need.**

## double negative

**double negative equals a positive** It is a truism of traditional grammar that double negatives combine to form an affirmative. Readers coming across a sentence like *He cannot do nothing* will therefore interpret it as an affirmative statement meaning "He must do something" unless they are prompted to view it as dialect or nonstandard speech. Readers will also assign an affirmative meaning to constructions that yoke *not* with an adjective or adverb that begins with a negative prefix such as *in-* or *un-,* as in *a not infrequent visitor* or *a not unjust decision.* In these expressions the double negative conveys a weaker affirmative than would be conveyed by the positive adjective or adverb by itself. Thus *a not infrequent visitor* seems likely to visit less frequently than *a frequent visitor.*

**double negative equals a negative** "*You ain't heard nothin' yet,*" said Al Jolson in 1927 in *The Jazz Singer,* the first talking motion picture. He meant, of course, "You haven't heard anything yet." Some 60 years later President Reagan taunted his political opponents by saying "*You ain't seen nothin' yet.*" These famous examples of double negatives that reinforce (rather than nullify) a negative meaning show clearly that this construction is alive and well in spoken English. In fact, multiple negatives have been used to convey negative meaning in English since the tenth century, and throughout most of this history, this form of the double negative was wholly acceptable. Thus Chaucer in *The Canterbury Tales* could say of the Friar, "*Ther nas no man nowher so vertuous,*" meaning "There was no man so virtuous anywhere," and Shakespeare could allow Viola in *Twelfth Night* to say of her heart, "*Nor never none/Shall mistress of it be, save I alone,*" by which she meant that no one except herself would ever be mistress of her heart.

**double negative equals trouble** But in spite of this noble history, grammarians since the Renaissance have objected to this form of negative reinforcement employing the double negative. In their eagerness to make English conform to formal logic, they conceived and promulgated the notion that two negatives destroy one another and make a positive. This view was taken up by English teachers and has since become sanctioned as a convention of Standard English. Now if you use a double negative to mean "no" in formal speaking or writing, you run the

risk of being considered an ignoramus. It's probably best to look smart and use the double negative only when you want to imitate speech or strike a folksy note.

**double negative with minimizing adverbs** The ban on multiple negatives also applies to the combination of negatives with adverbs such as *barely, hardly,* and *scarcely.* It is therefore incorrect to say *I couldn't hardly do it* or *The car scarcely needs no oil.* These adverbs have a minimizing effect on the verb. They mean something like "almost not at all." They resemble negative adverbs such as *not* and *never* in that they are used with *any, anybody,* and similar words rather than *none, nobody,* and other negatives. Thus we say *You barely have any time left,* just as we would say *You don't have any time left,* but we would not say *You barely have no time left,* since it would be an unacceptable double negative.

**exceptions to the rule** The ban on using double negatives to convey emphasis does not apply when the second negative appears in a separate phrase or clause, as in *I will not surrender, not today, not ever* or *He does not seek money, no more than he seeks fame.* You must use commas to separate the negative phrases in these examples. Thus the sentence *He does not seek money no more than he seeks fame* is unacceptable, whereas the equivalent sentence with *any* is perfectly acceptable and requires no comma: *He does not seek money any more than he seeks fame.*

More at **hardly, rarely,** and **scarcely.**

**double passive** You may sometimes find it desirable to conjoin a passive verb form with a passive infinitive, as in *The building is scheduled to be demolished next week* and *The piece was originally intended to be played on the harpsichord.* These sentences are perfectly acceptable. But it's easy for things to go wrong in these double passive constructions. They sometimes end in ambiguity: *An independent review of the proposal was requested to be made by the committee.* In this sentence, is the committee making the request or doing the review? What is worse, double passives often sound ungrammatical, as this example shows: *The fall in the value of the Yen was attempted to be stopped by the Central Bank.*

How can you tell an acceptable double passive from an unacceptable one? If you can change the first verb into an active one, making the original subject its object, while keeping the passive infinitive, the original sentence is acceptable. Thus you can say *The city has scheduled the building to be demolished next week* and *The composer originally intended the piece to be played on the harpsichord.* But you cannot make similar changes in the other sentence. You cannot say *The Central Bank attempted the fall in the value of the Yen to be stopped.*

This is all rather technical, however, and it may be easiest just to trust your ear. If a double passive sounds tinny, rewrite the sentence.

More at **verbs, voice of.**

**each**

***each* with singular or plural verb** The traditional rule holds that the subject of a sentence beginning with *each* is grammatically singular, and the verb and following pronouns must be singular. Thus you should say *Each of the apartments has* (not *have*) *its* (not *their*) *own private entrance* (not *entrances*). When *each* follows a plural subject, however, the verb and subsequent pronouns remain in the plural: *The apartments each have their own private entrances* (not *has its own private entrance*). But when *each* follows the verb with *we* as its subject, the rule has an exception. You can say either *We boys have each our own room* or *We boys have each his own room,* though the latter form may strike readers as stilted.

**each and every** The expression *each and every* is likewise followed by a singular verb and singular pronoun in formal style: *Each and every driver knows* (not *know*) *what his or her* (not *their*) *job is to be.*

**each with pronouns** For a discussion of which pronouns to use to refer to noun phrases using each, see **he** under *Gender.*

More at **every.**

### either

**either of more than two** A traditional rule holds that *either* should be used only to refer to one of two items and that *any* is required when more than two items are involved: *Any* (not *either*) *of the three opposition candidates still in the race would make a better president than the incumbent.* Remember that the rule applies only to the use of *either* as a pronoun or an adjective, as in *Either computer will run the software.* When using *either* as a conjunction, you can apply it to more than two elements in a series: *She left her glove either at the convenience store, the library, or the playground. Either the union will make a counteroffer or the owners will close the factory or the mayor will intervene.*

**either with singular or plural verb** When used as a pronoun, *either* is normally singular and takes a singular verb: *The two surgeons disagree with each other more than either does* (not *do*) *with the pathologist.* But when either is followed by *of* and a plural noun, it is often used with a plural verb: *Either of the parties have enough support to form a government.* As frequent as this usage may be, it is widely regarded as incorrect. Ninety-two percent of the Usage Panel rejected it in an earlier survey.

**either ... or and verb agreement** When all the elements in an *either ... or* construction (or a *neither ... nor* construction) used as the subject of a sentence are singular, the verb is singular: *Either Eve or Herb* has been *invited.* Analogously, when all the elements in the *either ... or* construction are plural, the verb is plural too: *Either the Clarks or the Kays* have been *invited.* When the construction mixes singular and plural elements, however, there is some confusion as to which form the verb should take. Some people argue that the verb should agree with whichever noun phrase is closest to it. The Usage Panel has much sympathy for this view. Fifty-five percent prefer the plural verb for the sentence *Either the owner or the players is going/are going to have to give in.* Another 12 percent find either verb acceptable, meaning that, overall, 67 percent accept the plural verb in such situations, and only 33 percent would require the singular. If none of these solutions satisfies you, the only alternative is to revise the sentence to avoid the *either ... or* construction.

**either ... or and parallelism** For a discussion of the parallel nature of *either ... or* constructions, see **parallelism** under *Style.*

More at **neither, or,** and **subject and verb agreement.**

**every** *Every* is representative of a large class of English words and expressions that are singular in form but felt to be plural in sense. The class includes, for example, noun phrases introduced by *every, any,* and certain uses of *some.* These expressions invariably take a singular verb; we say *Every car has* (not *have*) *been tested. Anyone is* (not *are*) *liable to fall ill.* But when a sentence contains a pronoun that refers to a previous noun phrase introduced by *every,* grammar and sense pull in different directions. The grammar of these expressions requires a singular pronoun, as in *Every car must have its brakes tested,* but the meaning often leads people to use the plural pronoun, as in *Every car must have their brakes tested.* The use of plural pronouns in such cases is common in speech, but it is still widely regarded as incorrect in writing.

The effort to adhere to the grammatical rule causes complications, however. The first is grammatical. When a pronoun refers to a phrase containing *every* or *any* that falls within a different independent clause, the pronoun cannot be singular. Thus it is simply not English to say *Every man left; he took his raincoat with him.* Nor can you say *No one could be seen, could he?* If you are unwilling to use plural forms in these examples, you must find another way of expressing your meaning, either by rephrasing the sentence so as to get the pronoun into the same clause (as in *Every man left, taking his raincoat with him*) or by substituting another word for *every* or *any* (as in *All the men left; they took their raincoats with them*).

The second complication is political. When a phrase introduced by *every* or *any* refers to a group containing both men and women, what pronoun should you use? Consider the example *Every person in this office must keep track of his* (*her? his or her? their?*) *own expenses.* This matter is discussed at **he** under *Gender.* More at **all, any, each, either, neither, none,** and **subject and verb agreement.**

**gerund** Gerunds are verb forms ending in *-ing* that act as nouns. They can be the subject of a sentence (*Skiing is her favorite sport*), the object of a verb (*She enjoys skiing*), or the object of a preposition (*She devoted her free time to skiing*). Gerunds can be modified like nouns (*That book makes for difficult reading*). But they can also act like verbs in that they can take an object (*Convincing him was never easy*) and be modified by an adverb (*Walking daily can improve your health*). **gerund and possessives (fused participle)** Some people insist that when a gerund is preceded by a noun or pronoun, the noun or pronoun must be in the possessive case. Accordingly, it is correct to say *I can understand his wanting to go,* but incorrect to say *I can understand him wanting to go.* But the construction without the possessive, sometimes called the *fused participle,* has been used by respected writers for 300 years and is perfectly idiomatic. Moreover, there is often no way to "fix" the construction by inserting the possessive. This is often the case with common nouns. Thus you can say *We have had very few instances of luggage being lost,* but not *. . . of luggage's being lost.*

Sometimes syntax makes using the possessive impossible. Consider the sentence *What she objects to is men making more money than women for the same work.* Changing *men making* to *men's making* not only sounds awkward, but it requires *women's* at the other end to keep the sentence parallel, and *women's* simply does not work. Perhaps for these reasons 53 percent of the Usage Panel finds the phrase *men making* acceptable in this sentence, and another 36 percent find it acceptable in informal contexts. Only 11 percent reject it outright.

However, when the construction is more complicated so that a word or phrase intervenes between the noun and the gerund, the panel is less sanguine. Only 25 percent accept the sentence *I can understand him not wanting to go*, where the negative *not* intervenes between the pronoun and the gerund. Thirty-one percent say this sentence is acceptable in informal contexts, leaving 44 percent who are naysayers. Panel acceptance drops even further when the syntax gets more complicated. Only 16 percent accept the sentence *Imagine a child with an ear infection who cannot get penicillin losing his hearing*, where both a phrase and a clause intervene between the noun *child* and the gerund *losing*. And only 17 percent find this sentence acceptable in informal contexts, so that 66 percent reject it roundly.

Be aware that sometimes nouns ending in *-s* can be confused with a singular noun in the possessive. Thus *I don't approve of your friend's going there* indicates one friend is going, and *I don't approve of your friends going there* indicates that more than one friend is going.
More at **participles.**

**had better** *Had better* is an idiomatic verb phrase meaning "ought to, must." It resembles an auxiliary verb in that its form never changes to show person or tense and that it can't follow another verb in a phrase (that is, you can't say *He will had better leave*, for example).

When speaking, people have a tendency to leave out *had: You better clean up your room!* But in writing, you had better keep *had*, either in full or as a contraction: *You had better not do that* or *You'd better not do that.*

**hardly** In Standard English, *hardly, scarcely*, and similar adverbs cannot be used with a negative. You cannot say *I couldn't hardly see him*. This violation of the double negative rule is curious because these adverbs are not truly negative in meaning. The sentence *Mary hardly laughed* means that Mary did laugh a little, not that she kept from laughing altogether. So why should *hardly* and *scarcely* be banned from use with a negative like *not*? Adverbs like *hardly* and *scarcely* may not have purely negative meaning, but they share some important features of negative adverbs. They combine with *any* and *at all*, which are characteristically associated with negative contexts. Thus you can say *I hardly saw him at all* or *I never saw him at all* but not *I occasionally saw him at all*. Similarly, you can say *I hardly had any time* or *I didn't have any time* but not *I had any time,* and so on. Like other negative adverbs, *hardly, scarcely*, and their companions cause inversion of the subject and auxiliary verb when they begin a sentence. Thus we say *Hardly had I arrived when she left* on the pattern of *Never have I read such a book* or *At no time has he condemned the movement*. Other adverbs do not cause this kind of inversion. You would never say *Occasionally has he addressed this question* or *To a slight degree have they changed their position*. What's more, adverbs such as *hardly* can be

said to have a negative meaning in that they minimize the state or event they describe. Thus *hardly* means "almost not at all"; *rarely* means "practically never"; and so forth. This is why they cannot be used with another negative such as *not* or *none*.
More at **double negative, rarely,** and **scarcely.**

**have to** The verb phrases *have to* and *have got to* express necessity and obligation. They differ subtly in meaning from the auxiliary verb *must*. While all of these verbs can be used to express a command or warning (*You have got to leave now. You must not shout*), *have to* and *have got to* are somewhat more forceful than *must* in expressing necessity. *There has* (or *has got*) *to be some mistake* conveys a bit more emphasis than *There must be some mistake*. Only *have to* can form verb phrases with *may, be,* and *have*. We can say *I may have to go* but not *I may have got to go*. We can say *You are having to do a lot more work these days* but not *You are having got to . . .* We can say *The town has had to repave its main road* but not *The town has had got to . . .* In spoken English people often drop the *have* from *have got to,* as in *We got to get up early*. But in formal writing *got to* is not ordinarily considered acceptable.
More at **auxiliary and primary verbs, must,** and **ought.**

**however**
**however beginning a sentence** *Sailing in rough weather can be very unpleasant. However, we found it exciting.* Some people say you should never begin a sentence with *however* when it means "nevertheless" or "on the other hand." They are probably in the minority. We asked the usage panelists if they observed this rule. Thirty-six percent said "usually or always," 19 percent said "sometimes," and 42 percent said "rarely or never."
**but however** For a discussion of this word combination, see **redundancy** under *Style*.
More at **and, but,** and **whatever.**

**like** *Tell it like it is. It's like I said. I remember it like it was yesterday.* As these familiar examples show, *like* is often used as a conjunction meaning "as" or "as if." In fact, writers since Chaucer's time have used *like* as a conjunction. But language critics and writing handbooks have condemned this use of *like* for more than a century, and a writer who uses it in formal style risks being tarred with their brush. If you want to avoid this fate, use *as* or *as if* instead: *Sales of new models rose as* (not *like*) *we expected them to. He ran as if* (not *like*) *his life depended on it.* Note, however, that there is sometimes a subtle difference between *like* and *as if.* With *like,* there is often a stronger suggestion that the following clause is true. For example, the sentence *The teachers treat her like she has real talent* is not exactly equivalent to *The teachers treat her as if she had real talent.* The sentence using *as if* implies that her talent could be in doubt.
　　*Like* is acceptable as a conjunction when used in informal contexts, especially with verbs such as *feel, look, seem, sound,* and *taste: It looks like we are in for a rough winter.* Constructions in which the verb is not expressed, such as *He*

*took to politics like a duck to water,* are acceptable even in formal style, since *like* in this case can be viewed as a preposition.
More at **as.**

## may

**may and might** *It may rain. It might rain.* What's the difference? Just as *could* is the past tense of *can, might* is the past tense of *may: We thought we might win the tournament.* But *might* can also be used as a substitute for *may* to show diminished possibility. Thus, saying *We might go to the movies* means that the likelihood of going is somewhat less than if you say *We may go to the movies.* When used to express permission, *might* has a higher degree of politeness than *may.* Thus, *Might I express my opinion* conveys less insistence than *May I express my opinion.*

**may can / might could** In many Southern varieties of English, *might* is used in the "double modal" construction with *could,* as in *We might could park over there.* Less frequently, one hears *may can* and *might should.* These constructions are not familiar to the majority of American speakers and are best avoided in formal writing.
More at **auxiliary and primary verbs** and **can.**

**more than one** Here's a riddle: How can you have more than one and still have only one? The answer: When you are skinning a cat. When a noun phrase contains *more than one* and a singular noun, the verb is normally singular: *There is more than one way to skin a cat. More than one editor is working on that project. More than one field has been planted with oats.*

When *more than one* is followed by *of* and a plural noun, the verb is plural: *More than one of the paintings were stolen. More than one of the cottages are for sale.*

When *more than one* stands alone, it usually takes a singular verb, but it may take a plural verb if the notion of multiplicity predominates: *The operating rooms are all in good order. More than one is* (or *are*) *equipped with the latest imaging technology.*
More at **subject and verb agreement.**

**must** The auxiliary verb *must* is used to express necessity, obligation, and probability: *Plants must have water in order to live. Swimmers must take a shower before entering the pool. You must be joking.* Unlike other auxiliaries like *can* and *may, must* has no past form like *could* or *might: They insisted we must wait until tomorrow.* In this regard *must* resembles *need* and *ought to.*
More at **auxiliary and primary verbs, have to, may, need, ought,** and **should.**

**need** Depending on the sense, the verb *need* behaves sometimes like an auxiliary verb (such as *can* or *may*) and sometimes like a main verb (such as *want* or *try*). When used as a main verb, *need* agrees with its subject, takes *to* before the verb following it, and combines with *do* in questions, negations, and certain other constructions: *He needs to go. Does he need to go so soon? He doesn't need to go.* When used as an auxiliary verb, *need* does not agree with its subject, does not take *to* before the verb following it, and does not combine with *do: He needn't go. Need he go so soon?* Unlike *can* and *may,* however, auxiliary *need* has no other form like *could* and *might* for the past tense: *He said we need not worry about that.*

More at **auxiliary and primary verbs, dare, have to, must,** and **ought.**

## neither

**neither or none** According to the traditional rule, *neither* is used only to mean "not one or the other of two." To refer to "none of several," *none* is preferred: *None* (not *neither*) *of the three opposition candidates would make a better president than the incumbent.*

**singular or plural** The traditional rule also holds that *neither* is grammatically singular: *Neither candidate is having an easy time with the press.* However, it is often used with a plural verb, especially when followed by *of* and a plural: *Neither of the candidates are really expressing their own views.*

**neither . . . (n)or** As a conjunction *neither* is properly followed by *nor,* not *or,* in formal style: *Neither prayers nor curses* (not *or curses*) *did any good.*

More at **either, every, none, nor,** and **or.**

**none** "*. . . and then there were none.*" The closing words of this well-known nursery rhyme should dispel the notion that *none* can only take a singular verb. People opposing the plural use base their argument on the fact that *none* comes from the Old English word *an,* meaning "one." But the citational evidence against restricting *none* is overwhelming. *None* has been used as both a singular and plural pronoun since the ninth century. The plural usage appears in the King James Bible as well as the works of John Dryden and Edmund Burke and is widespread in the works of respected writers today.

Of course, the singular usage is perfectly acceptable. Whether you should choose a singular or plural verb depends on the effect you want. You can use either a singular or a plural verb in a sentence such as *None of the conspirators has* (or *have*) *been brought to trial.* However, *none* can only be plural when used in sentences such as *None but his most loyal supporters believe* (not *believes*) *his story.*

More at **every, neither,** and **subject and verb agreement.**

**nor** The rules for using *nor* are neither simple nor easy to spell out. When using *neither* in a balanced construction that negates two parts of a sentence, you must use *nor,* not *or,* in the second part. Thus you must say *He is neither able nor* (not *or*) *willing to go.* Similarly, you must use *nor* (not *or*) when negating the second of two negative independent clauses: *He cannot find anyone now, nor does he expect to find anyone in the future. Jane will never compromise with Bill, nor will Bill compromise with Jane.* Note that in these constructions *nor* causes an inversion of the auxiliary verb and the subject (*does he . . . will Bill . . .*). However, when a verb is negated by *not* or *never,* and is followed by a negative verb phrase (but not an entire clause), you can use either *or* or *nor: He will not permit the change or* (or *nor*) *even consider it.* In noun phrases of the type *no this or that, or* is actually more common than *nor: He has no experience or interest* (less frequently *nor interest*) *in chemistry.*

*Or* is also more common than *nor* when such a noun phrase, adjective phrase, or adverb phrase is introduced by *not: He is not a philosopher or a statesman. They were not rich or happy.*
More at **neither** and **or.**

**not** You should be careful where you put *not* and other negatives in a sentence in order to avoid ambiguity. The sentence *All classes are not open to enrollment* could be taken to mean either "All classes are closed to enrollment" or "Not all classes are open to enrollment." Similarly, the sentence *Kim didn't sleep until noon* could mean either "Kim went to sleep at noon" or "Kim got up before noon."
More at **adverbs, also,** and **only.**

**nothing** According to the traditional rule, *nothing* is invariably treated as a singular, even when followed by an exception phrase containing a plural noun: *Nothing except your fears stands* (not *stand*) *in your way. Nothing but roses meets* (not *meet*) *the eye.*

**one** In formal usage, the pronoun *one* is sometimes used as a generic pronoun meaning "anyone": *One would hope that train service could be improved.* The informal counterpart of *one* is *you: You never know what to expect from her.* Trouble arises when you use *one* in a series of sentences. You must choose a relative pronoun to refer back to *one.* You can of course use *one* and *one's* repeatedly, as in *One tries to be careful about where one invests one's money.* But in a sequence of sentences this may start to become tedious. A traditional alternative has been to use *he, him,* and *his: One tries to be careful about his investments.* This has the drawback of raising the specter of gender bias. For a more detailed discussion of this problem, see the entry for **he** under *Gender.* Because of these problems, the temptation may arise to switch to *you,* but this will undoubtedly be distracting to your readers. It's better to use the same generic pronoun throughout.
**one of a greater number** When constructions headed by *one* appear as the subject of a sentence or relative clause, there may be a question as to whether the verb should be singular or plural. The sentence *One of every ten rotors was found defective* is perfectly grammatical, but sometimes people use plural verbs in such situations, as in *One of every ten rotors have defects.* In an earlier survey, 92 percent of the Usage Panel preferred the singular verb in such sentences.
**one of those who** Constructions such as *one of those people who* pose a different problem. Many people argue that *who* should be followed by a plural verb in these sentences, as in *He is one of those people who just don't take "no" for an answer.* Their thinking is that the relative pronoun *who* refers to the plural noun *people,* not to *one.* They would extend the rule to constructions with inanimate nouns, as in *The sports car turned out to be one of the most successful products that were ever manufactured in this country.*
But the use of the singular verb in these constructions is common, even among the best writers. In an earlier survey, 42 percent of the Usage Panel accepted the use of the singular verb in such constructions. It's really a matter of

which word you feel is most appropriate as the antecedent of the relative pro-noun—*one* or the plural noun in the *of*-phrase that follows it. Note also that when the phrase containing *one* is introduced by the definite article, the verb in the relative clause must be singular: *He is the only one of the students who has* (not *have*) *already taken Latin.*

**one or more** Constructions using *one or more* or *one or two* always take a plural verb: *One or more cars were parked in front of the house each day this week. One or two students from our department have won prizes.* Note that when followed by a fraction, *one* ordinarily gets a plural verb: *One and a half years have passed since I last saw her.* The fraction rule has an exception in that amounts are sometimes treated as singular entities: *One and a half cups is enough sugar.* Note also that the plural rule does not apply to these one-plus-a-fraction constructions that are introduced by the indefinite article. These are always singular: *A year and a half has passed since I last saw her.*

More at **more than one** and **subject and verb agreement.**

**only** Sometimes it seems that *only* only causes trouble. Because the adverb *only* can change the meaning of a sentence depending on where it is put, you have to be careful where you put it. Consider how the placement of *only* affects the meaning of the following examples:

> Dictators respect only force; they are not moved by words.
> Dictators only respect force; they do not worship it.
> She picked up the receiver only when he entered, not before.
> She only picked up the receiver when he entered; she didn't dial the number.

In general, it's a good policy to put *only* next to the word or words it modifies. Sticklers insist that this rule for placement of *only* should always be followed, but sometimes it sounds more natural for *only* to come earlier in the sentence, and if the context is sufficiently clear, there's no chance of being misunder-stood. Thus, the rule requires you to say *We can come to an agreement only if everyone is willing to compromise.* But you can say more naturally, with slightly different emphasis and with no risk of misunderstanding, *We can only come to an agreement if everyone is willing to compromise.*

More at **adverbs, also, not,** and **split infinitive.**

**or** When all the elements in a series connected by *or* are singular, the verb they govern is singular: *Tom or Jack is coming. Beer, ale, or wine is included in the charge.* When all the elements are plural, the verb is plural. When the elements do not agree in number, some people say that the verb should agree in number with the nearest element: *Tom or his sisters are coming. The girls or their brother is coming. Cold symptoms or a headache is the usual first sign.* But others object that these constructions are inherently illogical and that the only solution is to revise the sentence to avoid the problem of agreement: *Either Tom is coming or his sisters are. The first sign is usually cold symptoms or a headache.*

More at **either, neither, nor,** and **subject and verb agreement.**

## ought

**ought as auxiliary verb** *Ought* is an auxiliary verb that usually takes *to* with its accompanying verb: *We ought to go.* Sometimes the accompanying verb is dropped if the meaning is clear: *Should we begin soon? Yes, we ought to.* In questions and negative sentences, especially those with contractions, *to* is also sometimes omitted: *We ought not be afraid of the risks involved. Oughtn't we be going soon?* This omission of *to,* however, is not common in written English. Like *must* and auxiliary *need, ought to* does not change to show past tense: *He said we ought to get moving along.*

**ought in regional expressions** Usages such as *He hadn't ought to come* and *She shouldn't ought to say that* are common in many varieties of American English. They should be avoided in written English, however, in favor of the more standard variant *ought not to.*

More at **auxiliary and primary verbs, have to, must, need,** and **should.**

## participles

**uses of participles** A participle is a verb form that can be used as an adjective and is used with an auxiliary verb to form tenses and, in the case of the past participle, the passive voice. The present participle ends in *-ing* (*going, running*). The past participle for many verbs ends in *-ed* (*created, walked*); other past participles have a different form, and often a different vowel, from their base form (*made* from *make, ridden* from *ride, swum* from *swim*). The present participle is used with *be* to indicate continuing action or state (*I am going. They were laughing. We have been talking.*). The past participle is used with *have* to form past tenses (*We have climbed. She had ridden. They have sung.*) and with *be* to form the passive voice (*The floor is being scrubbed. The ball was kicked. The car has been driven.*).

**dangling participles** Participial phrases are used chiefly to modify nouns, as in *Sitting at his desk, he read the letter carefully* where the *sitting* phrase modifies *he.* It is important to remember that readers will ordinarily associate a participle with the noun or noun phrase that is adjacent to it. Thus readers will consider a sentence such as *Turning the corner, the view was quite different* to be an error, for the view did not do the turning. A sentence like this needlessly distracts the reader and would be better recast as *When we turned the corner, the view was quite different* or *Turning the corner, we had a different view.* The problem of dangling participles is treated more broadly under **dangling modifiers.**

**participles and absolute constructions** Be careful not to confuse a participial phrase that modifies a noun with an absolute construction that employs a participle. The difference is between sentences such as *Taking down the poster, he went inside* and *The poster having been taken down, he went inside.* Absolute constructions can dangle where they please since by their "absolute" nature they do not modify a specific element in the rest of the sentence. For more on this, see **absolute constructions.**

**participles as prepositions** A number of expressions originally derived from participles have become prepositions, and you can use these to introduce phrases that are not associated with the immediately adjacent noun phrase. Such expressions include *concerning, considering, failing, granting, judging by,* and *speaking of.* Thus you can say without fear of criticism *Speaking of politics, the elections have been postponed* or *Considering the hour, it is surprising that he arrived at all.*

**participles as adjectives** Many participles can also function as adjectives: *an interesting experience, an interested customer; the surprising results, the surprised researchers.* But it is often hard to tell when a participle is an adjective, especially with past participles. Linguists have a number of tests for confirming an adjective. Here are four of them:

1. Can the word be used attributively (i.e., before the noun it modifies), as in *an intriguing offer.*

2. Can it be used in the predicate, especially after the verb *seem,* as in *She thought the party boring* and *He seems concerned about you.*

3. Can it be compared, as in *We are even more encouraged now* and *The results are most encouraging.*

4. Can it be modified by *very,* as in *They are very worried about this.*

Some adjectives pass more of these tests than others and are thus more purely adjectival. *Disastrous,* for instance, passes tests 1, 2, and 3, but not 4. When used as adjectives, most participles pass all four tests, but modification by *very* is tricky. For more on this, see **very and past participles.**

You can tell that a past participle is really part of a passive verb—and not an adjective—when it is followed by a *by*-prepositional phrase that has a personal agent as its object. Thus, the participle *married* would be part of the verb in the sentence *Chuck and Wendy were married by a bishop* but used as an adjective in the sentence *Chuck and Wendy were happily married for about six months.* To confirm the adjectival status of a participle, try transforming the sentence to see if the participle can come before the noun: *For about six months Chuck and Wendy were a happily married couple.*

**plus** *You get the knife, the bowl, and the book. Plus you get the free knife sharpener.* The use of *plus* as a conjunction connecting clauses or starting a sentence that emphasizes an additional thought occurs frequently in sales pitches, but it is not well established in formal writing.

The use of *plus* to connect nouns presents a more complicated issue. When equations involving addition are written out in words, the verb is usually singular: *Three plus two is five.* Similarly, when *plus* connects nouns or noun phrases, the verb is usually singular: *Their strength plus their intelligence makes them formidable opponents.* Some people would argue that in these sentences *plus* functions as a preposition meaning "in addition to," but if this were true, you would be able to move the *plus* phrase to the beginning of the sentence, and this is clearly impossible. You cannot say *Plus their intelligence, their strength makes them formidable.* It makes more sense to view *plus* in these uses as a conjunction that joins two subjects into a single entity requiring a singular verb by notional agreement, just as *and* does in the sentence *Chips and beans is her favorite appetizer.* More at **subject and verb agreement.**

**possessive constructions** We all know that in English you form the possessive by adding an apostrophe and an *s*, or sometimes just an apostrophe, at the end of a noun. Pronouns have their own possessive forms (*my, your, his, her, its, our, their*); for a discussion of the rules used to make the possessives of individual nouns, see **Forming Possessives** under *Word Formation*. Of course, another way to indicate possession is to use a prepositional phrase using *of: the property of the town.*

It is important to remember that possessive constructions are often used with inanimate nouns (*a stone's throw, the water's edge*). And although we call them possessives, they often do not indicate simple possession but a number of other relations. These include source or origin (*the ambassador's letter, Hardy's novels*), description or classification (*the car's speed, the stadium's design, a month's salary*), and even purpose (*a women's college, boys' clothing*).

Listed below are some of the more troublesome constructions.

**both** "*A plague on both your houses!*" We know this familiar curse from Shakespeare's *Romeo and Juliet*. It means "a plague on the houses of both of you." While this "both your" construction is still idiomatic, you can be more precise grammatically by saying *of both*. Thus you would say *I gave copies of the book to the mothers of both* (rather than *both their mothers*) or *It's the fault of both* (rather than *both their fault* or *both's fault*).

**each other / one another** The possessive forms of *each other* and *one another* are written *each other's* and *one another's*, that is, with an apostrophe before the *-s: The boys wore each other's* (not *each others'*) *coats. They had forgotten one another's* (not *one anothers'*) *names.*

**else** When a pronoun is followed by *else,* the possessive form is generally written with the *'s* following *else: That must be someone else's* (not *someone's else*) *book.* Both *who else's* and *whose else* are in use, but not *whose else's: Who else's book could it have been? Whose else could it have been?*

**group possessive** You form the possessive for noun phrases by adding an *'s* or an apostrophe at the end of the phrase: *Jim and Nancy's house, the Department of Chemistry's new requirements, a three months' journey.* This construction gets cumbersome when the noun phrase is long, in which case you should probably use a prepositional phrase instead. Thus instead of saying *the house that overlooks the bay's property line,* you should say *the property line of the house that overlooks the bay.*

**of mine, of yours (double genitive)** People sometimes object to the "double genitive" construction, as in *a friend of my father's* or *a book of mine.* But the construction has been used in English since the 14th century and serves a useful purpose. It can help sort out ambiguous phrases like *Bob's photograph,* which could mean either "a photograph of Bob" (i.e., revealing Bob's image) or "a photograph that is in Bob's possession." *A photograph of Bob's,* on the other hand, can only be a photo that Bob has in his possession and may or may not show Bob's image. Moreover, in some sentences the double genitive offers the only way to express what is meant. There is no substitute for it in a sentence such as *That's the only friend of yours that I've ever met,* since sentences such as *That's your only friend that I've ever met* and *That's your only friend, whom I've ever met* are not grammatical.

**whose** You can use *whose* as a possessive to refer to both animate and inanimate nouns. Thus you can say *Crick, whose theories still influence work in laboratories around the world* or *Crick's theories, whose influence continues to be felt in laboratories around the world.* With inanimate nouns you can also use *of which* as an alternative, as in *Crick's theories, the influence of which continues to be felt in laboratories around the world.* But as this example demonstrates, substituting *of which* for *whose* is sometimes cumbersome.

More at **gerunds and possessives.**

### prepositions

**preposition ending a sentence** It was John Dryden, the 17th-century poet and dramatist, who first promulgated the doctrine that a preposition may not be used at the end a sentence. Grammarians in the 18th century refined the doctrine, and the rule has since become one of the most venerated maxims of schoolroom grammar. But sentences ending with prepositions can be found in the works of most of the great writers since the Renaissance. In fact, English syntax not only allows but sometimes even requires final placement of the preposition, as in *We have much to be thankful for* or *That depends on what you believe in.* Efforts to rewrite such sentences to place the preposition elsewhere can have comical results, as Winston Churchill demonstrated when he objected to the doctrine by saying *"This is the sort of English up with which I cannot put."*

Even sticklers for the traditional rule can have no grounds for criticizing sentences such as *I don't know where she will end up* or *It's the most curious book I've ever run across;* in these examples, *up* and *across* are adverbs, not prepositions. You can be sure of this because it is impossible to transform these examples into sentences with prepositional phrases. It is simply not grammatical English to say *I don't know up where she will end* and *It's the most curious book across which I have ever run.*

**participles as prepositions** Some participles, such as *concerning* and *considering,* are used as prepositions. For more on this, see **participles**.

**pronouns, agreement of** *A pronoun must agree with its antecedent in person, number, and gender.* Most people have heard this grammatical rule at some time in their lives. An *antecedent,* of course, is a noun or pronoun referred to by a pronoun. Usually an antecedent comes before its pronoun (as in *Dave played his guitar this morning*) but sometimes the pronoun anticipates the antecedent (as in *Although he knew he would be late, Mr. Stanton did not rush to get ready*).

The problems involving agreement of person are less inherent to the pronouns themselves than created by shifts in point of view. Sometimes it is difficult to stick to the same person when using generic pronouns, such as *one* and *you.* For more on this problem, see **one.**

Problems in number agreement are often initiated by indefinite pronouns such as *anyone, everybody,* and *somebody.* These problems often involve the related issue of gender. Which pronoun should you use in a sentence such as *Everyone thinks (he is/she is/they are) entitled to a raise this year?* Using the

plural pronoun in such constructions avoids the problem of gender bias but violates the rule of number agreement since indefinite pronouns like *everyone* are grammatically singular. Similar problems arise in sentences with singular antecedents of undetermined gender, such as *A good judge should never indulge (his/her/their) personal prejudices.* Perhaps the easiest solution here is to write in the plural: *Good judges should never indulge their personal prejudices.* For a more detailed discussion of these problems, see **he** under *Gender*.

More at **any, anyone, each, every,** and **none.**

**pronouns, personal** This entry treats personal pronouns only; usage issues involving interrogative, relative, and indefinite pronouns are addressed at entries for specific words (*that, who,* etc.).

A number of usage problems involving personal pronouns are questions of which case to use in a given situation. The cases of personal pronouns are listed in the table below as an aid in understanding the case problems discussed here.

| Nominative Case | Singular | Plural |
|---|---|---|
| First Person | I | we |
| Second Person | you | you |
| Third Person | he, she, it | they |

| Objective Case | Singular | Plural |
|---|---|---|
| First Person | me | us |
| Second Person | you | you |
| Third Person | him, her, it | them |

| Possessive Case | Singular | Plural |
|---|---|---|
| First Person | my | our |
| Second Person | your | your |
| Third Person | his, her, its | their |

**personal pronouns after *as*** *Your mother is just as proud as me,* said the father to the child with good grades. But should he have said, *Your mother is just as proud as I?* As with similar constructions using *than,* there is a traditional rule stating that the pronoun following *as . . . as . . .* constructions must be in the nominative case, demonstrated by the fact that *She is just as proud as I* is really a truncated version of the sentence *She is just as proud as I am.* Another way to put it would be to say that the second *as* functions as a conjunction, not as a preposition, in these sentences. Whatever the merits of this logic, the *as me* construction is very common in speech and appears regularly in the writing of highly respected writers. Moreover, you can argue that the second *as* is really a prepo-

sition in these constructions and demands the objective case. And there is the objection that *as I* constructions are overly formal, even pretentious. In short, both constructions are defensible and both are subject to attack. When you want to play it safe, use the *as I* construction, but throw in the verb to make it a clause: *She is just as proud as I am.*

**personal pronouns after forms of be** *That must be him on the phone. No, it must be he.* Traditional grammar requires the nominative form of the pronoun following the verb *be: It is I* (not *me*); *That must be they* (not *them*), and so forth. Nearly everyone finds this rule difficult to follow. Even if everyone could follow it, in informal contexts the nominative pronoun often sounds pedantic and even ridiculous, especially when the verb is contracted. Who would ever say *It's we*? But constructions like *It is me* have been condemned in the classroom and in writing handbooks for so long that there seems little likelihood that they will ever be entirely acceptable in formal writing.

The traditional rule creates additional problems when the pronoun following *be* also functions as the object of a verb or preposition in a relative clause, as in *It is not them/they that we have in mind when we talk about "crime in the streets" nowadays,* where the plural pronoun serves as both the predicate of *is* and the object of *have.* In this example, 57 percent of the Usage Panel prefers the nominative form *they,* 33 percent prefer the objective *them,* and 10 percent accept both versions. Perhaps the best strategy is to revise these sentences to avoid the problem. You can say instead *They are not the ones we have in mind, We have someone else in mind,* and so on.

**personal pronouns after but** Should you say *No one but I read the book* or *No one but me read the book*? If *but* is a conjunction in these sentences, you should use the nominative form *I.* If *but* is a preposition, you should use *me.* So which is it—conjunction or preposition? Although some grammarians have insisted that *but* is a conjunction here, they have had to admit that the objective form *me* is appropriate when the *but* phrase occurs at the end of a sentence, as in *No one has read it but me.* And in fact there is a strong case for viewing *but* as a preposition in all of these constructions. For one thing, if *but* were truly a conjunction, you would expect the verb to agree in person and number with the noun or pronoun following *but.* You would then say *No one but the students have read it,* but you normally say *No one . . . has read it.* What is more, a conjunction cannot be moved to the end of a clause, as in *No one has read it but the students.* You can tell this because you cannot use the similar conjunction *and* in this way. That is, you cannot say *John left and everyone else in the class.* For these reasons it seems best to consider *but* as a preposition in these constructions and to use the objective forms of pronouns such as *me* and *them* in all positions: *No one but me has read it. No one has read it but me.* These recommendations are supported by 73 percent of the Usage Panel when the *but* phrase precedes the verb and by 93 percent when the *but* phrase follows the verb.

**personal pronouns after except** Just like *but, except* in the sense of "with the exclusion of" or "other than" is generally viewed as a preposition, not a conjunction. Therefore, a personal pronoun that follows *except* should be in the objective case: *No one except me knew it. Every member of the original cast was signed except her.*

**personal pronouns after *than*** Grammarians have insisted since the 18th century that *than* should be regarded as a conjunction in all its uses. By this thinking, a sentence such as *Bill is taller than Tom* is really a truncated version of the sentence *Bill is taller than Tom is.* Accordingly, when a pronoun follows *than* in sentences like this, it should be in the nominative case since it is the subject of the verb that is "understood." Thus the rule requires *Bill is taller than he* (not *him*). But when applied to sentences in which the pronoun following *than* is the object of an understood verb, the rule requires that the pronoun be in the objective case. Thus you must say *The news surprised Pat more than me,* since this sentence is considered a truncated version of *The news surprised Pat more than it surprised me.* The rule is logical and neat, and no harm can come from following it in formal writing, but people often don't follow it, especially when speaking. In fact, *than* has been used as a preposition since the 1500s in sentences like *John is taller than me.* In these cases the pronoun is in the objective case where the rule would require the nominative. This construction appears in the writing of some of our most respected writers, among them Shakespeare, Johnson, Swift, Scott, and Faulkner. So if you choose to ignore the grammarian's rule, you are in good company. If you want even more justification, remember that *than* is clearly treated as a preposition in the *than whom* construction, as in *a poet than whom* (not *than who*) *no one has a dearer place in the hearts of his countrymen.* Still, if you find you have written a sentence such as *Mary is taller than him,* don't be surprised if some of your readers object.

**between you and I** "*All debts are cleared between you and I,*" writes Antonio to Bassanio in Shakespeare's *The Merchant of Venice.* Did Shakespeare commit a blunder, writing *I* where the objective form *me* is required?

When pronouns joined by a conjunction occur as the object of a preposition such as *between, according to,* or *like,* many people use the nominative form where the traditional grammatical rule would require the objective. They say *between you and I* rather than *between you and me,* and so forth.

Shakespeare can hardly have violated a rule of formal English grammar, since he and his contemporaries studied Latin grammar, not English. In fact, the rule outlawing *between you and I* did not get written until the 1860s. It has since become part of standard schoolroom grammar. Writing *between you and I* is now widely regarded as a sign of ignorance, even though the phrase occurs quite often in speech. So don't feel bad if you catch yourself saying it. Just remember: if you want to avoid trouble, stick to *between you and me* in formal speech and writing.

**personal pronouns in compound subjects** When pronouns are joined with other nouns or pronouns by *and* or *or,* there is a widespread tendency to use the objective form even when the phrase is the subject of the sentence: *Robert and her are not speaking to each other. Me and Kate are going to the store.* This usage is common in colloquial speech, but the nominative forms should be used in formal speech and writing: *John and she* (not *her*) *will be giving the talk.* When the form *I* is used, it is almost invariably the last element in the phrase: *Mr. McCarty and I have formed a partnership.*

**me for I did**—**the objective case as acceptable subject** *Who cut down the cherry tree?* What do you say to such a question when you feel the only responsible thing to do is to own up to it, *Me* or *I?* In such cases it is pedantic to apply the traditional rule that requires the nominative form of the pronoun when the objective form sounds more natural. Thus, we more colloquially say *Me,* even though you can argue that *I* must be correct here as a truncated version of *I did.*

When a pronoun is used as a subject together with a noun, people tend to use the objective form, as in *Us engineers were left without any technical support.* In formal speech or writing the nominative *we* would be preferable here. If you feel uncomfortable about either choice, you should rewrite the sentence to avoid the difficulty.

**pronouns, reflexive and intensive** The reflexive and intensive pronouns end in *-self* (singular) or *-selves* (plural):

> First person: *myself; ourselves*
> Second person: *yourself; yourselves*
> Third person: *himself, herself, itself; themselves*

These pronouns usually refer back to the subject of the sentence. They are called reflexive when they are the object of a verb or preposition or when they otherwise complete the meaning of a verb. Here are some examples:

> She freed herself from a difficult situation.
> They allowed themselves another break from work.
> He is not himself today.
> Their new business can't possibly pay for itself.

All of these uses are perfectly acceptable.

When the *-self* pronouns are used for emphasis, they are called intensive or emphatic pronouns:

> We ourselves would never have agreed to such a thing.
> She couldn't come herself.
> Myself, I wouldn't worry about it.

Sometimes the intensive pronoun does not refer to the subject of the sentence but is used as an emphatic substitute for a personal pronoun. This practice is particularly common in compound phrases, as in *Mrs. Evans or yourself will have to pick them up at the airport.* Although these usages have been common in the writing of reputable authors for several centuries, they may not sit well with your readers. A large majority of the Usage Panel disapproves of the use of *-self* pronouns when they do not refer to the subject of the sentence. Seventy-three percent reject the sentence *He was an enthusiastic fisherman like myself.* Sixty-seven percent object to *The letters were written entirely by myself.* The panel is even less tolerant of compound usages. Eighty-eight percent find this sentence unacceptable: *The boss asked John and myself to give a brief presentation.*

## rather

**would rather / should rather** *Which would you rather do—play professional baseball or sell used cars?* In expressions of preference *rather* is commonly preceded by *would: We would rather go to the lake than stay in town for the weekend.* In formal style, you sometimes see *should* instead of *would: I should rather my daughter attended a private school.*

**had rather** Sometimes *had* appears in these constructions, though this use of *had* seems to be growing less frequent: *I had rather work with Williams than work for him.* Language critics once condemned this use of *had* as a mistake. In truth the mistake was their own. They misunderstood sentences such as *I'd rather stay,* thinking the contraction was of *would.* But the contraction is a survival of the subjunctive form *had* that also appears in constructions like *had better* and *had best,* as in *We had better leave now.* This use of *had* goes back to Middle English and is perfectly acceptable.

**rather a** Before an unmodified noun only *rather a* is used: *It was rather a disaster.* When the noun is preceded by an adjective, however, both *rather a* and *a rather* are found: *It was rather a boring party. It was a rather boring party.* When *a rather* is used in this construction, *rather* qualifies only the adjective, whereas with *rather a* it qualifies either the adjective or the entire noun phrase. Thus *a rather long ordeal* can mean only "an ordeal that is rather long," whereas *rather a long ordeal* can also mean roughly "a long process that is something of an ordeal." *Rather a* is the only possible choice when the adjective itself does not permit modification. Thus we say *The horse was rather a long shot* but not *The horse was a rather long shot.*

More at **had better** and **should.**

## scarcely

**scarcely as negative adverb** *Scarcely* has the force of a negative and is therefore regarded as incorrectly used with another negative, as in *I couldn't scarcely believe it.* For more on this problem, see **double negative** and **hardly.**

**scarcely with a following clause** You should introduce a clause following *scarcely* with either *when* or *before.* The conjunction *than* is commonly used here, but such use is still considered unacceptable to some people. So you can say *The meeting had scarcely begun when* (or *before*) *it was interrupted,* but you should probably avoid saying *The meeting had scarcely begun than it was interrupted.*

## shall / will

**the traditional rules** The traditional rules state that you use *shall* to show what happens in the future only when *I* or *we* is the subject: *I shall* (not *will*) *call you tomorrow. We shall* (not *will*) *be sure to keep in touch. Will,* on the other hand, is used with subjects in the second and third persons: *The comet will* (not *shall*) *return in 87 years. You will* (not *shall*) *probably encounter some heavy seas when you round the point.* However, you can use *will* with a subject in the first person and *shall* with a subject in the second or third person to express determination, promise, obligation, or permission, depending on the context. Thus *I will leave tomorrow* indicates that the speaker is determined to leave. *You shall leave to-*

*morrow* has the ring of a command. The sentence *You shall have your money* expresses a promise ("I will see that you get your money"), whereas *You will have your money* makes a simple prediction.

**the reality** The English and some sticklers about usage are probably the only people who follow these rules, and then not with perfect consistency. In America, people who try to adhere to them run the risk of sounding pretentious or haughty. Americans normally use *will* to express most of the senses reserved for *shall* in British usage. Americans use *shall* chiefly in first person invitations and questions that request an opinion or agreement, such as *Shall we go?*, and in certain fixed expressions, such as *We shall overcome*. In formal style, Americans use *shall* to express an explicit obligation, such as *Applicants shall provide a proof of residence*, though *must* or *should* works just as well here. In speech you can get the distinctions in meaning delineated in the traditional rules by putting stress on the auxiliary verb, as in *I* will *leave tomorrow* ("I intend to leave"). You can also choose another auxiliary verb, such as *must* or *have to,* that is less open to misinterpretation, or you can make your meaning clear by adding an adverb such as *certainly.*

More at **auxiliary and primary verbs** and **should.**

## should

**should versus would** Just as they ignore the traditional rules governing the use of *shall* and *will,* Americans largely ignore the traditional rules governing the use of *should* and *would.* The two verbs are not always interchangeable, however. You can use either *should* and *would* in the first person to express the future from the point of view of the past, but keep in mind that *should* sounds more formal than *would: He swore that I should* (or *would* ) *pay for the remark.* The same principle applies to the verb in sentences that express a future condition: *If I had known that, I would* (or more formally, *should* ) *have answered differently.* In the second and third persons, however, you only use *would: She assured us that she would* (not *should* ) *return. If he had known that, he would* (not *should* ) *have answered differently.*

**should in conditional clauses** Choosing which verb to use in conditional clauses, such as those beginning with *if,* can be tricky. In certain clauses, you use *should* for all three persons: *if I* (or *you* or *he* ) *should decide to go, if it should begin to snow. Would* is not acceptable in these situations, but it does appear in other kinds of conditional clauses: *He might surprise you if you would give him a chance.* The best advice is to follow what sounds most natural. If you're really not sure, try a verb form in the indicative: *if it begins to snow.* You can also try the subjunctive: *if you were to give him a chance.*

**when only should is correct** To express duty or obligation, you use *should* as the equivalent of *ought to: I* (or *you* or *he* ) *should go.*

**when only would is correct** You use *would* (and not *should* ) to express willingness or promise (*I agreed that I would do it* ) and to express habitual action in the past (*We would walk along the canal at night* ). *Would* also has the advantage of being a polite substitute for *will* in requests: *Would you lend me a dollar?*

More at **auxiliary and primary verbs, shall / will,** and **subjunctive.**

## so

**so or so that in purpose clauses** Many people insist that *so* must be followed by *that* in formal writing when used to introduce a clause giving the reason for or the purpose of an action: *He stayed so that he could see the movie a second time.* But since many respected writers use *so* for *so that* in formal writing, it seems best to consider the issue one of stylistic preference: *The store stays open late so* (or *so that*) *people who work all day can buy groceries.*

**so or so that in result clauses** It is acceptable to use either *so* or *so that* to introduce clauses that state a result or consequence: *The Bay Bridge was still closed, so* (or *so that*) *the drive from San Francisco to the Berkeley campus took an hour and a half.*

**so as a connector in a narrative** *So the guy sits down at our table and pulls up his chair so he can be closer to me. So he starts telling us about his uncle. . . . So* is frequently used in informal speech to string together the elements of a narrative. But readers of formal writing generally expect connections to be made more explicit.

**so as intensive** People sometimes object to the use of *so* as an intensive meaning "to a great degree or extent": *We were so relieved to learn that the deadline had been extended.* This usage is most common in informal contexts, perhaps because unlike *very,* it presumes that the listener or reader will be sympathetic with the speaker's evaluation of the situation. Thus you would be more likely to say *It was so unfair of them not to invite you* than to say *It was so fortunate that I didn't have to put up with your company.* For just this reason, you can sometimes put intensive *so* to good use in more formal contexts to invite the reader to take the point of view of the speaker or subject: *The request seemed to her to be quite reasonable; it was so unfair of the manager to refuse.* Just remember not to overdo it.

More at **as.**

**split infinitive** *To boldly go where no one has gone before.* This phrase, so familiar to *Star Trek* fans, presents us with the dilemma of the split infinitive—an infinitive that has an adverb between the *to* and the verb. Split infinitives have been condemned as ungrammatical for nearly 200 years, but it is hard to see what exactly is wrong with saying *to boldly go.* Its meaning is clear. It has a strong rhythm than reinforces the meaning. And rearranging the phrase only makes it less effective. We may also want *to go boldly where no one has gone before,* but it doesn't sound as exciting. And certainly no one wants *to go where no one has gone before boldly.* That is a different voyage entirely.

In fact, the split infinitive is distinguished both by its length of use and the greatness of its users. People have been splitting infinitives since the 14th century, and some of the most noteworthy splitters include John Donne, Samuel Pepys, Daniel Defoe, Benjamin Franklin, Samuel Johnson, William Wordsworth, Abraham Lincoln, George Eliot, Henry James, and Willa Cather.

The only rationale for condemning the construction is based on a false analogy with Latin. The thinking is that because the Latin infinitive is a single

word, the English infinitive should be treated as if it were a single unit. But English is not Latin, and people split infinitives all the time without giving it a thought. Should we condemn compound infinitives, such as *I want to go and have a look*, simply because the infinitive *have* has no *to* next to it?

Still, if you dislike infinitives split by adverbs, you can often avoid them without difficulty. You can easily recast the sentence *To better understand the miners' plight, he went to live in their district* as *To understand the miners' plight better, he went to live in their district.* But as we saw with the *Star Trek* example, you must be careful not to ruin the rhythm of the sentence or create an unintended meaning by displacing an adverb.

If you plan on keeping your split infinitives, you should be wary of constructions that have more than one word between *to* and the verb. The Usage Panel splits down the middle on the one-adverb split infinitive. Fifty percent accept it in the sentence *The move allowed the company to legally pay the employees severance payments that in some cases exceeded $30,000.* But only 23 percent of the panel accepts the split infinitive in this sentence: *We are seeking a plan to gradually, systematically, and economically relieve the burden.* The panel is more tolerant of constructions in which the intervening words are intrinsic to the sense of the verb. Eighty-seven percent of the panel accepts the sentence *We expect our output to more than double in a year.*

Remember too that infinitive phrases in which the adverb precedes a participle, such as *to be rapidly rising, to be clearly understood,* and *to have been ruefully mistaken,* are not split and should be acceptable to everybody. And don't be deceived by *to*-constructions with a gerund, as in *He is committed to laboriously assembling all of the facts of the case.* Here what is split is not an infinitive but a prepositional phrase.

**subject and verb agreement** This entry provides an overview of subject and verb agreement. Problems that pertain to specific nouns, such as *data, number,* and *politics,* are treated at these entries under *Word Choice.* Other kinds of problems, such as those involving indefinite adjectives (like *every*) or conjunctions (like *either*), are treated at their respective entries in this chapter.

**?**

**grammatical agreement** *A verb must agree with its subject in person and number.* Singular subjects take singular verbs, and plural subjects take plural verbs. We've all heard this lesson more times than we care to remember. It's a good lesson, to be sure, but it's not quite as simple as it sounds.

One of the nice things about English is that its verbs do not change much to agree with a subject in number. In fact, for almost all verbs, there is only one change, adding *-s* or *-es* for third person singular, present tense. We say *He goes, She tries,* and *It matters.* All other persons require no changes to the verb. We say *I play, You play, We play,* and *They play.* The past tense requires its own changes to the verb, but (except for the verb *be*) these do not involve number. Thus we say *He walked and I ran, They walked and we ran,* and so on.

The modal auxiliaries are an exception to the agreement rule. They do not change to show number. We say *I can swim, He can swim, They can swim,* and so on. The primary verb *be* is a unique case in that it has many different forms—*am, are, is, was, were*—depending on the person, number, and tense of a specific use.

**notional agreement** It would be great if this was all there was to remember, but there is more than one kind of agreement. There is *grammatical agreement*, as discussed above, and agreement in meaning, or *notional agreement*. Usually grammatical agreement and notional agreement coincide. In the sentence *He laughs,* both are singular. In the sentence *We laugh,* both are plural. But in some sentences a subject can have a singular form and a plural meaning. Thus in the sentence *Her family are all avid skiers,* the noun *family* is singular in form but plural in meaning, and the verb is plural to agree with the meaning. In other words, there is notional agreement, but not grammatical agreement, between the subject and the verb. In the sentence *Everyone has gone to the movies,* the situation is reversed. The subject *everyone* is plural in meaning and singular in form, but the verb agrees in number with the form of its grammatical subject. There is grammatical agreement but not notional agreement.

Similarly, there are some nouns like *mumps* and *news* that are plural in form but take a singular verb: *The mumps was once a common childhood disease.* Amounts often take a singular verb: *Ten thousand bucks is a lot of money.* Here again we have notional, but not grammatical, agreement—the ten thousand bucks is considered a single quantity, and it gets a singular verb.

There are a number of words in English that can take a singular or plural verb depending on how they are used. Among these are collective nouns, pronouns such as *any* and *none,* and many nouns ending in *-ics,* such as *politics.*

**agreement by proximity** Certain grammatical constructions provide further complications. Sometimes the noun that is adjacent to the verb can exert more influence than the noun that is the grammatical subject. Selecting a verb in a sentence like *A variety of styles has been/have been in vogue for the last year* can be tricky. The traditional rules require *has been,* but the plural sense of the noun phrase presses for *have been.* While 59 percent of the Usage Panel insists on the singular verb in this sentence, 22 percent actually prefer the plural verb and another 19 percent say that either *has* or *have* is acceptable, meaning that 41 percent find the plural verb with a singular grammatical subject to be acceptable.

Sometimes syntax itself makes it impossible to follow the agreement rule. In a sentence like *Either John or his brothers are bringing the dessert,* the verb can't agree with both parts of the subject. Some people believe that the verb should agree with the closer of the two subjects. This is called *agreement by proximity.* For more on this subject, see **either** and **or**.

**compound subjects** In Modern English, a compound subject connected by *and* normally takes a plural verb: *Rebecca and Martha play in the same band. The house and the barn are on the same property. Their innovative idea, persistence, and careful research have finally paid off.* When a subject is followed by a conjoining prepositional phrase such as *as well as, in addition to,* or *with,* the verb should be singular: *Jesse as well as Luke likes jazz. The old school along with the playground is up for sale.*

Sometimes compound subjects are governed by a sense of unity and by notional agreement take a singular verb: *My name and address is printed on the box. His colleague and friend* (one person) *deserves equal credit.* This sense of unity is not simply a stylistic flourish. Using a singular or plural verb changes the meaning of the sentence. *Eating garlic and drinking red wine sometimes gives me a headache* means that the combination of garlic and red wine can cause a headache. With a plural verb (*give*), the sentence implies that garlic and red wine act separately; either can bring a headache.

## subjunctive

**the forms** *If she were coming, she would be here by now. I insist that the chairman resign! Their main demand was that the lawsuit be dropped.* These sentences all contain verbs in the subjunctive mood, which is used chiefly to express the speaker's attitude about the likelihood or factuality of a given situation. If the verbs were in the indicative mood, we would expect *she was coming* in the first sentence, *the chairman resigns* in the second, and *the lawsuit is dropped* in the third.

English has had a subjunctive mood since Old English times, but most of the functions of the old subjunctive have been taken over by auxiliary verbs like *may* and *should,* and the subjunctive survives only in very limited situations. It has a present and past form. The present form is identical to the base form of the verb, so you only notice it in the third person singular, which has no final *-s,* and in the case of the verb *be,* which has the form *be* instead of *am, is,* and *are.* The past subjunctive is identical with the past tense except in the case of the verb *be,* which uses *were* for all persons: *If I were rich . . . , If he were rich . . . , If they were rich. . . .*

The present subjunctive is most familiar to us in formulaic expressions such as *God help him, be that as it may, come what may,* and *suffice it to say.* It also occurs in *that*-clauses used to state commands or to express intentions or necessity:

> We insist that he *do* the job properly.
> The committee proposes that she *be* appointed treasurer immediately.
> It is essential that we *be* informed of your plans.

Other functions include use in some conditional clauses and clauses that make concessions or express purpose. In these cases the subjunctive carries a formal tone:

> Whether he *be* opposed to the plan or not, we must seek his opinion.
> Even though he *be* opposed to the plan, we must try to implement it.
> They are rewriting the proposal so that it not *contradict* new zoning laws.

The subjunctive is not required in such sentences, however, and you can use indicative forms if you prefer (*whether he* is *opposed . . .*).

The past subjunctive is sometimes called the *were* subjunctive, since *were* is the only subjunctive form that is distinct from the indicative past tense. It appears chiefly in *if*-clauses and in a few other constructions expressing hypothetical conditions:

If he *were* sorry, he'd have apologized by now.
I wish she *weren't* going away.
She's already acting as if she *were* going to be promoted.
Suppose she *were* to resign, what would you do then?

**if-clauses—the traditional rules** According to traditional rules, you use the subjunctive to describe an occurrence that you have presupposed to be contrary to fact: *if I were ten years younger, if America were still a British Colony.* The verb in the main clause of these sentences must then contain the verb *would* or (less frequently) *should: If I were ten years younger, I would consider entering the marathon. If America were still a British colony, we would all be drinking tea in the afternoon.* When the situation described by the *if*-clause is not presupposed to be false, however, that clause must contain an indicative verb. The form of verb in the main clause will depend on your intended meaning: *If Hamlet was really written by Marlowe, as many have argued, then we have underestimated Marlowe's genius. If Kevin was out all day, then it makes sense that he couldn't answer the phone.*

Remember, just because the modal verb *would* appears in the main clause, this doesn't mean that the verb in the *if*-clause must be in the subjunctive if the content of that clause is not presupposed to be false: *If I was (not were) to accept their offer—which I'm still considering—I would have to start the new job on May 2. He would always call her from the office if he was (not were) going to be late for dinner.*

Another traditional rule states that you are not supposed to use the subjunctive following verbs such as *ask* or *wonder* in *if*-clauses that express indirect questions, even if the content of the question is presumed to be contrary to fact: *We wondered if dinner was (not were) included in the room price. Some of the people we met even asked us if California was (not were) an island.*

**if-clauses—the reality** In practice, of course, many people ignore the rules. In fact, over the last 200 years even well-respected writers have tended to use the indicative *was* where the traditional rule would require the subjunctive *were.* A usage such as *If I was the only boy in the world* may break the rules, but it sounds perfectly natural.

**subjunctive after wish** Yet another traditional rule requires you to use *were* rather than *was* in a contrary-to-fact statement that follows the verb *wish: I wish I were (not was) lighter on my feet.* Many writers continue to insist on this rule, but the indicative *was* in such clauses can be found in the works of many well-known writers.

**would have for had** In spoken English, there is a growing tendency to use *would have* in place of the subjunctive *had* in contrary-to-fact clauses, such as *If she would have (instead of if she had) only listened to me, this would never have happened.* But this usage is still widely considered an error in writing. Only 14 percent of the Usage Panel accepts it in the previously-cited sentence, and a similar amount—but 16 percent—accepts it in the sentence *I wish you would have told me about this sooner.*

**didn't for hadn't** In speech people often substitute *didn't* for the subjunctive *hadn't* in *if*-clauses, such as *If I didn't have (instead of if I hadn't had) my seatbelt* *on, I would be dead.* This usage is also considered nonstandard, however. Seventy-one percent of the Usage Panel rejects it, although 18 percent feel it is acceptable in informal contexts.

**hadn't have** Another subjunctive form that is sometimes used in speech but is usually edited out of Standard English is the intrusive *have* occurring in negative constructions, as in *We would have been in real trouble if it hadn't have been for you.* In speech this *have* is always reduced, as *hadn't a'.* The *hadn't have* construction often appears in conjunction with the verb *happen,* as in *He would have been in real trouble if I hadn't have happened to be there* where standard practice requires *if I hadn't been there.* The Usage Panel has little affection for *hadn't have* in these situations; 91 percent of panelists find it unacceptable.

More at **should** and **wish.**

## that

**that / which (restrictive and nonrestrictive clauses)** The standard rule requires that you use *that* only to introduce a restrictive (or defining) relative clause, which identifies the person or thing being talked about; in this use it should never be preceded by a comma. Thus, in the sentence *The house that Jack built has been torn down,* the clause *that Jack built* is a restrictive clause telling which specific house was torn down. Similarly, in *I am looking for a book that is easy to read,* the restrictive clause *that is easy to read* tells what kind of book is desired.

By contrast, you use *which* only with nonrestrictive (or nondefining) clauses, which give additional information about something that has already been identified in the context; in this use, *which* is always preceded by a comma. Thus you should say *The students in Chemistry 101 have been complaining about the textbook, which* (not *that*) *is hard to follow.* The clause *which is hard to follow* is nonrestrictive in that it does not indicate which text is being complained about; even if it were omitted, we would know that the phrase *the textbook* refers to the text in Chemistry 101. It should be easy to follow the rule in nonrestrictive clauses like this, since *which* here sounds more natural than *that.*

Some people extend the rule and insist that, just as *that* should be used only in restrictive clauses, *which* should be used only in nonrestrictive clauses. By this thinking, you should avoid using *which* in sentences such as *I need a book which will tell me all about city gardening,* where the restrictive clause *which will tell me all about city gardening* describes what sort of book is needed. But this use of *which* with restrictive clauses is very common, even in edited prose. If you fail to follow the rule in this point, you have plenty of company. Moreover, there are some situations in which *which* is preferable to *that.* *Which* can be especially useful where two or more relative clauses are joined by *and* or *or: It is a philosophy in which ordinary people may find solace and which many have found reason to praise.* You may also want to use *which* to introduce a restrictive clause when the preceding phrase contains a *that: We want to assign only that book which will be most helpful.*

**omitting *that*** You can omit *that* in a relative clause when the subject of the clause is different from the word or phrase the clause refers to. Thus, you can say either *the book that I was reading* or *the book I was reading*. You can also omit *that* when it introduces a subordinate clause: *I think we should try again.* You should not omit *that*, however, when the subordinate clause begins with an adverbial phrase or anything other than the subject: *She said that under no circumstances would she allow us to skip the meeting. The book argues that eventually the housing supply will increase.* This last sentence would be ambiguous if *that* were omitted, since the adverb *eventually* could then be construed as modifying either *argues* or *will increase*.

***that* instead of *who*** *The man that wanted to talk to you just called back.* Some people say that you can only use *who* and not *that* to introduce a restrictive relative clause that identifies a person. But *that* has been used in this way for centuries. It is a quintessential English usage, going back to the Old English period, and has been used by our best writers. So it is entirely acceptable to write either *the man that wanted to talk to you* or *the man who wanted to talk to you*.

***that* with the verb *doubt*** For a discussion of when to use *that* after the verb *doubt*, see **doubt** under *Word Choice*.

More at **this, whatever, which,** and **who.**

**there** "*There once was a man from . . .*" "*There was an old woman who lived in a shoe . . .*" Lovers of limericks and nursery rhymes are familiar with the anticipatory *there* that functions as a "dummy subject," delaying the real subject until the end of the clause. In this use *there* is usually classified as a pronoun and is distinguished from its use as an adverb indicating location, as in *There's the glove I've been looking for.*

According to the standard rule, when the pronoun *there* precedes a verb such as *be, seem,* or *appear,* the verb agrees in number with the following grammatical subject: *There is a great Italian deli across the street. There are fabulous wildflowers in the hills. There seems to be a blueberry pie cooking in the kitchen. There seem to be a few trees between the green and me.* But people often disregard this rule and use a singular verb with a plural subject, especially when speaking or when using the contraction *there's.* The Usage Panel dislikes this construction, however. Seventy-nine percent reject the sentence *There's only three things you need to know about this book.* But when *there's* is followed by a compound subject whose first element is singular, the panel feels differently. Fifty-six percent of the Usage Panel accepts the sentence *In each of us there's a dreamer and a realist,* and 32 percent more accept it in informal usage. The panel is even more accepting of the sentence *When you get to the stop light, there's a gas station on the left and a grocery store on the right;* 58 percent accept it in formal usage, while 37 percent more accept it in informal usage. Although this usage would seem to violate the rules of subject and verb agreement, the attraction of the verb to the singular noun phrase following it is so strong that it is hard to avoid the construction entirely.

More at **subject and verb agreement.**

## this

***this* and *that*** *This* and *that* are both demonstrative pronouns that refer to a thought expressed earlier: *The letter was unopened; that* (or *this*) *in itself casts doubt on the inspector's theory. That* is sometimes viewed as the better choice in referring to what has gone before (as in the preceding example). When what is referred to has not yet been mentioned, only *this* is used: *This* (not *that*) *is what bothers me: we have no time to consider late applications.*

***this* as informal substitute for *a / an*** *This* is often used in speech and informal writing as an emphatic substitute for the indefinite article to refer to a specific thing or person: *You should talk to this friend of mine at the Department of Motor Vehicles. I have this terrible feeling that I forgot to turn off the water.* But it's best to avoid this substitution in formal writing except when you want to create a conversational tone. More at **that.**

**used to** We use the verb *use* in its past tense with an infinitive to indicate a past condition or habitual practice: *We used to live in that house.* Because the *-d* in *used* is not pronounced in these constructions, people sometimes mistakenly leave it out when writing. Thus it is incorrect to write *We use to play tennis.* When *do* occurs with this form of *use* in negative statements and in questions, the situation is reversed, and *use to* (not *used to*) is correct: *You did not use to play on that team. Didn't she use to work for your company?*

**verbs, mood of** A *mood* is a property of verbs that indicates the attitude of the speaker about the factuality or likelihood of what is expressed. The term mood is also applied to the sets of verb forms that convey this attitude. English has three moods. The *indicative mood,* which is by far the most common, is used to make statements. The sentences *Wilson enjoys music* and *The dog ran across the street* are in the indicative mood. The *imperative mood* is used to give direct commands, such as *Get out of here!* or *Stop shouting!* The *subjunctive mood* is used to indicate doubt or unlikelihood, as *were* in *If she were here, we wouldn't be in this fix.* The subjunctive has very limited use in English, having been largely supplanted by modal auxiliaries like *may* and *might.* Nonetheless, the subjunctive still has its uses and its usage problems. More at **subjunctive.**

**verbs, principal parts of** Verbs are words that express an action or a state of being. All English verbs that are not auxiliary verbs have four principal parts: a base form (the infinitive without *to*), a present participle, a past tense, and a past participle. The principal parts are used to form tenses. All present participles are formed by the addition of *-ing* to the base form: *making, breaking, crying.* Grammars usually classify verbs as regular and irregular. *Regular verbs* form their past tense and past participle by adding the suffix *-ed* to the base form. Thus we say *I walked, I have walked, They plodded, They have plodded, She tried, We had tried,* and so on. As these examples show, the spelling of these forms sometimes involves modification of the base form. The rules for spelling the principal parts of regular verbs are discussed under *Word Formation.*

*Irregular* verbs do not follow the *-ed* pattern of regular verbs. Most change their base form—and often its vowel—to make the past tense and past participle. Here are some examples of irregular verbs showing how varied they can be:

| Base Form | Past | Past Participle |
|---|---|---|
| bend | bent | bent |
| weep | wept | wept |
| think | thought | thought |
| speak | spoke | spoken |
| grow | grew | grown |
| ride | rode | ridden |
| tear | tore | torn |
| meet | met | met |
| find | found | found |
| stand | stood | stood |
| begin | began | begun |

Some irregular verbs, like *burst, cast, cut,* and *split,* do not change to form the past tense and past participle (*He cut the bread. He has cut the bread*). A few verbs, like *burn* and *spell,* have both regular (*burned, spelled*) and irregular (*burnt, spelt*) past tenses and past participles. Some, like *mow* and *saw,* have both regular and irregular past participles (*sawed, sawn*). Since English has so many irregular verbs, you should check your dictionary for the correct principal parts of particular verbs.

**verbs, tenses of** Verb tenses show time. English has present, past, and future tenses; these have three variations, simple, perfect, and progressive.
**simple tenses** The simple present is formed with a present form of the verb. The simple past uses the past form. The simple future requires the auxiliary *will* or *shall* and a bare infinitive.

| Tense | Uses | Examples |
|---|---|---|
| Present | current state or action | She *walks* in the park. |
| | habitual or repeated action | She *walks* in the park daily. |
| | future state or action | Her train *leaves* tonight. Tomorrow is pay day. |
| Past | past state or action | The book *fell* on the floor. |
| | habitual or repeated action | We *walked* in the garden every morning. |
| Future | future state or action | We *will walk* in the park. |
| | habitual or repeated action | We *will walk* in the park every morning. |

Future time can also be expressed by certain verb phrases like *be going to* (*The tree is going to bloom soon*), *be to* (*We're to have a meeting this morning*), and *be about to* (*They are about to start the race*).

**perfect tenses** The perfect tenses show completed state or action. The present perfect is formed with *has* or *have* and a past participle. The past perfect, also called the pluperfect, requires *had* and a past participle. The future perfect uses *will have* or *shall have* and a past participle.

| Tense | Uses | Examples |
|---|---|---|
| Present Perfect | state or action that occurred in the past and may continue to the present | He *has walked* in the park. I *have lived* in Arizona all my life. |
| Past Perfect (Pluperfect) | state or action that occurred before something else in the past | He *had walked* in the park that morning. I *had lived* in Arizona before moving to Oregon. |
| Future Perfect | state or action that will occur before something else in the future | He *will have walked* in the park by the time we arrive. Come March, I *will have lived* in Arizona for two years. |

**progressive tenses** The progressive tenses show a state or action that is continuing or in progress. The present progressive is formed with *am, is,* or *are* and a present participle. The past progressive requires *was* or *were* and a present participle. The future progressive uses *will be* or *shall be* and a present participle.

| Tense | Uses | Examples |
|---|---|---|
| Present Progressive | ongoing state or action | They *are walking* in the park. |
|  | future state or action | I *am going* to the museum tomorrow. |
| Past Progressive | state or action ongoing in the past | They *were walking* in the park. |
| Future Progressive | state or action ongoing in the future | They *will be walking* in the park all day. They *will be walking* in the park tomorrow. |

The perfect and progressive tenses are sometimes called *aspects* instead of tenses since they show how verb action is viewed or experienced with respect to time. The perfect and progressive tenses can be combined to show action in the past

that is ongoing and may continue to the point of reference: *They have been walking in the park all morning. Before we moved, we had been living in Arizona. By March, we will have been living in Arizona for two years.*

**sequence and consistency of verb tenses** It is important to keep verb tenses in the proper sequence so as not to disrupt the coherence of time in your writing. If the actions you are describing occur at the same time, keep the verbs in the same time:

> Once Jane gets angry, it takes a long time for her to calm down.
> When the timing belt broke, the engine stopped.
> The news broke while she was sleeping.

If the actions you are describing occur at different times, use tenses that make logical sense:

> We didn't go to the museum on our last visit, but this time we will certainly go there.
> After he had eaten the soup, everyone asked how it was.
> Although they will soon be moving out, they have enjoyed living here.

The most common problems with tenses arise when you have to shift back and forth from the present to the past and when you are converting direct speech to indirect speech. Consider the following example:

> I grew up in a neighborhood that surrounds a small park. We lived on a street that is lined with trees and has small, two-story houses. Many people park their cars on the street, but in the winter there's so much snow that it's difficult to find a space. My parents owned an old station wagon. Its heater had not worked for years.

In this narrative, the past events (growing up, owning a station wagon, and so on) are kept distinct from the conditions that continue into the present (the neighborhood surrounding the park, the street being lined with trees, and so on). While these conditions could have been described entirely in the past tense, the writer here wants to convey the sense of a continuing familiarity with the old neighborhood. There are, however, many conditions that continue into the present and must be conveyed by the present tense in almost any context: *Galileo discovered that Jupiter has* (not *had*) *moons. The explorers camped on the Illinois River near where it joins* (not *joined*) *the Mississippi.*

Sometimes writers shift from past to present tense when telling a story to add vividness to the events. This legitimate tense shift is a literary device called the *historical present.* It is familiar to readers of epic poetry, but people also use it when relating everyday anecdotes:

> I was walking down Delancey Street the other day when a guy *comes* up to me and *asks* me for the time.

When writing about literature, it's especially easy to mix up tenses. Suppose you are writing about Act V of a play in the present tense and refer back to something that happened in Act II using the past tense (after all, Act II is past in relation to Act V). Once writing in the past tense, you can then be tempted to continue it even when you write about Act V. For this reason it's best to write about literature in the present tense—whether you are in Act V or Act II: *Before he confronts Ophelia, Hamlet unburdens his soul in a soliloquy.* You may of course describe biographical details—how a writer lived or what a writer did—in the past tense, but you should keep this distinct from what a writer says or attempts to do in literature, which is eternally present. Thus you can say *Shakespeare portrays Hamlet as a very passionate man* and *Shakespeare presented many of his plays at the Globe Theater in London.*

When reporting indirect speech, you must convert direct speech in present tense to reported speech in past tense:

Direct Speech: "I am working for a law firm," she said.
Indirect Speech: She said that she *was working* for a law firm.

If the direct speech is in the past tense, the indirect speech must also be in the past or the past perfect:

Direct Speech: "The play opened last week," he said.
Indirect Speech: He said that the play *opened* (or *had opened*) the
    week before.

The second example raises the issue of whether the past perfect tense is falling out of use in such situations. The Usage Panel prefers the past perfect, but the simple past is often acceptable. Seventy-seven percent prefer *had talked* to *talked* in the sentence *I asked if he had talked to his doctor.* This leaves, of course, 23 percent for whom *talked* is unobjectionable. The panel is even more tolerant of the simple past in this example, which does not involve the reporting of discourse. In a sentence such as *Before I was introduced to her, I heard/had heard the rumor about her,* 59 percent would require *had heard,* while 41 percent would allow *heard.* Thus it seems likely that many readers will not notice the omission of *had*—that is, the use of the simple past in preference to the past perfect—in these situations.

But if the direct speech is in the perfect or past perfect tense, then the indirect speech must be in the past perfect:

Direct Speech: "I have been working as a plumber for six years," he
    said.
Indirect Speech: He said that he *had been working* as a plumber for six
    years.

More at **subjunctive.**

**verbs, transitive and intransitive** Most grammars classify verbs into transitive and intransitive. Transitive verbs take an object: *I read the book. She values your criticism. Priestley discovered oxygen.* Intransitive verbs do not take an object: *I sleep on a futon. She sings beautifully. The Kingsleys live in a brick house.* Many verbs, of course, sometimes take an object and sometimes do not. In other words, they can be transitive or intransitive depending on how they are used. The verb *read*, for example, is transitive in *I read the book* but intransitive in *I usually read in the evening*. Here are a few other examples:

| *Transitive* | *Intransitive* |
|---|---|
| She plays the saxophone beautifully. | She plays beautifully. |
| We won the game in overtime. | We won in overtime. |
| Jack opened the door slowly. | The door opened slowly. |
| We began the party with a song. | The party began with a song. |

**verbs, voice of** Transitive verbs have a property, known as *voice*, that allows you to express the relation between the subject and the action of the verb in one of two ways. Verbs in the active voice have the performer of the action as the subject and have the person or thing that is acted upon as the object. Thus the sentences *Marty found the kitten under the couch* and *The girls built a house of blocks today* have their verbs in the active voice. The performers of the action—Marty and the girls—are the subjects of the sentence, and the things acted upon—the kitten and the house—are the objects.

In the passive voice this situation is reversed. The person or thing that is acted upon becomes the subject, and the performer of the action gets put in a prepositional phrase beginning with *by* or is omitted from the sentence altogether. Thus in the passive voice the sentences would read *The kitten was found* (by Marty) *under the couch* and *The house of blocks was built* (by the girls) *today*.

Passive verb phrases normally consist of a form of the verb *be* followed by a past participle. Passive verbs can exist in any tense. They may or may not employ an auxiliary verb. Here are some examples:

| *Active* | *Passive* |
|---|---|
| Linda drives the car. | The car is driven by Linda. |
| Linda drove the car. | The car was driven by Linda. |
| Linda was driving the car. | The car was being driven by Linda. |
| Linda has driven the car. | The car has been driven by Linda. |
| Linda may have driven the car. | The car may have been driven by Linda. |

It is important not to confuse the passive voice with a progressive form of an active or intransitive verb. Like passive verbs, progressive verbs employ a form of the verb *be*, but progressive verbs always have a present participle (ending in *-ing*), whereas a passive verb always has a past participle. Passive verbs can have progressive forms, that is, they can employ the participle *being*, but it is always followed by a past participle. Here are some examples:

| *Active / Progressive* | *Passive / Progressive* |
|---|---|
| Jim is writing a book. | The book is being written by Jim. |
| Jim was writing a book. | The book was being written by Jim. |
| Jim had been writing a book. | The book had been being written by Jim. |

Don't be fooled by an adverb intervening between the form of *be* and the participle. The sentence *Jim is carefully writing a book* still has a progressive verb in the active voice, and *The book is being carefully written by Jim* still has its verb in the passive voice.

Some passive constructions use *get* instead of *be* with a past participle. In some of these sentences the subject may have a somewhat active role even when being acted upon by the verb. Thus you might say *The kitten got left in the basement,* which is no different from *The kitten was left in the basement.* But the sentence *Michelle got hired as a reporter* implies that Michelle's actions were instrumental in her securing the job. This passive with *get* is mostly limited to informal speaking and writing.

There are a few transitive verbs—called middle verbs—that cannot normally be made passive, such as: *fit, have, lack, resemble,* and *suit.* Thus you can say *That suit fits you* but not *You are fit by that suit; Our team lacks a good pitcher,* but not *A good pitcher is lacked by our team;* and so on.

One big reason for being aware of passive and active verbs in your writing is that overrelying on the passive voice can lead to prose that is boring, difficult to understand, and needlessly verbose. For more on these problems, see **passive voice** under *Style.*

More at **auxiliary and primary verbs, participles,** and **subject and verb agreement.**

**very and past participles** Why can you be *very pleased* with your raise but not *very praised* by your boss? In general usage *very* is not used alone to modify a past participle. Thus we may say of a book, for example, that it has been *very much praised* or *very much criticized* (where *very* modifies the adverb *much*), but not that it has been *very praised* or *very criticized.*

However, many past participle forms do double duty as adjectives, in which case modification by a bare *very,* or by analogous adverbs such as *quite,* is acceptable. Thus we say *a very celebrated singer* and *a performance that was quite polished.* In some cases there is disagreement as to whether a particular participle can be used properly as an adjective. Over the years people have objected to the use of *very* by itself with *delighted, interested, annoyed, pleased, disappointed,* and *irritated.* All these words are now well established as adjectives, as indicated by the fact that they can be used attributively, that is, in juxtaposition to a noun they modify, as in *a delighted audience, a pleased look, a disappointed young man.*

But the situation is not always clear. Some speakers accept phrases such as *very appreciated, very astonished,* or *very heartened,* while others prefer alternatives using *very much.* What is more, some participles allow treatment as adjectives in one sense but not another. You can speak of *a very inflated reputation,* for example, but not, ordinarily, of *a very inflated tire.* As a result, there is no sure way to tell which participles may be modified by a bare *very,* and you must trust your ear for what sounds natural. When in doubt, using *very much* is generally safer.

More at **participles.**

**what**

**what as subject of a clause** When *what* is the subject of a clause, it may take a singular or plural verb, depending on the sense. *What* is singular when taken as the equivalent of *that which* or *the thing which: I see what seems to be a dead tree.* It is plural when taken as the equivalent of *those which* or *the things which: He sometimes makes what* seem *to be thoughtless mistakes.*

**what in a clause that is the subject** When a clause that has *what* as its subject is itself the subject of a sentence, it may take a singular or plural verb, but how you decide this is more complicated. Most of these *what*-clauses are singular: *What they always wanted was a home of their own.* In fact, *what-* clauses are usually singular even when the verb is a linking verb, such as *be* or *seem,* followed by a plural noun or a series of nouns: *What she kept in her drawer was ten silver dollars. What truly commands respect is a large air force and a resolute foreign policy.*

In some cases, you can treat a clause with *what* as the subject as singular or plural, depending on the emphasis you want to convey. In *What excite him most* are *money and power,* the implication is that money and power are distinct elements; in *What excites him most is money and power,* the implication is that money and power are a single entity.

In other cases, *what-* clauses are plural. The *what-* clause as a whole is plural if it has a plural verb: *What seem to be two dead trees* are *blocking the road.* The *what* clause is usually plural if the verb in the main clause is a linking verb followed by a plural noun or noun phrase: *What most* surprise *me are the inflammatory remarks at the end of his article.*

There are also certain sentences that have a main verb followed by a plural noun or noun phrase whose sense requires that the *what*-clause be plural, as in *What traditional grammarians called "predicates" are called "verb phrases" by modern linguists* and *What the Romans established as military outposts were later to become important trading centers.* In these sentences, the plural nouns *predicates* and *outposts* give the *what*-clauses their plural meaning.

More at **subject and verb agreement** and **which.**

## whatever

**whatever or what ever** You can use either *whatever* or *what ever* in sentences such as *Whatever* (or *What ever*) *made her say that?* Critics have occasionally objected to the one-word form, but many respected writers have used it. The same is true of the forms *whoever, whenever, wherever,* and *however.* However, you must use the one-word form when *whatever* is used as an adjective: *Take whatever* (not *what ever*) *books you need.*

**whatever and commas** When a clause beginning with *whatever* is the subject of a sentence, do not use a comma: *Whatever you do is right.* Otherwise, a comma is fine: *Whatever you do, don't burn the toast.*

**never with *that*** When the phrase preceding a restrictive clause is introduced by *whichever* or *whatever, that* should not be used in formal writing. It is regarded as incorrect to write *whatever book that you want to look at;* instead you should write *Whatever book you want to look at will be sent to your office* or *Whichever book costs less* (not *that costs less*) *is fine with us.*

More at **that.**

**when** In informal style, *when* is often used after *be* in definitions: *A dilemma is when you don't know which way to turn.* The construction is useful, but it is widely regarded as incorrect or as unsuitable for formal discourse. In formal style, there is no alternative but to rephrase such definitions to avoid *is when.* The trick here is to make the first part of the sentence a full clause: *A dilemma is a situation in which you don't know which way to turn. You are in a dilemma when you don't know which way to turn.*

**where** *Where ya comin' from? Where ya goin' to? Where's the station at?* Questions like these also pose the question of how you use *where* in writing. When *where* is used to refer to a point of origin, the preposition *from* is required: *Where did she come from?* When it is used to refer to a point of destination, the preposition *to* is generally superfluous: *Where is she going?* rather than *Where is she going to?* When *where* is used to refer to the place at which an event or a situation is located, the use of *at* is widely regarded as regional or colloquial. So unless you want to convey the flavor of speech, write *Where is the station* not *Where is the station at.*

## which

**which referring to a clause or sentence** The relative pronoun *which* can sometimes refer to a clause or sentence, as opposed to a noun phrase: *She ignored him, which proved to be unwise. They swept the council elections, which could never have happened under the old rules.* While these examples are perfectly acceptable, using *which* in this way sometimes creates ambiguities. The sentence *It emerged that Martha made the complaint, which surprised everybody* may mean either that the complaint itself was surprising or that it was surprising that Martha made it. You can avoid the ambiguity by using other constructions such as *It emerged that Martha made the complaint, a revelation that surprised everybody.* It is important to remember that you can use *which* in this way only when the clause or sentence it refers to precedes it. When the clause or sentence follows, you must use *what,* particularly in formal style: *Still, he has not said he will withdraw, which is more surprising. Still, what is more surprising, he has not said he will withdraw.*
More at **that** and **what.**

**whichever** See **whatever.**

## who

**who and whom** *Who do you think is coming to the party? Whom did you give the invitations to?* The traditional rules that determine the use of *who* and *whom* are relatively simple: *who* is used for a grammatical subject, where a nominative pronoun such as *I* or *he* would be appropriate, and *whom* is used as the object of a verb or preposition. Thus, we write *The actor who played Hamlet was excellent,* since *who* stands for the subject of *played Hamlet,* and *Who do you think is the best candidate?* where *who* stands for the subject of *is the best candidate.* But we write *To whom did you give the letter?* since *whom* is the object of the preposition *to,* and *The man whom the papers criticized did not show up,* since *whom* is the object of the verb *criticized.*

This all seems straightforward enough, but with complicated sentences it is not so easy. A sentence such as *I met the man whom the government had tried to get France to extradite* requires you to have thought the sentence through before you have written it—you should know from the start that *whom* will be the object of the verb *extradite,* which is several clauses away. It is hard to be this calculating on a consistent basis, so it's not surprising that writers from Shakespeare onward often use *who* and *whom* interchangeably. In speech and informal writing, people tend to use *who,* even as the object of a verb or preposition. A sentence such as *Who did John say he was going to support?* is perfectly natural, despite violating the traditional rules. Using *whom* often sounds forced or pretentiously correct, as in *Whom shall I say is calling?* or *Whom did you give it to?* Nevertheless, many writers adhere to the rules, especially in formal style. These rules apply in the same manner to *whoever* and *whomever.*

**who in restrictive and nonrestrictive clauses** The relative pronoun *who* may be used in restrictive clauses, in which case it is not preceded by a comma, or in nonrestrictive clauses, in which case a comma is required. Thus you can say either *The scientist who discovers a cure for cancer will be immortalized,* where the clause *who discovers a cure for cancer* indicates which scientist will be immortalized, or *The mathematician over there, who solved the four-color theorem, is widely known,* where the clause *who solved the four-color theorem* adds information about a person already identified by the phrase *the mathematician over there.* More at **else** and **that.**

**whose** See **possessive constructions**.

**would** See **auxiliary and primary verbs, shall,** and **should**.

# Style

## *Parallelism, Passives, Redundancy, and Wordiness*

This chapter deals with some common writing problems that do not involve rules of grammar. These problems—of parallelism, redundancy, and the like—are more rhetorical than grammatical; that is, they involve choices you must make as a writer trying to create a certain style of expression. You must determine what stylistic choices will afford greater clarity and cogency to each of your efforts to communicate. We all make different choices when faced with different communicative tasks depending on what we feel will be most effective. An expression that is appropriate for a formal letter may be utterly off-putting in an informal message.

Of course, we also have to make these choices when we speak, but we are more likely to be aware of them in formal speech that we have conceived and outlined, if not scripted, in advance of its delivery than in off-the-cuff remarks or a routine conversation. And no doubt the audience in these more formal situations will have more exacting expectations of how we express ourselves than it would on more relaxed occasions.

A successful and distinctive writing style is an elusive bird of paradise. It is unmistakable once you see it but difficult to find. It involves many things: creating an appropriate voice for your purpose, choosing the right words for the subject and audience, constructing elegant sentences whose rhythm reinforces their meaning, presenting an argument in a logical fashion that is both engaging and easy to follow, finding vivid images to make thoughts accessible to your readers. You can probably add to this list. You may, for example, want to shock or jolt your audience rather than court it, and this strategy requires stylistic features that are quite different from those you would use for gentle persuasion.

The trouble with writing is that despite what many handbooks suggest, there are no hard and fast rules, no magic formulas, that make it an easy step-by-step process. You have to reconceive the rules every time you sit down to write because every occasion has its own specific requirements. Writing for university students is different from writing for business associates. Writing for older people is different from writing for teenagers. Writing about medicine is different from writing about sports. Writing to explain is different from writing to persuade.

At the same time, it is this challenge that makes writing so interesting and rewarding. It is a process of discovery, an exploration of uncharted territory.

And there are tools you can bring with you that will make the journey easier: a familiarity with your audience and your material, a sensitivity to words and their connotations, and a map of some of the pitfalls that have befallen others. We present one version of this map in the pages that follow.

## Parallelism

Most memorable writing has as one of its recognizable features the ample use of parallel grammatical structures. Consider these selections from famous political documents:

> We hold these truths to be self-evident, that all men are created equal, that they are endowed by their Creator with certain inalienable Rights, that among these are Life, Liberty, and the pursuit of Happiness. *(The Declaration of Independence)*

> It is rather for us to be here dedicated to the great task remaining before us—that from these honored dead we take increased devotion to that cause for which they gave the last full measure of devotion; that we here highly resolve that these dead shall not have died in vain; that this nation, under God, shall have a new birth of freedom; and that government of the people, by the people, for the people shall not perish from the earth. *(The Gettysburg Address)*

> Never in the field of human conflict was so much owed by so many to so few. (Winston Churchill's tribute to the Royal Air Force after the Battle of Britain)

These celebrated passages are moving in no small measure because of their elegant cadences and parallel structures. Both *The Declaration of Independence* and *The Gettysburg Address* contain a series of *that*-clauses whose rhythm reinforces the gravity of what is being said and puts great stress on the final elements in the sentence. In both passages the final elements themselves are constructed in parallel fashion. *Life, Liberty, and the pursuit of Happiness* is a series of nouns, with the last modified by a prepositional phrase. *Government of the people, by the people, for the people* presents a noun modified by a series of prepositional phrases, each with the same object so that the prepositions—commonplace words that usually have little meaning aside from connecting words together—have enormous significance and the word *people* is reinforced, thus emphasizing its underlying importance to the idea of government. Similarly, Churchill's famous line ends with a series of pronouns modified by the intensive *so*, which is repeated three times with prepositions indicating the relationship between the many (the British people) and the few (the heroic pilots).

A basic guideline about parallel constructions is to make sure that all the elements in a balanced pair or in a series have the same grammatical form.

That is, if you start with a *that*-clause, stick with *that*-clauses; if you start with an infinitive, stick with infinitives; if you start with a participle, stick with participles; and so on. What you don't want is a mixed bag, as in *She had a strong desire to pursue medicine and for studying literature* or *The scientist asked for volunteers with allergies but who had not given blood recently.*

A second point is to make sure that once you have chosen the kind of grammatical forms you want to make parallel, you structure them symmetrically. Remember that an initial article, preposition, auxiliary verb, or modifier will tend to govern all elements in the series unless it is repeated for each element. For example, if you set up a series of nouns with the first modified by an adjective, the reader will expect the adjective to modify the rest of the series as well. Thus you should say *The building has new lighting, plumbing, and carpeting* but not *The building has new lighting, plumbing, and different carpeting.* The same is true for articles: *He brought the rod, reel, and bait.* If you want to restrict a modifier to only one noun, repeat the article for each noun: *He brought the light rod, the reel, and the bait.*

Similarly, if you introduce a series of nouns with a single preposition, readers will expect that preposition to govern all the nouns: *He sent the letter to the provost, the dean, and the student who won the scholarship.* With contrastive conjunctions, it's best to repeat the preposition: *He sent the letter to the provost and the dean but not to the student or his parents.* An auxiliary verb will govern all the verbs in the series unless you construct each verb phrase separately: *We will always value her contributions, admire her fortitude, and wish her the best.*

When you spot a faulty parallel, recast the structure to give all the elements equivalent treatment. If your new parallel construction does not seem much of an improvement, rewrite the sentence completely to avoid the parallel construction. Better to have no parallel structures than to have parallel structures that sound overblown or stilted.

Faulty parallelism is all around us. We see and hear it every day—often without taking notice. How many times have you heard *Please leave your name, number, and a brief message?* After waiting for the tone, have you ever objected to the imperfect symmetry of this sentence? In our most recent ballot we presented some sentences with questionable parallelism to the usage panelists to see how tolerant they would be. As we expected, they had a range of opinions.

Sometimes making sure that all the elements in a parallel construction are equivalent is not as clear-cut as it sounds, and parallelism itself can be a matter of debate. Is a series of nouns that has some gerunds in it parallel? On this problem the panel is divided. Fifty-one percent approve, while 49 percent reject the sentence *The commmittee has the power of investigation, negotiation, arranging contracts, and hiring new employees.*

The panel is similarly divided when the first part of a compound verb has a series of objects, so that the second verb and its objects seem tacked on as the last element in the series. Fifty-four percent find unacceptable this example: *These services will use satellite, copper cable, fiber optics, cellular communications, and be accessible via suitably equipped computers.*

In other cases the panelists are more unified. They apparently see little harm in the imperfect telephone message cited above. Eighty-six percent accept the following example in which three nouns in the series are governed by the possessive *his*, while the fourth and final noun is modified by *the*: *In the hotel room the suspect had left his keys, briefcase, spare clothes, and the receipts for the cars he had rented.* This construction in fact has the virtue of adding emphasis to the final element. The receipts seem to be the most important piece of evidence that the suspect left behind.

When the situation is more clear-cut, however, and something in the construction is clearly out of balance, the panel is more insistent on restoring parallelism. This is the case with the coordinate conjunction *not only . . . but also*, where it is easy to spot when one element is out of place. Seventy-three percent reject the sentence *The film makers not only concentrate on Edward VIII's abdication over his love for divorcee Wallis Simpson but also his leaning toward Nazi Germany.*

Crafting sentences with flawless parallelism takes effort and practice. Even if your readers don't notice or object when you make mistakes, balance and symmetry are worth striving for in your writing. There are certain constructions that are notorious for throwing things out of whack. We list some of them below.

**both . . . and . . .** When using *both* and *and* to link parallel elements, make the words or phrases that follow them correspond grammatically. That is, whatever grammatical construction follows *both*, the same construction should also follow *and*. Thus you should say *Sales have risen in both India and China* or *Sales have risen both in India and in China*, but not *Sales have risen both in India and China*.

**comparisons with *as* and *than*** "*Did you know that more people are killed each year by hogs in Indiana than by sharks?*" says a writer in *Scuba Magazine*. You may well be wondering how many sharks there are in Indiana. In comparisons using *as* and *than* it is the second element that can give you trouble. It is easy to set up a faulty parallel, especially when prepositional phrases are involved. Consider this sentence:

> I want the photos in our brochure to look as impressive as their brochure.

Here the writer wants to compare photos in two different brochures, but the syntax compares the photos of one brochure with the entire brochure of the other organization. To be truly parallel, the sentence must read:

> I want the photos in our brochure to look as impressive as those in their brochure.

Note the addition of the pronoun *those* to counterbalance *photos* in the previous section of the sentence, and the repetition of the preposition *in*. You could, of course, repeat the noun *photos* instead of using a pronoun. Here is a similar example:

> They felt that the condition of the new buildings was not much better than the old ones.

In this sentence the condition of the new buildings is compared with the old buildings themselves, not with their condition. To make the sentence parallel, you must add the pronoun *that* to balance the noun *condition*. Again, you can repeat the noun if this is more to your liking, but in either case the prepositional phrase with *of* must follow:

> They felt that the condition of the new buildings was not much better than that (*or* the condition) of the old ones.

Sometimes it's only the second preposition that gets left out in these comparative constructions, as in *More cars are built in Canada than Mexico,* where perfect parallelism requires . . . *than in Mexico.*

*As* and *than* comparisons pose additional problems when the noun following *as* or *than* is the subject or object of an implied clause. Does the sentence *The employees are more suspicious of the arbitrator than the owner* mean that the employees distrust the arbitrator more than they distrust the owner or that the employees distrust the arbitrator more than the owner does? To be clear you must add a verb to the second element of the comparision: *The employees are more suspicious of the arbitrator than they are of the owner* or *The employees are more suspicious of the arbitrator than the owner is.*

Of course, sentences containing *as* and *than* comparisons may be unambiguous but still be in need of balancing. Here are two other examples:

> More than twice as many tons of corrugated cardboard are recycled
>     each year than (are tons of) newspaper.
> The factory is producing as many transmissions as (it did) last year.

The material in parentheses is often left out in sentences of this type, but parallelism requires it.

Making a syntactically imperfect comparison may not be the most grievous fault you can commit in writing, and nearly everyone makes these faults when speaking. But when you have the choice, why not be precise?

**compound verbs** *Jim knew that Candace had discovered the thief and felt it was OK to tell the reporters.* Here we have verbs that are parallel but ambiguous. Who felt it was OK to tell the reporters, Jim or Candace? When the first part of a compound verb is followed by a subordinate clause, the second part of the verb may appear to belong to the subordinate clause. In these cases, it's best to give the second verb its own subject: *Jim knew that Candace had discovered the thief, and he felt it was OK to tell the reporters.* As an alternative, you can recast the sentence to avoid the parallelism: *Once Jim knew that Candace had discovered the thief, he felt it was OK to tell the reporters.*

**either . . . or / neither . . . nor** You should follow both conjunctions in *either . . . or . . .* (or *neither . . . nor . . .*) constructions with parallel elements. If you follow *either* with a verb and an object, *or* must have a verb and an object as well. Thus you should say *She can either take the examination offered to all applicants or ask for a personal interview* but not *She can take either* *the examination offered to all applicants or ask for a personal interview.* Similarly, you should say *You may have either the ring or the bracelet* but not *You may either have the ring or the bracelet.*

**not only . . . but also** As with other correlative conjunctions, you should follow each part of the *not only . . . but also . . .* construction with an element of the same grammatical type. Thus, instead of *She not only bought a new car but also a new lawnmower,* you should write *She bought not only a new car but also a new lawnmower,* because in this version both *not only* and *but also* are followed by noun phrases.

Leaving out the *also* from this construction tends to intensify the first part of the construction rather than supplement it: *She is not only smart but brilliant. He not only wanted the diamond but wanted it desperately.*

**rather than** The phrase *rather than* consists of an adverb and a conjunction and often means "and not," as in *I decided to skip lunch rather than eat in the cafeteria again.* It is grammatically similar to *sooner than* in that it is used with a "bare" infinitive—an infinitive minus *to: I would stay here and eat flies sooner than go with them.*

*Rather than* can also be used with nouns as a compound preposition meaning "instead of": *I bought a mountain bike rather than a ten-speed.* But some people object to this use, insisting that *than* should be used only as a conjunction. They therefore object to constructions in which *rather than* is followed by a gerund, as in *Rather than buying a new car, I kept my old one.*

In some cases, however, *rather than* can only be followed by a gerund and not by a bare infinitive. If the main verb of the sentence has a form that does not allow parallel treatment of the verb following *rather than,* you cannot use a bare infinitive, and you must use a gerund. This is often the case when the main verb is in a past tense or has a participle. Thus, you must say *The results of the study, rather than ending* (not *end* or *ended*) *the controversy, only added to it.* If the main verb was in the present tense (*add*), you could use the bare infinitive *end.*

Curiously, when the *rather than* construction follows the main verb, it can use other verb forms besides the bare infinitive. Thus you can say *The results of the study added to the controversy rather than ended it.*

The overriding concern in all of this should be to avoid faulty parallels, as in sentences like *Rather than buy a new car, I have kept my old one* and *Rather than take a cab, she is going on foot.*

Clearly, it is grammatically defensible to follow *rather than* with a gerund, but if you prefer to avoid the controversy, use *instead of* with gerunds.

## Passive Voice

Writing handbooks usually include warnings about the passive voice—it is wordy and clumsy and leads to static rather than dynamic writing. There is

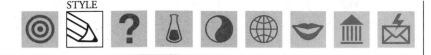

truth to this, certainly, but the passive voice also has legitimate uses, and in many instances it is preferable to the active voice.

The grammatical form of the passive voice is discussed in detail in the verbs section of the chapter *Grammar*. To summarize: the passive voice refers to verb forms that allow the subject to be the receiver (rather than the performer) of the verb's action. Passive verbs consist of a form of the verb *be* and a past participle: *is needed, was bought, has been delivered.*

**uses of the passive voice** The passive voice is a very versatile construction. It is particularly useful when the performer of the action is unknown or irrelevant to the matter at hand. Thus a police report might say *A car was broken into last night on Laurel Road* when the perpetrator is unknown. You might write in a memo *Office mail is now delivered twice a day* where what is important is the frequency of mail delivery, not the identity of the people working in the mailroom.

You can also use the passive voice to conceal the performer of an action or the identity of a person responsible for a mistake: *We had hoped to report on this problem but the data was inadvertently deleted from our files.* Who deleted the data? By using the passive voice the writer is able to avoid identifying the guilty party. This virtue of obscuring responsibility is in part what makes the passive voice so tempting to anyone working in an organization where something has gone wrong. Since the occasions for avoiding responsibility are multitudinous, passive verbs are bound to thrive for at least the foreseeable future.

Surprisingly enough, you can also use the passive voice to emphasize the performer of the action by putting the performer in a prepositional phrase using *by* at the end of the sentence: *The breakthrough was achieved by Burlingame and Evans, two researchers in the university's genetic engineering lab.* In this way the passive voice functions like a well-run awards ceremony. It creates suspense by delaying the announcement of the names.

Another virtue of passive constructions is that they allow you to emphasize a modifying adverb, as many politicians know well: *My remarks have been grossly distorted in the press.*

Scientists ordinarily use the passive voice to describe natural processes or phenomena under study. Here is a passage from an essay by the psychiatrist Paul R. McHugh, where he emphasizes real psychological processes in refuting the notion that children ordinarily suppress memories of trauma:

> . . . severe traumas *are* not *blocked* out by children but *remembered* all too well. They *are amplified* in consciousness, remaining like grief to *be reborn* and *reemphasized* on anniversaries and in settings that can simulate the environments where they occurred.

In technical and scientific articles, especially in the presentation of experimental methods, researchers use the passive voice as a conventional means of impersonal reporting. The passive voice allows them to avoid calling attention to themselves and to omit reference to any subjective thoughts or biases they might have brought to their work. The effect is to lend the article the air of objectivity. Here is a typical example from a paper in molecular biology:

> The protein concentration required to saturate the solid phase *was determined* and the amount of bound protein *was quantified* by the micro-bicinchoninic acid protein assay.

The experiment seems to run itself.

On some occasions you will want to use the passive voice to preserve the coherence of your writing. Suppose you are discussing a certain topic—immigrant labor in Europe, for example—from the point of view of an economist. Your subject then is how the various economies treat workers who come from other countries and are not citizens. Here is how one economist, John Kenneth Galbraith, discusses this subject:

> In the last forty years, in Germany, France, and Switzerland, and in lesser measure Austria and Scandinavia, the provision of outside workers for the task for which indigenous laborers are no longer available has been both accepted and highly organized. The factories of the erstwhile German Federal Republic are manned, and a broad range of other work is performed, by Turks and Yugoslavs. Those in France are similarly supplied by what amounts to a new invasion of the Moors—the vast influx from the former North African colonies.

In this passage there is not a single active verb. Galbraith thus violates one of the most common commandments of writing handbooks: "use active verbs." But would the passage be clearer or easier to read if Galbraith had made the workers the subject of the sentences?

> . . . Turks and Yugoslavs man the factories of the erstwhile German Federal Republic and perform a broad range of other work. What amounts to a new invasion of the Moors—the vast influx from the former North African colonies—supplies those in France.

For Galbraith's purpose—describing the economy rather than the social groups in European society—the passive voice works fine. In fact, using the active voice might seem oddly inappropriate and, hence, distracting to the reader.

The passive voice can also help you make smooth transitions. Here is a passage in which the astronomer Robert P. Kirschner discusses what happens to an aging star.

> . . . In some [very old] stars, carbon-rich matter from the core is dredged up by convection. The freshly synthesized matter then escapes, forming a sooty cocoon of graphite. Eventually fuel runs out, and the inner core of the red giant congeals into a white dwarf.
>
> A white dwarf is protected from total gravitational collapse not by the kinetic pressure of gases; the carbon and oxygen in its interior are in an almost crystalline state. The star is held up by the quantum repulsion of its free electrons.

Let's see how the same passage would read if the second paragraph were written with active verbs:

. . . Eventually the fuel runs out, and the inner core of the red giant congeals into a white dwarf.

It is not the kinetic pressure of gases that protects a white dwarf from total gravitational collapse; the carbon and oxygen in its interior are in an almost crystalline state. The quantum repulsion of its free electrons holds the star up.

The subject of discussion—the white dwarf—now seems secondary. The chemical and physical processes inside the star take precedence. As a result, the essay, rather than the star, is in danger of collapsing.

**abuses of the passive voice** Trouble can arise, however, when you use the passive voice on a sustained basis without an overriding reason to do so. And it is easy to do this, since written material full of passive verbs often sounds impressive. Perhaps because of the use of the passive voice in technical writing, a sequence of passive verb forms can have the air of authority, but what it often has is air. Passive constructions are by their nature more wordy than active ones, forcing you to rely on abstract nouns and strings of prepositional phrases to convey the bulk of your meaning. As a result, your meaning can get diffused in bloated sentences, and your writing can become tedious to read and hard to understand. Consider this example which stresses the importance of supervisors:

> Recognition and assessment of errors in quality control by the supervisors is required so that manufacturing procedures can be adjusted and the problems can be thereby eliminated.

The complicated syntax required to accomodate the passive verbs causes confusion. Are the errors recognized by the supervisors or committed by them? The prepositional phrases leave us unsure. Here is the same material rewritten with active verbs. Notice how much shorter it is:

> Supervisors must recognize and assess errors in quality control so that we can adjust manufacturing procedures to eliminate the problems.

When you're concentrating on the content and organization of your writing, it can be hard to tell if you've used too many passive constructions. A good test is to look down the page and circle (or make a note of) every form of the verb *be* (*is, are, was, were,* etc.) and any other weak verbs like *seem, appear,* and *exist.* If the page is covered with circles (or if you've grown tired of counting), you should consider rewriting the page using active verbs and the active voice. More at **wordiness.**

# Redundancy

A certain amount of redundancy is built in to the English language, and we would never consider getting rid of it. Take grammatical number, for instance.

Sentences such as *He drives to work* and *We are happy* contain redundant verb forms. The *-s* of *drives* indicates singularity of the subject, but we already know the subject is singular from the singular pronoun *he*. Similarly, *are* indicates a plural subject, which is already evident from the plural pronoun *we*. Number is also indicated redundantly in phrases like *this book* and *those boxes,* where the demonstrative adjective shows number and the noun does as well.

But there are redundant ways of saying things that can make the rest of your writing seem foolish. Many of these are common expressions that go unnoticed in casual conversation but that stick out like red flags in writing. Why say *at this point in time* instead of *now,* or *because of the fact that* when *because* will do? Something that is *large in size* is really just *large.* The trouble lies less in the expressions themselves than in their accumulated effect. Anyone can be forgiven for an occasional redundancy, but writing that is larded with redundancies is likely to draw unwanted laughs rather than admiration.

The usages that critics have condemned as redundancies fall into several classes. Some expressions, such as *old adage,* have become fixed expressions and seem harmless enough. Others, such as *consensus of opinion, close proximity, hollow tube,* and *refer back,* can be pointlessly redundant in some contexts yet defensible in others. In these cases the use of what is regarded as an unnecessary modifier or qualifier can sometimes be justified on the grounds that it makes a real distinction in meaning. Thus a *hollow tube* can be distinguished from one that has been blocked up with deposits, and a *consensus of opinion* can be distinguished from a *consensus of judgments* or a *consensus of practice.* In other cases the use of the qualifier is harder to defend. There is no way to *revert* without *reverting back* and no *consensus* that is not *general.*

Listed below are some of the more problematic redundancies.

**both** When you think about it, the conjunction *both* is often redundant. What exactly does *both* add to the meaning of this sentence: *Both Jack and Jill fell down the hill?* With *as well as, both* is even more redundant (if that's possible): *Both Jack as well as Jill fell down the hill.*

Verbs such as *agree* and *resemble* render *both* superfluous in its use as a pronoun and adjective: *Kevin and Conor both resemble their mother. Both researchers agree on this point.* The adjective *same* has the same effect. The sentence *They both have the same teacher* is no different in meaning from *They have the same teacher.*

But sometimes the mysterious effect of rhythm and emphasis counts for more than frugality in the use of words. If you like the way *both* sounds in constructions such as these, go ahead and use it.

**but . . . however** Too much contrast can ruin a photograph, and it can ruin a sentence as well. The contrastive conjunction *but* is redundant when used with *however.* It is hard to justify a sentence such as *But the management, however, went on with its plans.* Use one or the other, but not both.

**close proximity** Strictly speaking, the phrase *close proximity* says nothing that is not said by *proximity* itself. But like a few other common redundancies such as *old adage* and *mental telepathy*, this usage is too widespread and too innocuous to be worth objecting to.

**consensus** Many grammarians have condemned the expression *consensus of opinion* as redundant since a consensus itself entails a judgment about which there is general agreement. But many reputable writers have used *consensus of opinion*, and some have defended it on the grounds that a consensus may involve attitudes other than opinions; thus, there may be a *consensus of beliefs* or a *consensus of usage*. Nonetheless, the qualifying *of*-phrase can usually be omitted with no loss of clarity. The sentence *It was the consensus of opinion among the sportswriters that the game should not have been played* says nothing that is not said by *It was the consensus of the sportswriters that the game should not have been played*.

Expressions such as *overall consensus* and *general consensus* are harder to defend against the charge of redundancy. Ninety-five percent of the Usage Panel considers *overall consensus* to be objectionably redundant.

**consider as / deem as** *As* is sometimes used superfluously to introduce the complements of verbs like *consider, deem,* and *account: They considered it as one of the landmark decisions of the civil rights movement. The measure was deemed as unnecessary.* This usage may have arisen by analogy to *regard* and *esteem,* where *as* is standardly used in this way: *We regarded her as the best writer among us.* But the use of *as* with verbs like *consider* is not sufficiently well established to be acceptable in writing.

**cross section** Informally, we speak of a *cross section* of a population even if the group chosen is not statistically representative of the population as a whole. Thus you might say *You meet a cross section of Americans when you travel by interstate bus,* even though it is clear that some types of Americans are likely to be underrepresented among the people who ride interstate buses. When *cross section* is used in reference to the samples used in surveys and other investigations, the presumption is usually that the group has been chosen so as to be representative of the larger population, and here you must be more careful. Eighty-four percent of the Usage Panel finds the phrase *representative cross section* to be unacceptably redundant.

**else** *Else* is often used redundantly in combination with prepositions such as *but, except,* and *besides.* The sentence *No one else but Sam saw the accident* would thus do better without the *else.*

**empty rhetoric** In the ancient and medieval world, *rhetoric,* the study of persuasive argumentation, was an important branch of philosophy and a crucial skill to professional advancement. In recent years, however, people have been using the term chiefly in a pejorative sense to refer to pompous and devious language. This suspicion of rhetoric may result from a modern belief that language used in legitimate persuasion should be plain and free of artifice—

which is itself an argument from rhetoric. Thus, according to the newer sense of the term, you could construe as redundant the phrase *empty rhetoric,* as in *The politicians talk about solutions, but they usually offer only empty rhetoric.* It appears that the traditional meanings of rhetoric still carry a lot of weight, for only 35 percent of the Usage Panel judged this example to be redundant. Presumably, therefore, rhetoric can be other than empty.

**equally as** The adverb *equally* is generally regarded as redundant when used in combination with *as.* In an earlier survey, 63 percent of the Usage Panel found the following examples unacceptably redundant: *Experience is equally as valuable as theory. Equally as important is the desire to learn.* To get rid of the redundancy, you must delete *equally* from the first example and *as* from the second. Solving this usage problem usually involves using *as* alone when making an explicit comparison and *equally* alone when you want the comparison to be implied.

**free gift** What kind of gift isn't free? The kind that comes with strings attached. The widespread offering of gifts as part of product promotions has given the *free gift* a meaning all its own. A free gift ought, therefore, to be offered without an obligation to test-drive a vehicle, enroll in a book club, or open a savings account. Ought. Maybe the real problem is in using the word *gift* to refer to something that entails an obligation.

**from whence** *Send that dish back from whence it came!* A dyspeptic king might say that, but if uttered by a patron in most restaurants, it would be hard not to view it as anything but a joke. *Whence,* like *thence,* usually adds an archaic or highly formal tone to the passage in which it is used. It's great for creating an air of mock formality too.

Granting the king his royal license for formality to say *from whence it came,* would he then be open to criticism for redundancy? Language critics have attacked the construction *from whence* as redundant since the 18th century, and it is true that *whence* itself incorporates the sense of *from,* as in *a remote village, whence little news reached the wider world.* But *from whence* has been used steadily by reputable writers since the 14th century, most notably in the King James Bible: "*I will lift up mine eyes unto the hills, from whence cometh my help*" (Psalm 121). It is hard to label as incorrect a construction with such a respectable record of usage.

**inside of** People sometimes criticize the construction *inside of* as redundant or colloquial. But *inside of* is well established in formal writing, particularly in reference to periods of time: *They usually return the manuscript inside of* (or *inside*) *a month.*

**mental telepathy** If you are telepathic, are you also mental? The phrase *mental telepathy* ought to be regarded as redundant, but like some other fixed phrases, such as *hollow tube,* it has become so well established that the objection smacks of nitpicking.

**old adage** It is sometimes claimed that the expression *old adage* is redundant, inasmuch as a saying must have a certain tradition behind it to count as an *adage* in the first place. But the word *adage* is first recorded in the phrase *old adage,* showing that this redundancy itself is very old. A similar redundant phrase is *young whelp.*

**rarely ever / seldom ever** The use of *ever* after *rarely* and *seldom* is a classic redundancy that nevertheless appears to have a secure place in the language. *She rarely ever watches television* adds nothing to *She rarely watches television.* In an earlier survey, a large majority of the Usage Panel found this construction unacceptable in formal writing. Nonetheless, *ever* has been used as an intensive with *rarely* for several hundred years, and the construction is common in informal contexts. By contrast, the constructions *rarely* (or *seldom*) *if ever* and *rarely* (or *seldom*) *or never* are perfectly acceptable: *She rarely if ever watches television. She rarely or never watches television.*

**reason is because** A traditional rule holds that the construction *the reason is because* is redundant, and should be avoided in favor of *the reason is that.* The usage is well established, however, and can be justified by analogy to sentences in which *so that* follows *purpose,* as in *His* purpose *in calling her was* so that *she would be forewarned of the change in schedule.* A similar construction employs the conjunction *when* after the noun *time,* as in *The last* time *I saw her was* when *she was leaving for college.* You may find these constructions inelegant, however.

**reason why** A similar rule states that *why* is redundant in the expression *the reason why,* as in *The reason why he accepted the nomination is not clear.* It is true that *why* could be eliminated from such examples with no loss to the sense, but the construction has been used by reputable English writers since the Renaissance.

**refer back** You may have to *refer back* to an earlier chapter, but should you ever do it in writing? Many people consider *refer back* to be redundant, since the prefix *re-* means "back." Sixty-five percent of the usage panelists count themselves in this group. But when you think about it, *refer back* has some redeeming virtues. You can refer *back* to something that has already been mentioned or *refer ahead* to something that has not yet been mentioned. So you may want to *refer back* after all, if only to make sure your readers are looking in the right direction.

**revert back** You may be able to *refer ahead* but you can only *revert back.* Because the *re-* prefix means "back," you may find it simpler to do nothing more than *revert.* Seventy-eight percent of the Usage Panel considers *revert back* to be redundant.

**VAT tax** There are a number of recent expressions that add to an acronym the noun that the last letter of the acronym stands for. Thus, a *VAT tax* is a Value Added Tax tax. The *HIV virus* is the Human Immunodeficiency Virus virus.

An *ATM machine* is an Automated Teller Machine machine, and an *SAT test* is a Scholastic Assessment Test test, formerly known as the Scholastic Aptitude Test test. Seventy percent, or in some cases even more, of the Usage Panel is willing to overlook the redundancy of these expressions, probably because they have become fixed from so much use.

## Wordiness

In a world in which efficiency has become a prime value, most people view economy in wording as a sign of intelligence. Its opposite, therefore, is often considered a sign of stupidity. Most of us are busy and impatient people. We hate to wait. Using too many words is like asking people to stand in line until you get around to the point. It is irritating, which hardly helps when you are trying to win someone's goodwill or show that you know what you're talking about. What is worse, using too many words often makes it difficult to understand what is being said. It forces a reader to work hard to figure out what is going on, and in many cases the reader may simply decide it is not worth the effort. Another side effect of verbosity is the tendency to sound overblown, pompous, and evasive. What better way to turn off a reader?

It is easy to recommend concision in expression but much harder to figure out how to achieve it. In general, wordy writing has three distinguishing characteristics: weak verbs, ponderous nouns, and lots of prepositional phrases. The three are interconnected.

The key to writing clearly and concisely is to use strong active verbs. This means that you should only use the passive voice when you have a solid reason for doing so. (For more on this, see **passive voice** in this chapter and **verbs, voice of** under *Grammar*.) If you look down a page you have written and see that you are relying on forms of the verb *be* and other weak verbs like *seem* and *appear*, you can often boil down what you have written to a fraction of its size by revising with active verbs.

Relying on weak verbs forces you to shunt much of your meaning into nouns. These nouns tend to be abstract and Latinate, ending in *-ment, -tion*, and *-ence*. The nouns themselves need a proper grammatical home, and the only way to show how they relate to other parts of the sentence is to put the nouns in prepositional phrases. Here is an example:

> It is essential to acknowledge that one of the drawbacks to the increased utilization of part-time employees is that people who are still engaged full-time by the company are less likely to be committed to the recognition and identification of problems in the production area.

This passage has 45 words. We can boil it down to 14 by cutting out the unnecessary words, using active verbs, and using noun modifiers to do the work of prepositional phrases:

> Using more part-time employees often makes full-time employees less willing to report production problems.

Just as you can count weak verbs to test for wordiness, you can also count nouns in relation to active verbs. If there is a preponderance of nouns, consider revising the passage with strong verbs. It should be considerably shorter.

But in your efforts to write clearly, you must not lose sight of the fact that good writing has other virtues beside compactness. Just because a statement is concise does not make it moving. Consider the following passage from a speech by Winston Churchill voicing defiance during one of the most difficult times of World War II. It could certainly be made shorter with fewer repetitions, but it would hardly be more inspiring:

> We shall not flag or fail. We shall go on to the end. We shall fight in France, we shall fight on the seas and oceans, we shall fight with growing confidence and growing strength in the air, we shall defend our island, whatever the cost may be, we shall fight on the beaches, we shall fight on the landing grounds, we shall fight in the fields and in the streets, we shall fight in the hills; we shall never surrender.

A certain amount of repetition and redundancy has its uses. It never hurts to thank someone and add that you appreciate what was done. The recapitulation of the major points in a complicated essay can be a generous service to the reader, not a needless repetition. If you keep focused on what you are trying to accomplish and on what will help your readers or your listeners, you will have less need to remember formal rules of good writing. You will be able to trust your instincts and your ear.

# Word Choice

## *New Uses, Common Confusion, and Constraints*

This chapter treats usage problems that are inherent to individual words or entail a choice between words. It provides guidance on traditional difficulties such as when to use *between* instead of *among,* what the verb *decimate* means, and whether *politics* takes a singular or plural verb. It sorts out commonly confused words like *founder* and *flounder* or *blatant* and *flagrant.* And it assesses new usages, such as the verbs *empower* and *interface,* that have some popular appeal but may be seen as trendy or pretentious. Problems involving pronouns and conjunctions are treated under *Grammar.*

**a / an** In modern written English, we use *a* before a word beginning with a consonant sound, however it may be spelled (*a frog, a university, a euphemism*). We use *an* before a word beginning with a vowel sound (*an orange, an hour*). At one time, *an* was an acceptable alternative before words beginning with a consonant sound but spelled with a vowel (*an one, an united appeal*), but this usage is now entirely obsolete.

    *An* was also once a common variant before words beginning with *h* in which the first syllable was unstressed; thus 18th-century authors wrote either *a historical* or *an historical,* but *a history,* not *an history.* This usage made sense in that people often did not pronounce the initial *h* in words such as *historical* and *heroic,* but by the late 19th century, educated speakers were usually giving their initial *h*'s a huff, and the practice of writing *an* began to die out. Nowadays it survives primarily before the word *historical.* You may also come across it in the phrases *an hysterectomy* or *an hereditary trait.* These usages are acceptable in formal writing.

**able** The construction *able to* takes an infinitive to show the subject's ability to accomplish an action: *We were able to finish the project thanks to a grant from a large corporation. The new submarine is able to dive twice as fast as the older*

*model.* Some people think *able to* should be avoided with passive constructions involving forms of the verb *be*: *The problem was able to be solved by using a new method.* Since the problem has no ability to accomplish an action, this reasoning goes, it is not able to do anything; therefore *able to* should not be used. In such cases, you can usually substitute *can* or *could*: *The problem could be solved by using a new method.* Keep in mind, however, that passive constructions using the verb *get* ascribe a more active role to their subjects, and here you can use *able to*: *He was able to get himself accepted by a top law school.*

**about** The preposition *about* is traditionally used to refer to the relation between a narrative and its subject: *a book about Cezanne, a movie about the Boston Massacre.* Lately people have extended this use beyond narratives to refer to the relation between various kinds of nouns and the things they entail or make manifest: *The party was mostly about showing off their new offices. You don't understand what the women's movement is about.* This usage probably originates with the familiar expression *That's what it's all about,* but remains controversial. Fifty-nine percent of the Usage Panel rejected this use of *about* in the example *A designer teapot isn't about making tea; it is about letting people know that you have a hundred dollars to spend on a teapot.*

**not about to** When followed by an infinitive, *about to* means "presently going to, on the verge of," as in *I'm about to go downtown.* The construction *not about to* may be simply the negative of this, especially in response to questions: *I'm not about to go downtown. I'm about to go to the park.* But in most instances *not about to* expresses intention or determination, as in *We are not about to negotiate with terrorists.* A majority of the Usage Panel considers this usage acceptable in speech but not in formal writing.

**above** The use of *above* as an adjective or noun in referring to a preceding text is most common in business and legal writing. In general writing, its use as an adjective (*the above figures*) was accepted by a majority of the Usage Panel in an earlier survey, but its use as a noun (*read the above*) was accepted by only a minority.

**access** The verb *access* has become standard in reference to computers, as in *This program makes it considerably easier to access files on another disk.* In recent years, people have begun to extend *access* to nontechnical contexts, giving it the broader meaning "to obtain goods, especially by technological means." But this sense has yet to gain acceptability with the Usage Panel. Eighty-two percent reject the use of *access* in the sentence *You can access your cash at any of 300 automatic tellers throughout the area.*

**accompany** A traditional rule states that the preposition to use when *accompany* occurs in passive constructions should be *by* in the case of persons and *with* in the case of everything else. Thus you should say *The candidate was accompanied by six burly bodyguards,* but *The salmon was accompanied with a delicious salad.* However, *by* is quite commonly used in sentences of the second type, and the usage is grammatically defensible. The phrase introduced with *by* normally represents the subject of a related active sentence. You can see this by converting the sentence *The salmon was accompanied by a delicious watercress salad* to its active counterpart *A delicious salad accompanied the salmon.*

**acquiesce in / acquiesce to** When *acquiesce* takes a preposition, it is usually used with *in: No government acquiesces in its own overthrow.* The preposition *to* is less common, but also acceptable: *She acquiesced to her parents' wishes. Acquiesced with* is obsolete.

**act / action** The words *act* and *action* both mean "a deed" and "the process of doing." However, other senses of *act,* such as "a decision made by a legislative body," and of *action,* such as "habitual or vigorous activity," show that *act* tends to refer to a deed while *action* tends to refer to the process of doing. Thus people commit *sex acts* every day, but never *sex actions*. If they are seen, they are *caught in the act,* but not *in the action*. By the same token, they may want *a piece of the action,* but not *of the act*. As you can see, the demands of meaning or idiom often require one word or the other. But in cases where either can be used, either is acceptable: *My act* (or *action*) *was premature.*

**admission / admittance** Some people insist that *admittance* should be used only to refer to achieving physical access to a place (*He was denied admittance to the courtroom*) and that *admission* should be used to refer to achieving entry to a group or institution (*her admission to the club, China's admission to the United Nations*). There is no harm in observing this distinction, but don't be surprised if you see others ignoring it, for many people do. *Admission* is much more common in the sense "a fee paid for the right of entry": *The admission to the movie was five dollars.*

**adopted / adoptive** Children are adopted by parents, and we normally refer to an *adopted* child and to *adoptive* parents. By extension, *adoptive* can also refer to families and homes. When describing places, you can use either *adopted* or *adoptive: She enjoys living in her adopted country. San Francisco is their adoptive city.*

**advance / advancement** When used as a noun, *advance* indicates forward movement (*the advance of the army*) or progress or improvement (*an advance in molecular biology*). *Advancement* is usually used figuratively to indicate promotion or movement beyond an established norm: *career advancement*. Unlike *advance, advancement* often implies the existence of an agent or outside force. Thus *the advance of science* means simply the progress of science, whereas *the advancement of science* implies progress resulting from the action of an agent or force: *The purpose of the legislation was the advancement of science.*

**adverse / averse** Who isn't *averse* to getting *adverse* reactions to their ideas? *Averse* normally refers to people and means "having a feeling of distaste or aversion," as in *As an investor I'm averse to risk-taking.* People sometimes mistakenly slip in *adverse* for *averse* in these constructions with *to.* But *adverse* normally does not refer to people, rather to things that are antagonistic or contrary to someone's interests. Thus we say *We're working under very adverse* (not *averse*) *circumstances* and *All the adverse* (not *averse*) *criticism frayed the new mayor's nerves.*

**advise** The use of *advise* in the sense of "inform, notify" was found acceptable by a majority of the Usage Panel in an earlier survey, but many members prefer that this usage be restricted to business correspondence and legal contexts. Thus a sentence like *The suspects were advised of their rights* is perfectly acceptable, but one like *You'd better advise your friends that the date of the picnic has been changed* may come off as pretentious.

**affect / effect** *Affect* and *effect* are sometimes confused, but before you can sort them out, you must sort out the two words spelled *affect.* One means "to put on a false show of," as in *She affected a British accent.* The other can be both a noun and a verb. The noun meaning "emotion" is a technical term from psychology that sometimes shows up in general writing, as in this quote from a Norman Mailer piece about the Gulf War: "*Of course, the soldiers seen on television had been carefully chosen for blandness of affect.*" In its far more common role as a verb, *affect* usually means "to influence," as in *The Surgeon General's report outlined how smoking affects health.*

    *Effect* can also serve as a noun or a verb. The noun means "a result." Thus if you *affect* something, you are likely to see an *effect* of some kind, and from this may arise some of the confusion. As a verb, *effect* means "to bring about or execute." Thus, using *effect* in the sentence *The measures have been designed to effect savings* implies that the measures will cause new savings to come about. But using *affect* in the very similar sentence *These measures may affect savings* could just as easily imply that the measures may reduce savings that have already been realized.

**affinity** If there is an *affinity between* two friends, does one then have an *affinity for* the other? *Affinity* has a variety of meanings, ranging from "relationship by marriage" (its earliest) to "a resemblance or similarity" and extending to "a natural attraction" and even "a chemical attraction." The meanings are clear enough, but it's not always easy to know which preposition to use for each of these senses, especially since other factors can affect your choice, such as which verb you use. Thus you might say you feel a real *affinity for* (or *to* or *with*) your old neighborhood, and you might also say that the *affinity between* your old neighborhood and the people who once lived there is strong. Thus, while all of these usages are acceptable, there are some restrictions on which prepositions are acceptable with *affinity.* When *affinity* means "similarity or resemblance," the prepositions *with, to,* and *between* are standard, and it's hard to imagine a context where *for* would make sense. When affinity means "a feeling of kinship or sympathy," as in *I have an affinity for people in their situation, for* is perfectly acceptable. In some metaphorical uses, as in writing about food, *for* tends to predominate: *Lamb has a distinct affinity for red wines.* In chemical contexts, *for* is the preposition of choice: *the blood's affinity for oxygen, a dye with an affinity for synthetic fabrics.*

You might want to avoid using *affinity* as a simple synonym for *liking* since a majority of the Usage Panel in an earlier survey rejected the sentence *Her affinity for living in California led her to reject a chance to return to New York.* Nevertheless, the more sophisticated tone inherent in this use of *affinity* can lend an archness to certain contexts, as is evident when Barbara Tuchman writes of Kaiser Wilhelm's "*affinity for coarse physical jokes practiced upon his courtiers.*"

**affirmative** The expressions *in the affirmative* and *in the negative* are thought to come from military aviation, where pilots use *affirmative* and *negative* as synonyms for *yes* and *no* in radio transmissions. The idea is that the longer words are less likely to get lost in static. But when used in ordinary contexts, such as *She answered in the affirmative,* these expressions almost always sound pompous. *She answered yes* would be more acceptable even at the most formal levels of style.

**agenda** It is true that Cicero would have used *agendum* to refer to a single item of business before the Roman Senate, with *agenda* as its plural. But in Modern English *agenda* is used as a singular noun to denote the set or list of such items, as in *The agenda for the meeting has not yet been set.* If a plural of *agenda* is required, the form should be *agendas: The agendas of both meetings are exceptionally varied.*

**aggravate** *Aggravate* need not be an aggravating word. It comes from the Latin verb *aggravare,* which has two meanings: "to make heavier," that is, "to add to the weight of," and "to annoy," "oppress," "burden." When some people nowadays claim that *aggravate* should mean only "to make worse" and not "to irritate," they ignore not only an English sense in use since the 17th century but also one of the original Latin ones.

**alibi** You may be glad you have an alibi if you're hauled into court, but you may not want one if you're merely called on the carpet. When used as a noun in its nonlegal sense of "an excuse," *alibi* splits the Usage Panel in half. Forty-nine percent accept it in the sentence *He always had a ready alibi for the quality of his service.* When *alibi* is used as an intransitive verb meaning "to make excuses," as in *If you must alibi, at least try to be convincing,* it is unacceptable to 72 percent of the panel.

**all**

**all that** The construction *all that* is used informally in questions and negative sentences to mean "to the degree expected," as in *I know it won an Oscar, but the film is not all that exciting.* In an earlier survey, the Usage Panel rejected the use of this construction in formal writing.

**all in negative sentences** Be careful with sentences that have an *all . . . not . . .* form. They may be hazardous to your clarity. The sentence *All of the departments did not file a report* may mean that some departments did not file or that none did. If you want the first meaning, you can express it unambiguously by saying *Not all of the departments filed a report.* If you want the second meaning, try a paraphrase such as *None of the departments filed a report* or *All of the departments failed to file a report.* Note that the same problem can arise with other universal terms like *every* in negated sentences, as in the ambiguous *Every department did not file a report.*

**alleged** An *alleged* burglar is someone who has been accused of being a burglar but whose innocence or guilt has yet to be established. An *alleged* incident is an event that is said to have taken place but has not yet been verified. In their zeal to protect the rights of the accused, newspapers and law enforcement officials sometimes misuse *alleged.* A man arrested for murder may be only an *alleged* murderer, for example, but he is a real, not an *alleged,* suspect in that his status as a suspect is not in doubt. Similarly, if the money from a safe is known to have been stolen and not merely mislaid, then we can safely speak of a theft without having to qualify the description with *alleged.*

**all right / alright** Is it all right to use *alright?* Despite the appearance of *alright* in the works of such well-known writers as Flannery O'Connor, Langston Hughes, and James Joyce, the merger of *all* and *right* has never been accepted as standard. This is peculiar, since similar fusions like *already* and *altogether* have never raised any objections. The difference may lie in the fact that *already* and *altogether* became single words back in the Middle Ages, whereas *alright* (at least in its current meaning) has only been around for a little over a century and was called out by language critics as a misspelling. You might think a century would be plenty of time for such an unimposing spelling to gain acceptance as a standard variant, and you will undoubtedly come across *alright* in magazine and newspaper articles. But if you decide to use *alright,* especially in formal writing, you run the risk that some of your readers will view it as an error, while others may think you are willfully breaking convention.

**allude / allusion / refer / reference** All allusions are references, but are all references allusions? Many people, following the advice of language critics, like to make a distinction between *alluding* to something and *referring* to it. By this thinking, *allude* and *allusion* should apply to indirect references in which the source is not specifically identified: *"Well, we'll always have Paris," he told the travel agent, in an allusion to the movie* Casablanca. By contrast, *refer* and *reference* usually imply specific mention of a source: *I will refer to* Hamlet *for my conclusion: As Polonius says, "Though this be madness, yet there is method in't."* In practice, many writers do not follow this distinction, but it's certainly worthy of consideration.
More at **refer.**

**alongside / alongside of** Both of these forms are acceptable as prepositions. Thus you can say *The barge lay alongside* (or *alongside of* ) *the pier.*

### alternative

**two or more *alternatives*** You may find yourself in a situation with *no alternative*, with *only one alternative*, or with *more than one alternative*, but can you ever have *more than two alternatives?* Some traditionalists hold that *alternative* should be used only in situations where the number of choices involved is exactly two because of the word's historical relation to Latin *alter*, "the other of two." The Usage Panel is evenly divided on the issue, with 49 percent accepting the sentence *Of the three alternatives, the first is the least distasteful.*

The complexity of this situation arises from the multiplicity of senses that *alternative* has. It can mean "a choice or a situation that requires a choice between two things," as in *The only alternative to continuing down the river was to give up and hike out of the gorge.* From this it is a short leap in meaning to "one of a number of things from which only one can be chosen," and here is where we may be forced to choose *from several alternatives*.

**alternative used as an adjective** As an adjective, *alternative* can mean "allowing or requiring a choice between two or more things," as in *We wrote an alternative statement in case the first was rejected by the board.* It may also refer to a variant or substitute in cases where no choice is involved, as in *We will do our best to secure alternative employment for employees displaced by the closing of the factory.* In its latest usage, *alternative* indicates things that are outside established traditions or institutions, as in *the alternative press* or *alternative rock*.

Remember not to confuse *alternative* with *alternate*. Correct usage requires *The class will meet on alternate* (not *alternative*) *Tuesdays.*

**although / though** As conjunctions, *although* and *though* are generally interchangeable: *Although* (or *though*) *she smiled, she was angry. Although* usually occurs at the beginning of its clause (as in the preceding example), whereas *though* may occur elsewhere and is the more common term when used to link words or phrases, as in *wiser though poorer*. In certain constructions only *though* is acceptable: *Fond though* (not *although*) *I am of sports, I'd rather not sit through another basketball game.*

**altogether / all together** If you and your local scout troop go *all together* on a hike, you may be *altogether* tired when you get back. As this example shows, *altogether* and *all together* do not mean the same thing. We use *all together* to indicate that the members of a group perform or undergo an action collectively: *The nations stood all together. The prisoners were herded all together.* We use *all together* only in sentences that can be rephrased so that *all* and *together* may be separated by other words. Thus you can tell that *all together* is correct in the sentence *The books lay all together in a heap* since you can rephrase it as *All the books lay together in a heap.*

The adverb *altogether*, on the other hand, has several different meanings. It's easy to see how confusion might arise with the phrase *all together* when we use *altogether* to mean "all told, in all": *Altogether, there were fifty people at the wedding.* Most frequently, however, we use *altogether* as a synonym for *entirely* or *completely: The researchers tried an altogether different approach this time.* But we can also use it as a sentence adverb meaning "with everything considered, on the whole": *Altogether, I can understand why she took offense.*

**anticipate** Some people hold that you should never use *anticipate* as a synonym for *expect,* as in *We didn't anticipate that it would take so long to drive across Ohio.* They would restrict its use to situations in which advance action is taken either to forestall an occurrence (as in *She anticipated her opponent's next move*) or to fulfill a desire (as in *He anticipated my wish by making reservations at the Mexican restaurant*). In earlier surveys, however, a majority of the Usage Panel accepted the use of *anticipate* to mean "to feel or to realize beforehand" and "to look forward to." Thus by their lights it is OK to say *They really anticipate the joys of homeownership* or *We're anticipating a larger turnout at this year's school fair.*

**unanticipated** The word *unanticipated,* however, is not established as a synonym for *unexpected.* Seventy-seven percent of the Usage Panel rejected the sentence *They always set aside a little extra food for unanticipated guests,* inasmuch as guests for whom advance provision has been made cannot be said to be unanticipated, though they may very well be unexpected.

**antidote** Do you take an *antidote to, for,* or *against* something? In fact you can use any of these prepositions. Thus you can go to the movies as *an antidote to boredom,* be injected with *an antidote for snakebite,* or buy gold as *an antidote against inflation.*

**anxious** People have been using *anxious* as a synonym for *eager* for over 250 years, and for over 100 years language critics have been objecting to it. Objectors feel that *anxious* should be used only when the person it refers to is worried or uneasy about the upcoming event. By this thinking, it is OK to say *We are anxious to see the strike settled soon* but not *We are anxious to see the new show of contemporary sculpture at the museum.* The Usage Panel splits down the middle on this issue. Just 52 percent accept *anxious* in the second example.

So left to your own devices, what should you do? Using *anxious* to mean "eager" can have its own effectiveness, at least in colloquial discourse, since it adds emotional urgency to an assertion. It implies that the subject so strongly desires a certain outcome that frustration of that desire will lead to unhappiness. In this way, it resembles the informal adjective *dying* in sentences such as *I'm dying to see your new baby.* So use *anxious* when it fits your purpose.

**apparent** You might think that the meaning of a word like *apparent* would be, well, apparent. But language is never that easy. Used before a noun, *apparent* means "seeming": *For all his apparent wealth, Pat always had trouble paying the rent.* Used after a form of the verb *be,* however, *apparent* can mean either "seeming" (as in *His virtues are only apparent*) or "obvious" (as in *The effects of* *the drought are apparent to anyone who sees the parched fields*), so be careful that the meaning you want is clear from the context.

**arrant / errant** If you're unsure of the difference between these words, don't feel bad. *Arrant* was once a variant spelling of *errant,* which meant and still means "wandering." Thus an *errant* (or an *arrant*) thief was a bandit who roved the countryside. It was not a far stretch from this use to the meaning "notorious, outright, thoroughgoing," which is the meaning that *arrant* developed and kept. Now if you wander and rove, you can only be *errant.* And if you want an intensive adjective to add spice to insults, you want *arrant.* An *arrant fool* is a complete one.

**assure / ensure / insure** *Assure, ensure,* and *insure* all mean "to make secure or certain." Only *assure* is used with reference to a person in the sense of "to set the mind at rest": *The ambassador assured the Prime Minister of his loyalty.* Although *ensure* and *insure* are generally interchangeable, only *insure* is now widely used in American English in the commercial sense of "to guarantee persons or property against risk." If you want to keep them straight, it may be easier just to give these words separate roles: *I assure you that we have insured the grounds to ensure that we will be protected in case of a lawsuit stemming from an accident.*

**auger / augur** Don't confuse these words. An *auger* is a tool used for boring holes. An *augur* is a seer or soothsayer. The verb *augur* means "to foretell or betoken," as in *This development augurs change in the software business. Augur* is used most commonly as a verb without an object in phrases such as *augur well* or *augur ill,* as in *The rehearsal miscues did not augur well for opening night.*

**aural / oral** These words sound the same but have different meanings. *Aural* refers to the ear or to hearing: *aural disease. Oral* refers to the mouth or to speaking: *an oral vaccine, an oral examination.*

**author** As a verb, *author* first appeared in the late 16th century but fell out of use for 250 years. It was rejuvenated in the mid-20th century with the sense "to be the author of a written text." In most cases it refers to material that has been published—and not to unpublished texts such as love letters or diaries. Therefore it does not have quite as broad a meaning as the verb *write.* For this reason, it is unlikely that someone who has ghostwritten a book for a celebrity will be said to have "authored" the manuscript. Perhaps because of the relative newness of the verb, many usage critics have condemned it as illegitimate. The Usage Panel tends to sympathize with this view. Seventy-four percent reject the sentence *He has authored a dozen books on the subject.*

Journalists frequently use the verb *author* to apply to the creation or sponsoring of legislative acts, as in *The Senator authored a bill limiting uses of desert lands in California.* In these cases the lawmaker may not have actually written the bill that bears his or her name but rather promoted its idea and passage.

While a bit more tolerant of this legislative usage, the nays on the Usage Panel still have it. Sixty-four percent reject the example sentence cited above.

**coauthor** The verb *coauthor* is well established in reference to scientific and scholarly publications, where it serves a useful purpose since the people listed as authors of such works routinely include research collaborators who have played no part in the actual writing of the text but who are nonetheless entitled to credit for the published results. For more on this, see **author** under *Science Terms*.

**awhile / a while** People often confuse the adverb *awhile* with the noun phrase *a while*. This is hardly surprising because they sound the same and the noun phrase can function like an adverb. In many cases both forms are acceptable. You can say *It took a while to get down the hill,* where *a while* functions like other noun phrases such as *an hour* or *a long time.* You can also say *It took awhile to get down the hill,* where *awhile* functions like the adverb phrase *quite long* or the comparative adverb *longer.*

You may want to be careful using *a while* after prepositions, where traditional grammar calls for a noun as object. Thus you should write *I'll stay for a while,* but not *I'll stay for awhile.* Without the preposition, either form is acceptable: *I'll stay a while* or *I'll stay awhile.*

**backward / backwards** You can spell the adverb *backward* or *backwards.* The forms are interchangeable: *stepped backward, a mirror facing backwards.* But in Standard English the adjective has no *-s: a backward view.*

**bad / badly**

**bad as adverb** *Bad* is often used as an adverb in sentences such as *The house was shaken up pretty bad* or *We need water bad.* This usage is common in informal speech but is widely regarded as unacceptable in formal writing. In an earlier survey, 92 percent of the Usage Panel rejected the sentence *His tooth ached so bad he could not sleep.*

**want badly** The use of *badly* with *want* was once considered incorrect but is now entirely acceptable. So don't feel bad if you find yourself wanting to go to the beach *badly.*

**feel badly** If you say *I feel bad,* people may think you have a cold, or they may just as likely think your spirits need a lift. But what if you say *I feel badly?* Will you get sympathy, censure, or an aspirin? The adverb *badly* is often used after verbs such as *feel,* as in *I felt badly about the whole affair.* In fact, this usage bears analogy to the use of other adverbs with *feel,* such as *strongly* in *We feel strongly about this issue.* Many people like to restrict *feel badly* to refer to emotional distress and let *feel bad* cover physical ailments. There is nothing wrong with maintaining this distinction, but don't expect everyone else to share this view. It's another useful distinction that is often ignored. Be sure that readers will understand *feel badly* from its context.

**badly meaning "unwell"** In some regions people use *badly* to mean "unwell," as in *He was looking badly after the accident. Poorly* is also used in this way. You may want to be careful with this usage, however. In an earlier survey, 75 percent of the Usage Panel found it unacceptable in formal writing.

**baited / bated** If you wait for something with *baited breath*, people may well wonder what you have baited it with. The correct phrase is *bated breath*, which comes from the verb *bate,* meaning "to lessen or restrain," as in "*To his dying day he bated his breath a little when he told the story*" (George Eliot).

**baleful / baneful** *Baleful* and *baneful* overlap in meaning, but *baleful* usually applies to something that menaces or foreshadows evil: *a baleful look. Baneful* most often describes something that is actually harmful or destructive: *baneful effects of their foreign policy.*

**barbarism / barbarity** There is a significant difference in meaning between *barbarism* and *barbarity.* Both denote some absence of civilization, but the word *civilization* itself has several different senses, one the opposite of *barbarism,* the other the opposite of *barbarity.* On the one hand, *civilization* may refer to the scientific, artistic, and cultural attainments of advanced societies, and it is this sense that figures in the meaning of *barbarism.* The English word *barbarism* originally referred to incorrect use of language, but it is now used more generally to refer to ignorance or crudity in matters of taste, including verbal expression: *The* New Yorker *would never tolerate such barbarisms.* On the other hand, *civilization* may refer to the basic social order that allows people to resolve their differences peaceably, and it is this sense—that is, civilization as opposed to savagery—that figures in the meaning of *barbarity,* which refers to savage brutality or cruelty in actions, as in *The accounts of the emperor's barbarity shocked the world.*

**beside / besides** Some people argue that these two words should be kept distinct when they are used as prepositions. By this thinking, you should use *beside* only to mean "at the side of," as in *There was no one in the seat beside me.* For the meanings "in addition to" and "except for" you should use *besides: Besides replacing the back stairs, he fixed the broken bannister. No one besides Smitty would say a thing like that.* But this distinction is often ignored by widely respected writers. While it's true that *besides* can never mean "at the side of," you will often see *beside* used in place of *besides* in print. Watch out for ambiguity when using *beside* in this way. The sentence *There was no one beside me at the table* could mean that you had the table to yourself or that the seats next to you were not occupied.

**better**
*better and best Which do you think is best? The chocolate chip or the mocha supreme?* For a discussion of the use of superlatives to compare two things, see  **better / best** under *Grammar.*
*had better You better not.* Is it OK to leave the *had* out of *had better*? For an  answer to this question, see **had better** under *Grammar.*

## between

***between* and *among*** *"Between* is used for two, and *among* for more than two." This decree of grammar may still echo in your old classroom, but you would be wise to consider other reverberations as well. It is true that *between* is the only choice when exactly two entities are specified. For example, you must say *the choice between* (not *among*) *good and evil* and *the rivalry between* (not *among*) *Great Britain and France.* But when more than two entities are involved or when the number of entities is unspecified, the word choice depends on what you want to say. You use *between* when the entities are considered as distinct individuals and *among* when they are considered as a mass or collectivity. Thus in the sentence *The balloon landed between the houses,* the houses are seen as points that define the boundaries of the area where the balloon touched down. We assume, therefore, that the balloon did not land on any of the individual houses. In *The balloon landed among the houses,* the area of landing is considered to be the general location of the houses, taken together. It leaves open the possibility that the balloon came down on one of the houses. By the same token, we may speak of *a series of wars between the Greek cities,* which suggests that each city was an independent participant in the hostilities, or of *a series of wars among the Greek cities,* which allows for the possibility that the participants were shifting alliances of cities. For this reason, *among* is used to indicate inclusion in a group: *She is among the best of our young sculptors. There is a spy among you.* Use *between* when the entities are seen as determining the limits or endpoints of a range: *They searched the area between the river, the farmhouse, and the woods. The truck driver had obviously been drinking between stops.*

***between you and I*** This oft-maligned phrase is discussed as one of the case problems at **pronouns, personal** under *Grammar.*

## bimonthly / biweekly / semimonthly / semiweekly

If your therapy group has *semimonthly* meetings, how often should you expect to show up? A *bimonthly* meeting should take place "once every two months"; a *biweekly,* "once every two weeks." A *semimonthly* meeting should be held "twice a month" and a *semiweekly* "twice a week." That's *should.* These words are often confused, and to spare nervous attendees the suspense, the only decent thing to do is to use substitute expressions like *every two months* or *twice a month.*

In the publishing world, where confusion is a rarity, a *bimonthly* always comes out every two months, and a *biweekly* every two weeks.

## blatant / flagrant

Was that foul whistled by the referee *blatant* or *flagrant?* It could be either. It could be both (though you might think this a bit of overkill). *Blatant* and *flagrant* are often confused, which is not all that surprising since the words have overlapping meanings. Both attribute conspicuousness and offensiveness to certain acts, but the words differ in emphasis. *Blatant* means "offensively conspicuous," and thus emphasizes the actor's failure to conceal the act. *Flagrant,* on the other hand, means "conspicuously offensive," and emphasizes the serious wrongdoing inherent in the offense.

Thus a violation of human rights may be *blatant* or *flagrant.* If it was committed with contempt for public scrutiny, it is *blatant.* If its barbarity was monstrous, it was *flagrant.*

*Blatant* can also mean "unpleasantly loud." People sometimes use it to mean "obvious," as in *the blatant danger of such an approach,* but this use has not been established and is widely considered an error.

**boast** Some have objected to the use of *boast* as a transitive verb meaning "to possess or own a desirable feature," as in *This network boasts an audience with a greater concentration of professionals and managers than any other network.* This usage is by now well established, however, and is acceptable to 62 percent of the Usage Panel.

**born / borne** These words are both past participles of *bear.* Here's how to sort them out. Use *born* only in passive constructions referring to birth: *I was born in Chicago.* For all other uses, including active constructions referring to birth, use *borne: She has borne both her children at home. I have borne his insolence with the patience of a saint.*

**both** *Both* indicates that the action or state denoted by the verb applies individually to each of two entities. *Both books weigh more than five pounds,* for example, means that each book weighs more than five pounds by itself, not that the two books weighed together come to more than five pounds. *Both* is inappropriate where the verb does not apply to each of the entities by itself.

**both their fault / the fault of both** How do you make possessives for *both?* See **possessives** under *Grammar.*

**both . . . and . . .** See **parallelism** under *Style.*

## bring

**bring and take** When do you use *bring* and when do you use *take?* It depends on your point of view. We use *bring* to indicate motion toward the place of speaking or the place from which the action is regarded. Thus you normally *take* checks to the bank and *bring* home cash, although from the banker's perspective you have *brought* checks to the bank in order to *take* away cash.

When the point of reference is not the place of speaking itself, you can use either verb depending on the context. Thus you can say either *The labor leaders brought their requests to the mayor's office* or *The labor leaders took their requests to the mayor's office* depending on whether you want to describe things from the point of view of the labor leaders or the mayor. Perhaps for this reason, the distinction between *bring* and *take* is sometimes less clear than you might expect. A parent may say of a child, for example, *She always takes a pile of books home with her from school,* as the parent imagines the situation from the child's viewpoint. This usage may sound curious to those who are accustomed to observe the distinction more strictly, but there is really nothing wrong with it.

**bring and brung** The form *brung* is common in colloquial use in many areas, even among educated speakers, but it is not standard in formal writing.

**burgeon** *Burgeon* has gained greater acceptance in recent years in its use to mean not just "to put forth buds" but more generally "to grow and flourish." In 1969 only 51 percent of the Usage Panel accepted the phrase *the burgeoning population of Queens;* twenty years later 74 percent accepted the same phrase. However, it should be noted that in this use *burgeon* is more acceptable when it takes the form of the present participle. Only 29 percent of the panel accepts the sentence *News programs are less expensive to produce than entertainment series, and the public's appetite for them has burgeoned.*

**callous / callus** Do not confuse the adjective *callous* (as in *Years of dealing with criminals had left her callous*) with the noun *callus* (as in *I have a callus on my thumb*). You should also be careful not to mix up the verb *callous,* which means "to make or become callous," with the verb *callus,* which means "to form or develop hardened tissue."

**capital / capitol** When touring the *capital,* why not visit the *capitol? Capital* and *capitol* are terms that are often confused, mainly because they refer to things that are in some ways related. The term for a town or city that serves as a seat of government is spelled *capital.* The term for the building in which a legislative assembly meets is spelled *capitol.*

**careen / career** That sportscar went *careering* down the road. Or did it *careen? Careen* comes to us via Middle French from the Latin word *carina,* which meant "the keel of a ship." The original sense of the English verb was nautical and referred to the way a ship would lean to one side when sailing in windy conditions. Today, when used as a verb of motion, *careen* typically implies high speed. It often but not always entails a sideways motion or wavering. This sense probably came from the application of the nautical sense of the word to automobiles, which usually only *careen,* that is, lurch or tip over, when driven at high speeds.

Career, on the other hand, has always been on dry land. It comes from Middle French *carriere,* "race course," which comes from Latin *cararria,* "carriageway," and ultimately from Latin *carrum,* "cart, car." (The "occupation" sense is an extension of the "race course" meaning, although many might find this metaphor a bit of a stretch today.) As a verb, *career* originally meant "to move over a course." In the verb's first recorded usage, the course was the lane for each horse at a jousting tournament. But the kinds of courses and agents of motion soon proliferated, and the verb now means "to move forward at high speed."

In short, the sportscar can either *career* or *careen,* since both words are acceptable in this use.

**caring** Some people object to the use of *caring* as an adjective, and the acceptability of the usage seems to vary according to the relation between the source and object of the caring. Seventy-four percent of the Usage Panel accepts the sentence *A child has a right to certain things: a secure home, a healthful environment, and caring parents.* A smaller majority, 58 percent, accepts *We are looking for a few caring people to help with this program,* where the nature of caring appears vague and the object is any of a number of concerns that might arise. When *caring* is applied to circumstances instead of people, acceptability falls even further. Only 29 percent of the panel accepts *A child has the right to grow up in a healthful, caring environment.*

**celebrant** Although *celebrant* is most often used to describe an official participant in a religious ceremony or rite, a majority of the Usage Panel accepted the use of *celebrant* to mean "a participant in a celebration" in an earlier survey. Still, while *New Year's Eve celebrants* might be an acceptable usage, you may want to use the uncontroversial alternative *celebrator* in this more general sense (*New Year's Eve celebrators*).

**center** Can you *center on* something and *around* it at the same time? Traditionally, the verb *center* has been used with the prepositions *on, upon, in,* or *at,* but some language critics have denounced its use with *around* as illogical or physically impossible. Still, the fact that many writers persist in using this phrase in sentences such as *The discussion centered around the need for curriculum revision* suggests that many people perceive *center around* to best represent the true nature of what they are trying to say. *Center* can represent various relations involving having, finding, or turning about a center, and the choice of a preposition to accompany *center* depends on the meaning you want to convey. There is ample evidence for usages such as *Our hope centered in the young leader, His thoughts centered on the long journey before him,* and *The trade is centered at Amsterdam. Center around* is equally well established, as in *A storm of controversy centered around the king.* In this example, *around* seems to be the only appropriate choice. If using the phrase *center around* does not sit well with you, however, try *revolve around* instead.

**certain** If you think too much about it, you might conclude that *certain* is an absolute term like *unanimous* or *paramount* and cannot be modified. Something is either certain or it is not, you might say. There can be no in-between. But before you say much more, you may find yourself using *certain* in combination with adverbs such as *fairly, absolutely,* and *completely,* which would seem to imply that levels of certainty exist. In an earlier survey, a majority of the Usage Panel accepted the construction *Nothing could be more certain,* so you can be confident that modifying *certain* is a pretty safe bet.

**chord / cord** These two words are often confused—and with good reason, for they are really three. There are two words spelled *chord.* One comes from the word *accord* and refers to a harmonious combination of three or more musical notes. The other is an alteration of *cord,* taking its spelling from Greek *chorda,* "string, gut," by way of Latin. A mathematical chord is a line segment that joins two points on a curve.

*Cord* itself means "a string or rope." It has many extensions, as in *an electrical cord* and *a cord of wood.* When referring to anatomical structures, it can be spelled in general usage either as *cord* or *chord* (again by influence of Greek and Latin). Strict medical usage requires *cord,* however. Your doctor examines your *spinal cord* and *vocal cords,* never your *chords.*

When something *strikes a chord* with you, it is actually a metaphorical string that is being struck and not a triad of musical notes. But many of us feel harmonic overtones anyway.

**claustrophobic** You may feel claustrophobic in that cubicle, but is the cubicle therefore claustrophic as well? Clinically speaking, *claustrophobic* refers to an abnormal tendency to feel terror in closed spaces. But, like other terms used to describe psychological conditions (*schizophrenic* and *narcissism,* for example), *claustrophobic* has been applied more loosely in the general usage of our language over time. At first it referred to any kind of temporary feeling of being closed in or unable to escape (*Riding on trains makes me feel claustrophobic*). Then it became common to use it to refer to any kind of space that might make a person feel such a sensation (*The staff members are jammed into a nest of claustrophobic offices*). Seventy-four percent of the Usage Panel finds this latter usage unacceptable, implying that *claustrophobic* should be used only to describe a psychological state. Nevertheless, this usage is well established, and it follows a general tendency to combine adjectives with nouns according to a progressively looser interpretation of the relationship between the two. For example, the phrase *topless swimsuit* came to be followed by *topless dancers,* which led in turn to *topless bars, topless districts,* and *topless ordinances.* By the same token, a room that makes you feel a certain way may be described as sad or cheerful without objection, and there seems to be no reason for drawing the line at calling it *claustrophobic.*

**cohort** Education is not what you have learned but what you can still remember, and there are some today who remember from their second-year Latin that a "cohort" in Caesar's *Gallic Wars* was a unit of soldiers. There were six "centuries" (100 men) to a cohort, ten cohorts to a "legion" (therefore 6000 men). A century, then, would correspond to a company, a cohort to a battalion, and a legion to a regiment. The bodyguard of a Roman general was also called a *cohors.* Because of the word's history, some people insist that *cohort* should only be used to refer to a group of people and never to an individual person. In recent years, however, the use of *cohort* to refer to an individual rather than a group has become very common and is now in fact the dominant usage. Seventy-one percent of the Usage Panel accepts the sentence *The cashiered dictator and his cohorts have all written their memoirs,* while only 43 percent accept *The gangster walked into the room surrounded by his cohort.* Also, perhaps because of its original military and paramilitary associations, *cohort* usually has a somewhat negative connotation, and therefore critics of the President rather than his supporters might use a phrase like *the President and his cohorts.*

**commentate** *Commentate*, a back-formation from *commentator*, is normally used to mean "to serve as a commentator": *The retired tennis pro has agreed to commentate on the upcoming match.* It is sometimes used transitively to mean "to make a running commentary on," as in *She commentated the tennis match.* In an earlier survey, a majority of the Usage Panel found this transitive usage to be unacceptable.

**compare to / compare with** *Compare* usually takes the preposition *to* when it refers to the activity of describing the resemblances between unlike things: *He compared her to a summer day. Scientists sometimes compare the human brain to a computer.* It takes *with* when it refers to the act of examining two like things in order to discern their similarities or differences: *The police compared the forged signature with the original. The committee will have to compare the Senate's version of the bill with the version that was passed by the House.* When *compare* is used to mean "to liken (one) with another," *with* is traditionally held to be the correct preposition: *That little bauble is not to be compared with* (not *to*) *this enormous jewel.* But *to* is frequently used in this context and is not incorrect.

**complacent / complaisant** These words sound the same and are often confused. *Complacent* means "overly contented, self-satisfied," as in *After making a string of successes, the film director grew complacent.* The trouble arises in that *complacent* can also mean "eager to please," which is what *complaisant* means: *We were taken on a tour by an energetic and complaisant guide.* If you want to avoid the risk of being misunderstood, use *complacent* in the "contented" sense only.

**complement / compliment** *He complimented her on the way her sweater complemented her hair. Complement* and *compliment*, though quite distinct in meaning, are sometimes confused because they are pronounced the same. As a noun, *complement* means "something that completes or brings to perfection" (*The antique silver was a complement to the beautifully set table*); used as a verb it means "to serve as a complement to." The noun *compliment* means "an expression or act of courtesy or praise" (*They gave us a compliment on our beautifully set table*), while the verb means "to pay a compliment to."

**complete** Although *complete* is often held to be an absolute term like *perfect* or *chief*, and therefore not subject to comparison, it is actually often qualified as *more* or *less*. A majority of the Usage Panel accepts the example *His book is the most complete treatment of the subject.* For more on this, see **absolute terms** under *Grammar*.

 More at **equal, infinite, parallel, perfect,** and **unique.**

**compose / comprise** If you follow the traditional rule, you say that the whole *comprises* the parts and that the parts *compose* the whole. Thus you would say *The Union comprises fifty states* and *Fifty states compose* (or *constitute* or *make up*) *the Union.* While writers often maintain this distinction, *comprise* is increasingly

used in place of *compose*, especially in the passive: *The Union is comprised of fifty states.* Don't be surprised if this usage still elicits comments, however. In an earlier survey, a majority of the Usage Panel found this use of *comprise* unacceptable. More at **include.**

**conflicted** No conflict here! The adjective *conflicted* is most often associated with the jargon of New Age psychology. Almost the entire Usage Panel (92 percent) rejects its use in the sentence *Caught between loyalty to old employees and a recognition of the need to cut costs, many managers are conflicted about the reorganization plan.* This sentence might be better worded as *Caught between loyalty to old employees and a recognition of the need to cut costs, many managers have conflicting feelings about the reorganization plan.*

**contact** The verb *contact* is a classic example of a verb that was made from a noun and of a new usage that was initially frowned upon. The noun meaning "the state or condition of touching" was introduced in 1626 by Francis Bacon. Some 200 years later it spawned a verb meaning "to bring or place in contact." This sense of the verb has lived an unremarkable life in technical contexts. It was only in the first quarter of the 20th century that *contact* came to be used to mean "to communicate with," and soon afterward the controversy began. *Contact* was declared to be properly a noun, not a verb—and besides, it was argued, as a verb it was vague.

Neither of these arguments holds water. Turning nouns into verbs is one of the most frequent ways in which new verbs enter English. The examples are countless and familiar. *Curb, date, elbow, head, interview, panic, park,* and *service* are but a few. *Contact* is but another instance of what linguists call *functional shift* from one part of speech to another. As for *contact's* vagueness, this seems a virtue in an age in which forms of communication have proliferated. The sentence *We will contact you when the part comes in* allows for a variety of possible ways to communicate: by mail, telephone, computer, or fax.

But whatever you think of these issues, the main question is *contact's* acceptability in Standard English. It appears that the usefulness and popularity of this verb has worn down resistance to it. In 1969, only 34 percent of the Usage Panel accepted the use of *contact* as a verb, but in 1988, 65 percent of the panel accepted it in the sentence *She immediately called an officer at the Naval Intelligence Service, who in turn contacted the FBI.* More at **impact.**

**contemporary** When *contemporary* is used in reference to something in the past, its meaning is not always clear. *Contemporary critics of Shakespeare* may mean critics in his time or critics in our time. When the context does not make the meaning clear, you can avoid being misunderstood by using phrases such as *critics in Shakespeare's time* or *modern critics.*

**continual / continuous** These adjectives are sometimes confused because their meanings overlap. Both words can be used to mean "continuing without

interruption": *living in a continual state of fear, enjoying a continuous state of peace.* But *continual* usually refers to something that recurs or is interrupted periodically: *the continual pounding of the surf, the continual banging of the shutters in the wind.* Only *continuous* is used to refer to physical continuation: *The fans formed a continuous line around the field.*

**continuance / continuation** Both of these words mean "the act or fact of continuing," but only *continuance* is used to refer to the duration of a state or condition, as in *his continuance in office. Continuation* applies especially to prolongation or resumption of action (*a continuation of the meeting*) or to physical extension (*the continuation of the street*). The *continuation* of a story is that part of the story following a break in its narration.

**contrast** The noun *contrast* may be followed by *between, with,* or *to: There is a sharp contrast between his earlier and later works. In contrast with* (or less frequently, *to*) *his early works, the later plays are brittle and highly theatrical.* When *contrast* is used as a transitive verb, both *with* and *to* may follow, though *with* is more common: *He contrasts the naturalistic early plays with* (or *to*) *the brittle later comedies.*

**convince / persuade** According to a traditional rule, *convince* is used to indicate mental acceptance, and *persuade* to indicate mental acceptance followed by action. Thus you *convince* someone of the truth of a statement or proposition but *persuade* someone to do something. By extension you use *convince*, but not *persuade*, with a *that*-clause. Thus you should say *By convincing me that no good could come of staying, he persuaded me to leave.*

If you accept this distinction, then you should not use *convince* with an infinitive: *He persuaded* (not *convinced*) *me to go.* In an earlier survey, a majority of the Usage Panel upheld this distinction. But the use of *convince* with an infinitive has become increasingly common even among reputable writers. In addition, both *persuade* and *convince* see frequent use with *that*-clauses to indicate the acceptance of truth: *I convinced* (or *persuaded*) *the receptionist that the matter was urgent.* Thus, the traditional rule does not appear to have much of a future.

**could care less / couldn't care less** *I could care less!* you might say sometime in disgust. You might just as easily have said *I couldn't care less* and meant the same thing! How can this be? When taken literally, the phrase *I could care less* means "I care more than I might," rather than "I don't care at all." But the beauty of sarcasm is that it can turn meanings on their head, thus allowing *could care less* to work as an equivalent for *couldn't care less.* Because of its sarcasm, *could care less* is more informal than its negative counterpart and may be open to misinterpretation when used in writing.

The phrases *cannot but* and *can but* present a similar case of a positive and a negative meaning the same thing. For more on this, see **cannot** under *Grammar.*

**council / counsel / consul** *Council, counsel,* and *consul* are never inter-changeable as such, though their meanings are related. *Council* and *councilor* refer principally to a deliberative assembly (such as a city council or student council), its work, and its membership. *Counsel* and *counselor* pertain chiefly to advice and guidance in general and to a person (such as a lawyer or camp counselor) who provides it. *Consul* denotes an officer in the foreign service of a country.

## couple

**one or two** We like to think of a couple as one, but are they? When used to refer to two people who function socially as a unit, as in *a married couple,* the word *couple* may take either a singular or a plural verb, depending on whether the members are considered individually or collectively: *The couple were married last week. Only one couple was left on the dance floor.* When a pronoun follows, *they* and *their* are more common than *it* and *its: The couple decided to spend their* (less commonly *its*) *vacation in Quebec.*

**a couple of** Some people dislike the phrase *a couple of* for being inexact. After all, saying you had a couple of friends over could mean you entertained two, six, or even more. But this inexactitude of *a couple of* may serve a useful purpose, suggesting that the writer is indifferent to the precise number of items involved. Thus the sentence *She lives only a couple of miles away* implies not only that the distance is short but that its exact measure is unimportant. For more on this, see **collective noun** under *Grammar.*

**craft** *Craft* has been used as a verb since the Old English period and was used in Middle English to refer specifically to the artful construction of a text or discourse. In recent years, *crafted,* the past participle of *craft,* has been in vogue as a participle referring to well-wrought writing. *Craft* is more acceptable when applied to literary works than to other sorts of writing and is more acceptable as a participle than as a verb. Seventy-three percent of the Usage Panel accepts the phrase *beautifully crafted prose.* By contrast, only 35 percent accept the sentence *The planners crafted their proposal so as to anticipate the objections of local businesses.*

**credentialed** The use of the participle *credentialed* to refer to certified teachers and other professions is well established (*She became credentialed through a graduate program at a local college*), but its more general use to mean "possessing professional or expert credentials" is still widely considered jargon. The sentence *The board heard testimony from a number of credentialed witnesses* is unacceptable to 85 percent of the Usage Panel.

**credible / credulous** *Credible* is often used incorrectly where *credulous* would be appropriate. *Credible* means "capable of being believed" or "plausible": *She gave a very credible account of the incident. Credulous* means "believing too readily" or "gullible": *He was credulous enough to believe the manufacturer's claims.*

**crescendo** *Crescendo* is a music term referring to a gradual increase in the volume or intensity of a sound. It is sometimes used to refer to a climax or peak, as in noise level, rather than an increase. Many people dislike this usage, however. Fifty-five percent of the Usage Panel rejected it in the sentence *When the guard sank a three-pointer to tie the game, the noise of the crowd reached a crescendo.*

**criterion** Whether or not you get the job you applied for may come down to a single criterion. Like *phenomenon* it is a singular noun in Greek, and just as *phenomena* is the plural of *phenomenon,* so *criteria* is the plural of *criterion.* Since both *criterion* and *criteria* are in current use, you should use only *criterion* for the singular and only *criteria* for the plural.

**critique** Although *critique* has been used as a verb meaning "to review or discuss by using critical judgment" since the 18th century, it has not always had wide currency. But lately its use has increased. This is probably because the verb *criticize,* which once had the neutral meaning of "to use one's judgment regarding, evaluate," is now mainly used with the negative sense "to find fault with." When you criticize something, people normally assume you find something wrong with it. *Critique* thus presented itself as a neutral alternative. But this use of *critique* is still regarded by many as pretentious jargon, no doubt owing to its traditional use among literary critics. Sixty-nine percent of the Usage Panel rejects the sentence *As mock inquisitors grill him, top aides take notes and critique the answers with the President afterward.* There is no exact synonym, but in most contexts you can usually substitute *go over, review,* or *analyze.*

**czar / tsar** The word *czar* can also be spelled *tsar. Czar* is the most common form in American usage and virtually the only one employed in the extended senses "any tyrant" or, informally, "someone in authority." But *tsar* is preferred by most scholars of Slavic studies as a more accurate transliteration of the Russian and is often found in scholarly writing with reference to one of the Russian emperors.

**data** The word *data* is the plural of Latin *datum,* "something given," but does that mean you should treat it as a plural noun in English? Not always. The plural usage is still common enough, as this headline from the *New York Times* attests: *Data Are Elusive on the Homeless.* Sometimes scientists think of *data* as plural, as in *These data do not support the conclusions.* But more often scientists and researchers think of *data* as a singular mass entity like information, and most people now follow this in general usage. Sixty percent of the Usage Panel accepts the use of *data* with a singular verb and pronoun in the sentence *Once the data is in, we can begin to analyze it.* A still larger number, 77 percent, accepts the sentence *We have very little data on the efficacy of such programs,* where the quantifier *very little,* which is not used with similar plural nouns such as *facts* or *results,* implies that *data* here is indeed singular.

When plural, *data* has the unusual characteristic of not being capable of modification by cardinal numbers. You may have various data but you will never have five or ten data.

**debut** *Debut* is widely used as a verb, both intransitively (*Her new series will debut next March on network television*) and transitively (*The network will debut her new series next March*). These usages are well established in connection with entertainment and the performing arts but are not entirely acceptable when used of other sorts of introductions, as of products (*The company will debut the new six-cylinder convertible next fall*) or publications (*The national edition of the newspaper debuted last summer*), probably because of the association of the form with the language of show-business publicity.

**deceptively** Would you dive into a pool that is *deceptively* shallow? The question gives one pause. When *deceptively* is used to modify an adjective, the meaning is often unclear. Is the pool shallower or deeper than it appears to be? We asked the Usage Panel to decide. Fifty percent thought the pool is shallower than it appears. Thirty-two percent thought the pool deeper than it appears. And 18 percent said it was impossible to decide. Thus a warning notice worded in such a way would be misinterpreted by many of the people who read it, and others would be uncertain as to which sense was intended. When using *deceptively* with an adjective, be sure the context leaves no room for doubt. An easy way to remedy the situation is to rewrite the sentence without *deceptively: The pool is shallower than it looks* or *The pool is shallow, despite its appearance.*

**decimate** Discipline was unbelievably severe in the Roman army. If a soldier on guard duty didn't know the password, he was executed. If a cohort or legion mutinied, it was decimated, that is, the soldier standing in the first rank in the first file picked a number from one through ten out of a helmet, and the count-off continued from that number. When the count-off came to "ten" (*decem* in Latin), that soldier was executed, as was every tenth man after him; the other nine tenths got the message. Today people commonly extend the literal meaning of killing one tenth to the killing of any large percentage of a group. Sixty-six percent of the Usage Panel accepts this extension in the sentence *The Jewish population of Germany was decimated by the war,* even though it is common knowledge that the number of Jews killed was much greater than a tenth of the original population. But when the meaning is further extended to include large-scale destruction other than killing, as in *The supply of fresh produce was decimated by the accident at Chernobyl,* only 26 percent of the panel accepts the usage.

**deduction / induction** These words describe different forms of logical reasoning. When using *deduction* you reason from general principles to specific cases, as in applying a mathematical theorem to a particular problem or in citing a law or physics to predict the outcome of an experiment. When using *induction* you observe a number of specific instances and from them infer a general principle or law.

Some philosophers deny that induction truly has the force of logic, since observations of past instances may never be sufficient to give us certainty about what will happen in the future. Observing 100,000 white swans, for instance, does not give you the right to conclude that all swans are white. Observing as many car collisions gives you no right to predict that one will happen under similar conditions in the future. Think about this the next time you slam on the brakes.

**definite / definitive** *Definite* and *definitive* both apply to what is precisely defined or explicitly set forth. But *definitive* most often refers specifically to a judgment or description that serves as a standard or reference point for others, as in *the definitive decision of the court* (which sets forth a final resolution of a judicial matter) or *the definitive biography of Nelson* (i.e., the biography that sets the standard against which all other accounts of Nelson's life must be measured).

**denote / connote** Note the difference between this pair. *Connote* means "to signify indirectly" or "to suggest or convey what is not explicit." *Denote* has three meanings: first, "to mark, indicate," as in *Her frown denoted her increasing impatience;* second, "to serve as a symbol or name for," as in *A yellow light denotes caution;* and third, "to signify directly," as in *The word* river *denotes a moving body of water.* The confusion lies in these signifying senses, for *denote* describes the relation between the expression and the thing it conventionally names, whereas *connote* describes the relation between the word and the images or associations it evokes: *The word* river *connotes the relentlessness of time and the changing nature of life.*

**depend** In writing, *depend* is followed by *on* or *upon* when indicating condition or contingency, as in *It depends on who is in charge.* Leaving out the preposition is typical of casual speech.

**deprecate / depreciate** The first and fully accepted meaning of *deprecate* is "to express disapproval of." But the word has steadily encroached on the meaning of *depreciate.* It is now used, almost to the exclusion of *depreciate,* in the sense "to belittle or mildly disparage," as in *He deprecated his own contribution.* In an earlier survey, this newer sense was approved by a majority of the Usage Panel.

**dialogue** In recent years the verb sense of *dialogue* meaning "to engage in an informal exchange of views" has been revived, particularly with reference to communication between parties in institutional or political contexts. Although Shakespeare, Coleridge, and Carlyle used it, this usage today is widely regarded as jargon or bureaucratese. Ninety-eight percent of the Usage Panel rejects the sentence *Critics have charged that the department was remiss in not trying to dialogue with representatives of the community before hiring the new officers.*

**different from / different than** The phrases *different from* and *different than* are both common in British and American English. The British also use the construction *different to*. Since the 18th century, language critics have singled out *different than* as incorrect, though it is well attested in the works of reputable writers. If you want to follow traditional guidelines, use *from* when the comparison is between two persons or things: *My book is different from* (not *than*) *yours. Different than* is more acceptably used, particularly in American usage, where the object of comparison is expressed by a full clause: *The campus is different than it was twenty years ago.* You can use *different from* with a clause if the clause starts with a conjunction and so functions as a noun: *The campus is different from how it was twenty years ago.*

Sometimes people interpret a simple noun phrase following *different than* as elliptical for a clause, which allows for a subtle distinction in meaning between the two constructions. *How different this seems from Paris* suggests that the object of comparison is the city of Paris itself, whereas *How different this seems than Paris* suggests that the object of comparison is something like "the way things were in Paris" or "what happened in Paris."

**dilemma** In its main sense *dilemma* refers to a situation in which a choice must be made between alternative courses of action or argument. Although there is plenty of evidence that attests to widespread use of the term meaning simply "a problem" or "a predicament" and involving no issue of choice, the Usage Panel doesn't support this practice. Seventy-four percent of the panel rejects the sentence *Juvenile drug abuse is the great dilemma of the 1980s.*

It is sometimes claimed that because the *di-* in *dilemma* comes from the Greek prefix meaning "two," the word should be used only when exactly two choices are involved. But 64 percent of the Usage Panel accepts its use for choices among three or more options in the example *Ph.D. students who haven't completed their dissertations by the time their fellowships expire face a difficult dilemma: whether to take out loans to support themselves, to try to work part-time at both a job and their research, or to give up on the degree entirely.*

**discomfit / discomfort** It is true that *discomfit* originally meant "to defeat, frustrate" and that its newer use meaning "to embarrass, disconcert" probably arose in part through confusion with *discomfort*. But the newer sense is now the most common use of the verb in all varieties of writing and must be considered standard.

**discreet / discrete** As an individual, you might be *discreet*, but you are definitely *discrete. Discreet* means "prudent in speech and behavior": *He told me the news but asked me to be discreet about it.* The related word *discrete* means "separate, distinct": *The summer science program consists of four discrete units.*

**disinterested** In traditional usage, *disinterested* can only mean "having no stake in an outcome," as in *Since the judge stands to profit from the sale of the company, she cannot be considered a disinterested party in the dispute.* But despite critical disapproval, *disinterested* has come to be widely used by many educated writers to mean "uninterested" or "having lost interest," as in *Since she discovered skiing, she is disinterested in her schoolwork.* Oddly enough, "not interested" is the oldest sense of the word, going back to the 17th century. This sense became outmoded in the 18th century but underwent a revival in the first quarter of the early 20th. Despite its resuscitation, this usage does not have many fans on the Usage Panel. In our 1988 survey, 89 percent of the Usage Panel rejected the sentence *His unwillingness to give five minutes of his time proves that he is disinterested in finding a solution to the problem.* This is not a significantly different proportion from the 93 percent who disapproved of the same usage back in 1980.

**distinct / distinctive** A thing is *distinct* if it is sharply distinguished from other things; a property or attribute is *distinctive* if it enables us to distinguish one thing from another. *The warbler is not a distinct species* means that the warbler is not a clearly defined type of bird. *The warbler has a distinctive song* means that the warbler's song enables us to distinguish the warbler from other birds.

**dive** *The kids opened the box and dove into the pizza.* But should they have *dived?* The verb *dive* has two past tenses, *dived* and *dove,* and both are acceptable. *Dived* is actually the earlier form, and *dove* may seem strange in light of the general tendencies of change in English verb forms. Old English had two classes of verbs, called strong and weak. Strong verbs formed their past tense by a change in their vowel. Thus *drive* (past tense *drove*) and *fling* (past tense *flung*) are descendants of Old English strong verbs. Weak verbs formed their past tense by adding a suffix related to *-ed* in Modern English. The verbs *live* (past tense *lived*) and *move* (past tense *moved*) come from Old English weak verbs. But not all of the descendants of Old English verbs have preserved this pattern. Many verbs have changed from the strong pattern to the weak one; for example, the past tense of *help,* formerly *healp,* became *helped,* and the past tense of *step,* formerly *stop,* became *stepped.* Over the years, in fact, the weak pattern has become so prevalent that we use the term *regular* to refer to verbs that form their past tense by the addition of *-ed.* However, there have occasionally been changes in the other direction. For example, the past tense of *wear,* now *wore,* was once *werede;* that of *spit,* now *spat,* was once *spitede.* The development of *dove* is an additional example of the small group of verbs that have swum against the historical tide.
More at **snuck** and **wake.**

**doubt / doubtful**
***doubt* and *doubtful* with *that, whether,* or *if*** You can follow *doubt* and *doubtful* with clauses introduced by the conjunction *that, whether,* or *if.* Which conjunction you choose depends somewhat on the meaning you want to convey. We normally use *whether* to introduce indirect questions: *I asked whether he could come along. Whether* is therefore the traditional choice when the subject of *doubt* is in a state of genuine uncertainty about alternative possibilities: *Sue*

*has studied so much philosophy this year that she's begun to doubt whether she exists.* Similarly, when *doubtful* indicates uncertainty, *whether* is probably the word you want: *At one time it was doubtful whether the company could recover from its financial difficulties, but the government loan seems to have helped.*

On the other hand, you use *that* when you use *doubt* as an understated way of expressing disbelief. Thus you might say *I doubt that we've seen the last of* that *problem,* meaning "I think we haven't seen the last of that problem." *That* is also the usual choice when the truth of the clause following *doubt* is assumed, as in negative sentences and questions. Thus *I never doubted for a minute that I would be rescued* implies "I was certain that I would be rescued." By the same token, *Do you doubt that you will be paid?* seems to pose a rhetorical question meaning "Surely you believe that you will be paid," whereas *Do you doubt whether you will be paid?* may express a genuine request for information and might be followed by *Because if you do, you should make the client post a bond.*

In other cases, however, this distinction between *whether* and *that* is not always observed, and *that* is frequently used as a substitute for *whether.* You can also use *if* as a substitute for *whether,* but *if* is more informal in tone.

**doubt but** In informal speech, the clause following *doubt* is sometimes introduced with *but: I don't doubt but* (or *but what*) *he will come.* This construction has been used by many fine writers, but modern critics sometimes object to its use in formal writing.

**doubt with the subjunctive in *if*-clauses** For a discussion of when to use the subjunctive in *if*-clauses, such as those following *doubt,* see **subjunctive** under *Grammar.*

**drunk / drunken** As an adjective, the form *drunk* is used after a verb while the form *drunken* is now used only in front of a noun. Thus you should say *They were drunk last night* and *A drunken waiter at the restaurant ruined our evening.* Using *drunk* in front of a noun is usually considered unacceptable in formal style, but the phrases *drunk driver* and *drunk driving,* which have become fixed expressions, present an exception to this. *Drunk* and *drunken* are sometimes used to make a legal distinction, whereby a *drunk driver* is a driver whose alcohol level exceeds the legal limit, and a *drunken driver* is a driver who is inebriated.

**due to** *Due to* has been widely used for many years as a compound preposition like *owing to,* but some critics have insisted that *due* should be used only as an adjective. According to this view, it is incorrect to say *The concert was canceled due to the rain* but acceptable to say *The cancellation of the concert was due to the rain,* where *due* continues to function as an adjective modifying *cancellation.* This seems a fine point, however, and since *due to* is widely used and understood, there seems little reason to avoid using it as a preposition.

**elder / eldest** *Elder* and *eldest* generally apply to persons, unlike *older* and *oldest,* which also apply to things. *Elder* and *eldest* are used principally with reference to seniority: *elder sister, elder statesman, John the Elder.*

**elicit / illicit** You may elicit guffaws if you confuse these two. *Elicit* is a verb meaning "to bring or draw out something that is latent or potential," as in *Duke Ellington elicited some amazing sounds from his band*. By extension you can elicit a truth or principle, as from a discussion or inquiry. *Elicit* can also mean "to call forth a reaction," of which a guffaw is a good example. *Illicit*, on the other hand, is an adjective meaning "unlawful," as in *money acquired by illicit means*.

**empower** If you haven't been told that you are *empowered* lately, don't worry. Someone will tell you soon. The verb *empower* has become a buzzword in recent years, and its meaning seems to get vaguer with each use. Today teachers are empowering students to think for themselves. Computers empower us to become explorers on the information frontier. Women are empowering each other as professionals by using the services of other women. Politicians are empowering us to, well, have less to do with them.

The word *empower* is not new, having arisen in the mid-17th century with the legalistic meaning "to invest with authority, authorize." Shortly thereafter it began to be used with an infinitive in a more general way meaning "to enable or permit." Both of these uses survive today but are being overpowered by the word's use in politics and pop psychology.

Its modern use probably comes from the civil rights movement, which sought political *empowerment* for its followers. The word got taken up by the women's movement and its appeal has not flagged, as this 1992 quote from Karen Henry testifies: "*We need freedom from male domination and male-defined standards, so that we can create the fullness of our own lives, based on empowered choices.*" The word has also come to be used by politicians across the political spectrum.

Whether you feel empowered or not, should you use the verb *empower?* It depends on the context, at least in the opinion of the Usage Panel. In political contexts, the panel gives a strong yes vote to *empower*. Eighty percent approve of the example *We want to empower ordinary citizens*. But in other contexts the panel is markedly less enthusiastic. The sentence *Hunger and greed and then sexual zeal are felt by some to be stages of experience that empower the individual* garnered approval from only 33 percent of the panelists. The panel may frown on this kind of psychological empowering because it resonates of the self-help movement, which is notorious for trendy coinages.

**enormity / enormousness** *Enormity* is frequently used to refer simply to the property of being great in size or extent, but many people would prefer that *enormousness* (or a synonym such as *immensity*) be used for this general sense and that *enormity* be limited to situations that demand a negative moral judgment, as in *Not until the war ended and journalists were able to enter Cambodia did the world really become aware of the enormity of Pol Pot's oppression*. Fifty-nine percent of the Usage Panel rejects the use of *enormity* as a synonym for *immensity* in the sentence *At that point the engineers sat down to design an entirely new viaduct, apparently undaunted by the enormity of their task*. Even if

you side with the dissenting 41 percent and allow for *enormity's* largeness, you may want to avoid it in phrases like *the enormity of the President's election victory* and *the enormity of her inheritance,* where *enormity's* sense of monstrousness may leave your audience laughing when you don't want the laughs.

**enthuse** If you're *enthused* about something, don't say so! The verb *enthuse* is not well accepted; its use in the sentence *The majority leader enthused over his party's gains* was rejected by 76 percent of the usage panelists in an earlier survey. This lack of acceptance is often attributed to the word's status as a back-formation (it was formed from *enthusiasm*). Back-formations often meet with disapproval on their first appearance and only gradually become accepted. For example, *diagnose,* which was first recorded in 1861, is a back-formation from *diagnosis,* and *donate,* which first appeared in 1785, is a back-formation from *donation.* Both words are perfectly acceptable today. Since *enthuse* dates from 1827, there may be something more at play here than the simple eroding of popular resistance. Unlike *enthusiasm,* which denotes an internal emotional state, *enthuse* denotes either the external expression of emotion (as in *She enthused over attending the Oscar ceremonies*) or the inducement of enthusiasm by an external source (as in *He was so enthused about the diet pills that he agreed to do a testimonial for their television ad*). It is possible that a distaste for this emphasis on external emotional display and manipulation is sometimes the source of distaste for the word itself.
More at **intuit.**

**epithet** Strictly speaking, an epithet is not necessarily derogatory. Students of classical literature will remember the epithets of the Greek gods: *gray-eyed* Athena, *ox-eyed* Hera, *rosy-fingered* Dawn, and so on. But *epithet* is also used as a simple synonym for *term of abuse* or *slur,* as in the sentence *There is no place for racial epithets in a police officer's vocabulary.* Eighty percent of the Usage Panel accepts this usage.

**equable / equitable** Don't lose your equanimity over these look-alikes. *Equable* means "steady, unvarying," as in *an equable climate.* It is often extended to mean "unflappable, serene," as in *an equable disposition. Equitable* means "characterized by equity, fair": *an equitable distribution of gifts among the children.*

**equal** Some people say that *equal* is an absolute term, that is, that two quantities either are or are not equal and that *equal* therefore cannot be qualified in degree. Accordingly, it is illogical to speak of making *a more equal allocation of resources among the departments.* But in an earlier survey 71 percent of the Usage Panel accepted this example. Was the panel being illogical?

People who object to the *more equal* usage assume that mathematics and logic provide a model of accuracy that is appropriate to the everyday use of language. This supposition also underlies traditional grammatical discussions of other words, such as *unique, parallel,* and *center.* According to this account,

*equal* has its "precise" or "literal" meaning in the use of the equal sign in an arithmetic expression such as $5 + 2 = 7$, and more ordinary uses of *equal,* though they may be permissible, represent "loose" or "imprecise" extensions of the mathematical sense.

In fact the mathematical concept of equality is a poor model for using the word *equal* to describe relations between things in the world. As applied to such things, statements of equality are always relative to an implicit standard of tolerance. When someone says *The two boards are of equal length,* we assume that the equality is reckoned to some order of approximation determined by the needs of the situation. Thus the boards are not perfectly equal, just equal enough to be useful or acceptable for building a window frame or making some other object. If we did not think this way, we would always speak of physical objects such as boards as *nearly equal,* since true mathematical equality is unattainable with any measuring device.

What is more, we often speak of the equality of things that cannot be measured quantitatively, as when we say *The college draft was introduced in an effort to make the teams in the National Football League as equal as possible* or *The candidates for the job should all be given equal consideration.* In all such cases, equality is naturally a gradient notion and can be modified in degree. You can tell this from the existence of the word *unequal.* The prefix *un-* attaches only to gradient adjectives: we say *unmanly* but not *unmale;* and the word *uneven* can be applied to a surface (whose evenness may be a matter of degree) but not to a number (whose evenness is an either/or affair). For more on absolute terms, see **absolute terms** under *Grammar.*

More at **center, complete, infinite, parallel, perfect,** and **unique.**

**escape** Traditionally, *escape* is used with *from* when it means "break loose" and with a direct object when it means "avoid." Thus we might say *The forger escaped from prison by hiding in a laundry truck* but *The forger escaped prison when he turned in his accomplices in order to get a suspended sentence.* In recent years, however, *escape* has been used with a direct object in the sense "break free of": *The spacecraft will acquire sufficient velocity to escape the Sun's gravitational attraction.* This usage is well established and should be regarded as standard.

**everyplace / anyplace / someplace / no place** The forms *everyplace* (or *every place*), *anyplace* (or *any place*), *someplace* (or *some place*), and *no place* are widely used in speech and informal writing as equivalents for *everywhere, anywhere, somewhere,* and *nowhere.* These usages may be well established, but they are not normally used in formal writing. However, when the two-word expressions *every place, any place, some place,* and *no place* are used to mean "every (any, some, no) spot or location," they are entirely appropriate at all levels of style.

**exceptionable / exceptional** *Exceptionable* and *exceptional* are not interchangeable. Only *exceptionable* means "objectionable" or "debatable": *The teachers were relieved to find nothing exceptionable in the student newspaper.*

*Exceptional* means "uncommon" or "extraordinary": *That student has an exceptional memory.*

**fact** *Fact* has a long history in the sense "allegation of fact," as in "*This tract was distributed to thousands of American teachers, but the facts and the reasoning are wrong*" (Albert Shanker). This practice has led to the introduction of the phrases *true facts* and *real facts,* as in *The true facts of the case may never be known.* These usages may cause qualms among critics who insist that facts can only be true, but the usages are often useful for emphasis. And that's a true fact.

**factoid** *Factoid* is a recent coinage that may leave you wondering what is real and what is not. The *-oid* suffix normally imparts the meaning "resembling, having the appearance of" to the words it attaches to. Thus the *anthropoid apes* are the apes that are most like humans (from Greek *anthropos,* "human being"). In some words the *-oid* suffix has a slightly extended meaning—"having characteristics of, but not the same as." Science fiction fans will recognize a *humanoid* as a being that has human characteristics but is not really human. Similarly, *factoid* originally referred to a piece of information that has the appearance of being reliable or accurate, as from being repeated so often that people assume it is true. The word still has this meaning in standard usage. Seventy-three percent of the Usage Panel accepts it in the sentence *It would be easy to condemn the book as a concession to the television age, as a McLuhanish melange of pictures and factoids which give the illusion of learning without the substance.*

    *Factoid* has since developed a second meaning, that of a brief, somewhat interesting fact, that might better have been called a *factette.* The panel has less enthusiasm for this usage, however, perhaps because they see it as confusing. Only 43 percent of the panel accepts it in *Each issue of the magazine begins with a list of factoids, like how many pounds of hamburger were consumed in Texas last month.* Many panelists prefer terms such as *statistics, trivia, useless facts,* and just plain *facts* in this sentence.

**farther / further** Is it *the* further *you get in your trip, the* farther *you get in your book* or the other way around? Many writers since the Middle English period have used *farther* and *further* interchangeably. A relatively recent rule, however, states that *farther* should be reserved for physical distance and *further* for nonphysical, metaphorical advancement. Thus 74 percent of the Usage Panel prefers *farther* in the sentence *If you are planning to drive any farther than Ukiah, you'd better carry chains,* whereas 64 percent prefers *further* in the sentence *We won't be able to answer these questions until we are further along in our research.* In many cases, however, it is hard to see the difference. If we speak of *a statement that is far from the truth,* for example, we should also allow the use of *farther* in a sentence such as *Nothing could be farther from the truth.* But *Nothing could be further from the truth* is so common that it has become a fixed expression.

**faze / phase** Don't let *faze* faze you. The verb *faze* comes from Old English and means "to disrupt the composure of, disconcert." It is usually used in negative contexts: *She was not fazed by the setback but carried on as determined as ever. Faze* is sometimes mistakenly spelled *phase,* wherein lies the confusion. *Phase* is both a noun and a verb. It goes back to Greek (which is where we get *ph* with the sound of *f*). The noun has as its central meaning "a stage of development." The verb usually occurs in the phrases *phase in* and *phase out,* which entail introducing or ending something one stage at a time.

**fewer / less** The traditional rule says that you should use *fewer* for things that can be counted (*fewer than four players*) but *less* with mass terms for things of measurable extent (*less paper, less than a gallon of paint*). But people use *less* in certain constructions where *fewer* would occur if the rule were being followed. You can use *less than* before a plural noun that denotes a measure of time, amount, or distance: *less than three weeks, less than $400, less than 50 miles.* You can sometimes use *less* with plural nouns in the expressions *no less than* and *or less.* Thus you can say *No less than 30 of his colleagues signed the letter* and *Give your reasons in 25 words or less.*

**finalize** Even though *finalize* has been around since the early 1920s, people still object to it because they associate it with the language of bureaucracy. Seventy-one percent of the Usage Panel finds unacceptable the sentence *We will finalize plans for a class reunion.* Although *finalize* has no single exact synonym, you can always find a substitute among *complete, conclude, make final,* and *put into final form.*
More at **–ize.**

**firstly** Both *first* and *firstly* are well established to begin an enumeration: *Our objectives are, first* (or *firstly*), *to recover from last year's slump.* Whichever you choose, however, be consistent and use parallel forms in the series, as in *first . . . second . . . third* or *firstly . . . secondly . . . thirdly.*

**flammable / inflammable** Should you be careful with a solvent that's inflammable? Absolutely. The trouble with *flammable* and *inflammable* is that they mean the same thing. The prefix *in-* is not the Latin negative prefix *in-,* which is related to the English *un-* and appears in such words as *indecent* and *inglorious.* The *in-* in *inflammable* is an intensive prefix that is derived from the Latin preposition *in.* This prefix also appears in the word *enflame.* But many people are ignorant of all this and conclude that, since *flammable* means "combustible," *inflammable* must mean "not flammable" or "incombustible." Therefore, for clarity's sake, you should use only *flammable* to give warnings.

**flaunt / flout** *Flaunt* means "to exhibit ostentatiously": *She flaunted her diamonds.* To *flout* is "to show contempt for": *She flouted the proprieties.* For some time now people have been using *flaunt* in the sense "to show contempt for."

You should avoid this usage because people widely regard it as erroneous and you would be flaunting not your vocabulary but your lack of it.

**flotsam / jetsam** Your colleagues at work may jokingly refer to the flotsam and jetsam in your office but, technically speaking, they would be wrong unless you were truly adrift or sinking. *Flotsam* in maritime law applies to wreckage or cargo left floating on the sea after a shipwreck. *Jetsam* applies to cargo or equipment thrown overboard (jettisoned) from a ship in distress and either sunk or washed ashore. The common phrase *flotsam and jetsam* is now used loosely to describe any objects found floating or washed ashore.

**follow** You should use *as follows* (not *as follow*) regardless of whether the noun that precedes it is singular or plural: *The regulations are as follows.*

**foot** *Foot* and *feet* have their own rules when they are used in combination with numbers to form expressions for units of measure. You can say *a four-foot plank* but not *a four-feet plank*; you can also say *a plank four feet* (less frequently, *four foot*) *long* and *a plank four feet six inches long* (or *four foot six inches long*). But when you combine *foot* with numbers greater than one to refer to simple distance, use only the plural *feet: a ledge 20 feet* (not *foot*) *away. At that speed, a car moves 88 feet* (not *foot*) *in a second.*

**forceful / forcible / forced** *Forceful, forcible,* and *forced* have distinct but related meanings. *Forceful* describes someone or something that possesses or is filled with strength or force: *a forceful speaker, a forceful personality. Forceful measures* may or may not involve the use of actual physical force. You use *forcible,* however, for actions carried out by physical force: *There had been a forcible entry. The police had to use forcible restraint in order to arrest the suspect.* Use *forced* for an act or a condition brought about by control or an outside influence: *a forced smile, a forced landing, forced labor.*

**forego / forgo** If you are *foregoing* dessert, does that mean you are entering the dining room before it is brought in? The trouble here is that there are two *forego*s. The verb *forgo*—without the *e*—means "to do without" but has as an acceptable variant the spelling *forego.* Thus you can legitimately *forgo* or *forego* dessert. The other *forego* means "to go before, either in place or time," as in *A bad reputation often foregoes you.* This *forego* always has an *e*.

**former / latter** Some people insist that you should use the phrases *the former* and *the latter* only to refer to the first of two things and the second of two things, respectively: *"But Flynn preceded Casey, as did also Jimmy Blake, and the former was a lulu and the latter was a fake"* (Ernest Lawrence Thayer). It is easy to find violations of this rule in the works of good writers, but since *former* and *latter* are comparatives, many readers feel uneasy when the words are used in enumerations of more than two things, just as they would feel uneasy over the similar incorrect use of a comparative in a sentence such as *Her boys are 7, 9, and 13; only the younger was born in California.*

**fortuitous / fortunate** The word *fortuitous* is unfortunate since people argue about what it can and cannot mean. In its oldest sense, *fortuitous* means "happening by accident or chance." Thus *a fortuitous meeting* may have either fortunate or unfortunate consequences. Many people insist that this is all *fortuitous* can mean. But people for decades have used the word in reference to happy accidents, as in *The company's third-quarter profits were enhanced as the result of a fortuitous drop in the cost of RAM chips.* This use may have arisen because *fortuitous* resembles both *fortunate* and *felicitous.* Whatever its origin, the use is well established in the writing of reputable authors. The additional use of *fortuitous* to mean "lucky or fortunate" is more controversial, as in *He came to the Giants in June as the result of a fortuitous trade that sent two players to the Reds.* This use dates back at least to the 1920s, but people still widely regard it as incorrect, and you may want to avoid it.

**founder / flounder** People often confuse the verbs *founder* and *flounder.* *Founder* comes from a Latin word meaning "bottom" (as in *foundation*) and originally referred to knocking enemies down; people now use it also to mean "to fail utterly, collapse": *The business started well but foundered.* *Flounder* means "to move clumsily, thrash about" and hence "to proceed in confusion." Thus if John is *foundering* in Chemistry 1, he had better drop the course; if he is *floundering,* he may yet pull through.

**–ful** You usually form the plurals of nouns ending in *-ful* by adding *s* to the suffix: *cupfuls, glassfuls, spoonfuls.*

**fulsome** *Fulsome* is often used to mean "offensively flattering or insincere." But people also use the word, particularly in the expression *fulsome praise,* to mean simply "abundant," without any implication of excess or insincerity. This usage is all right, but it may invite misunderstandings in contexts in which someone could infer a deprecatory interpretation. You may unintentionally offend someone by saying *I offer you my most fulsome apologies,* where the use of an adjective like *full* or *abundant* would leave no doubt about the sincerity of your intentions.

**fun** Ten-year-olds nowadays are likely to say sentences such as *The carnival is funner than the Science Museum,* and their parents are likely to have given up trying to correct the sentence to *The carnival is more fun than the Science Museum.* This use of *fun* as an inflected adjective (*fun, funner, funnest*) became popular in the 1950s and 1960s and has persisted, so that a press release today will announce perfectly seriously: *The corporation believes that a spelling bee is a fun way to emphasize the critical importance of good basic communication skills in America's workplace.* The day will no doubt come when this use of *fun* is normal; yet at present the use of *fun* to modify nouns has a facetious or an informal tone. You should avoid it where a light tone would be inappropriate.

**gambit** Serious chess players know that a gambit is an opening move in which a minor piece like a pawn is risked or even sacrificed to gain a favorable position. Some critics familiar with the nature of chess gambits maintain that you should not use the word in an extended sense except to refer to maneuvers that involve a tactical sacrifice or loss for some advantage. But *gambit* is well established in the general sense of "maneuver" and in the related sense of "a remark intended to open a conversation," which carries no implication of sacrifice, just the risk of being shot down.

**gauntlet / gantlet** If you are not sure whether you should throw down the *gantlet* or the *gauntlet*, don't throw in the towel. There are two words spelled *gauntlet* and both have *gantlet* as a spelling variant, so you can't go wrong. One *gauntlet* comes from the Old French word *gantelet*, a diminutive of *gant*, "glove." It originally referred to a glove worn as part of medieval armor. Since its introduction in the 15th century, the word has had both *a* and *au* spellings. To *throw down the gauntlet* means to offer a challenge, which in medieval times was done by throwing down a glove or gauntlet.

The other *gauntlet* is a form of punishment in which the offender runs between two lines of men who beat him with sticks or other weapons, such as knotted cords. This word is an alteration of the obsolete word *gantlope*, which comes from the Swedish word *gatlopp*, a compound of *gata*, "lane," and *lopp*, "course." Shortly after *gantlope* appeared in English in the mid-17th century, the spelling *gauntlet* began to compete with it, in one of etymology's many mysteries. To *run the gauntlet* means to undergo this form of punishment. The expression has a rich history of metaphoric uses.

The *gantlet* variant of this second *gauntlet* has given birth to the railroad term *gantlet*, which is a section of track designed so that one rail of each track is inside the rails of the other to allow trains on separate tracks to pass through a very narrow space.

**get**
***get* in passive constructions** We feel there is a difference in tone or emphasis when we say *The demonstrators were arrested* as opposed to *The demonstrators got arrested*. The first example implies that the responsibility for the arrests rests primarily with the police. The example using *get* implies that the demonstrators provoked the arrest deliberately. For more on the use of *get* in passive constructions, see **verbs / voice** under *Grammar*.
***have got to*** For a discussion of this construction, see **have to** under *Grammar*. More at **got / gotten.**

**gift** *Gift* has a long history of use as a verb meaning "to furnish with a gift; endow" as in "*The world must love and fear him Whom I gift with heart and* *hand*" (Elizabeth Barrett Browning). This sense provides a useful distinction from *give*, for *give* can sometimes be confusing because it means both "to transfer physical possession" and "to transfer ownership." Unfortunately, the use of *gift* as a verb in Modern English is tainted by its association with the language of advertising and publicity (as in *Gift her with this copper warming plate*). A large majority of the Usage Panel rejected the usage in an earlier survey. When you want clarity, use a substitutes such as *give as a gift, bestow,* or *donate.*

**go** Parents reading picture books aloud to their infant children have always used *go* to produce nonlinguistic noises, as in *The train went "toot"* and *The cow goes "moo."* Now their grown-up infants use *go* to report speech, as in *Then he goes, "You think you're real smart, don't you?"* For speakers young enough to get away with it, this usage is useful when telling a story that has direct quotations, particularly when the user wishes to mimic the accent or intonation of the original speaker. You should restrict this sense of *go,* however, to the "narrative present" used in informal speech and omit it from more formal contexts.
More at **like.**

**good / well** People use *good* as an adverb all the time when speaking, as in *My car was just tuned and runs real good now* or *Burning the sauce stunk the kitchen up good.* In writing, it is perfectly acceptable to use the adjective *good* with linking verbs such as *be, seem,* or *appear: Plans for the reunion are looking good. The soup tastes good.* But the use of *good* as an adverb with other verbs is not common in writing and will in all likelihood be frowned on by your readers. Use *well* instead. Thus you should say *The dress fits well and looks good.*

Be careful when using *good* and *well* after the verb *feel.* While both of these adjectives can mean "healthy," your readers will probably interpret *She feels good* to mean "She is in good spirits." If they see *She feels well,* they may assume the reference is to her state of health, not to her mood.
More at **bad** and **well.**

**got / gotten** "There is no such word as *gotten,*" an irritated reader recently wrote to *The Boston Globe Magazine,* objecting to the use of the word by a usage commentator, who should have known better. The notion that *gotten* is illegitimate has been around for over 200 years and refuses to die. The word itself is much older than the criticism against it. As past participles of *get,* both *got* and *gotten* go back to the Middle Ages. In American English, *have got* is chiefly an intensive form of *have* in its senses of possession and obligation and can only be used in the present tense. *Gotten* sees regular use as a variant past participle of *get.* It can occur in a variety of past and perfect tenses: *Had she gotten the car when you saw her? I would not have gotten sick if I had stayed home.* In Britain, *gotten* has mostly fallen out of use.

There are subtle distinctions in meaning between the two forms. *Got* often implies current possession, where *gotten* usually suggests the process of

obtaining. *I haven't got any money* suggests that you are broke. *I haven't gotten any money* suggests that you have not been paid for your efforts. This sense of process or progression applies to many other uses of *gotten,* and in some of these cases *got* just doesn't sound as natural to the American ear: *The bridge has gotten weaker since the storm. We have finally gotten used to the new software. Mice have gotten into the basement.*

Remember that only *got* can be used to express obligation, as in *I have got to go to Chicago.* Note the difference in the sentence when *gotten* is used. *I have gotten to go to Chicago* implies that the person has had the opportunity or been given permission to go.

More at **get.**

**gourmet / gourmand / epicure** Your friend who likes to cook may be a *gourmet,* but is he also a *gourmand?* And could you also call him an *epicure?* Yes, and yes again. A *gourmet* is a person with discriminating taste in food and wine, as is a *gourmand.* But a *gourmand* can also be someone who enjoys food in great quantities. An *epicure* is pretty much the same as a *gourmet,* but the word may carry overtones of excessive refinement. This use of *epicure,* by the way, is a deliberate misrepresentation of Epicurean philosophy, which, while it professed that pleasure was the highest good, was hardly given to excessive concern with food and drink. It was concerned rather with personal happiness and freedom from pain. But rival philosophical schools took offense at Epicurus's doctrine of pleasure and distorted the name of his school.

**government** In American usage, *government* always takes a singular verb. In British usage, *government,* in the sense of a governing group of officials, takes a plural verb: *The government are determined to follow this course.* For more on this, see **collective noun** under *Grammar.*

**graduate** The verb *graduate* has denoted the action of conferring an academic degree or diploma since at least 1421. Accordingly, the action of receiving a degree should be expressed in the passive, as in *She was graduated from Yale in 1980.* This use is still current if slightly old-fashioned, and 78 percent of the Usage Panel accepts it. In general usage, however, the old sense has largely yielded to the much more recent sense "to receive a degree" (first attested in 1807): *She graduated from Yale in 1980.* Eighty-nine percent of the Usage Panel accepts this use. It is handy because it ascribes the accomplishment to the student rather than to the institution, which is appropriate in discussions of individual students. When the institution's responsibility is emphasized, however, you can still use the older sense. A sentence such as *The university graduated more computer science majors in 1987 than in the entire previous decade* stresses the university's accomplishment, say, of its computer science program. On the other hand, the sentence *More computer science majors graduated in 1987 than in the entire previous decade* implies that the class of 1987 was in some way a remarkable group.

The Usage Panel feels quite differently about the use of *graduate* to mean

"to receive a degree from," as in *She graduated Yale in 1980*. Seventy-seven percent object to this usage.

**graffito / graffiti** The word *graffiti,* like *spaghetti,* is a plural noun in Italian. In English *graffiti* is far more common than the singular form *graffito* (let alone *spaghetto,* which we don't use in English). *Spaghetti* is always used as a singular noun (only small children say *spaghettis*), and *graffiti* is often used as a singular, too. When the reference is to a particular inscription (as in *There was a bold graffiti on the wall*), the form *graffito* would be correct but might strike some readers as pedantic outside an archaeological context. There is no substitute for the singular use of *graffiti* when the word is used as a mass noun to refer to inscriptions in general or to the related social phenomenon. The sentence *Graffiti is a major problem for the Transit Authority Police* cannot be reworded *Graffito is . . .* (since *graffito* can refer only to a particular inscription) or *Graffiti are . . .*, which suggests that the police problem involves only the physical marks and not the larger issue of vandalism. In such contexts, the use of *graffiti* as a singular is justified by its usefulness.

**group** *Group* as a collective noun can be followed by a singular or plural verb. It takes a singular verb when the persons or things that make up the group are considered collectively: *The dance group is ready for rehearsal. Group* takes a plural verb when the persons or things that constitute it are considered individually: *The group were divided in their sympathies.* For more on this topic, see **collective noun** under *Grammar.*

**grow** *"Eventually you have to satisfy the customer and grow the business,"* the new chairman of Eastman Kodak said in 1993 at a news conference announcing his appointment. He was using the verb *grow* in a relatively new way—with an object that is not living. *Grow* has been used since medieval times as an intransitive verb meaning "to increase in size, quantity or degree," as in *Our business has been growing steadily for three years.* It has been used with an object since the 18th century, meaning "to produce or cultivate," as in *We grow beans and corn in our garden.* But the transitive use applied to business and nonliving things is quite new. It came into full bloom during the 1992 Presidential election, when nearly all the candidates were concerned with *"growing the economy."* Businessleaders and politicians may be fond of this usage, but should the rest of us? The Usage Panel thinks not. Eighty percent reject the phrase *grow our business.* The panel is more accepting of (but still not enthusiastic about) the phrase *grow our way,* perhaps because of *way*'s established use in expressions like *make our way* and *find our way.* Forty-eight percent of the panel accepted *We've got to grow our way out of this recession.* The panel had no affection for the odd but sometimes heard phrase *grow down.* Ninety-eight percent gave the thumbs down to *If elected, I shall do my utmost to grow down the deficit.*

**half** The phrases *a half, half of,* and *half a* or *half an* are all correct, though they may differ slightly in meaning. For example, *a half day* is used when *day*

has the special sense "a working day," and the phrase then means "four hours." *Half of a day* and *half a day* are not restricted in this way and can mean either four or twelve hours.

**hang** You should use *hanged* as the past tense and past participle of *hang* in the sense of "to put to death by hanging," as in *Frontier courts hanged many a prisoner after a summary trial.* A majority of the Usage Panel objects to *hung* used in this sense. In all other senses of the word, *hung* is the preferred form as past tense and past participle, as in *I hung my children's picture above my desk.*

**harebrained / hairbrained** Is that proposal to raise your taxes *harebrained* or *hairbrained? Harebrained* means "having or showing no more sense than a hare." It is a well-established word. Its first use dates to 1548. The spelling *hairbrained* also goes back to the 1500s, when *hair* was a variant spelling of *hare.* The *hair* variant was preserved in Scotland into the 18th century. The upshot of this is that it's impossible to tell exactly when people began writing *hairbrained* in the belief that the word means "having a hair-sized brain," but it's a good guess that it was a long time ago. Whatever the date of the first confused use of *hairbrained,* it continues to be used and confused to this day. If you want to give the impression that your brain is bigger than a hair and bigger than a hare's, use *harebrained.*

**headquarter** The verb *headquarter* occurs in both transitive and intransitive senses: *The magazine has headquartered the reporters in a building that houses many foreign journalists. The European correspondent will headquarter in Paris.* But this verb usage does not sit well with many people, and in an earlier survey a majority of the Usage Panel found both these examples unacceptable in formal writing. Although there is a lot of evidence for these usages, you would do best to use alternative expressions, for example: *The magazine has just assigned him to* (or *has stationed him in*) *a building that houses many foreign journalists. The European correspondent will make her headquarters in Paris* (or *will make Paris her headquarters*).

**headquarters** You can use the noun *headquarters* with either a singular or a plural verb. The plural is more common: *The corporation's headquarters are in Boston.* But when referring to authority rather than physical location, many people prefer the singular: *Division headquarters has approved the new benefits package.*

**healthy / healthful** Some people like to maintain a distinction between *healthy* and *healthful. Healthy,* they say, should be used to mean "possessing good health," and only *healthful* should mean "conducive to good health." People who hold this view are swimming against the tide of history, for *healthy* has been used to mean "healthful" since the 16th century. You can find the "healthful" use of *healthy* in the works of many distinguished writers, with this example from John Locke being typical: "*Gardening . . . and working in wood, are fit and healthy recreations for a man of study or business.*" Therefore, both *healthy* and *healthful* are correct in these contexts: *a healthy climate, a healthful climate; a healthful diet, a healthy diet.*

## help

**can help** Many people commonly use *help* in the sense conveyed in the sentence *Don't change it any more than you can help* (that is, "any more than you have to"). Others condemn this usage on the grounds that *help* in this sense means "avoid" and therefore logically requires a negative. But the expression is a well-established idiom.

**cannot help / cannot help but** For a discussion of these expressions, see **cannot** under *Grammar.*

## historic / historical
*Historic* and *historical* have different usages though their senses overlap. *Historic* refers to what is important in history: *the historic first voyage to the Moon.* It is also used of what is famous or interesting because of its association with persons or events in history: *a historic house. Historical* refers to whatever existed in the past, whether regarded as important or not: *a minor historical character. Historical* also refers to anything concerned with history or the study of the past: *a historical novel, historical discoveries.* While these distinctions are useful, don't be surprised if you see these words used interchangeably, as in *historic times* or *historical times.*

## holocaust
*Holocaust* has a secure place in the language when it refers to the massive destruction of human beings by other human beings. Ninety-nine percent of the Usage Panel accepts the use of *holocaust* in the phrase *nuclear holocaust.* Sixty percent accept the sentence *As many as two million people may have died in the holocaust that followed the Khmer Rouge takeover in Cambodia.* But because of its associations with genocide, people may object to extended applications of *holocaust.* The percentage of the panel's acceptance drops sharply when people use the word refer to death brought about by natural causes, and only 31 percent of the panel approves the sentence *In East Africa five years of drought have brought about a holocaust in which millions have died.* Just 11 percent approved the use of *holocaust* to summarize the effects of the AIDS epidemic. This suggests that other figurative usages such as *the huge losses in the Savings and Loan holocaust* may be viewed as overblown or in poor taste.

## hopefully

**hopefully as sentence adverb** If you use *hopefully* as a sentence adverb (as in *Hopefully the measures will be adopted*), be aware that many people find the usage unacceptable, including a large majority of the Usage Panel. It is not easy to explain why people dislike this use of *hopefully.* The use is justified by similar uses of many other adverbs: *Mercifully, the play was brief. Frankly, my dear, I don't give a damn.* And though this use of *hopefully* may have been a

vogue word when it first became frequent 30 years ago, it has long since lost any hint of jargon or pretentiousness for the general reader. The wide acceptance of the usage reflects popular recognition of its usefulness; there is no precise substitute. Someone who says *Hopefully, the treaty will be ratified* makes a hopeful prediction about the fate of the treaty, whereas someone who says *I hope* (or *We hope* or *It is hoped*) *the treaty will be ratified* expresses a bald statement about what is desired. Only the latter could be continued with a clause such as *but it isn't likely.*

**continued objections against *hopefully*** You might expect that people would have warmed to *hopefully* once the usage became well established. But instead they appear to have become more adamant in their opposition. In the 1968 Usage Panel survey, 44 percent of the panel approved the usage, but this dropped to 27 percent in our 1986 survey. There is plenty of evidence to suggest that the panel of the mid-1980s was less conservative than the panel of the 1960s, since it accepted once-condemned usages such as the employment of *contact* and *host* as verbs. And 60 percent of that same panel in the 1986 survey accepted the comparable use of *mercifully* in the sentence *Mercifully, the game ended before the Giants could add another touchdown to the lopsided score.* It is not the use of *hopefully* as a sentence adverb per se that bothers the panel. Rather, *hopefully* seems to have taken on a life of its own as a shibboleth.

**ambiguity of sentence adverbs** Like other sentence adverbs such as *bluntly* and *happily, hopefully* may occasionally be ambiguous. In the sentence *Hopefully, the company has launched a new venture,* you could construe the word *hopefully* as describing the point of view of either the speaker or the company. You can resolve such ambiguities either by repositioning the adverb (*The company has launched the new venture hopefully*) or by choosing a paraphrase (*We hope that the company has launched the new venture*). For more on sentence adverbs, see **adverbs, position of** under *Grammar.*

**host** People used *host* as a verb in Shakespeare's time, but this usage was long obsolete when the verb was reintroduced (or perhaps reinvented) in recent years to mean "perform the role of a host." The usage occurs particularly in contexts relating to institutional gatherings or television and radio shows, where the person performing the role of host has not personally invited the guests. People first resisted this usage perhaps because the verb involves a suspect extension of the traditional concept of hospitality. In a 1968 survey, only 18 percent of the Usage Panel accepted the usage in the sentence *The Cleveland chapter will host this year's convention.* Over time, however, the usage has become increasingly well established and has the useful purpose of describing the activities of one who performs the ceremonial or practical role of a host, as in arranging a conference or welcoming guests. In our 1986 survey, 53 percent of the panelists accepted the usage in the phrase *a reception hosted by the Secretary of State.* People are less inclined to accept *host* when it is used to describe the role of a performer who acts as a master of ceremonies for a broadcast or film, where the relation of *host* to the notion of "hospitality" is stretched still further. Only 31 percent of the panel accepted the use of the verb in the sentence

*Students have watched* Sex, Drugs and AIDS, *a graphic film hosted by actress Rae Dawn Chong.*

**cohost** The verb *cohost* is also well established to refer to those who collaborate in assuming responsibility for an occasion. Fifty-eight percent of the Usage Panel accepted this use in the sentence *The Department of Architecture and the Department of History will be cohosting a reception for conference participants.*

**identical** Some people insist that you should only use *with* after *identical.* But either *with* or *to* is now acceptable: *On this issue, the position of the Democrats is nearly identical with* (or *to*) *that of the Republicans.*

**identify** When used in the sense "to associate or affiliate (oneself) closely with a person or group," *identify* suggests a psychological empathy with the feelings or experiences of another person, as in *Most young readers readily identify* (or *identify themselves*) *with Holden Caulfield.* This usage derives originally from psychoanalytic writing, where it has a specific technical meaning, but like other terms from that field, it was widely regarded as jargon when introduced into wider use. In particular, some critics seized on the fact that in this sense the verb was often used intransitively, with no reflexive pronoun. In recent years, however, this use of *identify with* without the reflexive has become standard. Eighty-two percent of the Usage Panel accepts the sentence *I find it hard to identify with any of his characters,* whereas only 63 percent now accepts this same usage when the reflexive pronoun is used, as in *I find it hard to identify myself with any of his characters.*

**if**

***if* or *whether*** In informal writing, both *if* and *whether* are standard for introducing a clause indicating uncertainty after a verb such as *ask, doubt, know, learn,* or *see: We shall soon learn whether* (or *if* ) *it is true.* In such contexts, however, the use of *if* can sometimes create ambiguities. Depending on the intended meaning, the sentence *Let her know if she is invited* might be better paraphrased as *Let her know whether she is invited* or *If she is invited, let her know.*

***if* and the subjunctive** For a discussion of when to use the subjunctive mood in *if*-clauses, see **subjunctive** under *Grammar.*

**impact** The use of *impact* as a verb meaning "to have an effect" often has a big impact on readers. Eighty-four percent of the Usage Panel disapproves of the construction *to impact on,* as in the phrase *social pathologies, common to the inner city, that impact heavily on such a community.* Ninety-five percent disapprove of the use of *impact* as a transitive verb in the sentence *Companies have used disposable techniques that have a potential for impacting our health.* It's unclear why this usage provokes such a strong response, but it can't be because of novelty. *Impact* has been used as a verb since 1601, and its figurative use dates from 1935, allowing people plenty of time to get accustomed to it. It may be that its frequent appearance in jargon-riddled remarks of politicians, military officials, and financial analysts has made people suspi-

cious. Nevertheless, the use of *impact* as a verb has become so common in corporations and institutions that younger speakers have begun to regard it as standard. It seems likely, therefore, that the verb *impact* will eventually become as usual as the verb *contact* has become over the last 30 years.
More at **contact.**

**implement** People have been using *implement* as a verb meaning "to put into practice, carry out" since the 19th century. Some have objected to the verb as jargon, but its usefulness is obvious. Eighty-nine percent of the Usage Panel accepts the usage in the sentence *The mayor's office announced the creation of a special task force that will be responsible for implementing the new policy.*

**important** Some people object to the use of the phrase *more importantly* in place of *more important* as a means of introducing an assertion, as in *More importantly, there is no one ready to step into the vacuum left by the retiring senator.* But both forms are widely used, and there is no obvious reason for preferring one or the other.

**impracticable / impractical** The adjective *impracticable* applies to a course of action that is impossible to carry out or put into practice: *Refloating the sunken ship proved to be impracticable because of its fragility. Impractical* can also be used in this way, but it can also be weaker in sense, suggesting that the course of action would yield an insufficient return or would have little practical value. A plan for a new baseball stadium might be rejected as *impracticable* if the site was too marshy to permit safe construction, but if the objection were merely that the site was too remote for patrons to attend games easily, the plan would better be described as *impractical.*
More at **practicable.**

**in behalf of / on behalf of** A traditional rule holds that *in behalf of* and *on behalf of* have distinct meanings. Accordingly, you should use *in behalf of* to mean "for the benefit of," as in *We raised money in behalf of the earthquake victims.* And you should use *on behalf of* to mean "as the agent of, on the part of," as in *The guardian signed the contract on behalf of the child.* But as the two meanings are quite close, the phrases are often used interchangeably, even by reputable writers.

**incentivize / incent** Corporate executives, car dealers, and politicians often cite the need to *incentivize* people to act in certain ways. They may want salespeople to work harder, customers to be more eager to spend, or businesses to take more risks. *Incentivize* has been motivating people since the mid-1970s—the more informal *incent* came along about 10 years later. Both words mean the same thing, "to give an incentive to" or "provide a motivation for." Usually the incentive is in the form of a material reward—a bonus, rebate, or tax break. But although these two verbs are popular with business leaders, they curry little favor with the Usage Panel, which sees them as trendy jargon. Ninety-four percent of the panel rejects *incentivize* in the sentence *He's the*

*leader of this organization, and he's got to have the whole team of people incentivized to improve shareholder value.* Ninety-six percent reject *incent* in *The management incented the employees to improve the shareholder value of the company.* Panelists suggest *motivate, encourage,* and *give incentives to* as alternatives. More at **–ize.**

**include** Some writers insist that you should use *include* only when it is followed by a partial list of the contents of what the subject refers to. Therefore you may write *New England includes Connecticut and Rhode Island,* but you must use *comprise* or *consist of* to provide full enumeration: *New England comprises* (not *includes*) *Connecticut, Rhode Island, Massachusetts, Vermont, New Hampshire, and Maine.* This restriction is too strong. *Include* does not rule out the possibility of a complete listing. Thus the sentence *The bibliography should include all the journal articles you have used* does not entail that the bibliography must contain something other than journal articles, though it does leave that possibility open. When you want to make clear that the listing is exhaustive, use *comprise* or *consist of* to avoid ambiguity. Thus the sentence *The task force includes all of the Navy units on active duty in the region* allows for the possibility that Marine and Army units are also taking part, where the same sentence with *comprise* would entail that the task force contained only Navy forces. More at **compose / comprise.**

**incredible / incredulous** *Incredible* means "hard to believe, unbelievable": *His explanation of the cause of the accident was simply incredible.* It is often used more loosely to mean "astonishing," as in *The new pitcher has an incredible fastball. Incredulous* usually means "skeptical, disbelieving," as in *The incredulous reporters laughed at the manager's explanation of how the funds disappeared.* It is sometimes extended to mean "showing disbelief," as in *an incredulous stare.* You may occasionally see *incredulous* used where you would expect *incredible,* as in *an incredulous display of rudeness.* This usage is not well established, however, and is widely considered an error.

**individual** You normally use the noun *individual* to refer to an individual person as opposed to a larger social group or as distinguished from others by some special quality: "*This is not only a crisis of individuals, but also of a society*" (Raymond Williams). *She is a real individual.* Since the 19th century, however, there have been numerous objections to the use of the word to refer simply to "person" where no larger contrast is implied, as in *Two individuals were placed under arrest* or *The Mayor will make time for any individual who wants to talk to her.* This use of *individual* is common in official statements, as the examples imply, and lends a formal tone that you may find inappropriate for many contexts. Remember that the words *person* and *people* can do the same job perfectly well.

**infer / imply** People sometimes confuse *infer* with *imply,* but the distinction is a useful one. When we say that a speaker or sentence implies something, we

mean that information is conveyed or suggested without being stated outright: *When the mayor said that she would not rule out a business tax increase, she implied* (not *inferred*) *that some taxes might be raised.* Inference, on the other hand, is the activity performed by a reader or interpreter in drawing conclusions that are not explicit in what is said: *When the mayor said that she would not rule out a tax increase, we inferred that she had been consulting with some new financial advisers, since her old advisers were in favor of tax reductions.*

**infinite** *Infinite* is sometimes grouped with absolute terms such as *unique, absolute,* and *omnipotent,* since in its strict mathematical sense it cannot be modified or compared; that is, you cannot have a quantity that is *more infinite* than another or a set that is *somewhat infinite.* But *infinite* is different from other absolute terms in that it cannot be modified by *nearly* and *almost.* Either a set is infinite or it is not. It can't be almost infinite, since if it were, it would be finite.

In nontechnical usage, of course, *infinite* is often used to refer to an unimaginably large degree or amount, and in these cases it is acceptable to modify or compare the word: *We thought of retracing our steps to see where George might have lost his keys, but we soon realized that the possibilities were almost infinite.*

More at **center, complete, equal, parallel, perfect,** and **unique.**

**infrastructure** The term *infrastructure* has been around since 1927. It usually refers collectively to roads, bridges, rail lines, and similar public works that are required for an industrial economy, or a portion of it, to function. This often includes telecommunications facilities, such as telephone lines and microwave towers. The term has had specific application to the permanent military installations necessary for the defense of a country.

Perhaps because of the word's technical sound, people now use *infrastructure* to refer to any substructure or underlying system. Big corporations have their own financial infrastructure of smaller businesses, for example, and political organizations have their infrastructure of groups, committees, and admirers. This political sense may have originated during the Vietnam War in use by military intelligence officers, whose task it was to delineate the structure of the enemy's shadowy organizations. Today we hear that conservatism has an infrastructure of think tanks and research foundations and that terrorist organizations have an infrastructure of people who are sympathetic to their cause. This extended use referring to people does not sit well with the Usage Panel, however. Seventy percent found it unacceptable in the sentence *FBI agents fanned out to monitor a small infrastructure of persons involved with established terrorist organizations.*

**input** People have been using the noun *input* as a technical term for about a century in fields such as physics and electrical engineering, but its recent popularity grows out of its use in computer science, where it refers to data or signals entered into a system for processing or transmission. People now use *input* for the transmission of information and opinion, as in *The report questioned whether a President thus shielded had access to a sufficiently varied input to*

*have a realistic picture of the nation* or *The nominee herself had no input on housing policy.* In this last sentence the meaning of the term is uncertain: it may mean either that the nominee provided no opinions to the policymakers or that she received no information about housing policy. This vagueness in the nontechnical use of *input* may be one reason that some people object to it (including, in an earlier survey, a majority of the Usage Panel). Although the usage is well established, you should be careful not to use the word just to imply an unwarranted scientific precision.

**insignia** *Insignia* in Latin is the plural form of *insigne,* but it has long been used in English as both a singular and a plural form: *The insignia was visible on the wingtip. There are five insignia on various parts of the plane.* From the singular use of *insignia* we get the plural *insignias,* which is also acceptable. The Latin singular *insigne* is rare and may strike some readers as pedantic.

**intense / intensive** The meanings of *intense* and *intensive* overlap considerably, but the two adjectives often have distinctive meanings. When you describe human feeling or activity, *intense* often suggests a strength or concentration that arises from inner dispositions and is particularly appropriate for describing emotional states: *intense pleasure, dislike, loyalty,* and so forth. But you use *intensive* when the strength or concentration of an activity is imposed from without: *intensive bombing, intensive training, intensive marketing.* Thus a reference to *Mark's intense study of German* suggests that Mark himself was responsible for the concentrated activity, whereas *Mark's intensive study of German* suggests that the program in which Mark was studying was designed to cover a great deal of material in a brief period.

**interface** The noun *interface* has been around since the 1880s, meaning "a surface forming a common boundary, as between bodies or regions." But the word did not really take off until the 1960s, when it began to be used in the computer industry to designate the point of interaction between a computer and another system, such as a printer. The word was applied to other interactions as well—between departments in an organization, for example, or between fields of study. Shortly thereafter *interface* developed a use as a verb, but it never really caught on outside its niche in the computer world, where it still thrives. The Usage Panel has been unable to muster much enthusiasm for the verb. Thirty-seven percent accept it when it designates the interaction between people in the sentence *The managing editor must interface with a variety of freelance editors and proofreaders.* But the percentage drops to 22 when the interaction is between a corporation and the public or between various communities in a city. Many panelists complain of *interface* being pretentious and jargony. Certainly, there is no shortage of synonyms. *Cooperate, deal, exchange information, interact,* and *work* present themselves as ready substitutes.

**intrigue** People initially resisted the use of *intrigue* as a verb to mean "to arouse the interest or curiosity of" because it was an unnecessary French substitute for available English words such as *interest, fascinate,* or *puzzle,* but it now appears to be well established. Seventy-eight percent of the Usage Panel accepts it in the sentence *The special-quota idea intrigues some legislators, who have asked a Washington think tank to evaluate it,* whereas only 52 percent accepted it in a 1968 survey.

**intuit** The use of *intuit* as a verb is well established, but some object to it. Only 34 percent of the Usage Panel accepts it in the sentence *Dermot often intuits my feelings about things long before I am really aware of them myself.* People often attribute this lack of acceptance to the verb's status as a back-formation from *intuition,* but in fact the verb has existed as long as other back-formations, such as *diagnose* and *donate,* that are now wholly acceptable. The source of the objections most likely lies in the fact that the verb is often used in reference to more trivial sorts of insight than would be permitted by a full appreciation of the traditional meaning of *intuition.* In this connection, a greater percentage of the panel, 46 percent, accepts *intuit* in the sentence *Mathematicians sometimes intuit the truth of a theorem long before they are able to prove it.*
More at **enthuse.**

**ironic** In its nonliterary uses, *irony* often refers to a perceived incongruity between what is expected and what actually occurs, especially if what actually occurs thwarts human wishes or designs. People sometimes misuse the words *ironic, irony,* and *ironically,* applying them to events and circumstances that might better be described as simply *coincidental* or *improbable,* in that the events suggest no particular lessons about human vanity or folly. Thus 78 percent of the Usage Panel rejects the use of *ironically* in the sentence *In 1969 Susan moved from Ithaca to California where she met her husband-to-be, who, ironically, also came from upstate New York.* Some panelists noted that this particular usage might be acceptable if Susan had in fact moved to California in order to find a husband, in which case the story could be taken as exemplifying the folly of supposing that we can know what fate has in store for us. By contrast, 73 percent accepted the sentence *Ironically, even as the government was fulminating against American policy, American jeans and videocassettes were the hottest items in the stalls of the market,* where the incongruity can be seen as an example of human inconsistency.

**irregardless** *Irregardless* is a word that many people mistakenly believe to be correct usage in formal style, when in fact it is used chiefly in nonstandard speech or casual writing. The word was coined in the United States in the early 20th century, probably from a blend of *irrespective* and *regardless.* Perhaps this is why some critics insist that there is "no such word" as *irregardless,* a charge they would not think of leveling at a nonstandard word with a longer history, such as *ain't.* Since people use *irregardless,* it is undoubtedly a word. But it has never been accepted in Standard English and is usually changed by editors to *regardless* before getting into print.

**its / it's** *Its* is the possessive form of the pronoun *it* and is never written with an apostrophe: *The cat licked its paws.* The contraction *it's* (for *it is* or *it has*) always has an apostrophe: *It's the funniest show I've seen in years.*

**–ize** The suffix *-ize* has been and continues to be a productive means of turning nouns and adjectives into verbs, as in such well-established forms as *formalize, criticize, jeopardize,* and *hospitalize.* In many cases, *-ize* creates verbs with more than one meaning. Thus *computerize* may mean "to furnish with computers" (as in *The entire office has been computerized*) or "to enter on a computer" (as in *The records are not yet computerized*). In some cases this can cause ambiguity. For example, the sentence *Earthquake relief requirements must be prioritized* may mean that all relief requirements must be assigned a high priority or that the relative priority among requirements must be determined. It is important therefore that the context make clear which sense is intended.

Many words formed with *-ize* come from bureaucratic and corporate jargon, and for this reason they often meet with resistance when the general public first sees them. The verbs *Americanize, nationalize,* and *jeopardize* were all objected to when they were introduced, but they have since become standard. Although some recent words of this type have been quickly accepted—for example, *computerize, institutionalize,* and *radicalize*—many others cannot shake their association with bureaucratese. Among these are *accessorize, incentivize, prioritize, privatize,* and *finalize.* You should be careful with coinages of this sort, especially when writing for a general audience.
More at **finalize, incentivize,** and **prioritize.**

**kind** *These kind of errors make my blood boil!* The use of the *these* and *those* with *kind* and *sort,* as in *these kind* (or *sort*) *of films,* has been a traditional bugbear of American grammarians. By and large, British grammarians have been more tolerant. You can find the construction in the works of British writers from Pope to Churchill. Grammatically, the question boils down to whether *kind* and *sort* should be treated as head nouns (like *species* or *variety*) or whether they function more like adjectives (in the manner of *bunch* and *number* in the expressions *a bunch of friends, a number of reasons*). If *kind* and *sort* are nouns, you would expect to see only *this* or *that* and a singular verb accompanying them, as in *This kind of films is popular.* If they function as adjectives, however, you would expect *these* or *those* and a plural verb, as in *These kind of films are popular.* In fact, you can legitimately view the *kind of* construction in either way, which is doubtless one reason why writers don't follow a uniform pattern in usage.

Of course, when you use the plural *kinds,* you must use the plural *these* or *those,* and the verb must also be plural: *These* (not *this*) *kinds of films are* (not *is*) *popular.* By the same token, when both *kind* and the noun following it are singular, you must use a singular verb: *This kind of film is* (not *are*) *popular.* For more on this, see **subject and verb agreement** under *Grammar.*

**knot** In nautical usage, *knot* is a unit of speed, not of distance. It means "nautical miles per hour." Therefore, a ship travels at ten knots, not ten knots per hour, which would be "ten nautical miles per hour per hour." The speed of a ship travelling "per hour per hour" would be constantly changing, since the ship would be accelerating.

**kudos** Everyone likes to get kudos, but how much—or how many? *Kudos* means "praise." It comes from a Greek word that meant "glory" and is thus one of those words like *congeries* that look like plurals but are etymologically singular. So if you want to get the Greek right, you must use a singular verb: *Kudos is* (not *are*) *due her for her brilliant work.*

This is not to say you will never see *kudos* used with a plural verb or treated as if it were a count noun meaning "a praising remark," as in *They have received many kudos for their research.* It happens quite frequently. Some writers have tried to defend this use of *kudos* and even the singular form *kudo,* on the grounds that these usages follow the same pattern of words such as *pea* and *cherry.* These words were shortened from nouns ending in -*s* that were mistakenly thought to be plural. But if you decide to join in championing this view and offer someone a few kudos, don't be surprised if you are accused of being ignorant of *kudos's* Greek origins.

Oddly enough, people who are careful to treat the word only as a singular often pronounce it as if it were a plural. Etymology would require that the final consonant be pronounced as a voiceless (s), as we do in *pathos,* another word derived from Greek, rather than as a voiced (z). For more on this, see **kudos** under *Pronunciation.*

**lack** You normally use the verb *lack* in the sense of "to be wanting or deficient" as the present participle with *in: You will not be lacking in support from me.* When you use *lack* in the sense "to be in need of something," you often use *for* with it: *"In the terrible, beautiful age of my prime,/I lacked for sweet linen but never for time"* (E.B. White).

**late** If the late director of your glee club did a superb job, don't say so in public, for *late* can mean "having recently left office" or "having recently died." If the director is still alive, use *former* instead; it will ensure that you create no embarrassing misunderstanding.

**lay / lie** People have confused *lay* ("to put, place; prepare") and *lie* ("to recline; be situated") for centuries. They will probably continue to do so. *Lay* has been used to mean "lie" since the 1300s. Why? First, there are two *lays.* One is the base form of the verb *lay,* and the other is the past tense of *lie.* Second, *lay* was once used with a reflexive pronoun to mean "lie" and survives in the familiar line from the child's prayer *Now I lay me down to sleep.* It is not a long leap from *lay me down* to *lay down.* Third, *lay down,* as in *She lay down on the sofa* sounds the same as *laid down,* as in *She laid down the law to the kids.*

Here's how to keep them straight. *Lay* is a transitive verb—it takes an object. *Lay* and its principal parts (*laid, laid, laying*) are correctly used in the following examples: *She lays down her pen and stands up. He laid* (not *lay*) the *newspaper on the table. The table was laid for four. Lie* is an intransitive verb and cannot take an object. *Lie* and its principal parts (*lay, lain, lying*) are correctly used in the following examples: *She often lies* (not *lays*) *down after lunch. When I lay* (not *laid*) *down, I fell asleep. The rubbish had lain* (not *laid*) *there a week. I was lying* (not *laying*) *in bed when he called.*

There are a few exceptions to these rules. The phrasal verb *lay for* and the nautical use of *lay,* as in *lay at anchor,* though intransitive, are standard.

It's probably a good idea to keep the two verbs distinct in formal writing, since people will be looking for evidence of your education in your work. If you're submitting something for publication, the copy editor will almost certainly fix your *lays* and *lies* for you. But bear in mind that *lay* is often an expressive way to say "lie" and has a charmed existence in certain uses. Don't most dogowners at one time or another say *Lay down!* to their dogs? How many golfers *play it as it lays?* How many employers exhort their workers with *Let's not lay down on the job?* What if Bob Dylan, in a fit of zeal for correctness, had written "*Lie, Lady, Lie/Lie across my big brass bed?*" Somehow it's hard to imagine the lady sticking around.

**leave / let** You can use *leave alone* as a substitute for *let alone* in the sense "to refrain from disturbing or interfering." A majority of the Usage Panel in an earlier survey approved the following examples: *Leave him alone and he will produce. Left alone, he was quite productive.* Those who do not accept these examples generally feel that *leave alone* should mean simply "to depart from someone who remains in solitude": *They were left alone in the wilderness.*

Remember, however, that in standard usage you cannot use the simple verb *leave* as a substitute for *let* in the sense "to allow or permit." Thus in the following examples you can only use *let: Let me be. Let him go. Let us not quarrel. Let it lie.*

**legend** *Legend* comes from the Latin adjective *legenda,* "for reading, to be read," which referred only to written stories, not to traditional stories transmitted orally from generation to generation. This restriction also applied to the English word *legend* when it was first used in the late 14th century in reference to written accounts of saints' lives. But it's hard to keep a good story from being retold, and ever since the 15th century *legend* has referred to traditional stories as well. Today a legend can also be a person or achievement worthy of inspiring such a story—anyone or anything whose fame promises to be enduring, even if the renown is created more by the media than by oral tradition. Thus we speak of the *legendary* accomplishments of a major-league baseball star or the *legendary* voice of a famous singer. This "new" usage is common journalistic hyperbole. Fifty-five percent of the Usage Panel approves it.

**liable / apt / likely** People often use *liable, apt,* and *likely* interchangeably in constructions with infinitives, as in *John is liable to lose, John is apt to lose,* and *John is likely to lose.* But the three words have subtle distinctions in meaning. A traditional rule holds that you should use *liable* only if the subject (often a person) would be adversely affected by the outcome expressed by the infinitive. The rule therefore permits *Zach is liable to fall out of his chair if he doesn't sit up straight* but not *The chair is liable to be slippery.* Nevertheless, constructions of the latter type have long been common in good writing.

*Apt* usually suggests that the subject (whether a person or not) has a natural tendency enhancing the probability of an outcome and that the speaker is somewhat apprehensive about the outcome. Thus you would naturally use *apt* in a sentence like *The fuel pump is apt to give out at any day* but not in *Even the clearest instructions are apt to be misinterpreted by those idiots* (since "those idiots," not the instructions, are at fault). Similarly, you would not use *apt* in *The fuel pump is apt to give you no problems for the life of the car* (since there is no reason that the speaker should regard such an outcome as unfortunate).

*Likely* is more general than either *liable* or *apt.* It ascribes no particular property to the subject that would enhance the probability of the outcome. Thus, while *John is apt to lose the election* may suggest that the loss will result from something John does or fails to do, *John is likely to lose the election* does not. Nor does it suggest anything about the desirability of the outcome from the point of view of either the speaker or the subject.
More at **likely.**

**lifestyle** When *lifestyle* became popular a generation ago, some people objected to it as voguish and superficial, perhaps because it appeared to elevate habits of consumption, dress, and recreation to categories in a system of social classification. But the word has stayed with us, if only because such categories figure importantly in the schemes that Americans commonly invoke when explaining social values and behavior, as in *"an anticonventional lifestyle is no sure sign of feminist politics, or indeed, of any politics at all"* (Rachel Brownstein). The Usage Panel accepts the word, but more so when the context requires a term that implies categorization based on habits of consumption. Thus 53 percent of the Usage Panel accepts the word in *Bohemian attitudes toward conventional society have been outstripped and outdated by the lifestyles of millions of young people.* But 70 percent accept the word in *Salaries in the Bay Area may be higher, but it may cost employees as much as 30 percent more to maintain their lifestyles.*

**light** You can use either *lighted* or *lit* as past tense and past participle of *light.* Both forms are also well established as adjectives: *a lit* (or *lighted*) *pipe.*

## like

**instrusive *like*** You may have heard people complain about the use of *like* as a "meaningless" particle, as in *The waves were, like, really big* or *He wrote two best-sellers and then he, like, stopped writing.* Linguists call this "intrusive" or "focus" *like.* It can appear anywhere in a sentence and is used to set off the most significant new information—the focus—of the sentence. This use of *like* is a hallmark of spoken language and is used in writing almost solely in dialogue.

***like* indicating direct speech or an attitude** So I'm like, "Let's get out of here." Everyone has overheard this construction in casual conversation at the mall or in the park. It is used primarily by young people and appears to be gaining in popularity. It combines a form of the verb *be* and the adverb *like,* followed by a brief but dramatic pause. This *like* construction can introduce dialogue, just as *go* does, but it is also used to announce a brief performance or imitation of someone's behavior, often elaborated with gestures and facial expressions. So, for instance, if a woman says *So I'm like "Get lost, buddy,"* she may or may not have used those actual words to tell the offending person to leave. In fact, she may not have said anything, but is merely summarizing her attitude at the time by stating what she would have said if she had chosen to speak. This use of *like* is still restricted primarily to speech.

**like and as** Can *like* be a conjunction, or must you always use *as* instead? For an answer to this question, see **like** under *Grammar.*

More at **go.**

**likely** You normally use the adverb *likely* preceded by a modifier such as *very* or *quite: He will quite likely require some help with his classes.* But the unmodified use of *likely* is common enough in educated writing, and though it might be better avoided in highly formal style, it is perfectly acceptable: *They'll likely buy a new car this year.*

More at **liable.**

**lot** The common expression *a lot of* is a whole lot more complicated than you might think. It belongs to a class of words that include *deal* (in *a great deal of* ), *plenty,* and *load.* In phrases such as *a lot of strawberries,* the word *lot* is not really a head noun analogous to the word *bowl* in *a bowl of strawberries.* Rather, expressions like *a lot of, a whole lot of,* and *a great deal of* are best thought of as complex modifiers analogous to words like *many, much,* or *several. Lot* and *plenty* can occur with noncount nouns like *furniture* and with plural count nouns like *chairs.* The verb agrees in number with the noun in the *of*-phrase. Thus, when followed by a singular noun, *a lot of* takes a singular verb: *A lot of pizza was left on the table.* But when followed by a plural noun, it takes a plural verb: *A lot of the strawberries were ripe.*

Like *load, lot* has the further distinction of being used in the plural with similarly peculiar agreement rules. When followed by a singular noun, *lots of* takes a singular verb: *Lots of pizza was left on the table.* When followed by a plural noun, *lots of* is plural: *Lots of people were at the bookstore.*

*A lot* and some of its cousin phrases are also used as adverbs meaning "much" or "very much": *I'm feeling a whole lot* (or *lots* or *a great deal*) *better.* The phrase *a bit* or *a little bit* works in the other direction, meaning "somewhat."

Virtually all of the expressions discussed here have an informal tone, with the plural phrases like *lots of* having a decidedly more informal tone than the others. For more on this, see **subject and verb agreement** under *Grammar.*

**alot** Teachers of writing have seen this form in student papers more times than they care to remember, and they can expect to keep on seeing it. Even experienced writers find themselves writing *alot* for *a lot,* especially when working under pressure or dashing off a note. The fusion of an article and a noun into a single word is a normal linguistic phenomenon, having occurred in *another* and *awhile,* so it is very possible that we all may write *alot* one day. For the time being, however, keep in mind that *alot* is still considered an error in print, so don't be surprised if writing teachers and copy editors keep prying it apart.

**majority** When *majority* refers to a particular number of votes, it takes a singular verb: *Her majority was five votes. His majority has been growing by 5 percent every year.* When it refers to a group of persons or things that are in the majority, it may take either a singular or plural verb, depending on whether the group is considered as a whole or as a set of people considered individually. So we say *The majority elects* (not *elect*) *the candidate it wants* (not *they want*), since the election is accomplished by the group as a whole, but we say *The majority of the voters live* (not *lives*) *in the city,* since living in the city is something that each voter does individually.

*Majority* is often preceded by *great* (but not by *greater*) in expressing emphatically the sense of "most of": *The great majority approved.* The phrase *greater majority* is appropriate only when considering two majorities: *He won by a greater majority in this election than in the last.* For more on this, see **subject and verb agreement** under *Grammar*.

**masterful / masterly** Some people like to maintain a distinction between *masterful* and *masterly.* They think that *masterful* should be reserved for the sense "imperious, domineering" (as in *a masterful tone of voice*) whereas *masterly* should be the choice when the intended sense is "having the skill of a master" (as in *a masterly performance of the sonata*). The distinction can serve a useful purpose, but good writers have long been using *masterful* in the latter sense, and you should not consider this an error.

**materialize** In its original senses *materialize* is used without an object to mean "to assume material form" (as in *Marley's ghost materialized before Scrooge's eyes*) or with an object to mean "to cause to assume material form" (as in *Disney materialized his dream in a plot of orchard land in Orange County*). But these uses are probably less common nowadays than two extended senses of the verb. In the first, the meaning is roughly "to appear suddenly": *No sooner had we set the menu down than a waiter materialized at our table.* Some critics have labeled this use as pretentious or incorrect, but it has been around for more than a century, appears in the writing of highly respected writers, and seems a natural extension of the original sense. The second meaning is "to take effective shape, come into existence." In this use, *materialize* tends to be applied to things or events that have been foreseen or anticipated, and usually occurs in negative constructions: *The promised subsidies never materialized. It was thought the community would oppose the measure, but no new objections materialized.* While objections continue to materialize against this usage, it too is well established in reputable writing and follows a familiar pattern of metaphoric extension.

**means** In the sense of "financial resources," *means* takes a plural verb: *His means are more than adequate.* In the sense of "a way to an end," *means* may be treated as either a singular or plural. It is singular when referring to a particular strategy or method: *The best means of securing the cooperation of the builders is to appeal to their self-interest.* It is plural when it refers to a group of strategies or methods: *The most effective means for dealing with the drug problem have generally been those suggested by the affected communities.*

*Means* is most often followed by *of: a means of noise reduction.* But *for, to,* and *toward* are also used: *a means for transmitting signals, a means to an end, a means toward achieving social equality.*

**meantime / meanwhile** *Meantime* is more common than *meanwhile* as a noun: *In the meantime we waited.* As an adverb, *meantime* is less common than *meanwhile: Meanwhile we waited.* All of these uses are standard, however.

**media** The word *medium* comes from Latin. It has two plural forms—a Latin plural *media* and a normal English *-s* plural *mediums.* Trouble arises when the Latin plural is used as a singular noun in the fields of mass communications and journalism.

You may have come across *media* used as a singular noun to refer to a particular means of communication, as in *The Internet is the most exciting new media since television.* Many people regard this usage as incorrect, preferring *medium* as the singular instead.

People also use *media* with the definite article as a collective term to refer not to the forms of communication themselves so much as the communities and institutions behind them. In this sense, *the media* means something like "the press." Like other collective nouns, it may take a singular or plural verb depending on the intended meaning. If the point is to emphasize the multifaceted nature of the press, a plural verb may be more appropriate: *The media have covered the trial in a variety of formats.* Quite frequently, however, *media* stands as a singular noun for the aggregate of journalists and broadcasters: *The media has not shown much interest in covering the trial.* This development of a singular *media* parallels that of more established words such as *data* and *agenda,* which are also Latin plurals that have acquired a singular meaning.

Remember that you can't use the singular *medium* as a collective noun for the press. You can't say *No medium has shown much interest in covering the trial,* which would suggest that the lack of interest is in the means of communication itself rather than in its practitioners.

**methodology** Properly used, *methodology* refers either to the theoretical analysis of the methods appropriate to a field of study or to the body of methods and principles particular to a branch of knowledge. In this sense, you might hear of *objections to the methodology of an opinion survey* (that is, objections dealing with the appropriateness of the methods used). You might also hear the word used in phrases like *the methodology of modern cognitive psychology* (that is, the principles and practices that underlie research in the field).

But in recent years, people have begun to use *methodology* as a pretentious substitute for *method* in scientific and technical contexts, as in *The oil company has not yet decided on a methodology for restoring the beaches.* People may have taken to this practice by influence of the adjective *methodological,* which has come to mean "pertaining to methods." *Methodological* may have acquired this meaning because people had already been using the more ordinary adjective *methodical* to mean "orderly, systematic," and they needed another word for the "scientific method" sense. But however these words got entangled, you may want to keep them apart in your own writing, since you can thereby maintain an important conceptual distinction between the tools of scientific investigation (your *methods*) and the principles that determine how such tools are deployed and interpreted (your *methodology*).

**migrate / emigrate / immigrate** When used of people, *migrate* sometimes refers to a permanent change of settlement: *In the fifth century A.D. the Angles, Saxons, and Jutes began migrating to England.* In other contexts, *migrate* usually indicates a lack of permanent settlement, especially as a result of seasonal or periodic movement, as when birds or other animals migrate to a different region. *Emigrate* and *immigrate* are used only of people and imply a permanent move, generally across a political boundary. *Emigrate* describes the move relative to the point of departure: *After the Nazis came to power in Germany, many scientists emigrated* (that is, left Germany). By contrast, *immigrate* describes the move relative to the destination: *The promise of prosperity in the United States encouraged many people to immigrate* (that is, move to the United States).

**minimal / minimize** *Minimal* and *minimize* come from the Latin adjective *minimus,* "least, smallest," and people therefore use *minimal* to refer to the smallest possible amount, as in *The amplifier reduces distortion to the minimal level that can be obtained with present technologies.* In recent years, however, people have begun to use *minimal* more loosely to refer to a small amount, as in *If you would just put in a minimal amount of time on your homework, I am sure your grades would improve.* Language critics have objected to this usage, but it is fairly common. In one of our more recent surveys, we asked the Usage Panel what *minimal* meant in the sentence *Alcohol has a particularly unpleasant effect on me when I have a minimal amount of food in my stomach.* Under the strict interpretation of *minimal,* the sentence should mean "Alcohol has an unpleasant effect when I have eaten nothing." If the looser interpretation is allowed, however, the sentence can also mean ". . . when I have eaten a bit." Twenty-nine percent of the panel held to the strict interpretation (that is, "eaten nothing"); 34 percent said that it could have only the looser meaning (that is, "eaten a bit"); and 37 percent said that it could have either meaning. Thus 71 percent allowed the looser sense of *minimal,* so you should consider this sense acceptable, at least in nontechnical use.

The verb *minimize* has undergone a similar extension of meaning. In its strict sense it means "to reduce to the smallest possible level," but quite often the context requires us to interpret what the smallest possible level might be. Thus when a manager announces that *The company wants to minimize the risk*

*of accidents to assembly line workers,* we naturally think that the company plans to reduce the risk to the smallest level after considerations of efficiency and cost have been taken into account, not that risks are to be reduced to the lowest level regardless of disruptions and cost. People also use minimize more loosely to mean "to make appear to be of little importance; play down," as in *The President tried to minimize the problems posed by the nation's trade imbalance.* This sense is well established.

**modem** Like the word *fax, modem* is a computer term that originated as a noun for a piece of hardware and eventually developed into a verb as well. But where the verb *fax* has been around for nearly 20 years and is by now well established in general usage, the verb *modem* is a very recent coinage and has not gained much currency outside the confines of technical use. Only 34 percent of the Usage Panel accepts it in the sentence *To add to the debate in our special section on education reform, write, fax, or modem us your thoughts.* This hesitancy to embrace *modem* may stem from the fact that the widely used term *E-mail* presents itself as a more familiar usage in such contexts. By contrast, *fax* has no competing term. There is only one way to fax something, and that is to fax it. But even when the context is not one of interpersonal communication (as in *modeming information from one machine to another*), 71 percent of the panel dislikes *modem,* with many members preferring a more general term like *transmit* or even *send* instead.

**momentarily** *Momentarily* is widely used in speech to mean "in a moment," as in *The manager is on another line, but she'll be with you momentarily.* We've all heard remarks like this, in which the adverb *momentarily* means "in a moment." Many critics dislike this use, insisting that the adverb should only be used to mean "for a moment," as in *He hesitated momentarily before entering the room.* Fifty-nine percent of the Usage Panel agrees with them.

**moot** What do you get when you ask *a moot question?* An argument? A shrug? The adjective *moot* is originally a legal term going back to the mid-16th century. It derives from the noun *moot,* in its sense of a hypothetical case argued as an exercise by law students. Consequently, a *moot question* is one that is arguable or open to debate. But in the mid-19th century people also began to look at the hypothetical side of *moot* as its essential meaning, and they started to use the word to mean "of no significance or relevance." Thus *a moot point,* however debatable, is one that has no practical value. A number of critics have objected to this use, but 59 percent of the Usage Panel accepts it in the sentence *The nominee himself chastised the White House for failing to do more to support him, but his concerns became moot when a number of Republicans announced that they, too, would oppose the nomination.* So the next time you call something *moot,* be sure your readers will understand which sense of *moot* you mean.

**mutual** *Oh yeah? Well, the feeling is mutual!* Anyone who is in the habit of hurling insults is bound to hear this retort sooner or later. We use *mutual* to describe a reciprocal relationship between two or more things. Thus *their*

*mutual animosity* means "their animosity for each other" or "the animosity between them," and *a mutual defense treaty* is one in which each party agrees to come to the defense of the other. But many people also use *mutual* to mean "shared in common," as in *The bill serves the mutual interests of management and labor.* This usage is perhaps most familiar in the expression *our mutual friend,* which was widespread even before Charles Dickens used it as the title of a novel. While some language critics object to this usage because it does not include the notion of reciprocity, it appears in the writing of some of our greatest authors—among them Shakespeare, Edmund Burke, George Eliot, and James Joyce—and it continues to be used by well-respected writers today.

**myriad** Throughout most of its history in English, *myriad* was used as a noun, as in *a myriad of men.* In the early 19th century it began to be used in poetry as an adjective, as in *myriad men.* Both uses in English are acceptable, as in Samuel Taylor Coleridge's *"Myriad myriads of lives."* The poetic, adjectival use became so well entrenched generally that many people came to consider it as the only correct use. In fact, both uses in English are parallel with those of the original ancient Greek. The Greek word *murias,* from which *myriad* derives, could be used as either a noun or as an adjective, but the noun *murias* was used in general prose and in mathematics while the adjective *murias* was used only in poetry.

**nauseous / nauseated / nauseating** *Roller coasters make me nauseous*—or is it *nauseated?* Some people insist that you should use *nauseous* only to mean "causing nausea" and that it is incorrect to use it to mean "feeling sick to your stomach." The Usage Panel tends to support this notion. Seventy-two percent think you should be *nauseated* by roller coasters rather than made *nauseous.* But oddly enough the panel does not think *nauseous* is the best word to mean "causing nausea." Eighty-eight percent of the panel prefers *nauseating* in the sentence *The children looked a little green from too many candy apples and nauseating* (not *nauseous*) *rides.* Since there's plenty of evidence to show that *nauseous* is widely used to mean "feeling sick," it appears that people use *nauseous* mainly in the sense in which it is considered incorrect. In its "correct" sense it is being supplanted by *nauseating.*

**no sooner than / no sooner when** Because *sooner* in *no sooner* is a comparative adverb like *better* in *no better,* the expression should be followed by *than,* not *when: No sooner had she come than the maid knocked. I had no sooner left than she called.*

**number** As a collective noun, *number* may take either a singular or a plural verb. It takes a singular verb when it is preceded by the definite article *the: The number of skilled workers is increasing.* It takes a plural verb when preceded by the indefinite article *a: A number of the workers have learned new skills.* For more on this, see **collective noun** under *Grammar.*
More at **lot.**

**oblivious** You can use either *of* or *to* with *oblivious: The party appeared oblivious to* (or *of* ) *the mounting pressures for political reform.*

## off

**off meaning "from"** When *off* is used to indicate a source, it has an informal ring and should probably be avoided in formal contexts: *I borrowed the sander from* (not *off of* ) *my brother.*

**off of** The compound preposition *off of* also has an informal tone and is best avoided in formal speech and writing: *He stepped off* (not *off of* ) *the platform.*

## on

**on and onto** To indicate motion toward a position, you can use either *on* or *onto*. You can say *The cat jumped on the table* or *The cat jumped onto the table*. *Onto* is more specific, however, in indicating that the motion was initiated from an outside point. *He wandered onto the battlefield* means that he began his wandering at some point off the battlefield. *He wandered on the battlefield* may mean that his wandering began on the battlefield.

**on to** Don't confuse the adverb on when it is followed by the preposition to with the single word onto. Thus you should say *Let's move on to* (not *onto*) *another subject* and *We want to hold on to* (not *onto*) *our gains.*

**pair** The noun *pair* can be followed by a singular or plural verb. The singular is always used when *pair* refers to a set considered as a single entity: *This pair of shoes is on sale.* A plural verb is used when the members are considered as individuals: *The pair are working more harmoniously now.* After a number other than one, *pair* itself can be either singular or plural, but the plural is now more common: *She bought six pairs* (or *pair*) *of stockings.* For more on this, see **subject and verb agreement** under *Grammar.*

**paradigm** *Paradigm* comes from a Greek word meaning "an example or pattern." It first appeared in English with this meaning in the 15th century, and it still bears this meaning today: *Their company is a paradigm of the small high-tech firms that have recently sprung up in this area.* For nearly 400 years *paradigm* has also been applied to the patterns of inflections that are used to sort the verbs, nouns, and other parts of speech of a language into studiable groups. Anyone who has studied Latin will recall memorizing paradigms of word endings that distinguish the verbs belonging to different conjugations or the nouns of various declensions.

Since the 1960s *paradigm* has been used in science to refer to a theoretical framework, as when Nobel laureate David Baltimore cited the work of two colleagues that "*really established a new paradigm for our understanding of the causation of cancer.*" Once the scientists had paradigms to establish and overthrow, almost everyone else wanted to have them too. Researchers in many different fields, including sociology and literary criticism, began referring to the paradigms they were working in or trying to break out of. People have since used the term in an even wider range of contexts so that it often seems to mean "the prevailing view of things." The Usage Panel splits down the middle on these nonscientific uses of *paradigm*. Fifty-two percent disapprove of the sentence *The paradigm governing international competition and competitiveness has shifted dramatically in the last three decades.*

**parallel** In its mathematical usage, *parallel* is an absolute term. Two lines either are or are not parallel. Either they intersect, or they do not. They cannot be more parallel in one place than in another. Thus, in mathematics at least, *parallel* is a word that cannot be qualified by degree.

But some people would extend this restriction to uses of the word that fall outside the realm of mathematics. According to this logic, you cannot say *The two roads have been made more parallel.* But when we apply terms like *parallel* to the real world, it hardly makes sense to use them as if we were describing a geometrical ideal. A pair of rails or parked cars cannot be truly parallel in the mathematician's sense of the term but only more or less so, just as a road or shelf cannot be truly straight in the geometric sense but only very straight or relatively straight.

The objection to the modification of *parallel* by degree starts to look absurd when *parallel* is used metaphorically, as in *The difficulties faced by the Republicans are quite parallel to those that confronted the Democrats four years ago.* Here what is being described is the structural correspondence between two distinct situations, and concerns about the possibility of intersection seem remote indeed. In this sense, parallelism is clearly a matter of degree, so you should not hesitate to modify *parallel* accordingly. For more on absolute terms, see **absolute terms** under *Grammar.*

More at **center, complete, equal, infinite, perfect,** and **unique**.

**parameter** The term *parameter* has a number of specific meanings in fields such as astronomy, electricity, crystallography, and statistics. It is originally a term in mathematics, a field whose definitions can be so technical that they only make sense if you already know what they mean. Let us try nonetheless. In an equation, the parameter is one of the terms in an equation that can be varied to produce other equations of the same form. A parameter in the equation of a curve, for instance, can be varied to represent a family of curves. Applied more broadly to science, a parameter is one of a set of measurable factors, such as temperature and pressure, that define a system and determine its behavior. Thus the parameters of an experiment can be varied to produce different results.

Perhaps because of its ring of technical authority, people have applied *parameter* more generally in recent years to refer to any factor that determines a range of variations and especially to a factor that restricts what results from a process or policy. In this use it often comes close to meaning "a limit or boundary." Some of these new uses have a clear connection to the technical senses of the word. For example, the provisions of a zoning ordinance that limit the height or density of new construction can be reasonably likened to mathematical parameters that establish the limits of other variables. Therefore

you can say *The zoning commission announced new planning parameters for the historic Lamping district of the city.* But people often go one step further and use *parameter* as a highfalutin synonym for *characteristic* and end up sounding as if they are simply trying to add an aura of scientific precision to what would otherwise be an unremarkable point. The Usage Panel is not impressed by this "characteristic" use of *parameter.* Eighty percent reject the example *The Judeo-Christian ethic is one of the important parameters of Western culture.*

Some of the difficulties with the nontechnical use of *parameter* appear to arise from its resemblance to the word *perimeter,* with which it shares the sense "limit," though the two words differ in their precise meaning. This confusion probably explains the use of *parameter* in a sentence such as *U.S. forces report that the parameters of the mine area in the Gulf are fairly well established,* where the word *perimeter* would have expressed the intended sense more exactly. The Usage Panel does not cotton to this use of *parameter* either. Sixty-one percent find the "mine area" example unacceptable.

**pass** *Can what has passed between us be forever past?* So might one soap opera star breathe to another in impeccable, if overwrought, English. The past tense and past participle of *pass* is *passed: They passed* (or *have passed*) *our home. Time had passed slowly. Past* is the corresponding adjective (*in centuries past*), adverb (*drove past*), preposition (*past the crisis*), and noun (*lived in the past*).

**people / persons** As a term meaning "a body of persons sharing a culture," *people* is a singular noun, as in *As a people the Pueblo were noteworthy for their peacefulness.* Its plural is *peoples: the many and varied peoples of West Africa.* But when used to mean "human beings," *people* is plural and has no corresponding singular form. It is simply not English to say *A people came up and asked me what time it was.* If this seems odd, it really is not. A similar situation applies to the term for "people" in Spanish, Italian, Russian, and many other languages. Some grammarians have insisted that *people* is a collective noun that should not be used as a substitute for *persons* when referring to a specific number of individuals. By this thinking you should say *Six persons* (not *people*) *were arrested during the protest.*

But *people* has always been used in such contexts, and almost no one bothers with the distinction any more. *Persons* is still preferred in legal contexts, however, as in *Vehicles containing fewer than three persons may not use the left lane during rush hours.* Only the singular *person* is used in compounds involving a specific numeral: *a six-person car, a two-person show.* But *people* is used in other compounds: *people mover, people power.* These examples are exceptions to the general rule that plural nouns cannot be used in such compounds; note that we do not say *teethpaste* or *books-burning.*

**percent** Statistically speaking, you can increase a quantity by any percentage, but you cannot decrease a quantity by more than 100 percent. For example, once pollution has been reduced by 100 percent, it ceases to exist, and no further reduction is possible. In defiance of this logic, however,

advertisers sometimes refer to *a 150 percent decrease in lost luggage* or *a new dental rinse that reduces plaque on teeth by over 300 percent.* You can usually figure out the general idea of these examples, but this doesn't absolve them of being illogical.

*Percent* can take a singular or a plural verb, depending on how you view the quantity being described. Very often what determines the form of the verb is the noun nearest to it. Thus you might say *Eighty percent of the legislators are going to vote against the bill* or *Eighty percent of the legislature is set to vote the bill down.* In the second sentence the group of legislators is considered as a body, not as individuals. When you use *percent* without a following prepositional phrase, either a singular or plural verb is acceptable. For more on this, see **subject and verb agreement** under *Grammar.*

**percentage** When preceded by *the, percentage* takes a singular verb: *The percentage of unskilled workers is small.* When preceded by *a,* it takes either a singular or plural verb, depending on the number of the noun in the prepositional phrase that follows: *A small percentage of the workers are unskilled. A large percentage of the crop has spoiled.* For more on this, see **subject and verb agreement** under *Grammar.*

**perfect** Some people maintain that *perfect* is as an absolute term like *chief* and *prime* and therefore cannot be modified by *more, quite, relatively,* and other qualifiers of degree (for more on this, see **absolute terms** under *Grammar*). But the qualification of *perfect* has many reputable precedents (most notably in the preamble to the U.S. Constitution in the phrase "*in order to form a more perfect Union*"). Besides, *perfect* often means "ideal for the purposes," as in *There could be no more perfect spot for the picnic,* where modification by degree makes perfect sense.

More at **complete, equal, infinite, parallel,** and **unique.**

**periodic** In technical use, *periodic* means "occuring at regular or predictable intervals," as in the *Periodic Table of the Elements* that always appears in chemistry textbooks. But people often use *periodic* more loosely to mean "occasional, intermittent." This looser usage can be confusing to readers who are fond of the narrower sense of the word. Thus the writer who says *Jack's losses at the track were not covered by his periodic winners* invites readers to infer that Jack has a system that enables him to pick winners at regular intervals. In such situations you can avoid the ambiguity by using *occasional* instead.

**personality** Everyone *has* a personality but only a few people *are* personalities. Usually *personality* refers to the group of characteristics that are peculiar to a particular person, but *personality* can also mean "a celebrity." This usage is particularly common in popular journalism, as in *The show features interviews with entertainment personalities.* A case can be made for the usage, since many of the persons so described are best known simply for who they are rather than what they have done. Thus *personality* may be an appropriate

description of someone who is best known by virtue of his or her frequent appearances as a television host or a spokesperson for a certain product, but it is slighting when used of people whose renown is based on substantive achievements. Perhaps for this reason, 57 percent of the Usage Panel found this usage unacceptable in an earlier survey.

**peruse** *Are you perusing this note or just skimming it over? Peruse* has long meant "to read thoroughly" and is often used loosely when one could use the word *read* instead. Sometimes people use it to mean "to glance over, skim," as in *I only had a moment to peruse the manual quickly,* but this usage is widely considered an error. Sixty-six percent of the Usage Panel finds it unacceptable.

**phenomenon** The word *phenomenon* comes to us from Greek via Latin and usually keeps its Greek plural form *phenomena* when it means "an occurrence or fact that is perceptible to the senses." You may sometimes come across *phenomena* used as a singular noun, as in *This is a very strange phenomena,* but this usage may strike some readers as incorrect.

You can use *phenomenons* as the plural in nonscientific writing when the meaning is "extraordinary things, occurrences, or persons," as in *The Beatles were phenomenons in the history of rock 'n' roll.*

**plead** In strict legal usage, you can *plead guilty* or *plead not guilty* but you can never *plead innocent.* But in nonlegal contexts—that is, outside of the technical language of the law—people are often said to *plead innocent.* This is a widely used expression and should give you no reason to be suspicious.

**politics** Although it ends with an *-s, politics* takes a singular verb when used to refer to the art or science of governing or to political science: *Politics has been a concern of philosophers since Plato.* In its other senses, as when it refers to the activities or methods of a politician or a government, *politics* can take either a singular or plural verb: *"Politics are now nothing more than means of rising in the world"* (Samuel Johnson). *"American politics is a profession for amiable people eager to please and dedicated to the proposition that man's best friend is the compromise"* (George F. Will).

When *politics* means "political attitudes and positions," it usually gets a plural verb: *Her politics have not always been so radical.*

Many other nouns that end in *-ics* follow similar patterns. You should consult specific entries in your dictionary for precise information.

**pore / pour** You can't pour over a book unless you want to soak it. *Pour* means "to make a liquid flow, as from a container." *Pore* means "to read or study intently."

**possessed** *Possessed* is often followed by the prepositions *of, by,* or *with.* To show possession of a thing or an attribute, follow *possessed* with *of: She was pos-*

*sessed of a large estate. That child is possessed of a sharp tongue.* To indicate obsession or lack of self-control, use *by* or *with: The prosecutor described him as a man possessed by* (or *with*) *an urge to kill.*

**practicable / practical** It is easy to confuse these adjectives since they look so much alike and overlap in meaning. *Practicable* has only two meanings: "feasible" (as in *Sharon came up with a practicable plan*) and "usable for a specified purpose" (as in *A new more practicable entrance was added to the house*). Note that you cannot apply *practicable* to persons. *Practical* has at least eight meanings. These range from "acquired through practice rather than theory" (*I have practical experience using a lathe*) to "level-headed" (*He has always been a practical guy*) to "virtual" (*The party was a practical disaster*). It also has the sense "capable of being put into effect, useful," wherein the confusion with *practicable* arises. But there is a subtle distinction between these words that is worth keeping. If you have a *practical* knowledge of French, you can order coffee in a cafe, though it may not be *practicable* to try to learn the language of every country you visit.

**practically** *Practically* has as its primary sense "in a way that is practical": *We planned the room practically so we can use it as a study as well as a den.* The word has the extended meaning of "for all practical purposes," as in *After the accident the car was practically undrivable.* Here the idea is that you can still drive the car, but it is no longer practical to do so. Language critics sometimes object when the notion of practicality is stripped from this word in its further extension to mean "all but, nearly," as in *He had practically finished his meal when I arrived.* But this usage is widely used by reputable writers and must be considered acceptable.

**precipitate / precipitous** The adjective *precipitate* and the adverb *precipitately* were once applied to physical steepness but are now used primarily of rash, headlong actions: *Their precipitate entry into the foreign markets led to disaster. He withdrew precipitately from the race. Precipitous* currently means "steep" in both literal and figurative senses: *the precipitous rapids of the upper river, a precipitous drop in commodity prices.* But *precipitous* and *precipitously* are also frequently used to mean "abrupt, hasty," which takes them into territory that would ordinarily belong to *precipitate* and *precipitately: their precipitous decision to leave.* Many people object to this usage out of a desire to keep *precipitate* and *precipitous* distinct, but the extension of meaning from "steep" to "abrupt" is perfectly natural. After all, *a precipitous increase in reports of measles* is also an abrupt or sudden event. Although this extended use of *precipitous* is well attested in the work of reputable writers, don't be surprised if someone cites it as an error in your own writing.

**premiere** In entertainment contexts, the verb *premiere* has by now become the standard way of saying "to introduce to the public" or "to be introduced to the public." Because it emphasizes the very first time something is presented to the public, *premiere* gets a lot of use. Thus a movie can premiere in selected theaters, and a year later it can premiere again to a different audience on television. The verb first came out in the 1930s and acceptance of it in general usage has been slow. In 1969, only 14 percent of the Usage Panel accepted it. Twenty years later, however, when asked to judge the example *The Philharmonic will premiere works by two young Americans,* 51 percent accepted this usage. But only 10 percent of the panelists in the 1988 survey accepted the extension of the verb to contexts outside of the entertainment industry, as in *Last fall the school premiered new degree programs.* So if you are planning to premiere something, you should probably be in show business.

**prescribe / proscribe** If the doctor proscribes medicine, you'd better not take it. In its most common senses, *proscribe* means "to forbid or prohibit" and "to denounce." *Prescribe,* on the other hand, means to set down as a rule or guide, as in *The company handbook prescribes acceptable ways of reassigning an employee.* The medical sense, "to order the use of a medicine or treatment," is related to this.

**presently** The original use of *presently* to mean "at the present time, currently" goes back to the late 14th century. This usage seems to have disappeared from the written record in the 17th century, but it probably survived in speech, as it is widely found nowadays in both speech and writing. Perhaps because this sense was not treated in dictionaries until relatively recently, some language critics have argued that this usage is an error and that *presently* should only be used in its primary sense of "in a short time, soon," as in the shopkeeper's *I will be with you presently.* Apparently, many people are still persuaded by this criticism. Only 50 percent of the Usage Panel accepts the "currently" usage in the sentence *General Walters is presently the United States Ambassador to the United Nations.*

**principal / principle** *Our school principal—now there was a man of high principles.* It is easy to confuse these sound-alikes. Here is how to keep them straight. *Principle* is only a noun and usually refers to a rule or standard. *Principal* is both a noun and an adjective. As a noun, it has specialized meanings in law and finance, but in general usage it refers to a person who holds a high position or plays an important role: *a meeting among all the principals in the transaction.* As an adjective it has the sense of "chief" or "leading": *The coach's principal concern is the quarterback's health.*

**prioritize** It can be argued that *prioritize* serves a useful function in providing a single word to mean "arrange according to priority," but like many other recent formations with *-ize,* it is widely regarded as corporate or bureaucratic jargon. In an earlier survey, a large majority of the Usage Panel found *prioritize* to be unacceptable.
More at **–ize.**

**protagonist**
**protagonist in drama** The *protagonist* of a Greek drama was its first, or leading, actor; therefore there could only be one in a play. *Protagonist* is a pretty rare

word in ancient Greek, which also has words almost equally rare for second actor and third actor—*deuteragonist* and *tritagonist,* respectively. These latter two terms exist in Modern English also, but they are very rare, and writers use them, whether fortunately or unfortunately, only in technical discussions of drama. When the members of the Usage Panel were asked *How many protagonists are there in* Othello? the great majority answered *One* and offered substitutes such as *antagonist, villain, principal,* and *deuteragonist* to describe Desdemona and Iago. But as early as 1671 John Dryden used *protagonists* to mean simply "important actors" or "principal characters": *"Tis charg'd upon me that I make debauch'd persons…my protagonists, or the chief persons of the drama."* Some writers may still prefer to confine *protagonist* to its original singular sense, but it is useless by now to insist that the looser use is wrong.

**protagonist or proponent** Some people use *protagonist* to refer to a *proponent,* a usage that became common only in the 20th century and may have been influenced by a misunderstanding that the first syllable of the word is the prefix *pro-,* "favoring." Many readers will therefore find erroneous a sentence like *He was an early protagonist of nuclear power,* so it is probably better to use a word like *advocate* or *proponent* instead.

**prove** *We all thought that the prosecutor had proved her point.* Or should she have *proven her point?* Actually it can be either. The verb *prove* has two past participles: *proved* and *proven. Proved* is the older form. *Proven* is a variant. The Middle English spellings of *prove* included *preven,* a form which died out in England but survived in Scotland, and the past participle *proven* probably arose by analogy with verbs like *weave, woven* and *cleave, cloven. Proven* was used originally in Scottish legal contexts, such as *The jury ruled that the charges were not proven.* In the 20th century *proven* has made inroads into the the territory once dominated by *proved,* so that now the two forms compete on equal footing as participles. However, when used as an adjective before a noun, *proven* is now the more common word: *a proven talent.*

**provided / providing** In the past some critics have maintained that *provided* is preferable to *providing* as a conjunction meaning "on condition that." But both forms have been in use for centuries, with and without the additional word *that: You will receive a bonus provided* (or *provided that* or *providing* or *providing that) you finish the work on time.*

**quarter** When referring to the time of day, the article *a* is optional in phrases such as (*a*) *quarter to* (or *of, before,* or *till) nine* and (*a*) *quarter after* (or *past) ten.*

**quote** People have been using the noun *quote* as a truncation of *quotation* for over 100 years, and its use in less formal contexts is widespread today. Language critics have objected to this usage, however, as unduly journalistic or breezy. You may therefore want to avoid it in more formal situations. The Usage Panel, at least, shows more tolerance for the word as the informality of the situation increases. Thus only 38 percent accept the example *He began the* *chapter with a quote from the Bible,* but the percentage rises to 53 when the source of the quotation is less serious: *He lightened up his talk by throwing in quotes from Marx Brothers movies.*

People sometimes use *quote* as a synonym for "dictum, saying," as in *His career is just one more validation of Andy Warhol's quote that "in the future, everybody will be famous for fifteen minutes."* The Usage Panel has little liking for this usage. Seventy-six percent find it unacceptable.

**rack / wrack** If you are racked with doubt about this pair, you are not alone. There are seven words spelled *rack* in English. Two of these are variants of words spelled *wrack.* The *rack* we are immediately concerned with is familiar as a frame for holding or displaying things: *a hat rack.* This *rack* also refers to an implement of torture, consisting of a frame on which the body is stretched. From this has come the figurative meaning "pain or torment." In addition, *rack* can function as a verb, which means "to torture on a rack" and more commonly "to cause physical or mental suffering to," as in *For weeks after the accident he was racked with pain.* It is the verb that gives us torment today. It often appears in the compound *nerve-racking* and in the idiom *rack one's brains.*

On to *wrack,* of which, we noted, there are two. One means "destruction or ruin" and is familiar in the phrase *wrack and ruin.* The second *wrack* refers to wreckage cast ashore, but it is also a verb meaning "to cause the ruin of, wreck." Thus a business can be *wracked* by stiff competition. Both of these *wracks* have *rack* as an acceptable spelling variant, so a business can also be *racked* by competition, and the reader can never be sure if the business is in a state of metaphorical torment or if it is ruined—and in truth it may be both.

You can see how easy it is to mix these words up. If you want to avoid making a wreck of things, remember that the word *rack,* synonymous with pain, does not normally have *wrack* as a variant.

**rather** See **rather** under *Grammar.*

**regard / respect** If you are looking for another way to say "with reference to," look no further. *Regard* offers several variations: *regarding, in regard to, with regard to,* and *as regards.* All of these expressions are standard. The plural phrase *in regards to,* however, is not normally used in Standard English.

If these choices don't quite suit you, try *respect,* which offers *in respect to* and *with respect to.* There is also *in respect of,* but this is primarily used by British speakers. You may have also heard the preposition *respecting,* but this is not a standard usage.

If you still are not satisfied, try *about, concerning,* or *on.*

**repulse / repel** "*From where Yocke stood he could see that the left side of the vehicle's interior was covered with blood and tissue. Sights like this used to repulse him, but not now.*" If this quotation from Stephen Coonts's *Under Siege* gives you the jitters, it is probably not because of his choice of verbs.

A number of language critics have maintained that *repulse* should not be used to mean "to cause repulsion in" and that *repel* is the proper verb for this job. They add that *repulse* should only be used to mean "to drive away" (as in *The infantry repulsed the attack*) or "to spurn" (as in *She repulsed his rude advances with a frown*). But as the gritty passage cited above shows, many writers do not shy away from using *repulse* as a synonym for *disgust*. Besides, the related words *repulsion* and *repulsive* cause no controversy when used to mean "disgust" and "disgusting." So why should the verb be singled out for criticism? Still, *repel* presents itself as a perfectly good synonym, and is available if you are repulsed by *repulse*.

**research** If you are thinking of *researching* that topic before writing about it, go right ahead. Some language critics have objected to the use of *research* as a transitive verb, but the usage has ample historical precedent and is common in reputable writing. Eighty-one percent of the Usage Panel accepts it in the sentence *He spent a week at a funeral home researching mortuary procedures for his new novel.* The past participle *researched,* when used as an adjective, found even more favor with the panel. Ninety-one percent accept it in *The chapters on the internment are both readable and well researched.*

**responsible** Some critics have maintained that *responsible* should not be used to describe things, since only persons can be held accountable. The application to things is justifiable, however, when *responsible* is used to identify something as a source or cause. In an earlier survey, a majority of the Usage Panel accepted the sentence *Faulty construction was responsible for the crash.*

**restive / restless** These words overlap in meaning but have subtle distinctions. *Restive* usually indicates impatience or uneasiness caused by external coercion or restriction: *The government has done nothing to ease export restrictions, and domestic manufacturers are growing restive. Restive* also has a related sense, "stubbornly resisting control," and is sometimes applied to horses to mean "balky."

*Restless* can mean "characterized by a lack of rest," as in *a restless night*. It can also mean "constantly moving or acting," as in *restless seas* or *a plot hatched in his restless brain*. The confusion with *restive* arises when *restless* means "characterized by unrest, fidgety." But *restless* is usually not used in contexts involving external force or restriction: *The atmosphere in the office was congenial, but after five years she began to grow restless*. Still, if you are *restive* from impatience, you are probably fidgety, that is, *restless*, and in some situations either word will do.

**sacrilegious** *Sacrilegious,* the adjective form of *sacrilege,* is often misspelled *sacreligious* through confusion with *religious.*

**said** The adjective *said* is used primarily in legal and business writing, where it is equivalent to *aforesaid: the said tenant* (named in a lease), *said property.*

Outside of these contexts *said* is usually unnecessary. Simply saying *the tenant* or *the property* will suffice.

**same** The expressions *same* and *the same* are sometimes used in place of pronouns such as *it* or *one*, as in *When you have filled out the form, please remit same to this office.* As this example suggests, the usage is associated chiefly with business and legal language, and some critics have suggested that it should be reserved for such contexts. But though the usage often does sound stilted, it occurs with some frequency in informal writing, particularly in the phrase *lack of same*, as in *It is a question of money, or lack of same.*

**savings** There is a widespread tendency to use the form *savings* as a singular, as reflected in compounds such as *savings account* and *savings bond*. Compounds like these normally do not have plural nouns as their first component. No one has an *investments account*, for example. Nonetheless, *savings* usually takes a plural verb: *Your savings are safe in our bank.* But sometimes people think of savings as a lump sum and treat it as a singular noun, just as they would a sum of money: *Your savings* (or *Twenty thousand dollars*) *is enough to cover the down payment.* For more on this, see **subject and verb agreement** under *Grammar*.

Savings is also used in the phrase *a savings*, as in *a savings of $2,000*. While this phrase is increasingly common, it remains unacceptable to 57 percent of the Usage Panel. *A saving* is the only uncontroversial form.

**seasonal / seasonable** *Seasonal* and *seasonable*, though closely related, have different uses. *Seasonal* applies to what depends on or is controlled by the season of the year: *a seasonal rise in employment*. *Seasonable* applies to what is appropriate to the season (*seasonable clothing*) or timely (*seasonable intervention in the dispute*). Rains are *seasonal* if they occur at a certain time of the year. They are *seasonable* at any time if they save the crops.

**sensual / sensuous** Both of these adjectives mean "relating to or gratifying the senses." *Sensuous* can refer to any of the senses but usually applies to those involved in aesthetic enjoyment, as of art or music: *the sensuous imagery of a poem*. *Sensual* more often applies to the physical senses or appetites, particularly those associated with sexual pleasure. A *sensualist* is someone who is excessively devoted to eating, drinking, and sexual indulgence.

**series** *Series* is both a singular and a plural form. When it has the singular sense of "one set," it takes a singular verb, even when *series* is followed by *of* and a plural noun: *A series of lectures is scheduled.* When it has the plural sense of "one or more sets," it takes a plural verb: *Two series of lectures are scheduled: one for experts and one for laypeople.*

**service / serve** Aside from specialized senses in finance (*service a debt*) and animal breeding (*service a mare*), the verb *service* is used principally in the sense "to repair or maintain": *service the electric dishwasher.* In the sense "to supply goods or services to," *serve* is the most frequent or only choice: *One radio network serves three states.*

**set / sit** These verbs have been confused since the Middle Ages, so it is not surprising that they sometimes get mixed up today. Throughout its history *set* has been a transitive verb. It originally meant "to cause (someone) to sit" and also "to cause (something) to be in a certain position." This second sense survives as a basic meaning of the verb today: *She set the book on the table.* But since about 1300, *set* has been used without an object to mean "to be in a seated position, sit." *Set* is still common as a nonstandard or regional word meaning "sit," especially in rural speech: *Stop on by and set a spell.* The most familiar of *set*'s intransitive uses describes the motion of the sun at the end of the day. The sun only *sets;* it never *sits.*

This would seem a bit anomalous, since *sit* is mainly an intransitive verb. Its basic meaning is "to rest supported on the hindquarters," as in *He sits at the table.* It has a variety of other uses that entail occupying a location (*The house sits on a small lot*) or existing in a resting or unused state (*The skis sat gathering dust*). Nevertheless, *sit* has its transitive uses, some of which date back to the 14th century. It has taken over the meaning that originally belonged to *set,* "to cause (someone) to sit," so that we can now say *They sat the winning ticket holder back in his chair.* A more recent transitive use of *sit* is "to provide seats for," as in *The theater sits 5,000.*

But no matter how this sits with you, at least you don't have to worry about the chickens. A hen can *sit* or *set* on her eggs, so in this usage you can't possibly go wrong.

**shambles** A boy might sometimes transform his room into a battlefield, while his parents might only see a shambles. In fact, they could all be right. *Shambles* goes back to the sedate Latin word *scamnum,* "a stool or bench." Speakers of Old English borrowed the diminutive of this word, *scamillum,* as *sceamol,* which meant "a stool" and also "a table for selling goods." Old English *sceamol* became Middle English *shamel,* which developed the specific sense of "a table in a meat market." Soon it was used in the singular and plural to mean "a place where meat is butchered and sold, a meat market." From here it was a small step to the slaughterhouse, and in fact the Middle English compound *shamelhouse* meant "slaughterhouse." In the 16th century the plural form *shambles* also developed this sense, along with the figurative sense "a place or scene of bloodshed." So *shambles* just got bloodier and bloodier.

But no more. Our current, more generalized meaning "a scene or condition of disorder" is first recorded in 1926, and the blood has been draining from *shambles* ever since. Some people have resisted this modern sense of the word, insisting that a *shambles* must entail bloodshed, but theirs is a losing battle. Back in 1969, 85 percent of the Usage Panel found *shambles* acceptable when used in the "scene of disorder" sense. In fact, it is difficult to imagine most users of American English giving the word any other meaning.

**showcase** In its original meaning, a *showcase* is simply a case for displaying items, as in a store or museum. In theatrical language, a *showcase* is a production designed to display performers, and the verb *showcase* is used to refer to the act of exposure, whether of new talent—"*His productions showcased black singers but didn't cut them in on the lucrative action*" (James Wolcott)—or of established stars—"[The producer] *has crafted backgrounds which perfectly showcase* [the singer's] *vocals and driving rhythm guitar*" (Elijah Wald). Like other show business jargon, such as the verb use of *premiere*, this usage is properly exempt from criticism; we expect from P.T. Barnum a measure of exaggeration and grammatical license that we might not accept in other kinds of linguistic commerce.

But since its inception in the 1940s, the verb *showcase* has acquired a wider pattern of use. It is applied to the exposure of athletes and to the display of products: "*Recruiters promise a proud young man that he'll be a starter and a star, showcased for the pro scouts*" (Pete Axthelm). "*In the financial services section, stock-trading desks had been set up showcasing* [the company's] *computers*" (Boston Globe). "*The South Koreans . . . hope the Olympics will . . . showcase their country's breathtaking economic progress*" (Nancy Cooper). These uses clearly preserve the metaphoric sense of a showcase in which a commodity is displayed to advantage.

But other uses of the verb take it further from its original sense. It is sometimes used to mean simply "to hold up to admiration," even when the object is not something that can be hired or purchased: "*I feel great because Project Excellence is going to honor, to showcase, these youngsters who have risen above ridicule, hung in against myriad handicaps, and shown that they can be the best*" (Carl T. Rowan). It is also used to mean simply "to expose to public view," even when its object is neither admirable nor desirable: "*The Democrats were going to showcase all the wretchedness and decay and insolvency as a symbol of Republican not-so-benign neglect*" (Chicago Tribune). In this sense the verb is sometimes applied even to unintended exposure: "*But his news conference showcased once again his propensity for self-inflicted wounds*" (Newsweek). In these last two usages the verb no longer has any connection to the idea of a showcase, nor does it retain any hint of its theatrical character. The development of the verb nicely exemplifies how metaphors can become stripped of their original associations and so "die."

**slow** *Slow* may sometimes be used instead of *slowly* when it comes after the verb: *We drove the car slow.* In formal writing, *slowly* is generally preferred. *Slow* is often used in speech and informal writing, especially when brevity and forcefulness are sought: *Drive slow! Slow* is also the established idiomatic form with certain senses of common verbs: *The watch runs slow. Take it slow.*

**sneak** "*I ducked down behind the paperbacks and snuck out,*" writes Garrison Keillor in *Lake Woebegone Days.* Should he have *sneaked out* instead? The past tense *snuck* is an American invention. It first appeared in the 19th century as a nonstandard regional variant of *sneaked.* But widespread use of *snuck* has become more common with every generation. It is now used by educated speakers in all regions. Formal written English is more conservative than other varieties, of course, and here *snuck* still meets with much resistance. Many writers and editors have a lingering unease about the form, particularly if they recall its nonstandard origins. In fact, in 1990 a review of our citations, exhibiting almost 10,000 instances of *sneaked* and *snuck,* indicated that *sneaked* was preferred by a factor of seven to two. And 67 percent of the Usage Panel disapproved of *snuck* in our 1988 survey. Nevertheless, an examination of recent sources shows that *snuck* is sneaking up on *sneaked. Snuck* is almost 20 percent more common in newspaper articles published in 1995 than it was in 1985. Here are some examples from respected publications: "*He ran up huge hotel bills and then snuck out without paying*" (George Stade). "*In the dressing room beforehand, while the NBC technician was making me up, Jesse Jackson snuck up behind me and began playfully powdering my face*" (Bruce Babbitt). "*The Reagan administration snuck in some illegal military assistance before that*" (New Republic). "*He had snuck away from camp with a cabinmate*" (Anne Tyler).

More at **dive** and **wake.**

**so-called / self-styled** You should not use quotation marks to set off descriptions that follow expressions such as *so-called* and *self-styled,* which themselves relieve the writer of responsibility for the attribution: *his so-called foolproof method* (not "*foolproof method*").

**someday / some day / sometime / some time** *We should do that some day. Someday we will.* When should you use the single word, and when should you use the two-word phrase? The adverbs *someday* and *sometime* express future time indefinitely: *We'll succeed someday. Come sometime. Let's meet sometime when your schedule permits.* This sense can also be conveyed by *some day* and *some time.* But the two-word forms are always used when *some* is an adjective modifying and specifying a more particular *day* or *time: Come some day* (not *someday*) *soon. Choose some day* (not *someday*) *that is not so busy.*

**sometime** People most often use *sometime* as an adverb meaning "at some indefinite time in the future." The issue of when to use the single word *sometime* or the phrase *some time* is discussed at **someday.**

Since the 15th century people have used *sometime* as an adjective to mean "former," as in *our sometime colleague.* Since the 1930s people have also used it to mean "occasional," as in *the team's sometime star and sometime problem child.* A majority of the Usage Panel, however, finds this "occasional" use unacceptable.

**sooner than** *Sooner than* is a comparative construction combining an adverb and a conjunction. It sets up parallel structures in a sentence. For usage issues related to this, see **rather than** in **parallelism** under *Style.*

Sometimes people say *no sooner than,* sometimes *no sooner when.*

More at **no sooner than.**

**specious** A *specious* argument is not simply a false one but one that has the ring of truth. Those aware of the specialized use of the word may therefore sense a certain contradiction when an argument is described as *obviously specious* or *specious on the face of things*. If the fallaciousness is so apparent, the argument probably did not sound plausible to begin with.

**staunch / stanch** Should you call a pair of lifelong buddies *staunch* or *stanch friends?* Do you put pressure on a wound to *staunch* or *stanch the flow of blood?* These words are variant spellings of each other. The adjective and the verb are separate words. *Staunch* is more common than *stanch* as the spelling of the adjective. *Stanch* is more common than *staunch* as the spelling of the verb.

**stomp / stamp** The next time you *stomp* out of the office, don't *stomp* your foot in anger. You can use *stomp* and *stamp* interchangeably in the sense "to trample" or "to tread on violently": *stomped* (or *stamped*) *the poster of the candidate, stomping* (or *stamping*) *horses.* But only *stamp* is considered standard in the sense "to eliminate": *stamp out a fire, stamp out poverty. Stamp* is also standard in the sense "to strike the ground with the foot, as in anger or frustration," as in *He stamped his foot and began to cry.* A large majority of the Usage Panel in an earlier survey rejected the use of *stomp* with this sense.

**stratum** In Standard English, the singular form is *stratum;* the standard plural is *strata* (or sometimes *stratums*) but not *stratas.*

**suffer** In general usage, you should use *suffer* with *from,* not *with,* in constructions like *He suffered from hypertension.* Ninety-four percent of the Usage Panel rejects *suffered with* in the preceding example. In medical usage, *suffer with* is sometimes used in reference to the actual pain or discomfort caused by a condition, while *suffer from* is used more broadly in reference to a condition, such as anemia, that is detrimental but not necessarily painful.

**surveil** *Surveil* has encountered the same kind of critical resistance that was once accorded to other back-formations, such as *diagnose* and *donate.* It remains to be seen whether it too will eventually come to be regarded as useful and unexceptionable.

**teach** What's wrong with teaching school? Some grammarians have objected to the use of *teach* as a transitive verb when its object denotes an institution of learning, as in *Kim teaches grade school.* But this use of teach has been around since the 17th century and has wide currency at all levels. There's no reason to shy away from it.

**thusly** The adverb *thusly* was created in the 19th century as an alternative for *thus* in sentences such as *Hold it thus* or *He put it thus.* It appears to have been first used by humorists, who may have been echoing the speech of poorly educated people straining to sound stylish. The word has subsequently gained

some currency in educated usage, but it is still often regarded as incorrect. A large majority of the Usage Panel found it unacceptable in an earlier survey. In formal writing, *thus* can still be used as in the examples above; in other styles, expressions such as *this way* and *like this* are more natural.

**tight / tightly** You should always shut the door *tight*, but should you also shut it *tightly? Tight* is used as an adverb following verbs that denote a process of closure or constriction, such as *squeeze, shut, close, tie,* and *hold. In this use it is subtly distinct from the adverb *tightly. Tight* denotes the state resulting from the process, whereas *tightly* denotes the manner of its application. As such, *tight* is more appropriate when the focus is on a state that endures for some time after the activity has ended. The sentence *She closed up the house tight* suggests preparation for an impending blizzard. By the same token, it is more natural to say *The windows were frozen tight* than *The windows were frozen tightly,* since in this case the tightness of the seal is not likely to be the result of the manner in which the windows were frozen. With a few verbs *tight* is used in idioms as an intensive and is the only possible form: *sleep tight, sit tight. Tight* can be used only following the verb; before the verb use *tightly: The house was tightly* (not *tight*) *shut.*

**till / until** You can use *till* and *until* interchangeably in both writing and speech, though as the first word in a sentence *until* is more common: *Until you get that paper written, don't even think about going to the movies.*

If you've always thought that *till* is a shortened form of *until,* stop. As prepositions meaning "up to," both words appeared around 1200; the conjunction *till* is about 70 years older, with *until* not being used in this way until 1300. *Till* itself comes from a very old Old English word *til,* "to." *Until* was formed from *till* by the addition of the prefix *un-,* which meant "up to." So etymologically at least, *until* is a self-contained redundancy, meaning "up to up to."

The mistaken impression that *till* is a clipped form also has a few gray hairs. People started spelling it with an apostrophe in the 18th century, indicating they believed it to be a shortened form of *until.* Although *'till* is now nonstandard, *'til* is sometimes used in this way. It is a modern invention, dating from 1939, and is considered acceptable. But why bother with apostrophes when you can do without?

**too**

**not too** Some people object to the use of *not too* as an equivalent of "not very," as in *She was not too pleased with the results.* But in many contexts this construction is entirely idiomatic and should pass without notice: *It wasn't too long ago that deregulation was being hailed as the savior of the savings and loan industry. It was not too bright of them to build in an area where rock slides occur.* In these cases *not too* adds a note of ironic understatement.

**can't . . . too** Negation of *too* by *can't* may sometimes lead to ambiguities, as in *You can't check your child's temperature too often,* which may mean either that the temperature should be checked only occasionally or that it should be checked as frequently as possible.

**too beginning a sentence** *Too* meaning "in addition" or "also" is sometimes used to introduce a sentence: *There has been a cutback in federal subsidies. Too, rates have been increasing.* There is nothing grammatically wrong with this usage, but some critics consider it awkward.

**tortuous / torturous** Do you recall that *tortuous* mountain path that was so *torturous* to your feet? Although *tortuous* and *torturous* both come from the Latin word *torquere,* "to twist," their primary meanings are distinct. *Tortuous* means "twisting," as in *a tortuous road,* or by extension "complex" or "devious," as in *tortuous bureaucratic procedures* or *a tortuous explanation. Torturous* refers primarily to torture and the pain associated with it. However, *torturous* also can be used in the sense of "twisted" or "strained," and *tortured* is an even stronger synonym: *tortured reasoning.*

**toward** Some critics have tried to discern a semantic distinction between *toward* and *towards,* but the difference is entirely dialectal. *Toward* is more common in American English; *towards* is the predominant form in British English.

**tragedy / tragic** In literature a *tragedy* is a drama in which the main character is brought to ruin because of a personal fault, a moral weakness, or an inability to cope with circumstances. Usually the character contributes in some way to his or her downfall, and the extreme suffering that is brought upon the character tends to outstrip the audience's sense that it was justly deserved.

But in everyday usage people often use *tragedy* and the adjective *tragic* to refer to a regrettable event or a piece of misfortune. Some people object to this extended usage, noting it distorts the true meaning of these terms. But the Usage Panel has a more tolerant view. Eighty percent accept the example *The shooting was a tragic accident; the guard mistook the boy for a prowler.* If the circumstances of the event are less dire, the approval of the panel slips somewhat. Seventy-one percent approve of the use of *tragic* to refer to an idealistic student's dropping out of college in despair, and some panelists characterize this use as acceptable but hyperbolic.

**transpire** *What transpired last night transpires in the morning papers. Transpire* has been used since the mid-18th century in the sense "leak out, become publicly known," as in *Despite efforts to hush the matter up, it soon transpired that the colonels had met with the rebel leaders.* This usage has long been standard. It is a metaphorical extension of the word's oldest meaning, "to give off vapors containing wastes through the pores of the skin or the stomata of plant tissue."

The more common use of *transpire* to mean "occur" or "happen" has a more troubled history. Though it dates at least to the beginning of the 19th century, language critics have condemned it for more than 100 years as both

pretentious and unetymological. There is some sign that resistance to this sense of *transpire* is weakening, however. In a 1969 survey, only 38 percent of the Usage Panel found it acceptable; nearly 20 years later, 58 percent accepted it in the sentence *All of these events transpired after last week's announcement.* Still, many of the panelists who accepted the usage also remarked that it was pretentious or pompous.

**try and** The phrase *try and* is commonly used as a substitute for *try to,* as in *Could you try and make less noise?* A number of grammarians have labeled the construction incorrect. To be sure, the usage is associated with informal style and strikes an inappropriately conversational note in formal writing. Sixty-five percent of the Usage Panel rejects its use in written contexts as presented in the sentence *Why don't you try and see if you can work the problem out between yourselves?*

**unaware / unawares** *Unaware,* followed by *of* (expressed or implied), is the usual adjectival form modifying a noun or pronoun or following a linking verb: *Unaware of the difficulty, I went ahead. He was unaware of my presence. Unawares* is the usual adverbial form: *The rain caught them unawares* (without warning). *They came upon it unawares* (without design or plan).

**unexceptionable / unexceptional** Be exceptional! Don't confuse *unexceptional* and *unexceptionable. Unexceptionable* is derived from the word *exception* in its sense "objection," as in the idiom *take exception.* Thus *unexceptionable* means "not open to any objection," as in *A judge's ethical standards should be unexceptionable. Unexceptional,* in contrast, is related to the common sense of *exception* ("an unusual case") and generally means "not exceptional, not varying from the usual," as in *Some judges' ethical standards have unfortunately been unexceptional.*

**unique** Unique may be the foremost example of the absolute term—a term that, in the eyes of traditional grammarians, should not allow comparison or modification by an adverb of degree like *very, somewhat,* or *quite.* Thus, most grammarians believe that it is incorrect to say that something is *very unique* or *more unique than* something else, though phrases such as *nearly unique* and *almost unique* are acceptable, since in these cases *unique* is not modified by an adverb of degree. Most of the Usage Panel supports the traditional view. Eighty percent of the panelists disapprove of the sentence *Her designs are quite unique in today's fashion.*

Some criticism of the comparison and modification of *unique* no doubt stems from the word's use—and overuse—in advertising. For *unique* is everywhere. Who has not seen it in ad copy such as *Our city's most unique restaurant is now even more unique* or in claims like that for the automobile that is *So unique, it's patented?* In these examples *unique* is used as a classy-sounding synonym for *unusual* or *distinctive.*

But if you can't escape the modification of *unique* in advertisements, you

are also likely to find it in the work of many reputable writers, though without the exaggeration. When an art critic describes *the most unique of Beckman's self-portraits,* and a travel writer states that *Chicago is no less unique an American city than New York or San Francisco,* it is hard to see what is out of joint here. After all, if we were to use *unique* only according to the strictest criteria of logic, we might freely apply the term to anything in the world, since nothing is wholly equivalent to anything else. Clearly, then, when we say that a restaurant or painting is unique, we mean that it is in a class by itself. It might be easier to recognize that *unique,* like many absolute terms, has more than one sense and can be modified with grace in certain uses. For more on absolute terms, see **absolute terms** under *Grammar.*

More at **complete, equal, infinite, parallel,** and **perfect.**

**utilize** Some people complain that *utilize* is nothing but a pretentious substitute for *use.* It is true that you can often replace *utilize* with *use* with no loss to anything but pomposity. There seems little advantage of using *utilize* instead of *use* in sentences such as *Barbara utilized questionable methods in her analysis* or *We hope that many commuters will continue to utilize mass transit after the bridge has reopened.*

But *utilize* can also mean "to find a profitable or practical use for." Thus the sentence *The teachers were unable to use the new computers* might mean only that the teachers were unable to turn the computers on, whereas *The teachers were unable to utilize the new computers* suggests that the teachers could not find ways to employ the computers in instruction.

**various of** You sometimes see *various* used as a pronoun, as in *He spoke to various of the members.* Language critics have battered this usage for over 60 years as an unlicensed shift of an adjective to pronoun. But it is a justifiable usage since the pronoun *various* is used in much the same way that other quantifiers like *few, many,* and *several* are used. Be that as it may, 91 percent of the Usage Panel found *various* unacceptable as a pronoun in an earlier survey.

**verbal** With the possible exception of Samuel Goldwyn, who said "*A verbal contract isn't worth the paper it is written on,*" just about anyone who has ever made a *verbal* agreement knows that *verbal* sometimes means "spoken, not written." People have been using *verbal* in this way since the 16th century. Among the most prominent of these verbalists are Pepys, Swift, Fielding, and Dickens. This noble lineage has not deterred some language critics from insisting that *verbal* should only be used in the sense "by means of words" and that *oral* is the proper synonym for "spoken."

They may be wrong in ignoring the word's well-established use, but they are right that *verbal* can cause confusion. The phrase *modern technologies for verbal communication* may refer only to devices for spoken communication such as radio, the telephone, and the loudspeaker, or it may refer to all devices for linguistic communication, including the telegraph, the teletype, and the fax machine. In such contexts it's better to use *oral* or *spoken* to make your meaning unambiguous.

**wait on / wait upon** For more than 100 years, language critics have grumbled over the use of *wait on* and *wait upon* to mean roughly "await" or "wait for," as in *We are still waiting on management to approve the expenditure for new offices.* As the critics would have it, *wait on* should mean only "to serve the needs of someone." But it's hard to see why these phrasal verbs should be so restricted, especially when they have such widespread use as synonyms for *wait for* among educated speakers and writers. So don't wait on any more advice—go ahead and use them.

## wake

***wake, waken / awake, awaken*** The pairs *wake, waken* and *awake, awaken* have formed a bewildering array since the Middle English period. All four words have similar meanings, though there are some differences in use. Only *wake* is used in the sense "to be awake," as in expressions like *waking* (not *wakening*) *and sleeping, every waking hour.* *Wake* is also more common than *waken* when used together with *up,* and *awake* and *awaken* never occur in this context: *She woke up* (rarely *wakened up;* never *awakened up* or *awoke up*). Some writers have suggested that *waken* should be used only transitively (as in *The alarm wakened him*) and *awaken* only intransitively (as in *He awakened at dawn*), but there is ample literary precedent for usages such as *He wakened early* and *They did not awaken her.* In figurative senses *awake* and *awaken* are more prevalent: *With the governor's defeat the party awoke to the strength of the opposition to its position on abortion. The scent of the azaleas awakened my memory of his unexpected appearance that afternoon years ago.*
***woke and waked*** Regional American dialects vary in the way that certain verbs form their principal parts. Northern dialects seem to favor forms that change the internal vowel in the verb—hence *dove* for the past tense of *dive* and *woke* for *wake: They woke up with a start.* Southern dialects, on the other hand, tend to prefer forms that add *-ed* to form the past tense and the past participle of these same verbs: *The children dived into the swimming hole. The baby waked up early.* For more on this, see **verbs, principal parts of** under *Grammar.*
More at **dive** and **snuck**.

**want for** When *want* meaning "desire" is followed immediately by an infinitive construction, it does not take *for: I want you to go* (not *want for you to go*). When *want* and the infinitive are separated in the sentence, however, *for* is used: *What I want is for you to go. I want very much for you to go. Want* in its meaning of "have need, lack" normally takes *for: They'll not want for anything now that they've inherited his estate.*

## way

*Way* has long been an intensifying adverb meaning "to a great degree," as in *way off base* or *way over budget.* This usage is both acceptable and common but has an informal ring.

*Way* is also used in the slang of many younger speakers as a general intensifier, as in *way cool* and *way depressing*. If you are over 30, however, you may seem way ridiculous when you use it.

**way versus ways** In American English *ways* is often used as an equivalent of *way* in phrases such as *a long ways to go*. The usage is also acceptable but is usually considered informal.

**weaned on** *Almost immediately after their son was weaned from the bottle, he was weaned on wienies.* In recent years people have used *weaned on* to mean "raised on," as in *Moviegoers weaned on the* Star Trek *TV series will doubtless find the film to their liking*. At first blush, this would appear to be a mistake, since *wean* refers literally to a detachment from a source of nourishment. But the process of weaning involves a substitution of some other form of nourishment for mother's milk. So we sometimes hear that a child is *weaned onto* or *on sugar water*. The extension to figurative usages would seem to follow naturally. Thus a sentence like *Paul was weaned on Dixieland* suggests that Paul's exposure to this form of jazz began almost from the time he stopped nursing, that is, from a very early age.

**well** *George may look good, but he's not well.* English speakers have used *well* as an adjective as well as an adverb since Old English times, and the adjective *well* continues to enjoy a healthy existence. When applied to people, *well* usually refers to a state of health. Like similar adjectives such as *ill* and *faint, well* in this use is normally restricted to the predicate, as in the example above. *Well* does see occasional use as an attributive (that is, before a noun) as in Benjamin Franklin's "*Poor Dick eats like a well man, and drinks like a sick.*" It also appears in compound adjective *well-baby*, which is well known to pediatricians and recent parents.

*Good,* on the other hand, has a much wider range of senses that includes "attractive" (as in *She looks good*) and "competent" (as in *For a beginner, he's pretty good*) as well as "healthy."

**feel well / feel good** Some people insist that the expression *feel good* should not be used in reference to health but should be reserved to the description of a person's emotional condition. But in practice people don't often follow this distinction, and you should not assume that your readers will be aware of it. More at **bad** and **good**.

**wellness** Like the adjective *well-baby*, the noun *wellness* has the ring of a recent coinage and medical jargon, especially when used attributively, as in *a wellness clinic*, but the word is first recorded in 1654. Despite serving a useful function as a means of describing a state that includes not just physical health but fitness and emotional well-being, *wellness* has never received the acceptance of its antonym *illness*. Sixty-eight percent of the Usage Panel finds the word unacceptable in the sentence *A number of corporations have implemented employee wellness programs, aimed at enhancing spiritual values, emotional stability, fitness, and nutrition.*

**–wise** The suffix *-wise* has a long history of use to mean "in the manner or direction of," as in *clockwise, otherwise,* and *slantwise,* and these usages are fully acceptable. Since the 1930s, however, people have used the suffix in the vaguer sense of "with relation to," as in *This has not been a good year saleswise* or *Taxwise, it is an unattractive arrangement.* If these examples sound unremarkable, this may be because *-wise* has seen a lot of use in business writing and in informal speech. But the suffix has never gained respectability in more formal situations. A large majority of the Usage Panel rejected the examples cited above in one of our earlier surveys. You may save a few syllables by appending *-wise* to a noun, but you may thereby be injecting an unwanted note of informality into your writing. As an alternative, try paraphrases such as *This has not been a good year with respect to sales* and *As far as taxes are concerned, it is an unattractive arrangement.*

**wish** We normally use *wish* as a polite substitute for *want* with infinitives: *Do you wish to sit at a table on the terrace? Anyone who wishes to may leave now.* This usage is appropriate for formal style, where it is natural to treat the desires of others with exaggerated deference. Less frequently, we use *wish* with a noun phrase as its object, as in *Anyone who wishes an aisle seat should see an attendant.* Both usages may sound stilted in informal style, however, and you may want to use *want* instead.

**wish and was / were** Is it wrong to say *I wish I was rich* instead of *I wish I were rich?* For an answer to this question, see **subjunctive** under *Grammar.*

**world-class** The adjective *world-class* became current as a result of its original use to describe athletes capable of performing at an international level of competition, as in *A 10-second time in the 100-meter dash would put him in the first rank of world-class sprinters.* In recent years it has been extended to mean "of an international standard of excellence" and has been applied to a wide variety of categories. The Usage Panel generally accepts the word when it is used of things that naturally admit such comparison. Sixty-five percent accept the description *world-class restaurant,* and 53 percent accept *world-class sports car.* But the expression is not generally accepted as a vague way of emphasizing magnitude or degree. Only 7 percent accepted the sentence *Johann Sebastian Bach's 300th birthday will rank as a world-class anniversary,* and only 4 percent accepted a newspaper's description of AIDS as *a world-class tragedy.*

**wreak / wreck** *The boy wreaked havoc in the basement by wrecking his castle made of blocks. Wreak* in this sense of "to bring about, cause" is sometimes confused with *wreck,* "to cause the destruction of," perhaps because the wreaking of damage may leave a wreck. A storm should therefore only *wreak havoc,* never *wreck* it. The past tense and past participle of *wreak* is *wreaked,* not *wrought,* which is an alternative past tense and past participle of *work.* You may occasionally see the expression *work havoc* as well. This is an acceptable expression, but if you choose to use the past form *wrought havoc,*

don't be surprised if someone objects, for many people believe this is an error for *wreaked havoc*.

**yet** In formal writing, *yet* in the sense "up to now" is normally used with an accompanying verb in the present perfect rather than in the simple past. Thus you should say *He hasn't started yet*, not *He didn't start yet*. The use of *yet* with the simple past is common in speech and may be appropriate for informal writing.

# Science Terms

## *Distinctions, Restrictions, and Confusions*

The notes in this chapter discuss familiar words that have specific or specialized meanings in science and scientific terms that are easy to confuse. The chapter *Word Choice* discusses a few technical terms, such as *methodology, paradigm,* and *parameter,* that have been adapted for more generalized use.

**?**

**abductor / adductor** Standing upright. Riding a horse. Holding a glass, or a pen, or a paintbrush. Hitchhiking. Crossing your fingers. Spreading your toes apart so you can wiggle them in the sand. These are all activities that result from the actions of muscles known as *abductors* and *adductors*. Muscles that are abductors move body parts away from each other or from the trunk of the body itself. For example, an abductor muscle moves your thumb away from your index finger, allowing the popular "thumbs up" salute or the widely recognized sign for "thumbing" a ride. *Abductor* comes from Latin *abducere,* which is built of the prefix *ab-,* "away," and the verb *ducere,* "to bring." Adductor muscles, in contrast, bring body parts together or bring them closer to the body. It is a group of adductor muscles in the inner thigh, for example, that allows a rider to sit firmly astride a horse. Once the rider has dismounted, the same group of adductors works in concert with other thigh muscles to enable him or her to stand upright. *Adductor* comes from Latin *adducere,* which combines *ad-,* "to," and the verb *ducere.*

**absorption / adsorption** *Absorption* indicates an active ongoing process in which something is taken up by something else by various physical actions: *The absorption of spilled juice into a paper towel occurs by capillary action. Adsorption,* in contrast, describes the holding or accumulation of something, such as a gas, a liquid, or a solute (a substance that has been dissolved in another substance), on the surface of a solid or liquid: *The removal of dissolved gases from tap water is achieved by their adsorption onto a substance such as activated charcoal.*

**accuracy / precision** Imagine that you are a scientist with a measurement or calculation to your credit that has taken years of meticulous work. When your results are published, you find that your techniques are praised for their *precision* and your results are criticized for their lack of *accuracy.* How is this possible? We usually think of accuracy and precision as pretty much the same thing. But in science, these words are used in significantly different ways. A result is considered accurate if it is consistent with the true or accepted value for that result. The precision of a result, on the other hand, is an indication of how sharply it is defined. For example, the first few decimal places of the true value for the mathematical constant $\pi$ are 3.142, and the accepted value for the speed of light in a vacuum is $2.99792458 \times 10^8$ meters per second. Thus, 3.14 is an accurate value for $\pi$ to three digits precision, and $3.0 \times 10^8$ meters per second is an accurate value for the speed of light in a vacuum to two digits precision.

Consider the calculation of $\pi$ by William Shanks. In 1853 he published a calculation of $\pi$ to 607 decimal places. Twenty years later, he published a result that extended this work to 707 decimal places. This was the most precise numerical definition of $\pi$ of its time and adorned many classroom walls. In 1949 a computer was used to calculate $\pi$, and it was discovered that William Shanks's result was in error starting at a point near the 500th decimal place all the way to the 707th decimal place. Nowadays, with the benefit of a true value for $\pi$ to 100,000 decimal places, we can say that William Shanks's techniques generated a precise result, but the value he obtained was not accurate.

**albumin / albumen** The evolution of the words *albumin* and *albumen* represents a cockeyed sort of chicken and egg story. Did *albumin,* spelled with an *i* and representing a member of a class of proteins found in plants and animals, come first? Or was *albumen,* spelled with an *e* and describing the "white" of an egg, the progenitor? In this lexical tale, the egg wins. *Albumen* comes from Latin *albus,* "white," and as early as the 16th century, it was used to refer to the white of an egg. By the 1800s, *albumen* was being used to describe the substance that was a constituent of fluids and tissues of animals and of the roots and seeds of plants. Chemists in the mid-1800s, though, began to put a finer edge to things, determining that the type of protein represented by egg whites was part of a larger class of proteins that were chemically similar but had different forms and functions. The class of proteins came to be known as *scleroproteins* and the protein present in the white of an egg came to be called *albumin.* Thus we can say *The albumen of an egg is an excellent example of animal albumin. Albumin* comes from the combination of *album(en)* with the suffix *-in,* "neutral chemical compound." In addition to egg whites, this water-soluble, heat-coagulating protein is found in blood serum and milk.

**amount / concentration / level** How much is enough? What is the range for healthy individuals? Is it normal? These are but a few of the many questions often asked of health practitioners, nutrition gurus, and physical activity advocates by individuals worried about "numbers"—for cholesterol, body fat, vitamins, minerals, and more. And while the need to be precise about numbers can become a matter of personal pride, the usage of terms that give those numbers their proper perspective can become somewhat jumbled. In science, particularly medical science, *amount* describes a quantity or sum—the total quantity of a given component present in things such as solutions or preparations: *By the end of the experiment, the amount of reagent used exceeded 10 grams.* In medical usage, *concentration* is also used to describe a quantity but one that is set within the context of another quantity. Thus, the relative content of any substance that is dissolved or dispersed within a solution or mixture is referred to as the *concentration* of that substance. For example, the concentration of cholesterol in the blood is usually measured in terms of one quantity, *milligrams*, of cholesterol set within the context of another quantity, usually *deciliters*, of blood. The use of the term *level* within a medical context, in comparison, is usually descriptive rather than quantative, conveying a sense of the relation a particular range of concentrations has to a standard or normal concentration of a substance: *Although low compared with that of other individuals of her age and weight, her blood sugar level had remained consistent for the past five check-ups; therefore, no therapeutic action was considered necessary.*

**atomic / nuclear** The adjective *atomic*, although synonymous with *nuclear* when modifying *energy* and *weapons*, is quite distinct from *nuclear* when modifying *energy level* and *physics*. The difference is in the portion of the atom that is being described. *Nuclear* exclusively denotes the dynamics of particles associated with the core of an atom, including the protons and neutrons. This is where most of the mass of an atom is located. Thus, the nuclear binding energy between a neutron and proton in deuterium (an isotope of hydrogen) is 1.2 million electron volts. *Atomic*, when not synonymous with nuclear, denotes the dynamics of particles associated with the outer layers of the atom, the electrons. It is the configuration of electrons that determines the chemistry of an atom. Thus, the atomic binding energy of an electron in deuterium is 13.6 electron volts, a factor approximately 100,000 times smaller than the nuclear binding energy.

**author / writer** In February 1995, the discovery of the top quark spurred 2 4-page articles submitted to the journal *Physical Review Letters*, each including over 400 *authors*. Although an article with this number of authors submitted to a trade magazine might be an editor's worst nightmare, at a professional science journal 400 authors would be expected for a result 18 years in the making. Within scientific journals, the term *author* takes on a broader meaning than the term *writer*. An author is someone who has played a critical role in the outcome of an experiment or calculation. For example, an author might be the individual who maintains crucial laboratory equipment or develops a useful method of collecting data. In all cases, a writer is a person who has contributed to the actual writing of the article and is one of the authors.

The word *author* is sometimes used as a verb. For more on this, see **author** under *Word Choice*.

**average / arithmetic mean / median / mode** You may have asked yourself the question *Am I in an average family?* Other issues aside, the average number of people per family in the United States in March 1993 was 3.16 people. Depending on how you define 0.16 people, this is a pretty hard statistic to match. *Average*, in this sense, is identical with *arithmetic mean;* that is, the total of all items in a number of groups divided by the number of groups. Suppose that there are 25 families and that the sum of all the people in the 25 families is 79. Then the arithmetic mean for the number of people per family is 79/25 = 3.16 (the average number of people per family).

You may have had in mind a more meaningful statistic, however, when you considered the above question; that is, *Does the number of people in my family match the number of people in a mode family?* The *mode* is the most frequently occurring group. For example, suppose that 79 people in 25 families are distributed in the following manner:

| People per family | 2 | 3 | 4 | 5 | |
|---|---|---|---|---|---|
| Number of families | 10 | 6 | 4 | 5 | 25 families total |
| Number of people | 20 | 18 | 16 | 25 | 79 people total |

The most frequently occurring family is the 2-person family with 10 occurrences. Therefore, the mode family is the 2-person family.

Then again, you may wonder if the number of people in your family matches the *median* family. The *median* is the group with the number of cases above it equal to the number of cases below it. In our example, the qualities *above* and *below* refer to the number of people per family. Suppose that you make a list from 1 to 25 of the families shown above from the lowest number of people per family to the highest number of people per family: from 1 to 10 the list consists of 2-person families; from 11 to 16 the list consists of 3-person families; from 17 to 20 the list consists of 4-person families; and from 21 to 25 the list consists of 5-person families. The median point of this list is the 13th entry, because there are 12 entries before it and 12 entries after it. Since the 13th entry is a 3-person family, the median family is the 3-person family.

**axiom / postulate / theorem / corollary / hypothesis** The words *axiom* and *postulate* are synonymous in mathematics. They are statements that are accepted as true in order to study the consequences that follow from them. Suppose that you were studying a deductive system called Jabbermetry and the words *toves* and *mome* appeared in the statement "For every two toves *P* and *Q* there is a unique mome *PQ* that contains both *P* and *Q*." Given no other information, you would be unable to prove that this statement is true. In fact, this statement defines an important relationship between toves and momes; it is an axiom or postulate of Jabbermetry. Notice that if you are informed that Jabbermetry actually means Geometry, toves means points, and mome means line, the statement becomes more familiar: "axiom 1: For every two points *P* and *Q* there is a unique line *PQ* that contains both *P* and *Q*." Do not be misled by your familiarity with points and lines, however. It remains that this statement cannot be proven since you are given no other information and is thus an axiom or postulate.

Three other terms that occur in the hierarchy of deductive reasoning are *theorem, corollary,* and *hypothesis.* A *theorem* is a statement that is a logical consequence of axioms and other theorems. A theorem, unlike an axiom or postulate, exists only if a proof can be given for the statement. For example, if you allow the additional axioms "axiom 2: There exist three points not all in one line," and "axiom 3: Two lines $L$ and $M$ are parallel if they do not intersect or if $L = M$," then you can show that the statement "Two distinct lines intersect in at most one point" is a consequence of axioms 1-3; the proven statement is a theorem. A *corollary* is a trivial theorem, that is, a theorem that so closely follows another axiom or theorem that it practically does not require a proof. For example, a corollary of axiom 3 above is "If $L$ is a line, then $L$ is parallel to itself." The proof of this corollary is the definition of *equals:* "$L = L$ ." Finally, a *hypothesis* is a statement that has not been proven but is expected to be capable of proof. For example, you may hypothesize "If point $B$ is between points $A$ and $C$, then point $C$ is not between points $A$ and $B$." This is equivalent to a conjecture. If this statement does not follow from your present system of axioms, you may wish to include an additional axiom or make the hypothesis an axiom itself and see where it leads you. For the hypothesis given above, you may want to introduce an axiom that establishes a coordinate system.

Thus, axioms and postulates form the roots of a particular deductive system; theorems and corollaries are the logical consequences that fill out the deductive system; hypotheses drive theoretical development forward.

**bit / byte** The word *bit* is short for *bi*nary digi*t*, where a binary digit is a numeric symbol that can take on one of two values, usually 0 or 1. You are probably more familiar with *decimal digits*, that is, numeric symbols that can take on one of ten values: 0, 1, 2, 3, 4, 5, 6, 7, 8, or 9. The use of decimal digits seems natural to us because it is natural to begin our experience of counting using ten fingers. Within a computer, however, the natural system of counting is one that is based on two options: switches that are either on or off. You can think of it as an alphabet with only two characters. The table below indicates how you would count from 0 to 7 using bits.

| Decimal number: | 0 | 1 | 2 | 3 | 4 | 5 | 6 | 7 |
|---|---|---|---|---|---|---|---|---|
| Binary number: | 0 | 1 | 10 | 11 | 100 | 101 | 110 | 111 |

Notice that the higher you count, the more adjacent bits you need to represent the number. For example, it requires two adjacent bits to count from 0 to 3, and three adjacent bits to count from 0 to 7. This has important implications for coding and transmitting information. Suppose that you wish to assign a numeric code to each character on a typical computer keyboard and then you wish to transmit this information in bits. A typical keyboard has 101 keys. When you include the option of simultaneously pressing the shift key, a rough estimate tells you that you need to be able to count from 0 to 201. The minimum number of adjacent bits that we require in order to count this high is 8: 7 adjacent bits would allow you to count from 0 to 127 only, and 8 adjacent bits will allow you to count from 0 to 255. A sequence of 8 bits is so important that it has a name of its own: a *byte*. A handy mnemonic for *byte* is *binary digit eight*. Thus, it requires one byte of information (or 8 bits) to transmit one keystroke on a typical keyboard. It requires three bytes of information (or 24 bits) to transmit the three-letter word *the*.

**bug / insect** The word *bug* is often used to refer to any *insect* and sometimes even to spiders, which are not insects. Originally a term that meant a hobgoblin or scarecrow, *bug* had, by the early 1600s, metamorphosed into a term used to describe any of various insects or similar organisms, such as the centipede. But in strict biological usage, a *bug* (or *true bug*) is an insect having mouthparts that are adapted for piercing and sucking and are contained in a beak-shaped structure called a rostrum. Thus, an aphid, a leaf bug, and a stink bug are classified as bugs. All insects, including bugs, have six legs and a body divided into three sections—head, thorax, and abdomen. In fact, *insect* derives from Latin *insectum*, which is itself a translation of Greek *entomon*, "segmented, cut up," the source of our word *entomology*, "the study of insects." Spiders, on the other hand, belong to a group called *arachnids* and are characterized by having eight legs and two body sections—a cephalothorax consisting of a combined head and thorax and an abdomen.

**Calorie / calorie** An interesting question to consider is *How many calories do you burn just trying to understand what a calorie is?* First of all, we have to establish whether we are talking about *Calorie* with a capital *C* or *calorie* with a lowercase *c*. A *Calorie* with a capital *C* is defined as the amount of energy required to raise the temperature of 1 kilogram of water 1 degree Celsius (°C). Thus, it is a unit of energy equal to approximately 4,000 joules. *Calorie* with a capital *C* also goes by the names *large calorie, kilocalorie,* and *kilogram calorie.* This is the Calorie that you encounter when reading the cereal box in the morning or in any discussion of your diet. For example, you should read . . . *based on a 2,000 calorie diet* as . . . *based on a 2,000 large calorie diet.*

Alternatively, a *calorie* with a lowercase *c* is defined as the amount of energy required to raise the temperature of 1 gram of water 1 °C, or approximately 4 joules. *Calorie* with a lowercase *c* also goes by the names *small calorie* and *gram calorie.* Notice that 1,000 small calories equal 1 large calorie. The small calorie is the calorie that you encounter frequently in chemistry and physics class.

A precise understanding of calorie, however, requires an understanding of the nature of water. It turns out that the energy required to raise any mass of water 1 °C depends slightly on the temperature of the water. For example, the energy required to raise the temperature of 1 gram of water from 4 °C to 5 °C is 4.2045 joules, and the energy required to raise the temperature of 1 gram of water from 15 °C to 16 °C is 4.1855 joules. To remove this ambiguity, in 1950 the calorie was defined in terms of the joule exactly: 1 small calorie equals 4.184 joules exactly, or 1 large calorie equals 4,184 joules exactly. This definition corresponds closely to the energy required to raise the appropriate mass of water from 14.5 °C to 15.5 °C.

To answer the original question of this note: a 150 pound person (sitting) has burned approximately 1.5 large calories or 1,500 small calories since beginning to read this note. Work those neurons!
More at **Centigrade / Celsius / Kelvin.**

**catalyst / enzyme / vitamin** The word *catalyst* has been in use since the 1600s and comes from Greek *katalusis,* "dissolution." If this etymology seems slightly out of sync for a substance that helps other substances come together and react, consider that the term was first used to describe political situations, especially the breaking apart of governments. By the mid-1800s, though, the political meaning had been rendered obsolete and the term had become part of the lexicon of chemists. Today, a *catalyst* is a substance that increases the rate of a chemical reaction without undergoing any permanent chemical change itself. *Enzymes* are a special type of catalyst. They are biochemical in nature, are produced by living organisms, and are usually proteins. Deciding which term you should use depends upon the type of reaction you are describing. If the rate-enhancing compound is influencing the rate of an inorganic reaction, one that involves compounds that do not contain particular groups of atoms called *hydrocarbons,* the rate-enhancer is called a *catalyst.* If the agent of quickness is acting on hydrocarbon-containing compounds known as organics, the rate-enhancer is referred to as an *enzyme.*

Another type of compound that is often seen to behave as a reaction enhancer in the body is the *vitamin.* Like enzymes, these organic compounds are essential in small quantities for the normal functioning of the body. Unlike enzymes, vitamins are not made by the body; they must be obtained through the foods we eat. Originally thought to be incidental "ingredients" in food, vitamins were dubbed *accessory factors.* The term *vitamin* came into use in the early 1900s as a result of the research of Casimir Funk, a Polish-American biochemist. Funk discovered an organic compound that prevented a nerve-damaging illness known as *beri-beri* and named the substance *vitamine,* "live amine." Even though further research has shown that many vitamins do not contain an organic group known as an *amine,* the name stuck. Research has also shed more light on the pivotal role these nutritional necessities play in metabolism. In the body, nearly all vitamins are converted to *coenzymes.* In a manner roughly akin to that of an enzyme, a coenzyme acts by changing the location of groups of atoms, moving them from one type of molecule to another. This process, known as a *donor-acceptor* exchange, is important to the generation and storage of energy needed for the body's normal growth and functioning.

**cement / concrete** The terms *cement* and *concrete* are often used interchangeably—a usage that ignores the rich history and etymology of each term. The kinds of cement and concrete used today are similar to those used by the ancient Romans. After the Roman Empire fell in the fifth century, people lost the art of making cement and it was not rediscovered until the mid-1700s. *Cement,* from Latin *caementum,* "rough-cut stone," is made from limestone and clay that is crushed, heated, and ground into a powder. It is mixed with water and materials such as sand, gravel, and broken stone to make *concrete.* Cement and water form a paste that binds the other materials together as the concrete hardens, a process reflected in the etymology of the term itself. *Concrete* is a combination of the Latin prefix *com-,* "together," and *crescere,* "to grow." *Reinforced concrete* is made by pouring concrete around steel bars. Without this added strength, the building of modern skyscrapers would be impossible. *Prestressed concrete* is made by pouring concrete around steel cables stretched by jacks. When the jacks are released, the cables compress the concrete and strengthen it.

**centrifugal / centripetal / inertia** The word *centrifugal* is used to describe any feature that appears to "flee the center of," while *centripetal* is used to describe any feature that appears to "seek the center of." These terms have been used to describe the growth of flower petals and the transmission of nerve impulses. However, the most common use of centrifugal and centripetal is to describe the forces present in circular motion.

A centrifugal force is a force on an object that tends to move it away from a center of rotation and always results from the *inertia* of the object. *Inertia* is the property of an object proportional to mass that opposes acceleration. A centripetal force is a force on an object that tends to move it toward a center of rotation and can be a result of gravitation, electricity, or any other naturally occurring force. For example, if you hold a bucket of water by the handle and spin in a circle, you can feel the bucket pull your arms away from the center of your rotation. This is the centrifugal force and is a result primarily of the inertia of the bucket and the water. The effort that it requires to hold onto the bucket and keep spinning is the source of the centripetal force. You can "feel" the centrifugal force in this example, and you can observe (due to the circular motion) that a centripetal force is present. When Apollo 8 orbited the Moon in 1968, the centripetal force was provided by the gravitational attraction between the spacecraft and the Moon. The centrifugal force, which opposed gravity in this example, was provided by the inertia of the spacecraft and the astronauts. Because both gravity and inertia are proportional to the mass of an object, the astronauts could not "feel" either the centripetal or centrifugal force. This cancellation of effects that are proportional to mass is the source of weightlessness when in outer space.

More at **mass / weight** and **revolve / rotate.**

**Centigrade / Celsius / Kelvin** The history of naming temperature intervals can be considered a history of removing the ambiguity introduced by the word *degree.* In 1742, Anders Celsius, a Swedish astronomer, proposed dividing up the temperature interval between the boiling point of water and the freezing point of water into 100 steps. This is regarded as the origin of the *Centigrade* temperature scale. The prefix *centi-*, meaning "100" (as in *centipede*), is combined with the word *grade,* which is derived from the Latin word *gradus,* meaning "step." Thus, *Centigrade* means "100 steps."

In 1795, 53 years after Anders Celsius proposed a Centigrade temperature scale, the prefix *centi-* began to be used in the metric system to mean "$1/100$," as in *centimeter, centigram,* and *centiliter.* Later, in the 1850s, with the widespread introduction of the metric system, Centigrade started to cause confusion. This is because many European languages have a word similar to *grade* as their word for *degree.* For example, German has *Grad,* Swedish has *grad,* and Spanish and Italian have *grado.* Thus, scientific communications developed an ambiguity. When speaking of a Centigrade, did one mean the temperature scale or $1/100$ of some degree measure? In order to remove this confusion, scientists agreed in 1948 that the temperature unit *degree Centigrade* would henceforth be called *degree Celsius* and the symbol would be °C.

In 1954, the definition of the Celsius scale itself was changed. Rather than using the freezing and boiling points of water at 1 atmosphere of pressure, the degree interval Celsius was set equal to the degree interval *Kelvin,* and 0 °C was set equal to 273.15 degree Kelvin. Thus, the Kelvin scale became the fundamental temperature scale. Its fundamental unit was the *degree Kelvin,* with the symbol °K. Unfortunately, here also the word *degree* introduced complications as temperature measurements became finer. For example, the metric system dictates that 0.01 meter is equal to 1 centimeter. However, is 0.01 degree Kelvin equal to 1 centidegree Kelvin, or 1 degree centiKelvin? In order to remove this ambiguity, scientists agreed in 1967 that degree Kelvin would no longer be used to describe the fundamental temperature interval. The fundamental temperature interval would be called simply *kelvin* (with a lowercase *k*), and the symbol would be K without any degree symbol (°). The temperature interval in the Celsius scale, however, would retain the word *degree,* the capitalized *C* in Celsius, and the symbol °C.

Therefore, at the present time, the accepted way to indicate the freezing point of water at 1 atmosphere of pressure in the metric system is 273.15 kelvins, 273.15 K, 0 degrees Celsius, or 0 °C.

More at **heat / temperature.**

**characteristic / trait** You are going to the first hockey game of the season with someone you have never met. You have agreed upon a time and a place to meet and you have described what you look like—tall with curly hair, wire-rimmed glasses, and, in honor of the occasion, a Rangers jersey. What you have given your hockey chum is a list of your *characteristics.* A *characteristic* is a feature or quality that helps identify, tell apart, or describe recognizably a person or a group of people. The various features or qualities that qualify as characteristics can roughly be divided into two groups: acquired and inherited. Wire-rimmed glasses and a Rangers jersey represent acquired characteristics, while height and type of hair are inherited characteristics. Such inherited characteristics are technically referred to as *traits*, a term derived from Latin *tractus,*

"drawing out, line." In nontechnical usage, *characteristic* is often the term of choice, but in technical applications, *trait* is the preferred term to use when describing a genetically determined condition or feature.

**conduction / convection / radiation** The physical processes that are described by the words *radiation, convection,* and *conduction* all involve the transportation of heat energy. The difference between these processes is that each is associated with a particular type of medium and therefore a particular mode of heat transportation.

*Radiation* involves the transportation of heat through empty space, or the vacuum. Electromagnetic energy, such as light and radio waves, is transported by radiation. The light that warms your face from the Sun is a form of electromagnetic radiation that has traveled through 93 million miles of empty space. It is not necessary to have a complete vacuum present, however. When you heat a cup of tea in a microwave oven, the water is heated directly by microwave radiation, that is, by electromagnetic energy.

*Convection* involves the transportation of heat through fluids (either liquids or gases). Suppose that a portion of a fluid is heated. If there is another portion of the fluid that is colder, then the properties of most fluids dictate that a flow develops between the two regions that tends to mix them and bring them into thermal equilibrium. Suppose that you remove the hot tea from the microwave oven, and then you pour some cream into the water. Since water and cream are fluids, the method of heat transfer between them is convection. As the cream heats up and the tea cools down slightly, a flow develops and the cream mixes with the tea.

*Conduction* involves the transportation of heat through solids. In a solid, the constituent atoms are in fixed positions with respect to each other and flow is not possible. When a portion of the solid is heated, the atoms increase their rate of vibration at that point. This vibrating motion propagates to neighboring atoms—ones that are not vibrating as much—and thus propagates away from the source of the heat. Concluding with our hot cup of tea, suppose that you place a metal spoon in the cup and stir. The handle of the spoon that extends out of the tea heats up by conduction.
More at **fluid / liquid** and **heat / temperature.**

**congenital / heritable** The process during which a fertilized human egg develops from embryo to fetus to newborn is an exquisitely timed and delicately balanced one that is dependent upon the dictates of a multitude of genes. These genes carry a wealth of information including the *heritable* traits that elicit those post-birth coos from relatives and friends. Characteristics or conditions that are *heritable* are intrinsic to the genetic makeup of an individual and are capable of being passed from one generation to the next. Conditions or characteristics that are *congenital,* on the other hand, are usually not part of the organism's normal genetic makeup. *Congenital,* derived from Latin *com-,* meaning "together," and *genitus,* meaning "born," describes conditions or traits that are acquired either at birth or during the nine months of development in the uterus. Most often, *congenital* indicates that some factor, such as a drug, a chemical, an infection, or an injury, has upset the careful timing and balance of the developmental process in a way that adversely affects the fetus. Thus, a baby can have a *heritable* disease such as hemophilia, which can be passed on to future generations, or a *congenital* condition such as spina bifida, which cannot be passed on.

**contagious / infectious** *Contagious* refers to a disease that can be transmitted from one living being to another through direct contact (as with measles or AIDS) or indirect contact (as with cholera or typhus). The agent responsible for the contagious character of a disease is described as being *infectious,* the usual culprits being microorganisms such as viruses and bacteria or macroorganisms such as fungi or parasitic worms. Although an understanding of infectious agents didn't fully develop until the late 19th century, the notion of being contagious, or bringing about (disease) through physical contact, has a rich history. From the time of Hippocrates, disease was believed to be caused by miasmas, which were alterations of the atmosphere that arose from the earth and attacked the body. To the ancients, the miasmatic theory of contagion conveniently explained widespread diseases such as plague or smallpox. The scores of individuals who came in contact with these changes were inflicted with disease. Acceptance in the late 1800s of the germ theory of disease transmission—and its description of the role of infectious agents—laid the miasma line of thought to rest.

**diffuse / infuse / perfuse** The verbs *diffuse, infuse,* and *perfuse* have a "pour" relationship that is really quite close—etymologically close, that is. Each of these terms has as its basis the Latin word *fundere,* "to pour," with only their individual prefixes giving a glimmer of the fine distinctions in their usage. The Latin prefix *dis-,* "out, apart," that is a part of *diffuse* specializes the sense of pouring to that of spreading over a surface, through a space, or in a region: *A fluid or gas diffuses throughout a given space at a rate that is usually influenced by the surrounding temperature and pressure.* When used as an adjective, *diffuse* describes something that is spread out or dispersed and has a specific medical usage describing something, such as a disease, that widely affects the body or an organ: *The diffuse nature of the cancer ruled out surgery as a means of therapy.*

The verb *infuse* has the prefix *in-* as its first component. When a substance is infused, it is introduced, usually by injection, into something else so as to fill or cause filling: *A saline solution was infused into the animal's vein.* Chemists also have a specific usage for this verb. It describes the action of steeping or soaking a substance without boiling so as to extract its soluble properties. This activity is not just restricted to chemistry laboratories but is also one that is commonly conducted by many kitchen chemists who pop tea bags into cold water and set the concoction aside, allowing the tea to infuse the water with its flavors and colors.

In the verb *perfuse,* meaning "to cause to flow through," the prefix *per-*

is linked to *fundere*, thus giving a sense of "thorough, complete, or intense" to the pouring action. As with *diffuse* and *infuse, perfuse* has a particular medical usage. It is used to describe the action of artificially supplying an organ, a tissue, or the body with a fluid by circulating that fluid through blood vessels or other natural channels: *The organ was perfused with a solution containing a dye in order to determine the rate at which the solution diffused into tissues surrounding the blood vessels.*

**dissolve / melt** Suppose that you have a pot of boiling water and a tablespoon of salt. The salt is considered a solid and the water a liquid. When you mix the salt into the water, the solid disappears and you are left with a liquid, apparently. Did the salt *melt*, or did the salt *dissolve?* When a substance melts, it changes phase from a solid to a liquid by the application of heat. In the above example, if the salt melted, then a portion of the salt-water liquid is composed of pure liquid salt. Alternatively, when a substance dissolves, a homogenous solution is formed that is composed of two or more substances. The pure phase of the dissolved substances within the solution can be solid or gas. Since you do not know the pure phase of the salt within the salt-water liquid, you do not know whether the salt has melted or dissolved.

To decide the issue, you continue to mix more salt into the water. You will discover at a certain point that the solid phase of the salt no longer disappears as it is mixed into the water. Thus, the solid phase of the salt did not change, even after the application of heat from the water. The salt did not melt; it merely dissolved into the liquid water. At a certain point, the solution became saturated with salt, and additional crystals could no longer be dissolved into it. If you continue to boil off the water, you will be left with the original phase of salt as a solid. The actual melting point of table salt is 801 °C, well above the boiling point of water.

In the example above, a solid (table salt) was dissolved into a liquid. A gas can also be dissolved into a liquid. The carbonated water that is present in a typical soft drink is a solution of carbon dioxide gas that is dissolved into water at high pressure. If you open a soda bottle with carbonated water in it at regular atmospheric pressure and leave it open, the carbon dioxide gas separates from the water (much the same way that the boiling water separated from the salt crystals) leaving only the water, and other flavorings, behind. At such a point, the soda is said to have gone "flat."
More at **heat / temperature.**

**endemic / epidemic** "*The endemic and epidemic diseases in Scotland fall chiefly, as is usual, on the poor.*" So wrote the British economist and sociologist Thomas Robert Malthus in his 1798 treatise on population. In this work, Malthus gave dire warnings of the poverty and distress that would result if the world's population continued to grow unchecked. Yet the only population controls he could conceive of were famine, war, and disease, especially endemic or epidemic diseases. *Endemic,* built from the prefix *en-,* "in or within," and Greek *demos,* "people," describes a disease that is restricted to a particular region, such as cholera and plague in parts of Asia. *Epidemic*, built from the prefix *epi-*, "upon" and *demos*, is used to refer to a disease that involves many more people than usual in a particular community or a disease that spreads into regions in which it does not normally occur. Occurrences of influenza often result in epidemics. In fact, Hippocrates described such an epidemic that occurred in 412 B.C. But history has at least one example of an influenza epidemic that was so vicious it outgrew the classification of epidemic and became *pandemic*, or worldwide, in scope. The 1918 influenza pandemic killed 20 million people—548,000 in the U.S. alone—a toll that made it a tragic example of the effectiveness of one of Malthus's methods for population control.

Widespread disease in populations of animals other than humans is referred to as being *epizootic*, a term constructed from *epi-*, Greek *zoo*, "living being," and the suffix *-otic*, "specified condition or disease." Epizootic diseases spread rapidly, simultaneously affecting a large number of animals in a region. Foot-and-mouth disease is an example of a disease that can be epizootic. Some diseases that are transmitted among animals also can be transmitted to humans. Such diseases are known as *zoonotic* diseases, a term derived from *zoo* and Greek *nosos*, "disease." Anthrax and rabies are examples of epizootic diseases that can also become zoonotic.

**entropy** When the German scientist Rudolf Clausius introduced the word *entropy* into the lexicon of thermodynamics in 1865, he used a simple formula to construct the word based on his understanding of the etymology of *energy*. Intending for the prefix *en-* to mean *contents*, and the segment *-trop-* to mean *transformation*, he spliced together *entropy* to mean "contents that have been transformed." Although his goal must have been to give an unambiguous meaning to a newly defined thermodynamic quantity, he could not have anticipated how the various meanings of this word over time could be a case study in disorder and uncertainty.

Originally, Clausius intended for the entropy of a system to be associated with the amount of thermal energy put into a system that could not be extracted as mechanical work. Quantitatively, if a system is held at constant temperature $T$, and an amount of heat $Q$ is added to the system, then the change in entropy $S$ is given by the formula $S = Q/T$, where $T$ is the temperature given in absolute units, such as *kelvins*. Clausius was also the source of the thermodynamic principle "The entropy of an isolated, closed system is either numerically constant or increases with time."

As the scientific understanding of entropy evolved, a subjective sense of entropy developed that associated entropy with energy that is irreversibly lost and with disorder. Here, *disorder* means the number of ways that you can rearrange a system so that it looks exactly the same. For example, when an ice sculpture melts, the water molecules go from a fixed arrangement to a relatively free arrangement. Because there are far more ways to rearrange water molecules in a puddle (so that it looks like a puddle) than there are ways to rearrange water molecules in an ice statue (so that it looks like the same ice

statue), the entropy of the puddle is greater than the entropy of the ice statue. The disorder of the ice statue has increased through melting. This particular understanding of entropy was first mathematically demonstrated in 1896 by another German scientist, Ludwig Boltzmann.

In the late 19th century, the concept of entropy suggested to philosophers a physical means by which the universe would ultimately wind down. The combination of entropy as disorder and the principle of Clausius evolved into a narrative that could be stated: *the disorder and randomness of our world is only increasing.* In more recent years, as people have tried to explore the implications of this principle, *entropy* has been defined as broadly as "*the smashing down of our world by random forces that don't reverse*" (Stephen Leacock) and as "*the assassin of the truths of the Modern Age*" (Jeremy Rifken). In these uses, entropy is no longer seen as a thermodynamic quantity; it has become a dark force in the universe.

Despite the narrative force that the concept of entropy appears to evoke in everyday writing, in scientific writing entropy remains a thermodynamic quantity and a mathematical formula that numerically quantifies disorder. When the American scientist Claude Shannon found that the mathematical formula of Boltzmann defined a useful quantity in information theory, he hesitated to name this newly discovered quantity *entropy* because of its philosophical baggage. The mathematician John Von Neumann encouraged Shannon to go ahead with the name *entropy,* however, since "*no one knows what entropy is, so in a debate you will always have the advantage.*"

**exon / intron / axon** In 1844, when the American inventor Samuel Finley Breese Morse transmitted "*What hath God wrought*" as a series of dots, dashes, and pauses along a telegraph wire stretched between Washington, D.C., and Baltimore, Maryland, he inadvertently mimicked a cipher system nature has used for millenia—DNA and RNA. Each of the genes contained in DNA and RNA is composed of a particular arrangement of discrete "dots" or "dashes" of information, punctuated by "pauses" of noninformation. When adeptly translated by specialized cellular components, this coded information yields millions of protein "messages" that allow the body to function. The molecular dots or dashes are called *exons;* the punctuations of silence are known as *introns.* The terms *exon* and *intron* were first introduced into the scientific literature in the late 1970s when research began to show that a gene was not simply read from one end to another when a protein was formed. Instead, genes were found to be composed of information units that could be read, or *expressed,* in a variety of combinations, thus making any one gene the template to any number of proteins. *Exon,* then, is built from *ex*pressed and the suffix *-on,* "fundamental unit," a suffix that also is used in such words as *photon* and *electron.* Research also showed that exons did not exist in an unbroken string within a gene but were separated by *introns,* units of nonexpression that, at least according to current understanding, serve no function other than to provide silent patches between the information-laden exons. *Intron* comes from the combination of *intr*agenic, which means "within the gene," and the suffix *-on.*

The similar-sounding term *axon* is neurological rather than genetic and refers to the filamentous process of a nerve cell. Its function is to conduct nerve impulses away from the body of the nerve cell and toward other nerve cells or other cells or tissues. *Axon* comes from Greek *axon,* "axis," and first appeared as a neurological term in scientific literature in the early 1900s.

**fluid / liquid / gas** In science, the use of the word *fluid* applies to both *liquids* and *gases.* A *fluid* is a substance that does not have a fixed shape, and one whose molecular constituents move freely past one another. Thus, fluids take on the shape of their containers. The distinguishing feature between a liquid and a gas is that a *liquid* is a fluid that has a relatively fixed volume, and a *gas* is a fluid that does not have a fixed volume: gases can be compressed and can expand to fill a container entirely.

One exception to this scientific use of *fluid* is *bodily fluids.* Here the word *fluid* applies to liquids only.

**frequency / pitch / pitch class** In the vernacular of music, the *pitch* of a sound is completely determined by its *frequency* of vibration. Typical pitch standards in Western music assign a given frequency to one of the twelve notes in an octave: C, C#, D, D#, E, F, F#, G, G#, A, A#, B, and another symbol to indicate the relative position of the octave. For example, American Standard Pitch uses a subscript to indicate octave, and assigns to $C_4$ (middle C) a frequency of 261.63 vibrations per second. Thus, a sound with the frequency 261.63 has the pitch $C_4$ in American Standard Pitch. The *pitch class* of a sound is determined only by its note assignment and not by the octave in which the note occurs. Therefore, there are twelve pitch classes in Western music. $C_3$ and $C_4$ are in the same pitch class, but they have different pitches.

In acoustics, a sound is also quantified by its frequency of vibration. However, scientists refer to another quality of sound called *pitch* that is a subjective measure of the combination of the frequency and intensity of a sound. This is related to but distinctly different from the vernacular use of *pitch* in music. In acoustics, a unit of pitch called the *mel* (from *mel*ody) has a dependence on the frequency and the intensity at which a note is heard. For example, in acoustics, the note $C_4$ heard with an intensity of $10^{-4}$ watts per meter$^2$ has a different pitch than the note $C_4$ heard with an intensity of $10^{-2}$ watts per meter$^2$. In music, however, both of these sounds are considered to have the same pitch.

**fruit / vegetable** If only it were as simple as the difference between apples and oranges. But trying to tell the difference between a *fruit* and a *vegetable* often leaves people confused—and often makes guesswork out of complying with the admonition to eat 2-4 servings of fruit and 3-5 servings of vegetables a day. This is because *fruit* has two meanings—one popular and one scientific. In popular usage, a fruit is a plant part that is eaten as a dessert or a snack because it is sweet. This is why we consider apples and peaches fruit, but not peppers or lentils. But botanically speaking, a fruit is the mature ovary of a plant; it is a self-contained vehicle for reproduction of the type of plant from which it developed. A peach, for example, contains a pit that can sprout a new peach tree, while the seeds known as peas hold the potential for another pea vine. To a botanist, apples, peaches, peppers, peas, and cucumbers are all fruits.

A *vegetable* is a plant that is grown primarily because it produces an edible part, such as the leaf of spinach, the root of a carrot, the flower of broccoli, or the stalk of rhubarb. By this reasoning, all fruits must come from vegetables. Of course any child knows that we usually make the further distinction that vegetables are by definition not very sweet and are not served for dessert.

**genotype / karyotype / phenotype** Can you roll your tongue? Not bend it so that the tip points toward the back of your mouth, but roll it, bringing the outside edges together to form a tube of your tongue? If you can, you are one of 7 in 10 people whose genetic constitution, called their *genotype,* contains the gene for tongue-rolling. As the numbers indicate, a lot of people are able to roll their tongues, or as a geneticist might say, the *phenotype* of many people includes the ability to tongue-roll. *Phenotype* comes from Greek *phainein,* "to show." It describes a person's physical and biochemical expression of his or her genotype as well as a person's physical manifestation of various environmental influences. For example, a person's natural color of hair and eyes, blood type, and fingerprints are phenotypic expressions of genetically determined traits. An individual's hair style, altered hair or eye color, and style of eyeglasses or sunglasses are examples of phenotypic expressions of environmental influences.

Analyzing a cell's chromosomes, the cellular structures that convey genetic information, can give clues to a person's *genotype* and, ultimately, his or her phenotype. One method for doing such an analysis involves making photographic enlargements of the chromosomes after they have been arranged in an orderly manner, such as from largest to smallest. Such photographs are called *karyotypes.* An example of such an analysis is a prenatal test, a procedure in which chromosomes taken from a fetus are analyzed to determine whether any genetic diseases or disorders are present. An analysis of the karyotype of these chromosomes can help determine whether the baby's genotype would result in a phenotype marked by Down syndrome, Klinefelter's syndrome, or a similar disorder that affects physical and mental development.

**germ / microbe / microorganism** It's a classic line, "Don't eat that now, it has *germs* on it!" It, of course, is food that has perhaps fallen on the floor, slipped from a plate onto a roadside picnic table, or been shared with the family pet. The culprit called a *germ,* from Latin *germen,* "bud," is a nontechnical term describing a living organism, especially one not visible to the naked eye, that is capable of causing disease. A term that has a similar meaning but is equally nontechnical is *microbe,* derived from the Greek prefix *mikro-,* "small," and *bios,* "life." For situations that demand the meaning carried by *germ* and *microbe* but need the added benefit of technical rigor, the term to choose is *pathogen.* Derived from Greek *pathos,* "suffering" and the suffix *-gen,* "producer," *pathogen* describes an agent that causes disease, especially a bacterium, fungus, or other microorganism. The term *microorganism,* built from the prefix *micro-,* "small" and the noun *organism,* is a general term that describes all one-celled microscopic organisms, both disease-causing and benign.

**heat / temperature** *Heat* and *temperature* represent two different but related properties of matter. *Heat* can be derived from the entire energy of a quantity of matter, which is the sum of the kinetic and potential energies of each molecular or atomic constituent. Kinetic energy is the energy associated with the motion of each particle of matter, and potential energy is the energy stored in a particle as a result of its position or condition, as opposed to its motion. Notice that there are no restrictions on the kinds of energy that can be heat. The energy of an exothermic chemical reaction generates heat, as well as the energy $E = mc^2$ derived from the energy content of matter in a nuclear reaction.

*Temperature,* on the other hand, is a measure of the average kinetic energy per molecular or atomic constituent. Notice that two qualifiers are included in this statement: temperature is related to the kinetic energy only; and temperature describes an average property per constituent particle. Consider a large kettle of boiling water. If you measure the temperature of the water, you will find that it is 100 °C. Suppose that you capture the steam that is rising off the surface of the kettle and measure its temperature. You will find that the temperature of the steam is also 100 °C. Even though the temperature of the steam and the water are identical, the energy content per molecule of each is different. The molecules of water in the steam are at a higher potential energy than the molecules of water in the liquid water since it requires additional energy to overcome the molecular attraction that binds water molecules together in liquid form. This is the reason that being burned by steam at 100 °C is more damaging than being burned by water at the same temperature. The kinetic energy of the molecules are identical, but the potential energy of the steam is higher. Temperature is related to the kinetic energy only.

Next, consider a large kettle of water and a small teapot of water. Suppose that the small teapot has one-fourth the volume of the large kettle. Starting from the same temperature, it takes more energy to boil the large kettle of water than it takes to boil the small teapot of water. For every molecule of water in the small teapot that has an increase in kinetic energy, there are four molecules in the large kettle that require the same average increase in kinetic energy. It requires four times as much energy, and therefore four times as much heat, to excite the molecules in the large kettle to the same temperature as that of the small teapot. Thus, *heat* is a measure of the total energy, while *temperature* is an average property per molecule or atom.

**law / theory** Although the language of science strives for precision, there are terms that are used solely in their historical context even when other meanings may be more familiar. Because of this, it is easy to introduce an ambiguity into discussion. Take the term *law,* for example. In a legal sense, a law is a body of rules governing the affairs of a community. When applied to the natural world, the word *law* has the connotation of unwavering fact: a law of science tells you that this is the way that the world works. In the 17th century, when Newton devised his laws of motion and gravitation, the predictive success of this work was unprecedented. As far as could be practically determined at that time, Newton's laws always held. In fact, in 1846 these laws were responsible for the discovery of one of the planets—two hundred years after Newton's time. By analyzing the inconsistencies in the orbit of the planet Uranus, the Parisian astronomer Leverrier was able to predict the position of the as yet unseen eighth planet from the Sun, Neptune. Ultimately, however, unresolvable inconsistencies did turn up between Newton's laws and observed phenomena in the solar system. For example, the orbit of Mercury deviates slightly from that predicted by Newton's laws. By historical precedent, however, Newton's laws retained their names. New theories were put forward to account for these inconsistencies, as well as other problems in physics. The most successful theories to date have been Einstein's *Theories of Special and General Relativity*. These works account for the discrepancies in Mercury's orbit; they also predict many other new phenomena not even imagined in Newton's time. Thus, we have the curious state of affairs where Newton's constructions are referred to as *laws* and Einstein's constructions are referred to as *theories*, even though Einstein's theories have enjoyed far more predictive success than Newton's laws.

**mass / weight** Although most hand-held calculators can translate pounds into kilograms, an absolute conversion factor between these two units is not technically sound. A pound is a unit of force, and a kilogram is a unit of *mass*. When the unit pound is used to indicate the force that a gravitational field exerts on a mass, the pound is a unit of *weight*. Mistaking weight for mass is tantamount to confusing the electric charges on two objects with the forces of attraction (or repulsion) between them. Like charge, the *mass* of an object is an intrinsic property of that object: electrons have a unique mass, protons have a unique mass, and some particles, such as photons, have no mass. *Weight*, on the other hand, is a force due to the gravitational attraction between two bodies. For example, one's weight on the Moon is $1/6$ of one's weight on Earth. Nevertheless, one's mass on the Moon is identical to one's mass on Earth. The reason that hand-held calculators can translate between units of weight and units of mass is that the majority of us use calculators on the planet Earth at sea level, where the conversion factor is constant for all practical purposes.

**matter / substance / material** In chemistry, a distinction is often made between the use of the terms *matter* and *substance*. The term *matter* is used as a label according to one of the broadest criteria possible: whether an item possesses mass while it is stationary. If an item has mass when it is stationary, then it is part of the *matter* of the universe. Otherwise, it is classified as *energy*. At the level of subatomic particles, an example of matter is the electron, and an example of energy is the photon.

We now consider a narrower criterion. Consider the myriad of chemical properties that any large amount of matter can possess. The term *substance* is used as a label for a collection of matter with specific chemical properties. The smallest unit of a substance is an atom. The largest unit of a substance is a molecule.

Consider the sentence *Matter can exist in one of three states: a solid, a liquid, or a gas.* This statement is meant to indicate that *all* of the matter in the universe exists in one of three states. The focus is not on specific chemical properties unique to some molecules or atoms. On the other hand, consider the statement *Air is composed of the substances nitrogen, oxygen, argon, carbon dioxide, neon, and helium.* This statement illustrates two points; first, air is a mixture of substances and is not considered a substance itself; second, the chemical properties of nitrogen are distinct from those of oxygen, argon, carbon dioxide, neon, and helium.

*Matter* is a term that classifies everything in the universe according to mass. *Substance* is a term that classifies objects according to specific atomic and molecular properties. Between these two levels of classification, there is the vernacular classification we make use of every day—when we speak of metals, paper, and ink, for example. At this level of classification, we are not especially concerned with the specific, microscopic details of matter. A term that is sometimes used to classify the characteristics of an object at this level is *material.* For example, in a chemistry laboratory, the laboratory bench may be constructed of the material wood, the flask may be constructed of the material glass, and the safety goggles may be constructed of the material plastic.

**meteor / meteorite / meteoroid** Originally, the word *meteor* was used to indicate any type of atmospheric phenomena. People spoke of rain, hail, and snow as *aqueous meteors;* of wind as *airy meteors;* of the aurora borealis as *luminous meteors;* and of shooting stars as *fiery meteors.* Nowadays, this sense of *meteor* lingers on in *meteorology,* which is the study of the atmosphere and weather conditions. The word *meteor* itself, however, has narrowed in meaning to indicate fiery meteors only. As the name suggests, meteors were considered to be of atmospheric origin. Prior to the 19th century, the possibility that they came from interplanetary space was considered unbelievable among the general public. Thomas Jefferson claimed in 1809 that people would rather *"believe that Yankee professors would lie, than that stones would fall from heaven."* Popular explanations for meteors and the stones found where they fell ranged from clouds sweeping up dirt and raining down rocks, to bolts of lightening simply striking stones already in the earth. The term for a stone associated with the meteor phenomena is *meteorite.* Note the *-ite* suffix, which is commonly used to indicate a rock or mineral. Thus, *meteorites* are the terrestrial stones that appear to be associated with the fiery meteor phenomena, and *meteor* is used to indicate the streak of light produced in the atmosphere. The term *meteorite* is the second oldest term of the three, and the first citations for it in *The Oxford English Dictionary* place it in the 1820s. It was at this time that scientific opinion about the source of meteorites was beginning to change. An American scientist instrumental in this change was Huburt Anson Newton, a Yale astronomy professor. He predicted an 1866 meteor shower by associating the meteor phenomena with a comet that was due to be observed that year. Newton is attributed with the first citation for *meteoroid* in *The Oxford English Dictionary:* "*The term meteoroid will be used to designate such a body before it enters the earth's atmosphere.*" Thus, the terminology for Earth-bound stones from interplanetary space is partitioned according to the stones' stages of descent: a *meteoroid* is a stone in interplanetary space ranging in size from a speck of dust to a chunk about 100 meters in diameter—just shy of being an asteroid; a *meteor* is the bright flash of light produced by a meteoroid as it hits Earth's atmosphere and is also used to refer to the stone itself while it is in Earth's atmosphere; finally, a *meteorite* is a meteoroid that has survived the transition through Earth's atmosphere and rests on Earth's surface.

**mitosis / meiosis** Cells divide in two ways—by *meiosis* or *mitosis*. *Meiosis*, coming from the Greek word meaning "less," occurs in two distinct phases, each phase containing several stages. The activity of the first phase produces two cells. During the second phase, these two cells split again, yielding a total of four cells called *gametes*. Each gamete contains half the number of chromosomes—called the *haploid* number—that other cells of the body have. In mammals, these gametes are called eggs when they reside in the female and sperm when they are produced by the male. The other process of cell division is called *mitosis*, from Greek *mitos*, "thread of a warp," and the suffix *-osis*, "action" or "process." It occurs in four stages and produces cells that contain a full array—called the *diploid* number—of chromosomes. These cells, known as *somatic* cells, are used for the maintenance, functioning, and growth of the body and its parts.

**rad / rem / roentgen / gray / sievert** A complete understanding of the biological effects of high-energy electromagnetic radiation and corpuscular radiation is not currently available. In the face of this, scientists have devised a system for measuring the amount of energy that is transferred from radiation to an object as well as for estimating the relative damage that a particular kind of radiation can cause. The units that are used currently for sorting out the differences are the *gray* and the *sievert*. The gray and the sievert appear to be identical units because they are both expressed in terms of joules of radiation energy per kilogram of object. It is important to keep in mind their difference, however: the gray describes a measurable property of radiation while the sievert describes an estimated property.

The *gray* describes an objective property of radiation that can be expressed in simple terms: the amount of energy transferred by radiation to an object. An absorbed dose of one gray is equal to the absorption of one joule of radiation energy by one kilogram of matter. For example, the average person absorbs about 450 micrograys of cosmic radiation in the course of a year. The gray was adopted internationally as a unit of absorbed dose in 1976. Prior to the gray, there was the *rad,* short for *r*adiation *a*bsorbed *d*ose. The difference between the rad and the gray is a proportionality factor: 100 rads equals one gray. Finally, prior to either of these units, there was another measure of radiation absorption called the *roentgen*. Although the roentgen describes a different property from energy absorbed per unit mass, the effect of one roentgen on dry air is roughly equal to the rad. The *roentgen* is defined as the amount of x-ray or gamma ray radiation (electromagnetic radiation) that produces $1/3 \times 10^{-9}$ coulomb of electric charge in one cubic centimeter of dry air at standard conditions.

A measurement of "energy absorbed per unit mass" does not tell the entire story, however. Consider the difference between radiation composed of electromagnetic energy and radiation composed of charged particles. It is known that for a fixed amount of energy that is absorbed, the amount of biological cell damage is greater when the radiation is composed of charged particles than when it is composed of electromagnetic energy only. For example, beta rays are streams of electrons and alpha rays are streams of helium nuclei. Both of these types of radiation cause more biological damage per energy absorbed than x-rays and gamma rays, which are forms of high-energy electromagnetic radiation. An estimate of this damage is embodied in the unit *sievert*, which measures the radioactive dose equivalent. One sievert is equal to one gray multiplied by a relative biological effective factor, $Q$, and a factor that takes into account the distribution of the radiation energy, $N$. Specifically, if $E$ represents the radioactive dose equivalent in sieverts, and $D$ is the absorbed dose in grays, then $E = QND$. The factor $Q$ varies from 1 for electromagnetic radiation to 20 for radiation consisting of high-energy charged particles. Suppose that the distribution of energy of cosmic radiation is identical for both charged particles and electromagnetic energy and is equal to one: $N = 1$. If the 450 micrograys of absorbed cosmic radiation consist solely of gamma rays (high energy electromagnetic radiation), then $Q = 1$, and the average person absorbs 450 microsieverts of radiation in one year. Alternatively, suppose that the 450 micrograys of absorbed cosmic radiation consists solely of alpha particles (helium nuclei) with energies of 10 million electron volts. In this case, $Q = 20$, and the average person absorbs 9,000 microsieverts of radiation in one year.

The sievert is the correct unit to use when you wish to monitor the biological danger of radiation. The gray is the correct unit to use when you wish to monitor energy absorbed per unit mass. Prior to the sievert, the unit used to monitor the biological effectiveness of radiation was called the *rem*, short for *r*oentgen *e*quivalent *m*an. Similar to the difference between the rad and the gray, the difference between the rem and the sievert is a proportionality factor: 100 rems equal one sievert.

See also **conduction / convection / radiation.**

**reflection / refraction** In everyday writing, the word *refraction* occurs much less frequently than *reflection: They reflected on their achievements. This new theory was a reflection of her intelligence.* In nature, however, the process of refraction occurs just as often as reflection.

Refraction and reflection describe two different options that the front of a light wave, sound wave, or any wave can take when it encounters a boundary between two media. The media can be two dissimilar substances, such as glass and air, or it can be a single substance with regions that are in different states, such as air with regions that are at different temperatures. *Reflection* occurs when a wavefront hits the boundary and returns to its original medium. *Refraction* occurs when a wavefront passes from one medium to another and deviates from a straight-line path. For example, light passing through a prism is bent when it enters the prism and again when it leaves the prism; it is, thus, refracted. Light striking a mirror bounces away from the silver backing and is reflected.

The boundary between the media does not have to be abrupt for reflection or refraction to occur. Consider the fact that light travels slower through air than through a vacuum, and its speed through air is dependent on the temperature of the air. On a hot day, the air directly over the surface of an asphalt road is at a higher temperature than the air further from the surface. Because the speed of light is different in these two regions, we observe an image that shimmers. This is due to refraction. A similar effect is found in the upper atmosphere of Earth at night. The "twinkling" of stars is due to temperature fluctuations in the upper atmosphere and is also an example of refraction.

**renin / rennet / rennin** It was probably just another recipe swapped among Renaissance homemakers. To make cheese, first slaughter a calf, then remove the inner lining of the fourth stomach, pour in milk, allow it to curdle, remove the curds, squeeze them together to remove all the liquid, and set the unripened cheese aside to age. The initial component for this concoction—the bag made of a calf's stomach lining—was called *rennet*, a word linked to an Old English and Old German verb meaning "to flow" or "to run." Exactly why the rennet caused milk to curdle remained unanswered for a couple of centuries. Investigations in the late 1800s revealed the curdling was produced by a compound known as an *enzyme* present in the juices of the stomach. This compound, it was shown, helped break apart a protein called *casein* in the milk and, in the process, triggered the formation of another compound that then bonded to the calcium in the milk, forming curds. The enzyme was dubbed *rennin*, a combination of *renne*t and the suffix *-in*, "neutral chemical compound." This suffix appears in the names of other enzymes such as *trypsin*, the compound produced in the pancreas that breaks proteins into smaller bits for use by the body.

While the stomach is the site of rennin production, the kidneys are the source for *renin. Renin*, in fact, comes from Latin *renes*, "kidneys," combined with *-in*. When a major upset such as dehydration or hemorrhage causes the body's blood pressure to become dangerously low, specialized cells in the kidneys begin to produce renin. The renin circulates in the bloodstream ready to perform its very specialized task: it clips two component parts, called *amino acids*, from another blood-borne protein known as *angiotensin*. This newly abbreviated protein, now called *angiotensin I*, is clipped further by another blood-carried compound to form *angiotensin II*. This substance causes blood vessels to constrict, thus raising blood pressure back to normal levels and ensuring the continued proper functioning of the body.

**revolve / rotate** The verbs *revolve* and *rotate* are used in everyday writing to indicate cyclic patterns. For example, *revolving debt* is debt that is carries over from one credit card statement to the next; *crop rotation* refers to the successive planting of different crops on the same land. Although they are used as synonyms in everyday writing, this is not so in scientific writing. The difference between the two terms lies in the location of their central axis. If an object is orbiting another object, as the Moon is Earth, then one complete orbit is called a *revolution*. On the other hand, if an object is turning about itself, or rather, about an axis that passes through itself, then one complete cycle is called a *rotation*. This difference is epitomized in this statement: *Earth rotates on its axis and revolves about the Sun.*

**solar year / sidereal year / aphelion / perihelion** A *solar year* and a *sidereal year* both refer to the amount of time it takes Earth to revolve about the Sun. The difference between the two measures is in the reference point for one revolution. The Latin root of *sidereal* is *sidereus*, "starry," which itself comes from *sides*, "star, constellation." The Latin root of *solar* is *solis*, "sun." Thus, the difference between a solar year and a sidereal year is the difference in time between one complete revolution of Earth relative to the Sun, and one complete revolution of Earth relative to the constellations.

Consider the solar year. In order to establish the reference points for the motion of Earth relative to the Sun, we need to examine closely the orbit of Earth. The orbit of Earth about the Sun is not a perfect circle; it is an ellipse and the distance between Earth and the Sun varies over the course of a year. When Earth is nearest to the Sun, this point in Earth's orbit is called the *perihelion*. When Earth is farthest from the Sun, this point in Earth's orbit is called the *aphelion*. The time from perihelion to perihelion, or from aphelion to aphelion, is one solar year.

Suppose that at successive occurrences of aphelion (to the minute), you observed the position of Earth with respect to the constellations. You would notice a slight difference from year to year. You would need to wait an extra 20 minutes after reaching aphelion for Earth to be in the same position with respect to the constellations that it was at the previous aphelion. Obviously, this variation of Earth's orbit about the Sun with respect to the stars is slight. Since the constellations do not affect seasons on Earth to the extent that the Sun does, the difference between the solar year and the sidereal year is not of immediate importance. However, one direct result of the difference between a solar year and a sidereal year is the shifting of the North Star. When the Sumerians lived in the fourth millennium B.C., the North Star was Thuban in the constellation Draco. Nowadays, the celestial North Pole is near the star Polaris, on the handle of the Little Dipper. By A.D. 14,000 the North Pole will be near the star Vega. It will be 26,000 years before the North Star is near Polaris again.

**stalactite / stalagmite** A seemingly timeless usage problem in geology is the difference between *stalagmites* and *stalactites*. They are both examples of mineral deposits that form in caves, or speleothems. The source of each word can be traced back to the Greek word *stalassein,* meaning "to drip." This is appropriate since the source of each in nature is the dripping of mineral-rich water within caves. The difference is in their orientation: a *stalactite* is an icicle-shaped mineral deposit that hangs from the roof of a cavern, and a *stalagmite* is a conical mineral deposit that extends up from the floor of a cavern.

**transcription / translation** It is a concept that is accepted by most everyone these days: The double helix of genetic material known as DNA is the fundamental unit of heredity. These molecular maps use a unique copying process to duplicate their information, thus allowing then to continually send out the information needed to guide an organism's growth and functioning. This copying process is called *transcription,* built from the Latin prefix *trans-,* "across," and *scribere,* "to write." Far more than a simple letter-for-letter replication, transcription results in a strand of genetic material that is *complementary* to one of the two strands of DNA; that is, it is built of molecular entities that are the perfect partners to the components in that strand of DNA. This complementary molecule is known as *mRNA* or messenger RNA. True to its name, mRNA serves as an information carrier, moving from the area of the cell containing the DNA, known as the *nucleus,* to the area surrounding the nucleus, known as the *cytoplasm.* Once in the cytoplasm, mRNA takes up residence in cellular workstations known as *ribosomes,* locations that make it available to another form of RNA, known as *tRNA* or transfer RNA. Each tRNA carries an organic compound known as an *amino acid.* By interpreting the directions contained in mRNA, tRNAs position their amino acids in a particular sequence, a sequence that ultimately forms a particular protein, one of the multitude of proteins vital to the body's functioning. This process of interpretation is called *translation,* from Latin *trans-* and *latus,* "brought." Thus, through the cellular processes of transcription and translation, the information of DNA is neatly noted and cleverly transformed into a proteinic language that is readily understood—and used—by the body.

**turgor / torpor** *I can't talk about it now, I'm too stressed out.* Dealing with day-to-day events that cause stress can produce such symptoms as headaches, shortened tempers, and even silence. If the stress is long-term, the physiological changes can be extensive. The physical and mental distress, for example, of victims of *post-traumatic stress disorder* can range from flashbacks to episodes of violent behavior to a lessening of verbal skills and short-term memory. While many of the events we think of as stress-producing are the result of human-human interaction, so-called natural stresses such as heat or cold also trigger a variety of symptoms, or responses in living organisms.

Two such responses are the wilting of plants and sleeping in animals or, on a technical level, decreased *turgor* and increased *torpor. Turgor* comes from Latin *turgere,* "to be swollen." It describes the normal fullness or tension pro-

duced by the fluid present in plant or animal cells or by blood in the body's vessels and capillaries. When, for example, a plant is stressed by drought, the fluids held in specialized cellular structures called *vacuoles* diminish, lessening the pressure that the internal contents of the cell place on the cell wall. Less pressure, less opportunity to stay rigid. The cell walls buckle and the plant wilts. In contrast to this concept of pressure or tension, *torpor*, from Latin *torpere*, "to be stiff," is a metabolic response exhibited by some mammals. It describes a temporary physiological state in which an organism's body temperature drops and its metabolic rate is reduced. Thus, an animal is said to be in a state of torpor when it *hibernates* to avoid the stresses of cold and, perhaps, food shortages or when it *estivates* to avoid excessive heat or drought.

**xylem / phloem** *Up the xylem, down the phloem* may sound like a call to woodland insurrection. Instead, it is a useful device for determining which of these botanical terms is involved in what type of botanic activity. The vascular system of a plant consists primarily of the sturdy upward-conducting tissue known as *xylem* (from the Greek word *xulon* meaning wood) and the soft downward-conducting tissue known as *phloem* (from the Greek word *phloios* meaning bark). In herbaceous plants, for example, water moves from the roots to the leaves by way of the xylem. Nutrients from the leaves are, in turn, distributed down and throughout the plant via the phloem.

# Gender

## *Sexist Language and Assumptions*

Some of the most interesting changes that have taken place in the English language over the last 30 years have been driven by the desire to avoid, if not banish, sexism in the language. This reform movement is noteworthy for its differences from most previous reform movements, which have usually been inspired by a desire for English to be more logical or more efficient in expression. Historically, most proposed language reforms are ignored and end in failure. The few reforms that have become standard include the ban on *ain't* and the double negative, along with a scattering of "more rational" or simpler spellings like *primeval, rime, tenor,* and *theater*.

But the reforms involving gender are explicitly political in intent and represent a quest for social justice rather than a wish for more consistent logic. And unlike other political language reforms, which tend to be limited to individual names for ethnic groups, gender reforms involve basic grammatical components like pronouns, basic grammatical rules like pronoun agreement, and basic words like *man, father, male* and *female*. Some of these elements have been in the language for over a thousand years. It is not surprising, therefore, that the effort to undo them can often be a difficult and untidy business.

Despite this, the movement to reduce sexism in English has been remarkably successful by historical standards. Whether you agree with these efforts or not, there is no denying that they are widespread both in speech and in writing. A glance at any newspaper or five minutes in front of the television news will produce evidence to show that people are changing their language to accommodate concerns about fairness to both sexes. It is undeniable that large numbers of men and women are uncomfortable using constructions that have been criticized for being sexist. Since there is little to be gained by offending people in your audience, it makes sense to educate yourself about the issues involved and to try to accommodate at least some of these concerns.

Even if you are not convinced of the need for reforms to reduce gender bias, you ought to recognize that the use of language that has been called out as sexist can sometimes lead to ambiguity. Using a term like *policemen*, for instance, may leave your readers wondering whether you are excluding women police officers from the discussion or whether you are tacitly allowing *policemen* to stand for the entire police force. You owe it to your readers to be clear.

Of course, not everyone perceives sexist language the same way. People have different levels of sensitivity on these matters, and you must find a level

that suits you. Some people are comfortable using generic *he* but avoid the generic use of compounds ending in *-man*. Some people find compounds using *master-* to be sexist and avoid using the term *fellow*, as in *fellow colleagues*, to refer to women. Practice in these matters is mixed, and it would behoove us all to acknowledge the difficulty inherent in many of these usages and to agree to disagree.

Finally, it is important to remember that avoiding sexist terms and constructions is no guarantee that what you have written will be free of gender bias. Sexist stereotypes, such as the assumption that all nurses are women or that all executives are men, can seem like the status quo—the way the world "is"—especially when you are distracted by a deadline or concerned about some other feature of your writing, such as its organization or its tone. Sexist assumptions can be insidious. A headline that reads *Allegations Embroil Financier and Woman* may seem innocuous at first, but if the article shows the woman to be a financier as well, you have to wonder about the politics of the headline editor, who has assumed that a financier must naturally be a man and that a woman's professional status is somehow not worth mentioning.

The trouble with gender bias is that it often takes real effort to uncover it, even in your own writing, and you have to train yourself to look for it. You can begin by reading the following entries.

**alumna / alumnus** *Alumnae* and *alumni* are women and men who have been reared or nourished by their *alma mater,* their "nourishing mother." *Alumnus, alumna,* and *alma* are all derived from the Latin verb *alere,* "to nourish." *Alumnus* is a masculine noun whose plural is *alumni,* and *alumna* is a feminine noun with the plural *alumnae.* Coeducational institutions usually use *alumni* for graduates of both sexes. But those who object to masculine forms in such cases prefer to use *alumni and alumnae* or the form *alumnae/i,* which is the choice of many women's colleges that have begun to admit men.

**blond / brunet** Terms that came into English from French to designate hair color, such as the pairs *blonde/blond* and *brunette/brunet,* are sometimes treated in English as in French: the gender-marked form of the adjective or noun, ending in *—e* or *—te,* is used when referring to a female, and the non-gender-marked form is used when referring to a male. However, this has not always been the case. In fact, the history of these terms shows a mixed usage. As early as 1481 the adjective *blounde* was used of men's hair, and in 1683 Prince George of Denmark was described as being *blonde.* In 1860 George Eliot wrote of "*the blond girl,*" and in the 1930s James Thurber wrote, "*He was a quiet, amiable blonde youth.*" And there are numerous citations in modern prose of *blond* referring to females.

Recently, the usage of *blond* or *brunet* to refer to members of either sex has become more widespread among writers. This trend makes sense when you consider other French-derived words that have more recently come into wide usage in English and can refer to either males or females: *entrepreneur,*

*gourmand, restaurateur.* The obvious discrepancies in usage between words such as *blond/blonde,* which have tended to be gender-marked in English, and words such as *entrepreneur* and *gourmand,* which have not, suggests to some that the usage has at its base a sexist stereotype: that women are primarily defined by their physical characteristics.

Furthermore, you still see both *blonde* and *brunette* used with some frequency as nouns to refer to females, while *blond* and *brunet* do not have a history of this usage when referring to males. When you read about *a blond* (or *a blonde*) *entering the room,* you automatically assume it is a woman. In other words, it is easier for speakers of English to equate a woman with her hair color than to do the same to a man.

If you agree that these usages are sexist, you should use the adjectival forms *blond* and *brunet* to modify the noun *hair* or one of its synonyms (*a woman with blond hair,* not *a blond woman*). You should also avoid noun usages of these terms.

**domestic partner** Many people would now agree that the concept of family can include persons living together who may not be married or who may not be of opposite sexes. Few can agree, however, on how to refer to such persons. Many new words have been tried out in the 1980s and 1990s, but most of these have been dropped from general usage. Thus the linguistic situation seems to reflect the continuing flux of the social situation.

One term, *significant other,* which has been in use since at least 1985, is an all-purpose word for describing a lover, whether gay or straight, or a spouse, but this term is now considered somewhat outdated. *Spousal equivalent* or *spouse-equivalent,* dating from about 1990, is not widely used and in fact may be considered offensive in that it implies that legal marriage between heterosexual partners is the standard to which everything else is to be compared.

Another term, one originally used as a U.S. Census Bureau designation, is *POSSLQ* (person of the opposite sex sharing living quarters), pronounced (pŏs′əl-ky$\overline{oo}$). This term is problematic in that it is unwieldy and limits the liaison to one of opposite-sex partners. On the other hand, it is vague enough to include roommates who are not romantically involved.

A term that is gaining in popularity and is being used by some companies and organizations in drafting benefits plans that include all members of such nontraditional families is *domestic partner,* which has also been in use since about 1985. A newer term that is also gaining in use is *life partner.* And there are other terms that have a long history of usage, such as *companion, lifelong* (or *longtime*) *companion,* and *partner.* Some people consider these terms euphemistic when applied to gays and lesbians. These terms can also be misleading, even in general application, and you should probably not use them for this reason.

**epicene pronouns** People have long noted the need in English for a third person singular pronoun that can refer to a person of either sex, thus liberating us from dependence on masculine *his* in sentences like *Someone left ___ hat* and *A smart student keeps ___ papers in ___ notebook.* What many people do not realize is that English once had such a pronoun, but it fell out of use, probably because the linguistic need to specify gender was so overwhelming.

That pronoun is *a*—not the article *a*, but a reduced form of the Middle English third person pronouns *he*, which referred to a male, and *heo*, which was used for a female. These pronouns, which derive from Old English, came to be nearly indistinguishable when pronounced, and in some dialects they were reduced to a short syllable, spelled *ha* or *a*. Thus there existed a native English pronoun that could refer to a third person of either sex, at least in the nominative case. Unfortunately, this development created a problem that is the opposite of our modern one: people sometimes couldn't tell which gender was being referred to! *Would that be a (he) or a (she)?* In part to differentiate the genders, Middle English speakers began using *she* for the female pronoun. Just where *she* comes from is a matter of some debate, but it probably was an alternate pronunciation of *heo* that received wider use because it could be distinguished from *he*.

The common-gender pronoun *a* still survives today in some British dialects, along with the forms *un* and *hoo* or *u*, as a relic of Middle English *he* and *heo*. But for most speakers of English, an epicene pronoun is devoutly to be wished for. And people have been wishing for a long time. Artificial epicene pronouns for English have been proposed at least since the mid-19th century. Dennis Baron in his book *Grammar and Gender* has compiled a list of some eighty of these modest proposals that have been put forth over the years. We present a selection on page 174. Some of these proposals have been invented independently more than once. Some have been taken or adapted from other languages. Note that many are inflected for grammatical case just as *he* and *she* are.

In addition, concerned readers have sent their own pronoun proposals to the editors of *The American Heritage Dictionary of the English Language.* Among these are *che, chim, chis* (1985); *per, pers, pem* (1992); *ne, nes, nem* (1995); and *wun* (1995). *Wun*, whose plural would be *wuns* or *wen*, would also function as a substitute for generic *man*, and be used in compounds as well, as in *gentlewuns* and *wunkind*. No doubt other dictionary publishers have their own files of epicene pronouns proposed by readers.

Like most efforts at language reform, these well-intended suggestions have been largely ignored by the general English-speaking public, and the project to supplement the English pronoun system has proved to be an ongoing exercise in futility. Pronouns are one of the most basic components of a language, and most speakers appear to have little interest in adopting invented ones. This may be because in most situations people can get by using the plural pronoun *they* or using other constructions that combine existing pronouns, such as *he/she* or *he or she*.

Epicene pronouns have enjoyed some success in certain forms of writing, especially science fiction. Some Internet discussion groups also make a habit of using these pronouns.

More at **he.**

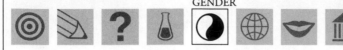

| Date | Pronoun | Date | Pronoun |
|------|---------|------|---------|
| about 1850 | ne, nis, nim<br>hiser | 1972 | tey, term, tem<br>shis, shim, shims,<br>shimself |
| 1868 | en | | ze, zim, zees, zeeself<br>per, pers |
| 1884 | thon, thons<br>hi, hes, hem<br>le, lis, lim<br>hiser, himer<br>ip, ips | 1973 | na, nan, naself<br>s/he<br>him/er<br>his-or-her |
| 1888 | ir, iro, im | 1974 | en, es, ar<br>hisorher<br>herorhis |
| 1890 | e, es, em | | |
| 1912 | he'er, him'er, his'er,<br>his'er's | 1975 | ey, eir, em |
| 1927 | ha, hez, hem<br>on<br>hesh, hizzer, himmer | 1977 | e, ris, rim<br>em, ems |
| about 1930 | thir | 1978 | ae<br>hir |
| 1935 | himorher | 1979 | et, ets, etself<br>shey, sheir, sheirs |
| 1938 | se, sim, sis | 1980 | it |
| 1945 | hse | 1981 | heshe, hes, hem |
| 1970 | she (since it contains *he*), heris, herim<br>co, cos<br>ve, vis, ver | 1984 | hann |
| | | 1985 | herm |

**—ess** Many people feel that sexist connotations may be implicit in the use of the suffix *-ess* to indicate a female, as found in words like *sculptress, waitress, stewardess,* and *actress.* According to this view, the sexism lies in the nonparallel use of terms to designate men or women: the ending for men, *-er* or *-or,* seems neutral or unmarked in a word like *sculptor,* and *sculptress* by comparison seems to be marked for gender, suggesting that a man in that role is what is expected and a woman is somehow unexpected or different.

While it is true that the specific terms *actress* and *waitress* are in wide use and are largely acceptable, in general the use of such pairs of terms as *actor/actress, steward/stewardess,* and *waiter/waitress* to indicate gender is sometimes considered offensive and is often unnecessary. For occupational titles, the use of *-ess* is usually considered inappropriate and has been almost completely replaced by newly formed gender-neutral compounds or by the *-er/-or* forms. When you board an airplane, for example, you are now assisted by a *flight attendant* instead of *steward* or *stewardess.* British peerage titles formed with *-ess,* such as *duchess* and *countess,* however, are technically correct and unlikely to offend.

The suffix has a long history dating to the Middle Ages. But several similar suffixes, such as *-ette,* as in *suffragette,* and *-trix,* as in *aviatrix,* also have long histories and have proved no match for the neutral *-er/-or* ending. So it appears likely that *-ess* will meet the same fate.

**–ette** The suffix *-ette,* used to mean "female," as in *usherette* or *drum majorette,* was attacked on etymological grounds long before it was widely considered sexist. Historically, *-ette* is the feminine form of the French diminutive suffix *-et* that occurs in borrowings such as *banquet, clarinet,* and *tablet.* This feminine form occurs in such words as *cigarette* and *lorgnette.* In the 20th century, *-ette* became fairly productive as an English diminutive in inanimate nouns, as in *kitchenette, laundrette, luncheonette,* and *novelette.*

But the use of *-ette* to form nouns referring to women is a separate development that probably comes from its use in French to form feminine versions of masculine names, as in *Antoinette* and *Paulette.* The suffix was first applied in this sense to an English common noun in *suffragette,* which became the recognized term for women involved in the suffrage movement in England. *Suffragette* was always considered insulting by the suffragists in the United States. Nonetheless, *suffragette* served as the model for a number of words that referred to women who occupied positions once reserved for men, such as *chaufferette* and *sailorette,* but of these only *usherette* and *drum majorette* have survived. Even in these two terms, the use of *-ette* in this sense is often considered sexist for the same reason that people criticize the use of *-ess:* it implies that the unmarked form of the term, reserved for males, is the standard. But *-ette* carries with it the additional insult of being at heart a diminutive and therefore may be viewed as patronizing and belittling.

**father** People have been using the verb *father* to mean "to perform the child-rearing functions of a father" since at least 1987. Its use as a verbal noun, as in *He devoted the day to fathering,* is now quite common and is recorded in such respectable sources as *Newsweek, The Washington Post,* and *The Arizona Republic.* But its use as a verb, as in *He felt he was fathering as much as he could,* is rare.

Like the analogous sense of *parent,* however, this sense of *father* is still stigmatized by the Usage Panel: 64 percent of the members find the term unacceptable. This may be because of tension between the child-rearing usage and the word's older meaning of "to beget."
More at **parent.**

**female / male** Contrary to popular opinion, the word *female* is not derived from *male,* nor is it even related. In this case, women preceded men. *Female* comes from the Latin word *femella,* "young woman, girl," which was a diminuitive of *femina,* "woman." *Female* came into English by way of Old French

around 1330 and was first spelled *femele*. *Male* came along in 1373, also from Latin via Old French. But *male* derives from the Latin *masculus*, a diminutive of *mas*, "male." As early as 1380 *femelle* began to be influenced by *male*, and spellings with an *a* began to appear. Eventually, *female* became the standard English spelling.

When used to refer to persons, *male* and *female* should be used in parallel and only when relevant: *Male and female guards were assigned to the rest rooms.* Often people use *female* and *male* in a way that draws attention to something perceived as unusual without realizing they are doing this. When the sex of the person performing a job is irrelevant, phrases like *a female police officer* and *a male nurse* are viewed by many as offensive, since the gender marking is gratuitous and carries the implication that the norm in certain professions, such as police work, is to be a man and that the norm in other professions, such as nursing, is to be a woman.

As nouns, *male* and *female* are generally used in technical, medical, or scientific writing, often to refer to groups of subjects in an experiment, whether humans or other animals: *The control group consisted of twelve females and eleven males.* Since *male* and *female* are used so much in zoology to designate animals, their application to people can sometimes have comical overtones. Nevertheless, they represent a convenient way to avoid repeating phrases like *a boy or a man* and *girls and women: This disease usually affects females.*

**feminist** The word *feminist* first appeared in print in 1894 and was coined as the adjective for *feminism*, which appeared in 1851. The agent noun *feminist* is first recorded in print in 1904. Originally, *feminist* only referred to women supporters of women's rights. But the word—whether noun or adjective—now refers to a person of either sex, as in *Yes, men can be feminists.* Eighty-six percent of the Usage Panel approves of this usage.

**gender / sex** Traditionally, writers have used the term *gender* to refer to the grammatical categories of masculine, feminine, and neuter, as in languages such as French or Spanish whose nouns and adjectives carry such distinctions. In recent years, however, more people have been using the word to refer to sex-based categories, as in phrases such as *gender gap* (as in voting trends) and *politics of gender.* Anthropologists especially like to maintain a distinction between the terms *gender* and *sex,* reserving *sex* for reference to the biological categories of male and female and using *gender* to refer to social or cultural categories, such as different gender roles in a religious organization. According to this distinction, you would say *The effectiveness of the treatment appears to depend on the sex* (not *gender*) *of the patient* but *In society, gender* (not *sex*) *roles are clearly defined.* A majority of the Usage Panel approves of this distinction, but opinions are mixed. In a sentence similar to the first one above, 51 percent choose *sex,* 31 percent choose *gender,* and 17 percent would allow both. Similarly, for the example *Sex/gender differences are more likely to be clearly defined in peasant societies,* 47 percent prefer *gender,* 38 percent would use *sex,* and 15 percent would allow both words.

**guy** Used in the singular, *guy* is an informal noun that refers to a man or boy. Its feminine equivalent is the equally informal, though probably less common, term *gal*. So, for example, if you are separating two groups of students for a session in line dancing, everyone will know what you mean when you say, "*Guys* to the left and *gals* to the right." Similarly, every girl knows how to interpret a "Guys Only" sign outside her brother's bedroom door.

In the plural, *guy* is used to refer to a group of men, to a mixed group of men and women, or even (though less frequently) to a group of girls or women.

## he

***he* as generic pronoun** Many writers of English have traditionally used the pronouns *he, him,* and *his* as generic or gender-neutral singular pronouns in formal writing, as in *A novelist should write about what he knows best* and *No one seems to take any pride in his work anymore.* However, whether *he* really refers to both genders or can be considered gender-neutral is questionable, since many people feel that it can only designate a male who is supposed to be taken as the representative member of the group referred to. When many occupations and public offices were held exclusively by men, using *he* in this way was unremarkable. For example, the sentence *Each member of Congress is answerable to his constituents* could raise no objections throughout most of U.S. history, as Congress was occupied exclusively by men, and there was scant possibility of women holding office. But the argument for the continued use of the so-called masculine generic in formal English gets more shaky every day, with women becoming more visible in all aspects of public life; instead the singular masculine pronouns now seem best used when referring to a group of men—and when used in this way they parallel the singular feminine pronouns.

Nonetheless, the use of the masculine pronoun as generic still has its advocates: in a series of sample sentences such as *A taxpayer who fails to disclose the source of _____ income can be prosecuted under the new law,* 37 percent of the Usage Panel completed the sentences with the masculine pronoun.

But if you don't like the traditional usage or feel it is sexist, you will want to avoid generic *he.*

### alternatives to *he*

***she* as generic pronoun** Some writers avoid generic *he* simply by using *she,* as if to make up for *she*'s neglect over the centuries. This practice is more common than you might think. In a 1989 article from the *Los Angeles Times,* for example, writer Dan Sullivan notes, "*What's wrong with reinventing the wheel? Every artist has to do so in her search for the medium that will best express her angle of vision.*" And Alice Walker writes in 1991, "*A person's work is her only signature.*" You may find this usage needlessly brings the issue of gender to the forefront of the discussion, distracting the reader, but the same argument can be leveled against using generic *he.* Using *she* still carries an air of unconventionality, which may be why only three percent of the Usage Panel recommends it in sentences like *A taxpayer who fails to disclose the source of _____ income can be prosecuted under the new law.*

**alternating *he* and *she*** Some writers switch between *he* and *she* in alternating sentences, paragraphs, or chapters. This practice has been gaining acceptance. You see it especially in books about child development (where the need for a generic pronoun is pervasive) and in academic journals, where you might see a passage such as *The researcher should note that at this point in the experiment she may need to recheck all data for errors* followed later in the same section by *The researcher should record his notes carefully at this stage.* At first glance, you might find this cumbersome, but if the context clearly requires generic pronouns, alternating between *he* and *she* can offer a balanced way of proceeding.

**compound and coordinate forms** Forms such as *he/she, she/he, he or she, her or him,* and so on, offer another solution to this problem. The Usage Panel looks favorably on many of these alternatives, especially in formal writing. For the sentence *A patient who doesn't accurately report _____ sexual history to the physician runs a risk of misdiagnosis,* 51 percent of the panel would use *his or her,* and another 8 percent would use *his/her* or *her/his.* These forms are grammatically unexceptionable, but they can be cumbersome in situations requiring their repeated use.

**zero pronoun / indefinite or definite articles** There are occasions when you do not need to use a pronoun at all, although people often do anyway. The sentence *A writer who draws on personal experience for _____ material should not be surprised if the reviewers seize on that fact* is actually complete as it stands and needs no pronoun. It is good policy to try sentences like these without the pronoun to see how they sound.

In other situations the indefinite or definite article will serve nicely. Thus you can complete sentences like *A child who develops this sort of rash on _____ hands should probably be kept at home for a couple of days* and *Every student handed in _____ assignment* with the definite article *the.* And you can use the indefinite article *a* or *an* in sentences like *A parent who feels _____ child has been treated unfairly should bring the matter up with the principal* and *Every student handed in _____ assignment.* In such cases these solutions are perfectly acceptable, but it may not always be idiomatic to replace a pronoun with an article.

**the plural / *they*** Perhaps the easiest and most effective alternative to generic *he* is to write in the plural: *All the students handed in their assignments, Taxpayers must appear for their hearings in person,* and so on.

***they* with singular antecedent** The alternative to the masculine generic with the longest and most distinguished history in English is the third-person plural pronoun. Recognized writers have used *they, them, themselves,* and *their* to refer to singular nouns such as *one, a person, an individual,* and *each* since the 1300s. For example, in 1759 the Earl of Chesterfield wrote, "*If a person is born of a…gloomy temper…they cannot help it,*" and, echoing this sentiment, W. M. Thackeray wrote in *Vanity Fair* in 1848, "*A person can't help their birth.*"

Modern writers of note, from George Bernard Shaw to Anne Morrow Lindbergh, have also used this construction, in sentences such as *To do a per-*

*son in* means *to kill them* and *When you love someone you do not love them all the time.* The practice is widespread and can be found in such mainstream publications as *Christian Science Monitor, The Washington Post, Discover,* and *Wall Street Journal.*

The use of the plural pronoun to refer to a singular noun or pronoun is hardly restricted to writing, however. Its use is so common in speech as to go without being noticed. And it is a favorite among advertisers, as in the slogan *In matters of taste, to each their own.*

When people shy away from using *they* to refer to a singular antecedent, it is usually out of respect for the traditional grammatical rule concerning pronoun agreement. Most of the Usage Panel rejects the use of *they* with singular antecedents as ungrammatical, even in informal speech. Eighty-two percent find the sentence *The typical student in the program takes about six years to complete their course work* unacceptable. Interestingly enough, panel members seem to make a distinction between singular nouns, such as *the typical student* and *a person,* and pronouns that are grammatically singular but semantically plural, such as *anyone, everyone,* and *no one.* Sixty-four percent of panel members accept the sentence *No one is willing to work for those wages anymore, are they?* in informal speech. Many writers might now consider this too fine a distinction—rejecting *they* for singular nouns but allowing it for singular pronouns that are plural in meaning—perhaps because they feel it will be missed by readers, who might merely think that the writer is being inconsistent.

**epicene pronouns** Some writers use common-gender pronouns that people have invented. These range from the somewhat common (*s/he*) to the downright obscure (*ip, wun*). Writers who use these forms often are trying to make a point about the role of the masculine generic in maintaining the invisibility of women in society. Books written using only these specially coined pronouns have the unusual virtue of concealing the sex of a character.

More at **epicene pronouns**.

**hero / heroine** Many writers now consider *hero,* long restricted to males, to be a gender-neutral term. Its use to refer to admired men or women is increasing; 63 percent of the Usage Panel approves of the word as used to describe Rosa Parks, the woman who galvanized the civil rights movement in the United States by refusing to give up her seat on a Montgomery bus. The word *heroine* is still useful and acceptable, however, in referring to the principal female character of a fictional work such as a novel or a dramatic production: *Jane Eyre is a well-known literary heroine.* Ninety-four percent of usage panelists accept this usage.

**lady** *Lady* is normally used as a parallel to *gentleman* to emphasize norms expected in polite society or in situations requiring courtesies: *Ladies and gentlemen, your attention, please.* If you are trying to describe a woman with a strict adherence to rules of correct behavior, you might call her a *lady;* and if you use the word *lady,* it will probably be interpreted in this way. In much the same way, *gentleman* brings to mind a man of refinement. Thus, you might say *I met a nice woman at the zoning board meeting last night* but *My five-year-old behaved like a lady throughout the afternoon tea party.*

Many people consider the attributive use of *lady*, as in *lady doctor*, offensive and outdated. When the sex of a person is relevant, the preferred term for this usage is *woman*.

*Lady* also sees productive use in speech as a sarcastic epithet for a rude or inept woman who is a stranger, as in *Hey, lady, I was in line before you!*

**man** Traditionally, many writers have used *man* and certain compounds derived from it to designate any or all members of the human race regardless of sex. This practice has the strength of history on its side. In Old English the principal sense of *man* meant "a human being"; the words *wer* and *wyf* (or *woepman* and *wifman*) were used to refer to "a male human being" and "a female human being" respectively. But in Middle English *man* displaced *wer* as the term for "a male human being," while *wyfman* (the word that evolved into present-day *woman*) was retained for "a female human being." Despite this change, *man* continued to carry its original sense of "a human being" as well, and so the result is an asymmetrical arrangement that many criticize as sexist: *man* can stand for all people, but *woman* cannot. Because of a growing belief that *man* and words formed from it are not inclusive of women, more and more writers are showing an unwillingness to use the word *man* in its sense of "a human being" or *men* in its sense of "members of the human race."

Another concern about the use of generic *man* is that it can often be ambiguous, at least in the plural, since *men* can refer exclusively to adult human males, and for this reason too you may want to avoid it. There are a number of ways to reword such sentences as *The capacity for making tools is unique to men*, for example. When you are talking about the human race, you may substitute such words as *humans, humanity, humankind,* or *the human race.* And in sentences such as *Man has* (or *men have*) *long yearned to unlock the secrets of the atom,* you may substitute the word *people* for *man* or *men*, often with a gain in clarity.

Sometimes these alternative wordings sound tinny. This is because they are not monosyllables, and rhythm sometimes makes a monosyllable like *man* particularly alluring. Consider titles, for instance. There is a strong iambic beat to Jacob Bronowski's *The Ascent of Man,* and a strong finish to Victor McKusick's *Mendelian Inheritance in Man.* Somehow *The Ascent of Humanity* and *Mendelian Inheritance in Humans* are just not as musical. Here if you want to avoid *man,* you simply have to bid farewell to the old song and compose an entirely new construction with a rhythm that benefits from polysyllabic words.

Despite the objections to the generic use of *man,* a majority of Usage Panel members still approve of it. Not surprisingly, the women members are significantly less enthusiatic than the men. For example, the sentence *If early man suffered from a lack of information, modern man is tyrannized by an excess of it* is acceptable to 81 percent of the panel—but a breakdown by sex shows that only

58 percent of the women panelists accept it, while 92 percent of the men do.

A majority of the panel also accepts compound words derived from generic *man.* The sentence *The Great Wall is the only man-made structure visible from space* is acceptable to 86 percent, and in this case the gender gap narrows: 76 percent of the women accept it, as well as 91 percent of the men. The sentence "*The history of language is the history of mankind*" (James Bradstreet Greenough and George Lyman Kittredge) is acceptable to a majority of 76 percent, which includes 63 percent of the women and 82 percent of the men. Such compounds are significantly less acceptable when applied to women, however; only 66 percent of the panel members (57 percent of the women and 71 percent of the men) accept the use of the word *manpower* as it applies specifically to women.

A related set of problems is raised by the use of *man* in forming the names of occupational and social roles, such as *businessman, chairman, spokesman, layman,* and *freshman,* as well as in formations like *unsportsmanlike* and *showmanship.* For more on this, see **-man compounds**.

*Man* is also used as a verb. This is another time-honored usage, going back to the Middle Ages, that many people consider sexist when the subject includes or is limited to women. Fifty-six percent of the Usage Panel rejects the verb when it is used in the sense "to take stations at" to refer to an activity performed by women in the sentence *Members of the League of Women Voters will be manning the registration desk.* As a verb *man* was originally a military or nautical term and like the pronoun *he* is unobjectionable in most historical contexts: in the days when only men manned the decks, there was no need for a different word to include women. But a wise man would admit that those days are past.

More at **he.**

**-man compounds** There are many compounds in English that are formed with *man* as the second element: words that describe occupations, such as *alderman, councilman, deliveryman, fireman,* and *postman;* words that describe one's place in society, such as *nobleman* and *workingman;* even words that describe skills, such as *craftsmanship, horsemanship, showmanship,* and *sportsmanship.* In the past people have usually used these words of men and women indiscriminately, but now writers are increasingly using other, more inclusive terms in place of these, especially in the area of occupational titles.

In general, the Usage Panel is more accepting of *-man* compounds in words describing social roles, such as *layman* and *freshman,* than in occupational terms, such as *spokesman* and *businessman.* This may be because the panel views the occupational distinctions as having unjust economic consequences. A majority of the panel also accepts words based on *-man* when they refer to a role or class in the abstract, but when they refer specifically to a woman, the panel tends to reject them. However, as with the use of the so-called generic or gender-neutral *man,* the men on the panel are much more accepting of *-man* compounds than the women. The general use of *chairman* is acceptable to 67 percent of the panel (including 52 percent of the women

and 76 percent of the men) in the sentence *The chairman will be appointed by the Faculty Senate.* But only 48 percent accept the use of the word in *Emily Owen, chairman of the Mayor's Task Force, issued a statement assuring residents that their views would be solicited,* where it is applied to a woman—and in this case the gender split is not nearly so dramatic, only 8 percent.

To many writers, however, the distinction between general use and use in reference to women seems only a fine one, and they choose not to use such restrictive *-man* words at all. There are several strategies for replacing compounds formed with *man*. When referring to women, you can use parallel terms like *businesswoman, spokeswoman,* and *chairwoman.* You can also use common-gender terms coined with *person,* such as *businessperson, spokesperson,* and *chairperson.* For occupational titles ending in *-man,* new standards of official usage have been established by the U.S. Department of Labor and other government agencies. In official contexts, terms such as *firefighter* and *police officer* are now generally used in place of *fireman* and *policeman.*

In addition, there are some entirely new, more inclusive phrases, such as *first-year student* for *freshman, letter carrier* for *mailman,* and *workers' compensation* for *workmen's compensation,* with which you can replace older terms based on the *-man* model. You can also reword with a phrase, such as *member of the clergy* for *clergyman,* or try a clipped form, such as *chair* for *chairman.* English also has a number of long-standing gender-neutral agent nouns, such as *cleric* and *head,* that you can avail yourself of.

Of course there are some words, such as *unsportsmanlike* or *showmanship,* for which there are no exact synonyms. In cases like these you may need to completely reword the sentence if you want to avoid using a *-man* compound.

Since most of the new terms can give no offense to traditionalists, it only makes sense to use them and thereby avoid alienating the nontraditionalists in your audience.

**master** Like *man, master* is a word that has produced many familiar compounds and other usages in English. The compounds include *masterpiece, mastermind, masterstroke, concertmaster, master bedroom,* and *master plan,* to name a few. If you have an original document to copy, you may refer to it as the *master,* and if you have conquered a particularly difficult problem, you might say you have *mastered* it. However, also like *man,* for many people *master* has masculine associations because of its sense "a man who serves as the head of a household."

Many senses of *master,* such as the noun sense "an expert" and the verb sense "to make oneself an expert at," have long been considered gender-neutral and are in wide use. Some words, like *masterpiece* and *master plan,* have lost most, if not all, of their associations with maleness. They exist as distinct words, and people do not usually think of them as a combination of parts each containing a different meaning. Despite this, some people are offended by the use of *master* in any context—whether by itself or in compounds—because of its connotation of maleness and its associations with the institution of slavery.

**Ms.** Many of us think of *Ms.* or *Ms* as a very recent invention of the women's movement, but in fact the term was first suggested as a convenience to writers of business letters by such publications as the *Bulletin of the American Business Writing Association* (1951) and *The Simplified Letter,* issued by the National Office Management Association (1952). Along with many others, champions of women's rights saw the virtues of the term and soon advocated its use in more general contexts, as is evidenced by the founding of *Ms.* magazine in 1972.

The form *Ms.* or *Ms* is now widely used in both professional and social contexts. Thus the term stands as a highly successful language reform—probably because people value its usefulness. As a courtesy title, *Ms.* serves exactly the same function as *Mr.* does for men, and like *Mr.* it may be used with a last name alone or with a full name: *Ms. Pemberton; Ms. Miriam E. Pemberton.*

Using *Ms.* obviates the need for the guesswork involved in figuring out whether to address someone as *Mrs.* or *Miss:* you can't go wrong with *Ms.* Whether the woman you are addressing is married or unmarried, has changed her name or not, *Ms.* is always correct. And the beauty of *Ms.* is that this information becomes irrelevant, as it should be—and as it has always been for men.

Of course, some women may indicate that they prefer to use the title *Miss* or *Mrs.*, and in these cases it only makes sense to follow their wishes.

**née** *Née* or *nee,* originally a French word meaning "born," is used to indicate the name at birth of a married woman who has since changed her name. In English *née* or *nee* is usually followed only by a family name. Thus you should say *Mary Parks, née Case,* not *née Mary Case.* The word has been used since 1758, though now it is usually restricted to society columns and obituaries. Since this term now usually sounds outdated or affected, you may want to avoid it outside of these contexts. Finding substitutes, such as *born* or *formerly known as,* is easy enough: *Mary Parks, formerly known as Mary Case.*

**parent / parenting** The verb *parent* is one of those intriguing words that are used metaphorically before a primary or concrete meaning has established itself. Its original sense, meaning "to produce," dates from the 17th century. The meaning "to act as a parent to" has been around since the late 19th century, but again metaphorically: governments "parent" certain citizens, for example. These uses are rare, however, and *parent* is most familiar now in its use as a gerund meaning "raising children," as in *Men need to be initiated into primary parenting.* This use has been around since the 1950s, and *parenting* is now widely used in newspapers and magazines. The verb *parent* itself, as in *I've found more time to parent since I started working half-time,* is rarely used in print.

With parental leave for new parents gaining in practice and fathers more involved in child-raising, both the term *parenting* and the job of parenting have risen to new heights of acceptance: even President Clinton has said, "*I think parenting is the most important job in this society.*"

Nonetheless, the term *parenting* has had many critics, perhaps because it derives from a verb that was made from a noun in the manner of *contact* and *modem.* Back in 1988, the Usage Panel could not muster much affection for it. Only 46 percent accepted it in formal writing in this example: *In choosing foster homes we give preference first to relatives and second to families with prior experience in parenting.* But given the word's widespread usage, it is likely that more panel members would accept it today.

**pert / sassy / vivacious** There are certain words in English that we tend to think of as sex-specific, even though they are not defined that way in dictionaries. In a recent survey we polled the Usage Panel on a number of these words. Two-thirds of the panel feels that *vivacious* can only be used of a female subject, as in the example _____ *can be so vivacious at times,* while more than 70 percent of the panelists believe only men or boys can be *debonair.* Similarly, a majority of panelists feel that *saucy, sassy, pert,* and *demure* can apply only to women or girls.

Surprisingly, 43 percent of the Usage Panel believes that *wanton* can apply to either women or men, and 64 percent believe the same of *prim.* If you use the words *urbane, suave,* or *lecherous,* however, a majority of panel members believe you should refer to a man.

Other interesting controversies include the adjective *suave* and the noun *fellow.* Sixty percent of the panel thought these words should be limited to men, leaving 40 percent who would in theory at least allow a woman to be described as a *suave fellow.*

**same-sex** *Same-sex* is a relatively recent coinage that arose to refer to activities and arrangements that involve one gender but not the other. Thus, it has appeared in phrases like *same-sex friends* (as opposed to one's friends of the opposite sex) and *same-sex support system* (in which members of one gender help each other in the manner of an "old boy network"). The single-gender usage continues today, especially in reference to education: A *same-sex school* is all-male or all-female. More recently, *same-sex* has been used as a substitute for *homosexual* in contexts that do not warrant explicit reference to sexuality. It occurs frequently in phrases like *same-sex couples, same-sex dating,* and *same-sex marriage.* Both usages are acceptable to the Usage Panel.

**she** The feminine pronoun *she* has been used since the Middle Ages to refer to such inanimate objects as Earth, the sea, and ships. It has also been frequently used to refer to female personifications of nations and cities, as in *"San Francisco never failed to surprise her summertime visitors"* (Edwin Chen). This practice may have originated, and was certainly encouraged by, reference to words that were grammatically feminine in the language from which they had been translated. Thus, the soul was sometimes conceived as female at least in part because it is a feminine noun in Latin (*anima*). A further influence was the personification of certain objects, such as the Moon, and certain ideas, such as fortune or philosophy, as goddesses by ancient writers.

Whatever its origin, many writers still observe this usage today. People commonly refer to cars, musical instruments, and other objects with which they

have close association with the pronoun *she*. But others find this practice objectionable because it seems to ascribe stereotypically feminine characteristics to these entities and because it lacks balance in that people tend not to personify objects as masculine. These objections contributed to the decision by the National Weather Service to discontinue its practice of identifying hurricanes by women's names only. Now you can be subjected to a hurricane of either sex.

# Names and Labels

## *Social, Racial, and Ethnic Terms*

One of the most basic ways of showing respect for others is to refer to them by the names with which they have chosen to identify themselves and to avoid using names that they consider offensive. This applies to ethnic groups and to other people who are identified according to their stage in life (such as older people), a condition with which they must live (such as people who have a disability), a category that society has placed them in (such as aboriginal peoples), or their sexual orientation.

Of course the difficulty comes in knowing what terms a particular group has accepted and what terms that group finds offensive and why. Some groups, such as African Americans and Hispanics, refer to themselves by more than one name, and the opinions of insiders are mixed about which should be the term of choice. In some cases the linguistic situation is in flux. Over time traditional terms can accumulate a certain amount of historical and emotional baggage, and some groups have periodically changed their names as a means of reasserting their dignity. Some groups "reclaim" terms that they once considered offensive—*Indian* is an example—as a way of voicing ethnic pride.

The notes listed below focus on accepted and in some cases controversial ways of referring to specific social groups. Blatantly offensive terms, whose usage is not a matter of debate, are not included. The notes have been written from the point of view of a neutral outsider, reviewing current usage, summarizing the arguments that have been made for and against specific terms, and giving advice about how to refer to groups you may not belong to and may know little about.

As a general rule, it is good to remember that you should only refer to a person by category when it is relevant or necessary to the discussion at hand. That is, you should ordinarily view people as individuals and not mention their racial, ethnic, or other status, unless it is important to your larger purpose in communicating. But when reference to another's status is appropriate, you can inform yourself about some of the current issues in American society by reading the notes that follow.

**aborigine / aboriginal** An *aborigine* is simply a member of the original or earliest known inhabitants of a region, that is, one of the people who are already established in a region when the first migrant or explorer from somewhere else arrives. As a noun, *aborigine* is now used primarily of the indigenous peoples of Australia and in that context (though in no others) it is generally capitalized. When referring to other native peoples, such as American Indians or the early Celts of Britain, you may wish to use a phrase such as *aboriginal inhabitants* or *indigenous peoples* instead of *aborigines*. While there is nothing offensive in the notion of prior habitation—indeed, it is a point of considerable pride among most native peoples—the lowercase noun *aborigine* may well evoke an unwelcome stereotype.

More at **native.**

**African American / Afro-American** During American colonial and early national times, black slaves and freemen alike were often referred to as *Africans,* even after several generations' residence in America. That this practice was common among blacks as well as whites is obvious from the number of churches and institutions founded during this period with names such as the African Methodist Episcopal church and the Free African Society. However, this usage fell out of favor in the 19th century, and it was not until the Black Power movement of the late 1960s and early 1970s that black Americans' African heritage was again acknowledged in popular terminology. *Afro-American,* which gained rapid acceptance alongside *black* during this period, expressed a growing, sometimes defiant pride in black American culture and its African origins. Afro hairstyles and African dress became popular in many parts of the black community, while Afro-American studies programs proliferated on university campuses.

But in the following decades *Afro-American* lost some of its popularity, especially in referring to people, so that today a phrase such as *the election of two new Afro-Americans to Congress* sounds somewhat dated. To a large degree its place has been taken by the similar term *African American,* popularized in the late 1980s by Jesse Jackson and other black leaders and quickly adopted by many columnists and commentators, black and white alike. *African American* has the virtue of conforming to the standard model of ethnic American names such as *Asian American, Irish American,* and *Italian American.* Like *Native American,* it is most appropriately used by outsiders in public discourse, as in articles, broadcasts, and speeches, where it communicates respect by emphasizing ethnicity over race. It has the further advantage that, unlike *black,* its use as a noun in referring to a particular person or persons is unproblematic; you can say *My teacher is an African American* where you probably would not say *My teacher is a black.* But there is little indication that *African American* is poised to push *black* aside as that term earlier pushed aside *Negro.* Indeed, recent surveys among black Americans, while confirming widespread acceptance of *African American,* indicate a strong continued preference for *black.*

As a noun, *African American* should be spelled without a hyphen. The adjective can be styled either with or without a hyphen.

More at **black** and **hyphenated Americans.**

**Amerasian** *Amerasian* is not a synonym for *Asian American*. An *Amerasian* is a person of mixed Asian and American parentage, especially the child of an Asian mother and an American father. The term, which dates to the Korean War in the early 1950s, came into wider use during the Vietnam War, when the prolonged presence of American servicemen in South Vietnam and other Southeast Asian countries resulted in an increased number of such children. Since American servicemen are of varying racial and ethnic backgrounds, there is no fixed racial connotation to *Amerasian* apart from a supposition that one parent, generally the mother, is an ethnic Asian.
More at **Asian American** and **Eurasian.**

**American Indian** For those who are convinced that *Indian* is inherently offensive, the compound *American Indian* may seem just as unacceptable, but for others the term offers a useful alternative where *Native American* might seem too formal or anachronistic and *Indian* alone either too casual or ambiguous. In principle, *American Indian* can apply to all native peoples throughout the Americas except the Eskimos and Aleuts, but in practice it is generally restricted to the peoples of the United States and Canada. For native peoples of Mexico, Central America, the Caribbean, and South America, *Indian* or the less frequent *Amerindian* are better choices: *the Indian civilizations of Mexico and Peru, the Amerindians of the Guyana highlands.*
More at **Indian** and **Native American.**

**Amerindian** The contractions *Amerindian* and *Amerind* occur infrequently in modern American English and are likely to sound stilted or old-fashioned when used in referring to contemporary Native Americans. They are somewhat more common in anthropological contexts or when used of South American cultures.
More at **American Indian, Indian,** and **Native American.**

**Anglo** *Anglo* is used in the United States primarily in distinguishing a white English-speaking person from a person of Hispanic heritage. This usage originated in the Southwest, where historical patterns of settlement resulted in three distinct, relatively stable cultural groups: Native American, Hispanic, and most recently Anglo (short for *Anglo-American*). While *Anglo* is used exclusively of whites, it is not strictly limited in this context to persons of English ancestry—German Americans, Polish Americans, Irish Americans, and others can all be viewed as Anglos so long as their primary language is English. Outside of the Southwest and southern California, however, *Anglo* is less widely used as a general label for non-Hispanic whites. In areas where there is no large Hispanic population to be measured against or where ethnic distinctions among various European groups remain strong, *Anglo* is less commonly used as a catch-all term.

 *Anglo* is also used in non-Hispanic contexts. In Canada, where its usage dates at least to 1800, the distinction is between persons of English and French descent. And in American historical contexts *Anglo* is apt to be used

more strictly to refer to Americans of English descent, as in this passage by Benjamin Schwarz describing the politics of nation-building in pre-Revolutionary America: "*The 'unity' of the American people derived . . . from the ability and willingness of an Anglo elite to stamp its image on other peoples coming to this country*" (the *Atlantic Monthly*, May 1995).

**Asian** *Asian* is now strongly preferred in place of *Oriental* for persons native to Asia or descended from an Asian people. Both terms are rooted in geography rather than ethnicity, but where *Asian* is neutral, *Oriental* sounds outdated and to many people even offensive.

The usual objection to *Oriental*—meaning "of or situated in the East"—is that it identifies Asian countries and peoples in terms of their location relative to Europe. However, this objection is not usually made of other terms, such as *Near Eastern* and *Middle Eastern,* stemming from the same accident of geography that led the earliest European travelers eastward rather than westward into Asia. The real problem with *Oriental* is more likely that it comes freighted with connotations from an earlier era, when Europeans viewed the regions east of the Mediterranean as exotic lands full of romance and intrigue, the home of despotic empires, fabulous cities, and mysterious customs. Such common expressions as "Oriental splendor" and "the inscrutable Orient" testify to the rich—and now generally offensive—associations that have attached to this term in previous centuries.

It is worth remembering, though, that *Oriental* is not an ethnic slur to be avoided in all situations. It is most objectionable in contemporary contexts and when used as a noun, as in *the appointment of an Oriental to head the commission.* In these cases *Asian* (or a more specific term such as *Vietnamese, Korean,* or *Asian American,* if appropriate) is the only acceptable term. But in certain historical contexts, or when its exotic connotations are integral to the topic, *Oriental* remains a useful term.

Asia is the largest of the continents with more than half the world's population. Though strictly speaking any of the peoples indigenous to the continent can be termed *Asian,* in normal contexts this designation tends to be restricted to persons from East, South, and Southeast Asia. Indonesians and Filipinos are usually included under *Asian* as well, but not the Melanesians, Micronesians, and Polynesians of the central and southern Pacific Ocean, who are often known collectively as *Pacific Islanders.* The predominantly Muslim and Christian peoples of Southwest Asia and the former Soviet republics—including Turks, Arabs, Armenians, and Iranians—are usually designated *Middle* or *Near Eastern* rather than *Asian.*

**Asian American** An American of Asian descent is an *Asian American,* not an *Amerasian,* the latter term being largely restricted to children fathered by American servicemen stationed in Asia during the Korean and Vietnam wars. As with *Latin American* and *Euro-American,* the designation *Asian American* can apply to many different people with different national origins and widely varying cultural backgrounds. Wherever appropriate you should consider

using a more specific term, such as *Chinese American* or *Korean American,* in place of the comprehensive one.

As a noun, *Asian American* should be spelled without a hyphen. The adjective can be styled either with or without a hyphen.

More at **Amerasian, Eurasian,** and **hyphenated Americans.**

**Asiatic** Like *Oriental, Asiatic* tends to evoke stereotypical and generally offensive images of Asian peoples and cultures. The only acceptable term in most modern contexts is *Asian.*

**Australoid** The term *Australoid,* referring to the group of peoples indigenous to Australia and certain of the large islands to the north, belongs to the racial classification system proposed by European anthropologists in the 18th and 19th centuries. These terms are largely outdated and potentially offensive today. When referring to the indigenous peoples of this region, you should consider using the appropriate ethnic name, if known, or a term such as *native Australian* or *native Bornean.*

More at **race.**

**black** *The Oxford English Dictionary* contains evidence of the use of *black* in reference to African peoples as early as 1400; no doubt it was used orally before then, and certainly it has been in continual use ever since. Though it never descended to the level of a racial epithet, *black* was often looked upon with disfavor by earlier generations of African Americans. This was especially true during the period following the Civil War, when emancipated slaves and their descendants rejected *black* and its semantic twin *negro*—the terms most closely associated with two and a half centuries of servitude—in favor of *colored.* During the first part of the 20th century *colored,* in turn, lost ground to a newly capitalized *Negro,* which remained as the preferred racial label until the social and political upheavals of the 1960s.

The Black Power movement that followed on the heels of the decades-long civil rights struggle called, among other things, for the adoption of *black* as a term of racial pride. The campaign for the acceptance of *black* is remarkable for the swiftness with which it accomplished its purpose as well as for its success in altering the status of a word that had often been regarded by both blacks and whites with suspicion. Today *black,* or *Black,* remains the preferred term at most if not all levels of discourse. While *African American* has gained wide acceptance, especially in the media, recent polls in the black community continue to show a strong preference for *black.*

**capitalization of *black*** *Black* is sometimes capitalized in its racial sense, especially in the black press, though the lowercase form is still widely used by authors of all races. The capitalization of *Black* does raise ancillary problems for the treatment of the term *white.* Orthographic evenhandedness would seem to require the use of uppercase *White,* but this form might be taken to imply that whites constitute a single ethnic group, an issue that is certainly debatable. Uppercase *White* is also sometimes associated with the writings of

white supremacist groups, which for many people would of itself be sufficient reason to dismiss it. On the other hand, the use of lowercase *white* in the same context as uppercase *Black* will obviously raise questions as to how and why the writer has distinguished between the two groups. There is no entirely happy solution to this problem. In all likelihood, uncertainty as to the mode of styling of *white* has dissuaded many publications from adopting the capitalized form *Black*.
More at **African American.**

**blind** There is no reason to avoid the word *blind* in referring to a person who is sightless or whose vision is so severely restricted as to be useless for ordinary purposes. As with *deaf*—but unlike *cripple*—the substitution of a euphemistic expression for *blind* could itself be objectionable if perceived as implying that blindness is too piteous a condition to be stated in plain language. In particular, you should not substitute *visually impaired* for *blind* except in referring to a range of vision problems that includes less than total or legal blindness.
More at **impaired.**

**brown** As a description of skin color, *brown* stands apart from *white, black, red,* and *yellow* in that it is not strongly associated with any specific racial group. In certain contexts it denotes a relatively light skin color in a person of mixed white and black ancestry. In other contexts it is simply used to mean *nonwhite* or *non-European*. While *brown* is often used with positive connotations, it can also sound condescending or offensive when used by whites. The term *people of color* is generally preferable to either *nonwhite* or *brown-skinned peoples* when referring to peoples of other than European origin.
More at **person of color.**

**Caucasian / Caucasoid** *Caucasian* and its more restricted synonym *Caucasoid* belong to the system of racial classification proposed by European anthropologists in the 18th and 19th centuries. These terms refer to a broad group of peoples indigenous to Europe, western Asia, northern Africa, and much of the Indian subcontinent. *Caucasian* and *Caucasoid* are in some ways the most problematic of the traditional racial terms, not so much for any offensive character as for their widespread misuse as a synonym for "white" or "European." Many of the peoples traditionally included in this category, such as the Berbers of North Africa and the various Hindu and Muslim peoples of northern India, have skin color noticeably darker than most Europeans and as such are not usually considered to be white. Obviously they are not European either. Yet in casual usage, in police reports, and even in many dictionaries, *Caucasian* is often used interchangeably with those two terms. You should take care to avoid this imprecision.

 *Caucasian,* but not *Caucasoid,* is also a geographic term referring to the Caucasus (the mountainous region between the Black and Caspian Seas for which the racial category was named) or to any of its indigenous peoples including Azerbaijanis, Armenians, and Ossetians. When using *Caucasian* in

this sense you may wish to provide an initial context so as to avoid any ambiguity; instead of *a Caucasian people* you might include a phrase such as *a people inhabiting* (or *from*) *the Caucasus*.
More at **race.**

**challenged** People who object to the terms *handicapped* and *disabled* as being too negative sometimes propose the substitution of *challenged* instead, especially in the phrase *physically challenged*. While this usage may have its place, as in referring to athletes with physical disabilities, it has failed to gain general acceptance in broader contexts. Indeed, it is frequently ridiculed as an awkward and condescending euphemism and is better avoided in ordinary contexts.
More at **differently abled.**

**Chicana** A Mexican-American woman or girl can be referred to as either a *Chicana* or a *Chicano,* though the masculine form might in some cases be considered inappropriate.
More at **Latina.**

**Chicano** *Chicano* is derived from Mexican-Spanish *mexicano,* in which the *x* is pronounced as a strongly aspirated *h*. It is used only of Mexican Americans, not of Mexicans living in Mexico. *Chicano* was originally an informal term in English (as in Spanish), and the spelling of the first recorded instance in an American publication followed the Spanish custom of lowercasing nouns of national or ethnic origin. However, the literary and political movements of the 1960s and 1970s among Mexican Americans established *Chicano* as a term of ethnic pride, and it is properly written today with a capital.
     While there is little danger of offense in using *Chicano* in a context related to Mexican-American politics, demographics, or the arts, it should be used with care by outsiders in ordinary discourse. There are also regional differences in usage throughout the Southwest. When unsure of how *Chicano* will be received, you should use either *Mexican American* or the more general *Latino* or *Hispanic*.

**color** The color names traditionally assigned to the various peoples and races of the world are notoriously inexact. Most *white* people's skin is not truly white, nor is most *black* people's skin black, to say nothing of the inexactitude of *red* and *yellow*. Of the familiar color labels, only *brown* has much claim to objective accuracy, though it is so broad a term that it can be used of virtually any skin of any group except untanned northern Europeans.
     Of course the standard color terms are not really used as objective descriptions of skin tones—that is left to a more expressive vocabulary containing such words as *bronze, copper-colored, milky,* and *ebony. White, black, red,* and *yellow* serve rather as shorthand racial labels, and in this usage they have met with varying fates in American English. While *white* and *black* are

used at all levels with complete naturalness, *red* and *yellow* are now rarely encountered and in most contexts are looked on as offensive.
More at **black, brown, red, white,** and **yellow.**

**colored** *Colored,* or *coloured,* is recorded in its racial sense as early as 1611, but it did not become widespread in American English until after the Civil War, when the newly freed black population began to embrace it as a respectful alternative to *black* or *negro.* Well into the 20th century *colored* remained a self-chosen term of pride, as evidenced by its use in the name of the NAACP (the National Association for the Advancement of Colored People) founded in 1909 and continuing under that name even today. By midcentury, however, the term *colored* had been largely supplanted among black Americans, first by the recently capitalized *Negro* and later by *black* and *African American.* As *colored* lost favor in the black population, its use by outsiders became more clearly offensive.

In the United States, *colored* has usually been spelled lowercase and has been virtually synonymous with *black* or *Negro* as those terms are used in American society, that is, with reference to any person of African ancestry regardless of mixture with European or other non-African peoples. In South Africa it is written uppercase—*Coloured*—and has long been applied specifically to persons of mixed-race parentage as opposed to racially unmixed blacks, whites, and Asians.

**crippled** The adjective *crippled* and the corresponding noun *cripple* are now considered offensively blunt when used of a person with a hindering or incapacitating physical condition. The current preference in most cases is for *disabled,* as in *an accident that left her disabled* or *improved access for the disabled.* But when the emphasis shifts from the person to the impairment itself, there is generally no reason to avoid the stronger term. Thus while you might choose to say *He was increasingly disabled by multiple sclerosis,* you might describe the disease itself as *crippling,* especially if your purpose is to stress the seriousness of its physical effects. There is a great difference between the insensitive labeling of a particular person as a *cripple* and the deliberate use of such a word for its vivid effect, as in this quote from the *Washington Post:* "*There is no more devastating blow to the human psyche than to be transformed in microseconds from a healthy robust human being into a cripple.*"
More at **disabled.**

**deaf** The rise of the Deaf Pride movement in the 1980s has introduced a distinction between the lowercase *deaf* and the capitalized form *Deaf.* A person who is unable to hear or whose hearing is only minimal is properly termed *deaf.* A deaf person who belongs to the community that has formed around the use of American Sign Language as the preferred means of communication is said to be *Deaf* or a member of *Deaf culture.* The issue of capitalization is different with *deaf* than it is for *black.* In the case of *black,* the decision whether to capitalize is essentially a matter of personal or political preference;

use of the capitalized form, though, does not differentiate one black person from another. With *deaf,* on the other hand, the capitalized form has a different meaning than the lowercased form, and the two should be carefully distinguished so as to avoid misunderstanding. Only if a person is self-identified as belonging to Deaf culture should you refer to him or her as *Deaf.*

The expression *hearing-impaired* is not an exact equivalent of *deaf.* Though *hearing-impaired* can logically denote total deafness and *deaf* can be used of different degrees of hearing loss, the former strongly suggests that a person retains some capacity to detect sound.
More at **impaired.**

**deaf and dumb** *Deaf and dumb* has a long history in English, the earliest citation in *The Oxford English Dictionary* occurring in 1225 and in reverse order— "dumbe & deaf." The *dumb* in *deaf and dumb* does not, of course, mean "lacking intelligence" but rather "incapable of speech," but even when this point is clear the expression is offensive in any but a historical or figurative context.
More at **dumb.**

**deaf-mute** Though it may sound somewhat less offensive than *deaf and dumb*, the term *deaf-mute* is similarly objectionable for its implicit equation of deafness with an incapacity for speech or communication.
More at **dumb.**

**differently abled** The term *differently abled* is sometimes proposed as a substitute for *disabled* or *handicapped. Differently abled* emphasizes the fact that many people with disabilities are quite capable of accomplishing a particular task or performing a particular function, only in a different manner or taking more time or effort than people without the disability in question. It can also be taken to mean that a person who is incapable of one act may nevertheless be capable of many or even most others. These are useful reminders, but the fact remains that *differently abled* has won little acceptance among the general public and is often criticized as being both awkward and condescending.

An even more notorious example is the use of *challenged* in combinations, such as *physically challenged*, that are normally formed with *handicapped* or *disabled.* The purpose of this proposed substitution is to emphasize the positive aspect of the challenge that a particular condition presents over the negative aspect of hindrance or incapacity. However, the widespread parody of this usage in such expressions as *vertically challenged* for "short" or *melanin challenged* for "white" has effectively eliminated this construction as a serious alternative to *disabled* or *handicapped.*

**disabled / disability** *Disabled* is the clear preference in contemporary American English in referring to people having either physical or mental impairments, with the impairments themselves preferably termed *disabilities. Handicapped*—a somewhat euphemistic term derived from the world of sports gambling—is still in wide use but is sometimes taken to be offensive, while more

recent coinages such as *differently abled* or *handicapable* are generally perceived as condescending euphemisms and have gained little currency.

The often-repeated recommendation to put the person before the disability would favor *persons with disabilities* over *disabled persons* and *person with paraplegia* over *paraplegic*. Such expressions are said to focus on the individual rather than on the particular functional limitation, and they are preferred by many people who themselves have disabilities. Respect for the wishes of this group calls for observing this rule, but the "person-first" construction has not found wide acceptance with the general public, perhaps because it tends to sound unnatural or possibly because in English the last word in a phrase usually has the greatest weight, thus undercutting the intended purpose.

**dumb** The sense of *dumb* meaning "stupid" is much more recent in English than the sense of "lacking the power of speech." However, the later sense has overwhelmed the earlier to such a degree that any reference to a person who cannot speak as *dumb* is clearly offensive. Indeed, *dumb* now has such strong connotations of dimwittedness that even using it of animals, as in *the dumb creatures of the forest,* is likely to cause either mirth or misunderstanding.

But the offensiveness of a phrase such as *deaf and dumb* is due only in part to the confusion between the two senses of *dumb*. Equally objectionable is the implication that deafness is an insurmountable obstacle to acquiring speech, or, on the other hand, that vocal utterance is the only form of speaking. Whether with surgical implants to enhance residual hearing, through learning a signed language, or by a combination of these and other methods, deaf children today are far more likely than in the past to lead lives rich in communication and language, making any expression such as *deaf and dumb* or *deaf-mute* not only offensive but in most cases simply inaccurate.

**Dutch** A number of English expressions formed with the word *Dutch* are objectionable because of the unflattering stereotypes they perpetuate. Some of these, such as *Dutch uncle* (a stern critic) and *Dutch courage* (courage gained by drinking liquor), seem to be passing from the language unassisted. Others, however, such as *in Dutch* (in trouble) and *go Dutch* (to pay one's own expenses on a date), have retained their currency. Most people today are only vaguely aware of the stereotypes evoked by these phrases, but it is probably best to avoid them.

## elder

*elder as an adjective* *Elder* is not a synonym for *elderly*. In comparisons between two persons, as in a family, *elder* simply means "older" but not necessarily "old": *My elder sister is going off to college.* In other contexts it does denote relatively advanced age but with the added component of respect for a person's position or achievement: *an elder statesman, an elder chief of the tribe.* If it is age alone that you wish to express, you should use *older* or *elderly: a survey of older Americans, an elderly waiter.*

*elder as a noun* As with the adjective, the noun *elder* can be used comparatively without necessarily implying old age: *He is my elder by three years.* It can

also refer to an office in certain churches or, more broadly, to a position of authority or respect conferred by age and experience: *an elder in the Presbyterian Church, a tribal elder.* The use of *elder* in the sense of "an elderly person" is uncommon in contemporary English, though it is widely used as an attributive in such phrases as *elder care* and *elder services.*

**elderly** *Elderly* applies to the stage of life that begins at the end of middle age. When used as a noun in referring to older persons in general, it is relatively neutral, denoting a group of people whose common characteristic is advanced age: *policy issues of special interest to the elderly.* However, when used as an adjective in describing a particular person, *elderly* has a range of connotation that goes beyond the denotation of chronological age to include the various effects of aging. On the one hand, it can suggest dignity; on the other, frailty or diminished capacity. While there is no reason to avoid *elderly* as an adjective, you should keep in mind that a phrase such as *the elderly couple in the second row* is likely to conjure a more specific—and probably older—image than if the couple were described as *older.*

**ethnicity / ethnic** Who is more ethnic—a WASP or a Jew? A Russian or a Mexican? A Catholic or a Buddhist? The English word *ethnic* can be traced ultimately to the Greek word for "people" in the sense of "foreign nation." ("People" meaning "the general populace" was expressed in Greek by *demos.*) Thus the idea of otherness, as measured by such attributes as nationality, religion, language, or race, is central to ethnicity. But the question is, other than what? When the adjective *ethnic* is applied to such cultural items as food and dress, the presumption is generally of a difference from a surrounding norm; Thai food is considered ethnic fare in the United States but not in Bangkok. When it comes to people, the same assumption of departure from a presumed norm is sometimes made, as in this passage from *Newsweek* magazine describing the Greek-American presidential candidate Michael Dukakis: *"For a lot of people, the governor of Massachusetts was too liberal, too ethnic, too cold—maybe even too short."* However, the concept of ethnicity as it relates to a society as a whole is today generally considered to include all groups, each of which is equally "other" in relation to the rest. That is, we generally consider our own group—WASP, Jew, Russian, or whatever—to be just as *ethnic* as anyone else's, and we respond to questions about our *ethnicity* as readily when we belong to the majority population as when we belong to the minority.

**Eurasian** In its ethnic as opposed to its geographic sense, *Eurasian* denotes a person of mixed European and Asian parentage. It was first used in the 19th century in referring to someone of European—especially British—and East Indian birth; in a contemporary American context the parents are more often a white American—that is, of European descent—and a person of East or South Asian origin.

The geographic sense of *Eurasian* is quite distinct, referring to the land mass comprising the European and Asian continents and especially to the large indeterminate region where they join. Peoples indigenous to this region can also be termed *Eurasian,* creating a potential ambiguity when used of an individual as opposed to a group or culture. If the ambiguity is not resolved by context, you may wish to use a descriptive phrase such as *a member of a Eurasian people* or *a person of European and Asian parentage* for clarity.

**Euro-American / European American** *Euro-American* and its near twin *European American* have gained a certain currency in recent years as designations for white Americans, that is, Americans of European descent. *Euro-American* is first recorded as a noun in a passage by the anthropologist Margaret Meade written in 1949, but its growing use outside of anthropology is probably a response to the popularity in American English of compound ethnic designations such as *Hispanic American, Asian American, Native American,* and more recently *African American.* The addition of *Euro-American* and *European American* to this list offers a useful alternative to *white* or *white American,* terms that emphasize skin color over cultural heritage. However, the general public has so far been slow to adopt them.

**gay** *Gay* is now standard in its use to refer to the American homosexual community and its members; in this use it is generally lowercased. *Gay* is distinguished from *homosexual* primarily by the emphasis it places on the cultural and social aspects of homosexuality as opposed to sexual practice. Many writers reserve *gay* for homosexual men, but the word is widely used with reference to both sexes; when the intended meaning is not clear in the context, the phrase *gay and lesbian* should be used. Like other names of social groups that are derived from adjectives (for example, *black*), *gay* may be regarded as offensive when used as a noun to refer to particular individuals, as in *There were two gays on the panel.* In such cases you should substitute the phrase *gay people* for gays. But there is no objection to the use of the noun in the plural to refer to the general gay community, as in *Gays have united in opposition to the policy.* More at **lesbian.**

**handicap / handicapped** In recent years *handicap* has lost ground to *disability* in describing conditions that restrict or prevent certain physical or mental functions. *Handicap* is sometimes held to imply a helplessness that is not suggested by the more forthright *disability.* The stigma that has attached to *handicap* may have developed from a mistaken belief that the original phrase *hand in cap* referred to a beggar holding out a cap to collect coins (though that would more logically come from *cap in hand*). In fact, *hand in cap* (or *hand i' cap*) was a 17th-century game of chance in which participants drew items from a cap. A later sense, still in use today, refers to an advantage or compensation given to different contestants to equalize the chances of winning. By its nature, a sports handicap encourages competitiveness, not helplessness, and a contestant who loses with a handicap has the satisfaction of knowing that under other circumstances the outcome might well have been

different. In contrast a *disability*, strictly speaking, is a condition that makes performance not just more difficult but impossible. But logic is one thing, and respect for a group's preferences is another; the clear choices today are *disability* and *disabled*.

While *handicapped* is probably best avoided as a noun, as in *programs designed for the handicapped*, it is more acceptable in phrases such as *handicapped parking* or *handicapped accessible*.
More at **disabled / disability.**

**Hispanic** *Hispanic* and *Latino* are both widely used in American English as terms for a person of Spanish-language heritage living in the United States. Though often used interchangeably, they are not identical, and in certain contexts the choice between them can be significant. *Hispanic*, from the Latin word for "Spain," is arguably the broader term, potentially encompassing all Spanish-speaking peoples in both hemispheres and emphasizing the common denominator of language among communities that sometimes have little else in common. *Latino*, which is probably derived from the Spanish word for "Latin American," refers more exclusively to persons or communities of Latin American origin. Of the two, only *Hispanic* can be used in referring to Spain and its history and culture; a native of Spain residing in the United States is a *Hispanic*, not a *Latino*, and you cannot substitute *Latino* in the phrase *the Hispanic influence on native Mexican cultures* without garbling the meaning.

In practice, the geographic distinction between *Hispanic* and *Latino* is of little significance when referring to residents of the United States, since the great majority of people in this group are of Latin-American origin and can be denoted by either word. A more important difference stems from the claim that *Latino* is a term of ethnic pride in a way that *Hispanic*, with its perceived echo of Spanish imperialism, is not. According to this view, *Hispanic* lacks the authenticity and flavor of *Latino*, which is derived directly from Spanish and can change to *Latina* to indicate female gender. A further objection to *Hispanic* is that it is the term most often used in formal or official contexts—as on government applications or census forms—and as such bears the stamp of an establishment that to some seems far removed from the community (or communities) these words refer to.

While these views are strongly held by many, they are by no means universal, and the division is as much geographical as it is political. *Latino* is overwhelmingly preferred in California whereas *Hispanic* is the clear choice in Florida as well as in Texas and most of the Southwest (though in these regions *Chicano* is also widely used). In other areas and in the national media, usage tends to be mixed. An outsider is best advised to follow the prevailing custom wherever it can be determined, but you need not worry in most situations about giving offense, since both terms remain current and in many contexts continue to overlap.

Note that *Hispanic* and *Latino* refer only to language and culture; neither term should be thought of as specifying racial makeup. You should also keep in mind that the growing Hispanic population of the United States is made up

of people from many different national and ethnic backgrounds who do not necessarily compose a single unified community. Whenever possible you should consider substituting a term such as *Mexican American, Cuban American,* or *Puerto Rican* for the broader *Hispanic* or *Latino.*

**homosexual** Many people now avoid using *homosexual* because of the emphasis this term places on sexuality, and indeed *gay* and *lesbian,* which stress cultural and social matters over sex, are frequently better choices. But you need not conclude that *homosexual* is always or even usually offensive. It is most objectionable when used as a noun in referring to a particular person or persons; here *gay man* (or *men*) and *gay woman* (or *women*) are called for. However, when used adjectivally, as in *homosexual issues* or *a homosexual legislator,* or collectively, as in *the rights of homosexuals to marry,* it is usually deemed unobjectionable.

Historically, the *homo-* of *homosexual* derives from the Greek word meaning "same," as in *homonym* or *homophone,* rather than from the Latin word meaning "man," as in *Homo sapiens.* However, a popular reanalysis of the prefix has led many to assume that the literal meaning of *homosexual* is something akin to "man-sex" as opposed to its true meaning of "same-sex," causing some people to erroneously conclude that the word applies only to men.

**hyphenated Americans** Naturalized immigrants to the United States and their descendants are sometimes referred to as *hyphenated Americans,* a term that dates to the end of the 19th century and that reflects an earlier tendency in American English to hyphenate such forms as *Irish-American, German-American,* and *Mexican-American* both as nouns and as adjectives. Contemporary usage frowns on hyphenating these constructions, especially when used as nouns; thus, *The new mayor is an Asian American; she is the first Asian-American* (or *Asian American*) *mayor in the city's history.* In the case of *Native American,* neither the noun nor the adjective is usually hyphenated.

The term *hyphenated American* has itself come under strong criticism as suggesting that those so designated are not as fully American as "unhyphenated" citizens, and you would do well to avoid this term except in historical contexts.

**impaired** The use of *impaired* in such expressions as *hearing-impaired* or *visually impaired* is a recent addition to the vocabulary of disability. When used as euphemisms for *deaf* or *blind,* these terms are superfluous at best and may even be offensive if taken to imply that deafness and blindness are too disturbing to mention directly. However, the notion of impairment is useful in describing conditions involving less than total loss of capacity. Thus a person is best described as *hearing-impaired* if he or she has a partial hearing loss and as *deaf* if the loss is profound. When referring to a group of people with varying degress of sensory loss, from partial to total, you should use the term formed with *impaired* since it more readily suggests a range of conditions than the more absolute-sounding *deaf* or *blind.*

**Indian** Assuming that he had reached the Indies, Columbus called the people on the islands his ships visited "indios," or "Indians," and the misnomer has stuck ever since. It is natural that people would propose alternatives to this term, whether to avoid confusion between the inhabitants of America and India or to indicate respect for the original occupants of the American continents. Thus *Native American* has become widely established in American English, being acceptable in most contemporary contexts and preferred in many, especially in formal or official communication.

However, the acceptance of *Native American* has not brought about the demise of *Indian.* Unlike *Negro,* which was quickly stigmatized once *black* became preferred, *Indian* never fell out of favor with a large segment of the American population. It is firmly rooted in English in such common terms as *Plains Indian, French and Indian War,* and *Indian summer* as well as in numerous plant and place names. In locutions of this kind there is no possibility of substitution.

The criticism that *Indian* is hopelessly tainted by the ignorant or romantic stereotypes of popular American culture can be answered, at least in part, by pointing to the continuing use of this term among American Indians themselves. Indeed, Indian authors and those sympathetic to Indian causes often prefer it for its unpretentious familiarity as well as its emotional impact, as in this passage from the Kiowa writer N. Scott Momaday's memoir *The Names* (1976): "*It was about this time that* [my mother] *began to see herself as an Indian. That dim native heritage became a fascination and a cause for her.*"

**Jew** It is widely recognized that the attributive use of the noun *Jew,* in phrases such as *Jew lawyer* or *Jew ethics,* is both vulgar and highly offensive. In such contexts *Jewish* is the only acceptable possibility. Some people, however, have become so wary of this construction that they have extended the stigma to any use of *Jew* as a noun, a practice that carries risks of its own. In a sentence such as *There are now several Jews on the council,* which is unobjectionable, the substitution of a circumlocution like *Jewish people* or *persons of Jewish background* may in itself cause offense for seeming to imply that *Jew* has a negative connotation when used as a noun.

**Latina** The use of the feminine forms *Latina* and *Chicana* as nouns in referring to a woman or girl is perfectly proper in American English, and failure to do so (as in *She is a Latino*) may sometimes be resented. The use of these forms as modifiers, however, poses problems that English does not usually have to solve. Is it wrong to use a masculine form such as *Chicano* to modify *woman*? Is the phrase *Chicana woman* redundant? Should you say *She is a Latino novelist,* or is *Latina novelist* required? And is the novel that such a person writes a *Latino* or a *Latina novel*?

There is no one answer to these questions, though a few guidelines can be offered. First, the rules of adjective-noun agreement required by Spanish grammar do not normally affect English usage; thus the choice between *She is the city's first Latino mayor* and *She is the city's first Latina mayor* does not

depend on the gender of the Spanish word for mayor. Second, the use of the masculine form as a modifier with reference to a woman is common and unremarkable in English, as in *"Bush Appoints Latino Woman to U.S. Court"* (headline in the *Sacramento Bee*) and *"Juror 1427, a Latino woman who works for the Los Angeles County assessor"* (the *Los Angeles Times*). Third, the use of the feminine form to modify words like *woman* or *girl* is often, though not always, associated with a liberal feminist viewpoint, as in *"I came to know Chicana women living in a barrio who were organizing women's health-care programs"* (*Ms.* magazine). And finally, there are many cases in which the feminine modifier provides significant information that would be lost by using the masculine, as in *"Goldie Hawn plays a bleeding-heart liberal lawyer who rehabilitates the waifs and strays crossing her path* [including] *a pair of docile Chicana illegals"* (the *Village Voice*).

**Latino** American English usage is fairly evenly divided between *Latino* and *Hispanic* in referring to Americans who trace their origins to a Spanish-speaking country or culture. These terms are often used interchangeably, but there are important differences between the two.
More at **Hispanic.**

**lesbian** If *gay* can refer to either sex, why are such seemingly unnecessary expressions as *gay and lesbian* or *lesbians and gay men* so common when referring to groups that include both men and women? While the answer is undoubtedly complex, one aspect is probably the natural linguistic process by which two words with shared or inclusive meanings tend to become specialized over time. Thus the growing use of *lesbian* as a term of pride among many homosexual women in the 1970s created a certain linguistic pressure for a comparable term limited to homosexual men. But homosexual men (and, of course, many women who would later call themselves *lesbian*) had already come of political age under the banner of gay liberation, and *gay* was their strongly preferred term. While *gay* has never lost its inclusiveness, it has tended to become more closely associated with men, making the dual term *gay and lesbian* not only respectful but in many cases necessary for clarity.
More at **gay.**

**minority** Socially speaking, a *minority* is an ethnic, racial, religious, or other group having a distinctive presence within a larger society. Some people object to this term as negative or dismissive, and you should generally avoid it in contexts where a group's status with regard to the majority population is irrelevant. Thus you would normally say *a tour of the city's ethnic* (not *minority*) *restaurants* or *a poem celebrating the diversity of cultures* (not *minorities*) *in America,* where in both cases the emphasis is cultural as opposed to statistical or political. But in the appropriate context, as when discussing a group from a social or demographic point of view, *minority* is a useful term that you need not avoid as offensive.

A different problem arises when *minority* is used to refer to an individual

rather than a group, as in the sentence *As a minority, I am particularly sensitive to the need for fair hiring practices.* Seventy-two percent of the Usage Panel finds this example unacceptable, possibly because it is felt that an individual cannot have the same relationship to society as a group. However, when the word is used in the plural without a numeral or a quantifier like *many* or *some*—as in *The firm announced plans to hire more minorities and women*—the panelists are more approving, with only 27 percent judging an example such as this one unacceptable. The discrepancy in these opinions can be explained by the fact that in this type of plural usage, the word is understood as referring to the members of a group taken collectively rather than as individuals.

**Mongoloid** In its anthropological sense, *Mongoloid* refers to the group of peoples indigenous to central and eastern Asia, some of whom in all probability crossed to the Western Hemisphere and populated North and South America. Like the other terms proposed by anthropologists in the 18th and 19th centuries as human racial classifications, *Mongoloid* is now considered outdated and potentially offensive. In particular, you should take care not to confuse *Mongoloid* with *Mongolian*, which is occasionally used in the anthropological sense but which primarily refers to the central Asian region of Mongolia or to its peoples.

The use of *Mongoloid* or *Mongolism*—capitalized or not—in a medical sense is now clearly offensive. The preferred term for the congenital disorder is now *Down syndrome* or, somewhat less acceptably, *Down's syndrome.*
More at **race.**

**mute** *Mute* as an adjective meaning "incapable of speech" as opposed to "refraining from speaking" is often considered objectionable, primarily for its association with the more clearly offensive *deaf-mute.* As a noun used of a person who cannot speak, it is even more likely to cause offense. On the other hand, there is no good alternative for *mute* in this sense, either as an adjective or a noun. A person who has lost the ability to speak due to a pathological condition is best described as *aphonic,* from the noun *aphonia,* but this term does not cover a deaf person who is physiologically capable of producing vocal sounds yet who does not or can not speak. For such a person, oral speech is usually both difficult and problematic. In fact, many deaf people today are brought up in a sign-oriented community that rejects the notion that speaking is necessary or, to some, even desirable; they are best referred to simply as *deaf,* or, if appropriate, *Deaf.*
More at **deaf.**

**native** The earliest known inhabitants of a region can variously be called *native, indigenous,* or *aboriginal* peoples. Of these terms, *native* and *aboriginal* stand out as having acquired certain stereotypical connotations that render them offensive to many people. The images they tend to evoke (such staples as grass huts, throbbing drums, and warriors brandishing spears) derive in large part from the experience of early European colonists in

Africa, Asia, and the Americas, with further elaboration in the books and movies of popular culture. Of course the stereotyping of unfamiliar peoples out of ignorance and cultural arrogance is by no means limited to Europeans, but that fact is of little help in deciding how to refer to indigenous peoples in Modern English.

As is often the case with words that name peoples, the use of the noun is considerably more problematic than the use of the adjective. Thus *the aboriginal inhabitants of the South Pacific* and *the peoples native to northern Europe* are much more acceptable wordings than if you were to substitute the nouns *aborigines* or *natives*. Interestingly enough, the adjective *native* has recently lost most of its stigma and even gained positive connotations when attached to a geographical noun, as in *Native Alaskan* or *native Australian*. This locution has the further benefit of being equally acceptable as either adjective or noun—*a member of a native Australian people* can just as acceptably and less wordily be called *a native Australian*. Of terms formed on this model, those referring to indigenous American peoples generally capitalize the adjective—as in *Native American, Native Alaskan,* and *Native Hawaiian*—while others are almost always lowercase.

As usual, you should use a specific ethnic name wherever possible in lieu of a broader or vaguer categorization—*a Cherokee* instead of *a Native American, a Yupik* instead of *a Native Alaskan*—unless your intention is to emphasize membership in the larger group.

**Native American** *Indian* has always been a misnomer for the earliest inhabitants of the Americas. Many people have come to prefer *Native American* both as a corrective to Columbus's famous mistake and as a means of avoiding the Hollywood stereotypes so often associated with *Indian*. But while *Native American* has gained popularity in many circles, *Indian* remains in wide use as well, leaving room for choice in most situations.

There are solid arguments in favor of *Native American*. It eliminates any confusion between indigenous American peoples and the inhabitants of India, making it the preferred term in many formal or official contexts. It is also historically accurate, despite the insistence by some that Indians are no more native to America than anyone else since their ancestors are assumed to have migrated here from Asia. But one sense of *native* is "being the original inhabitants of a particular place," and Native Americans' claim to being the original inhabitants of the Americas predates all others by some twelve to twenty and possibly forty thousand years.

Accuracy aside, however, the choice between the two terms is often made on political grounds. For many, *Native American* is the only choice for expressing a sense of pride in or an attitude of respect toward the indigenous cultures of America; *Indian* is seen as wrong and potentially offensive. For others, *Native American* smacks of bureaucracy and the attempt to manipulate language for political purposes. In this view *Indian* is the natural English term, its inaptness made irrelevant by five centuries of consistent usage.

It should be noted that this controversy has subsided somewhat in recent

years, and it is now common to find the two terms used interchangeably in the same piece of writing. Furthermore, the issue has never been particularly divisive between Indians and non-Indians. While generally welcoming the respectful tone of *Native American,* Indian writers have continued to use the older name at least as often as the newer one.

Note that *Native American* is not generally hyphenated as either a noun or an adjective.

More at **American Indian, Indian,** and **hyphenated Americans.**

**Negro** *Negro* was borrowed into English from the Spanish and Portuguese words for *black* long before the first Africans were sold to settlers in Virginia in 1619, and it has undergone a series of ups and downs, at least in American English, ever since. Throughout the 17th and 18th centuries *negro,* generally spelled lowercase, was the most common label for referring to Africans or persons of African descent. After emancipation, however, black Americans tended to reject both *negro* and *black* as part of the vocabulary of slavery, with *colored* becoming the preferred name instead. But neither of the earlier terms disappeared, and by the end of the 19th century many black writers, such as Booker T. Washington and W.E.B. Du Bois, were using *negro* and *black* as readily as *colored.*

The 20th century saw a dramatic rise in the use of *negro.* Du Bois and the NAACP led a protracted and ultimately successful nationwide campaign for its capitalization, and by the 1930s *Negro* was established in most of the mainstream American press as the preferred racial label for black Americans. During the civil rights movement of the 1950s and 1960s, it was *Negro* that speakers and writers most often chose, whether they were expressing racial pride or demanding social justice. But the ensuing Black Power movement swept *Negro* aside in a remarkably short time, establishing *black* as the new term of pride. Today *Negro* is at best outmoded and in many contexts could well be considered offensive.

**Negroid** *Negroid,* one of the terms proposed by European anthropologists in the 18th and 19th centuries as part of a system of human racial classification, refers to the indigenous peoples of Africa south of the Sahara Desert. It is sometimes applied to certain peoples native to Indonesia, New Guinea, Melanesia, and the Philippines as well. In all cases it is now considered both out of date and likely to cause offense.

More at **race.**

**nonwhite** Many people object to the term *nonwhite* for referring to people by what they are not rather than what they are. Of course there are occasions, as when discussing an exclusionary policy such as the former system of apartheid in South Africa, when this emphasis is entirely appropriate. In many other cases, however, you should consider an alternative term such as *person of color* or *people of color* in place of *nonwhite.*

More at **person of color.**

**old** *Old* is the most straightforward term to use when referring to advanced age. It strongly suggests at least a degree of physical infirmity and age-related restrictions. Although people often claim to find euphemisms more offensive than direct speech, you should be careful in labeling a person or group as *old* on the basis of chronological age alone. Where inappropriate, as with people just reaching retirement age and those leading active lives, or where bluntness might offend, you would do well to consider a less definitive term such as *elderly* or *older*.

**older** As a comparative form, *older* would logically seem to indicate greater age than *old*. Except when a direct comparison is being made, however, the opposite is generally true. *The older man in the tweed jacket* suggests a somewhat younger man than if you substitute *old*. Where *old* expresses an absolute, an arrival at old age, *older* takes a more relative view of aging as a continuum—older, but not yet old. As such, *older* is not just a euphemism for the blunter *old* but rather a more precise term for someone between middle and advanced age. And unlike *elderly*, *older* does not particularly suggest frailness or infirmity, making it the natural choice in many situations.

**Oriental** *Oriental* is now generally considered outmoded and even offensive when used of an Asian or an Asian American.
More at **Asian.**

**person of color** Dissatisfaction with the implications of *nonwhite* as a racial label has contributed to the revival of the phrase *person of color* or similar terms, such as *woman of color,* based on the same construction. In effect, *person of color* stands *nonwhite* on its head, substituting a positive for a negative. Furthermore, the almost exclusive association in American English of *colored* with *black*—that is, with Americans of African descent—does not carry over to terms formed with "of color." Indeed, the somewhat artificial sound of *person of color* serves to emphasize that something other than *colored person* is probably intended, so that when Jesse Jackson proclaims that "*These are profound tendencies which strike at the middle class as well as the poor, at whites as well as people of color,*" he is encouraging his audience to think more inclusively than if he had juxtaposed *white* with *black*. In this light, the term *person of color* and its related forms are welcome additions to the vocabulary of race and ethnicity.

**race** In its anthropological sense, a *race* is a group of humans distinguished from other similar groups by genetically inherited characteristics. Though the perception of distinctive physical differences between peoples is undoubtedly as old as the history of human migration, the search for a scientific basis for race is a more recent undertaking. The earliest efforts of physical anthropologists involved elaborate descriptions of such characteristics as skin color, hair color and texture, body proportions, and skull measurements. Modern studies tend to ignore these superficial features in favor of more precisely measurable

criteria, especially the analysis of blood types and of metabolic processes.

The attempt to classify humans into discrete racial groups is greatly complicated by the fact that human populations have been migrating and intermingling for hundreds of centuries. There are no pure races in any meaningful sense, only large geographical groupings whose genetic histories can never be fully known. The traditional names for these groupings—*Negroid, Mongoloid, Caucasoid* (or *Caucasian*), and in some systems *Australoid*—are now controversial in both technical and nontechnical contexts and are likely to give offense no matter how they are used. *Caucasian* does retain a certain currency in American English, but it is used almost exclusively—and erroneously—to mean "white" or "European" rather than "belonging to the Caucasoid racial group," a group that includes a variety of peoples generally considered to be nonwhite. This ambiguity, along with the growing aversion among many people to the racial terminology of earlier anthropologists, suggests that *Caucasian* may soon go the way of the *-oid* words and disappear even from local police blotters.

Of course, the existence of racial differences between peoples remains an obvious, if scientifically indefinite, fact with important social implications. But the terminology of race has shifted in recent years from anthropological classifications toward a more flexible language of geography, culture, and color.

More at **Australoid, Caucasian, Mongoloid,** and **Negroid.**

**red** Experts disagree as to why Native Americans came to be known as *red men*. One theory holds that the term was first used by early European explorers in describing the mysterious Beothuk people of Newfoundland, who were reported to paint their bodies liberally with red ocher. According to this view, the now-extinct *Red Men* gave their nickname to the rest of the peoples native to North America. While there is no doubt that the Beothuks did paint their bodies red, it is more likely that the adjective *red* was applied to Native Americans as a whole in the same manner in which other color labels were given to non-European peoples, in recognition of the perceived difference between the color of their skin and the paler skin of most Europeans.

As a racial label, *red* has never gained the wide acceptance of *black* and *white*. While *red* has often been used with positive connotations, particularly in the expressions *red man* and *Red Indian*, these are generally dismissed today as the romantic stereotypes of a former era when Indians were viewed as the model of the "noble savage." The term *redskin* evokes an even more objectionable stereotype—the crafty foe of pioneers and the western cavalry now further reduced to caricature status as the mascot of American sports teams. It is true that *red* has frequently been appropriated by contemporary Native Americans as an ironic or defiant term of pride, as in the Red Power movement or the title of Lakota author Vine Deloria, Jr.'s book *God is Red*. However, reference to American Indians by their purported skin color is almost certain to cause offense when coming from outsiders.

**Scottish** *Scottish* is the full, original form of the adjective. *Scots* is an old Scottish variant of the form, while *Scotch* is an English contraction of Scottish that at one time also came into use in Scotland (as in Robert Burns's "*O thou, my Muse! guid auld Scotch drink!*") but subsequently fell into disfavor. To some extent these facts can serve as a guide in choosing among the many variant forms of related words, such as *Scot, Scotsman* or *Scotswoman,* or *Scotchman* or *Scotchwoman,* for one of the people of Scotland; *Scots, (the) Scotch,* or, rarely, *(the) Scottish* for the people of Scotland; and *Scots, Scotch,* or *Scottish* for the dialect of English spoken in Scotland. The forms based on *Scotch* are English and disfavored in Scotland, while those involving the full form *Scottish* tend to be more formal. In the interest of civility, forms involving *Scotch* are best avoided in reference to people. But there is no sure rule for referring to things, since the history of variation in the use of these words has also left many expressions in which the choice is fixed, such as *Scotch broth, Scotch whisky, Scottish rite,* and *Scots Guards.*

**senior** *The Oxford English Dictionary* traces the use of *senior* in the sense of "an older person" to the 14th century. In contemporary American English, however, *senior* is generally taken to be a shortening of the more recent *senior citizen,* and those who object to the compound are apt to object to the shortened form as well. As with the compound, though, you may have difficulty finding a good alternative. When speaking of older people as a group you can of course use *the elderly,* but when referring to individuals, as in *There were several seniors in the cast,* there is no clear alternative besides *older people,* which you may not feel is a significant improvement.

**senior citizen** Some people object to *senior citizen* as a patronizing or demeaning euphemism. Though clearly euphemistic in tone, it is not so easy to say exactly what *senior citizen* is a euphemism for. Most synonyms for "an older person," such as *oldster, old-timer,* and *golden ager,* are far more condescending or offensive, and one is left with compounds such as *older person, elderly man,* or *old woman,* which are not always better alternatives.

*Senior citizen* is a well-established term, first recorded in 1938, that rarely gives real offense and that, when used appropriately, can offer certain advantages over other choices. Unlike expressions based on *old* or *older, senior citizen* acknowledges that age is not necessarily the only relevant factor in describing people who are advanced in years. Strictly speaking, a senior citizen is a person who has reached an agreed-upon retirement age (though who has not necessarily retired) and whose relation to society—in the form of certain benefits and privileges—has changed accordingly. Thus *senior citizen* denotes not only age but also social or civic status, making it the natural term to use when discussing an older person in a political or social context. It is when *senior citizen* is used more loosely in contexts other than the societal that it draws the sharpest criticism.

**welsh** Etymologists can find no firm evidence that the verb *welsh,* meaning "to swindle a person by not paying a debt" or "to fail to fulfill an obligation,"

is derived from *Welsh,* the people of Wales. However, many Welsh themselves harbor no doubt on this subject and hold the verb to be a pointed slur. You would do well to avoid this informal term in ordinary discourse; *renege* or *cheat* can usually be substituted.

**white** Although *white* in its racial sense has never been stigmatized in the same way as other color labels, especially *yellow* and *red,* there are many people who would prefer to dispense with all color terms in referring to people in favor of a more neutral vocabulary of national or geographic origin. The proposal to replace *white* with *European* or *Euro-American* has a certain merit, especially in view of the recent acceptance of *African American* as an alternative to *black.* But the fact remains that *black* and *white* are not only familiar and convenient labels but in some cases terms of group pride as well, and as such they are not likely to disappear from American English anytime soon.

You should not confuse *white* with *Caucasian* or *Caucasoid. White* refers to the light-skinned peoples of Europe and adjacent areas of western Asia, whereas *Caucasian* and *Caucasoid* refer to a proposed geographical race that includes peoples from northern Africa, the Near and Middle East, and the Indian subcontinent along with Europeans.

Though *black* is sometimes capitalized when referring to African Americans or their culture, *white* is almost always spelled lowercase.
More at **black** and **Caucasian.**

**yellow** Of the color terms used as racial labels, *yellow,* referring to Asians, is perhaps the least used and the most clearly offensive. Its primary associations in contemporary English are with the expressions *yellow horde* and *yellow peril,* references to the supposed threat posed by Asian peoples who, according to a scenario popular around the turn of the 20th century, were poised to overwhelm the rest of the world, especially whites. Needless to say, *yellow* is not a term to be used by outsiders in ordinary discourse today.

# Pronunciation Challenges

*Confusions and Controversy*

*The affluent and choleric comptroller heinously inveigled herbs from the impious valet who often harasses the dour governor with aplomb.* The funny thing about this sentence (aside from the fact that it really doesn't make any sense) is that it is mostly made up of words that can be pronounced in at least two distinctly different ways, regardless of the speaker's accent or regional dialect. That is, when pronouncing these words, the speaker has a choice, whether to stress one syllable or another, or to pronounce a letter that for other people is silent, or to substitute or lose certain sounds. Because of all these choices, many speakers hesitate when pronouncing these words. The entries listed below will inform you about these words, and, we hope, will make you more comfortable about pronouncing them.

People commonly complain about the inadequacies of the English spelling system and about the difficulties that arise when they try to pronounce unfamiliar words. Many other languages are not plagued with these problems. Native speakers of English who are learning Czech, Finnish, Spanish, or Polish are delighted to discover that the pronunciation of a word in these languages can be predicted with a high degree of accuracy by its spelling. And conversely, the correct spelling of a word can be fairly easily deduced from its pronunciation. Unfortunately, in English the correlation between spelling and pronunciation is not as close. Just consider, for example, the letter *a*, which represents a different vowel sound in each of the following words: *pat, mane, father, any, village, waffle, wall, was.* Or consider the short *e* sound in *pet*, which may also be spelled *a (any), ae (aesthetic), ai (said), ay (says), ea (thread), ei (heifer), eo (leopard), ie (friendly), oe (roentgen),* and *u (burial).*

How did this situation come about? English adopted its alphabet, except for the letters j, u, and w, from the one used by the Romans to represent the sounds of Latin, and the fit was not an exact one. English is a Germanic language that has borrowed many words from French, Dutch, and other languages, and the result is a phonological mishmash in which certain letters are pronounced differently depending on the origin of the words they appear in. Nonetheless, English sound and spelling were not all that far apart until the advent of printing in the 15th and 16th centuries, which helped to freeze English spelling while its pronunciation underwent dramatic changes, principally in the system of long vowels, which is known as the Great Vowel Shift. As a result of these changes Middle English *name*, pronounced (nä′mə), became Modern English *name;* Middle English *sweete*, pronounced (swā′tə), became Modern English *sweet;* Middle English *ride*, pronounced (rē′də), became Modern English *ride*, and so forth. It was also during this period that final *e* became silent. Printers, however, preserved the spellings used in medieval manuscripts, so that our modern spellings actually reflect more accurately the medieval pronunciations of words before all these changes took place.

Today, enormous variety in pronunciation also exists because English is so widespread, with 350 million native speakers worldwide, which makes the existence of a universal standard impossible. Traditionally, however, varieties of English have been divided into two types, British English and American English, each with its own more or less acknowledged standard. Within the United States, home to 232 million native speakers of English, there is no single perceived standard of pronunciation. There are certain norms based on the variety of English spoken in the northern United States (not including New England) that have been adopted for use by news broadcasters, but even these are subject to more regional variation than most people might suppose. Thus, generally speaking, standards in the U.S., if they exist at all, tend to be regional. And with regard to the pronunciation of vowels in particular an enormous variation is tolerated across regional boundaries.

The list of entries that follows is composed of words whose pronunciation has a history of variation or controversy, or for one reason or another has been problematic for speakers. A few of the entries simply address various processes of phonologic change, such as assimilation and dissimilation, which are natural processes that occur in all living languages. Other entries, as at *C* and *G*, concern aspects of pronunciation that are taken for granted or ignored by most speakers but that are interesting nevertheless from a historical point of view.

The symbols used to render pronunciations are those that are used in *The American Heritage Dictionary of the English Language, Third Edition* (1992). These symbols are phonemic rather than phonetic. That is, they are designed to help you distinguish meaningful units of sound, such as the difference between *cat* and *cad* or *pat* and *pet*. They are not designed to represent the specific pronunciation of any individual or of any particular speech community. Thus they allow people from different speech communities to pronounce words correctly in their native dialect. In the discussions that follow, the term *long vowel* can refer to any of the following sounds: (ā), (ē), (ī), (ō), (ä), and (o͞o); it can also refer to the diphthongs (ou) and (oi). The term *short vowel* can refer to any of these sounds: (ă), (ĕ), (ĭ), (ŏ), (ŭ), and (o͝o). A full pronunciation key can be found on page 211.

# Pronunciation Symbols

A list of the pronunciation symbols used in this book is given here in the column headed *Symbols*. Next to each symbol, in the column headed *Examples,* is a word or words chosen to illustrate how the symbol is pronounced. The letters that correspond in sound to the symbols are printed in boldface type.

| Symbols | Examples | Symbols | Examples |
|---|---|---|---|
| ă | pat | o͞o | boot |
| ā | pay | ou | out |
| âr | care | p | pop |
| ä | father | r | roar |
| b | bib | s | sauce |
| ch | church | sh | ship, dish |
| d | deed, milled | t | tight, stopped |
| ĕ | pet | th | thin |
| ē | bee | *th* | this |
| f | fife, phase, rough | ŭ | cut |
| | | ûr | urge, term, firm |
| g | gag | v | valve |
| h | hat | w | with |
| ĭ | pit | y | yes |
| ī | pie, by | z | zebra, xylem |
| îr | pier | zh | vision, pleasure, garage |
| j | judge | | |
| k | kick, cat, pique | ə | about, edible, circus |
| l | lid, needle | | |
| m | mum | ər | butter |
| n | no, sudden | | |
| ng | thing | **Stress** | |
| ŏ | pot | Primary stress (′) | **global** (glō′bəl) |
| ō | toe | | |
| ô | caught, paw | Secondary stress (′) | **globalize** (glō′bə-līz′) |
| oi | noise | | |
| o͝o | took | | |

**a** The indefinite article is generally pronounced (ə), as in *a boy, a girl.* When stressed for emphasis, it is pronounced (ā), as in *not a person was left.* The form *an,* which is used before vowels, also has a stressed and an unstressed variant.

**aberrant** Traditionally this word has been pronounced with stress on the second syllable. However, a newer pronunciation with stress on the first syllable has apparently gained a lot of ground and is now equally acceptable. In a recent ballot, 45 percent of the Usage Panel preferred the older pronunciation, and 50 percent preferred the newer one. A small percentage of the panelists use both pronunciations. Perhaps one reason for the shift is the association of *aberrant* with *aberration* and *aberrated,* which are both stressed on the first syllable.

**acumen** The pronunciation (ə-kyōō′mən), with stress on the second syllable, is an older, traditional pronunciation reflecting the word's Latin origin. An Anglicized variant pronunciation with stress on the first syllable, (ăk′yə-mən), is equally acceptable and may be more common in British English.

**–ade** This noun suffix can be traced back to Latin through French, and then Provençal, Spanish, Portuguese, or Italian, which undoubtedly accounts for the variety of ways in which it can be pronounced. Most English words ending with *-ade* were adopted from French with no change in spelling: *accolade, balustrade, charade, comrade, esplanade, façade, lemonade, masquerade, serenade.* The usual pronunciation in English is (-ād), although many of these words, such as *accolade,* have a variant with the pronunciation (-äd), and for some, such as *esplanade* and *façade,* (-äd) may be the most common or only acceptable pronunciation. No one will have trouble pronouncing the words that are commonly used, but with unfamiliar words the pronunciation (-ād) is probably safest.

**aerate** The pronunciation (âr′ē-āt′), which may raise a few eyebrows in some circles, is an example of *intrusion,* a phonological process that involves the addition or insertion of an extra sound for no obvious reason. The usual pronunciation of *aerate* has only two syllables, (âr′āt′).
More at **intrusion.**

**affluence / affluent** Most people pronounce these two words with stress on the first syllable, (ăf′lōō-əns; ăf′lōō-ənt). The pronunciation with stress on the second syllable, (ə-flōō′əns; ə-flōō′ənt), is a newer pronunciation that has developed in American English, and probably occurs more frequently among younger educated people.

**–age** This noun suffix appears in many words that are borrowed from French, such as *barrage* (a dam), *barrage* (heavy artillery fire; an outpouring), *damage, espionnage, garage, heritage, homage, language, manage, marriage, personage, reportage, sabotage, umbrage, usage, visage, voyage.* The pronunciation of *-age* in these words can range from (-äzh) to (-äj) to (-ĭj) depending on the degree to which the pronunciation has become Anglicized. In words formed in English on the same model, such as *luggage, poundage, orphanage, parsonage, breakage,* and *wreckage,* the pronunciation of *-age* is always (-ĭj).

**agoraphobia** The pronunciation (ăg′ər-ə-fō′bē-ə) is the one most widely accepted in educated speech. Likewise *agoraphobe* should be pronounced (ăg′ər-ə-fōb′) and *agoraphobic* (ăg′ər-ə-fō′bĭk).

**ague** This somewhat old-fashioned word is properly pronounced (ā′gyō͞o), with two syllables.

**albumen / albumin** Both of these words generally have stress on the second syllable, and, in fact, sound the same except for the final vowels, which may be slightly emphasized to preserve a distinction between the two. A pronunciation with the stress on the first syllable does occur, however, probably more often in British English.

**alms** The older and more widely accepted pronunciation is (ämz), but the spelling pronunciation (älmz) is increasingly common.
More at **L** and **spelling pronunciation.**

**alumni / alumnae** *Alumni,* the Latin plural of *alumnus,* is usually pronounced (ə-lŭm′nī), according to the pronunciation rules for Anglicized Latin. Likewise *alumnae,* the Latin plural of *alumna,* is usually pronounced (ə-lŭm′nē). Confusion comes about in part because in English *i* has several possible pronunciations and *ae* is an unusual combination. Also, in classical Latin pronunciation, which attempts to approximate the pronunciation of ancient Roman times, the opposite would be true, that is, the final vowel sound of *alumni* would be (ē), and the final vowel sound of *alumnae* would be (ī).

**analogous** This word is properly pronounced (ə-năl′ə-gəs), with a hard *g* sound, never (ə-năl′ə-jəs), with a *j* sound.
More at **G.**

**anesthetist** The pronunciation (ə-nĕs′tĭ-tĭst) is an example of *assimilation,* a phonological process that involves one sound being influenced by another sound, usually a following sound, so that the sounds become more alike or identical. In the case of *anesthetist,* the (th) becomes (t) by assimilating to the following (t), with the result that the sound segment (tĭ) occurs twice. In careful speech the word should properly be pronounced (ə-nĕs′thĭ-tĭst).
More at **assimilation.**

**angina** The pronunciation (ăn′jə-nə), which more accurately reflects the word's Latin pronunciation, is more common in medicine. Both pronunciations, the one with stress on the second syllable and the one with stress on the first syllable, are acceptable in all circumstances, however.

**Antarctic** The original spelling of the word *Antarctic* in English left out the first *c*, which was reintroduced into the spelling apparently at the beginning of the 17th century, most likely in a conscious effort to make the English word conform more closely to its Greek ancestor. The spelling with the *c* is now, of course, the only acceptable one, but the pronunciation with the *c* is not. Both (ănt-ärk′tĭk) and (ănt-är′tĭk) are equally acceptable.
More at **Arctic.**

**apartheid** This word from Afrikaans, the language of the Dutch settlers of South Africa, is pronounced in many ways in English including (ə-pärt′hīt′), (ə-pärt′hāt′), (ə-pär′tīt′), (ə-pär′tāt′), (ə-pär′tīd′), (ə-pär′tād′). Any of these pronunciations is generally acceptable. The pronunciation that most closely approaches the one in Afrikaans is (ə-pärt′hāt′).

**aplomb** Confusion arises with the pronunciation of this word probably because the sequence *omb* has several conspicuously different ways of being pronounced—(ŏm) as in *bomb,* (ōm) as in *comb,* (o͞om) as in *tomb.* You can pronounce *aplomb* (ə-plŏm′) or (ə-plŭm′).

**arctic / Arctic** *Arctic* was originally spelled in English without the first *c,* which was later reintroduced after the original spelling in Greek. Both (ärk′tĭk) and (är′tĭk) are equally acceptable pronunciations.
More at **Antarctic.**

**argot** The pronunciation (är′gō), a remnant of the word's French origin, still appears to be the most common one, although (är′gət) is also acceptable, especially in American English.

**ask** The pronunciations (ăks) and (ăst) are both considered nonstandard, although they may occur fairly frequently, especially in the southern or middle sections of the country. The pronunciation (ăst) for *asked,* on the other hand, is extremely common all over and can be considered standard.

**assimilation** *Assimilation* is a phonological process that occurs when the articulation of one sound is influenced by another adjacent or nearby sound, usually a following one, so that the two sounds become more alike or even identical. An example of a partial assimilation is the pronunciation (ĭng′kŭm′) for *income,* where (n), which is made near the front of the mouth, becomes (ng), made near the back of the mouth, before (k), also made near the back of the mouth. An example of a total assimilation is the pronunciation (hôrsh′sho͞o′) for *horseshoe,* where (s) before (sh) becomes (sh). The main result of assimilation, as with other types of historical sound change, is that articulation is made easier for a speaker, particularly when speech is rapid. Particular instances of assimilation, such as those above, or the pronunciations (lĕnth) and (strĕnth) for *length* and *strength,* or (pŭng′kĭn) for *pumpkin,* may draw adverse criticism despite the fact that such criticism is groundless from a historical or phonological point of view.

**asterisk** This word is properly pronounced (ăs′tə-rĭsk′). The pronunciation (ăs′tə-rĭks′), which is frowned on in educated speech, illustrates a linguistic process known as *metathesis,* which refers to a transposition of sounds, syllables, or words in a particular sequence.
More at **metathesis.**

**athlete** The pronunciation (ăth′ə-lēt′) is an example of *intrusion,* a phonological process that involves the addition or insertion of an extra sound within a word or between words in speech. Most people pronounce *athlete* (ăth′lēt′), with just two syllables.
More at **intrusion.**

**auxiliary** The pronunciations (ôg-zĭl′yə-rē) and (ôg-zĭl′ə-rē) are probably the most common. Other acceptable pronunciations are (ôg-zĭl′ē-ĕr′ē), (ôg-zĭl′ē-ə-rē), and (ôg-zĭl′rē).

**banal** Here's a word whose pronunciation vexes just about everyone, including our Usage Panel. In a recent ballot, 46 percent of the panelists preferred the pronunciation (bə-năl′), rhyming with *canal;* 38 percent said they used (bā′nəl), rhyming with *anal;* 14 percent said (bə-näl′), second syllable rhyming with *doll;* and 2 percent used (băn′əl), rhyming with *panel.* In this situation, there really is no right or wrong choice. Use any of the first three and you will have lots of company.

**barbiturate** Originally this word had its main stress on the third syllable (bär′bĭ-tŏor′ĭt, -āt′, -tyŏor′-), a pronunciation that is still used sometimes in medicine. As the word passed into the general vocabulary the stress shifted to the second syllable (bär-bĭch′ər-ĭt, -ə-rāt′), bringing the stress pattern more in line with words like *acculturate* and *saturate.* Either way is considered correct now. Since at least the early 1960s the pronunciation (bär-bĭch′ə-wĭt), without the second *r,* has been considered nonstandard despite the fact that many people pronounce the word that way.

**blackguard** This rather old-fashioned and now chiefly literary word dates back to the 16th century when it was spelled and most likely pronounced as two distinct words and probably referred literally to a guard of soldiers or perhaps some kind of attendants. By the 18th century the two words had become a hyphenated or a solid compound with the meaning "scoundrel." As the two parts of the compound lost their separate meanings, so they eventually lost their separate pronunciations. *Blackguard* is pronounced (blăg′əd) in British English and (blăg′ərd) or (blăg′ärd′) in American English.

**boatswain** Usually pronounced (bō′sən), this word, like *blackguard,* has a pronunciation that is not easily predictable from the spelling. But whereas *blackguard* is never pronounced as two words, *boatswain* is often pronounced (bōt′swān′)—by landlubbers, of course—and that is not considered incorrect.

The variant spellings *bosun, bo's'n,* and *bos'n,* reflecting the sailors' pronunciation, have been around for well over a hundred years. Other nautical words with tricky pronunciations include *bowline, forecastle, gunwale, mainsail,* and *topgallant,* to name just a few.
More at **pronunciation spelling** and **spelling pronunciation.**

**bogeyman** We are all frightened by this mysterious character, but we cannot seem to agree on what to call him. His aliases include *bogeyman, bogyman, boogeyman, boogyman, boogieman,* and also *boogerman, boogarman,* and *buggerman.* The original word was probably *bogey* or *bogy* with the other forms springing up as pronunciation spellings. Pronunciation options include (bō′gē), (bōō′gē), (bōōg′ē), or (bōōg′ər), (bōō′gər), or even (bŭg′ər). According to the *Dictionary of American Regional English,* the form *boogerman* prevails in the South, and *boogeyman* everywhere else in the United States.

**bouquet** When used to refer to a bunch of flowers, this 18th-century borrowing from French may be pronounced (bō-kā′) or (bōō-kā′) in American English. When used to refer to an aroma, as of wine, this word is usually pronounced (bōō-kā′).

**bowline** This nautical word is traditionally pronounced (bō′lĭn), but the pronunciation (bō′līn′) is also correct.
More at **spelling pronunciation.**

**breeches** The noun meaning "trousers" rhymes with *itches,* and may be spelled *britches.*

**brooch** This word, which can also be spelled *broach,* is pronounced (brōch), and less often (brōōch).

**bulimia** The older pronunciation in English is (byōō-lĭm′ē-ə), which is still used in medicine. In popular usage the word is now more commonly pronounced (bōō-lē′mē-ə).

**buoy** Traditionally and in Britain this word is pronounced like *boy,* (boi). In the United States the more common pronunciation seems to be (bōō′ē), except in the compound *life buoy,* where (boi) is entrenched. The pronunciation (bwoi), which is also traditional, is now rarely heard in either Britain or the U.S.

**C** Our letter *c* comes from the Roman alphabet and is a descendant of Greek gamma, which the Romans adapted and used to represent the sound (k) as well as (g). (Later they developed the form *G* and assigned the (g) sound to it.) In Latin and the Romance languages the pronunciation of (k) before *e, i,* and *y* gradually changed resulting in the sound (ch) or the "soft" *c* pronounced like (s). Middle English scribes continued the use of (soft) *c* before *e, i,* and *y* in words borrowed from French and began to use *k* more frequently for the hard *c* sound before these vowels in native English words. In Modern English, *c* is, with very few exceptions, soft before *e, i,* and *y* and hard before *a, o, u,* and consonants.

**cabal** Either (kə-băl′) or (kə-bäl′) is acceptable.

**cache** This early 19th-century borrowing from French sounds like *cash.* The pronunciation (kă-shā′) goes with *cachet,* another French borrowing.

**cadre** This 19th-century borrowing from French has a variety of pronunciations in English including (kăd′rē), (kä′drē), (kăd′rā) and (kä′drā). The first of these was popularized by the United States military, and (kä′drē) and (kä′drā) have sprung up probably through the association of *cadre* with *padre.* The pronunciation (kä′dər), which is the most common in British English, is closest to the French pronunciation. Any of these pronunciations is acceptable.

**catacomb** The final syllable of this word usually rhymes with *comb* in American English and *comb* or *tomb* in British English.

**Celt / Celtic** In general, scholars pronounce these words with an initial (k) sound, but many people pronounce them with an (s) sound.

**centenary** The pronunciation with the main stress on the first syllable is the correct historical pronunciation, but the pronunciation with stress on the second syllable, which probably came about through association with *centennial,* is now equally common.

**cerebral** The pronunciation with stress on the first syllable is the older Anglicized one, but the pronunciation with stress on the second syllable, which is especially common in American English, is equally acceptable.

**Ch** In Old English the sounds (k) and (ch) were both represented by the letter *c.* Later, under the influence of French spelling, Middle English scribes inserted an *h* after *c* to indicate the (ch) sound at the beginning of words, as in *child.* (The sequence *tch* became the usual way to represent this sound following short vowels, as in *catch.*) In English words of Greek origin the digraph *ch* represents a transliteration of Greek X (chi), and so is usually pronounced (k), as in *chorus, architect.* And in English words borrowed from French, *ch* is often pronounced (sh), as in *charlatan, cachet.*

**choleric** The older pronunciation, which is the only one recognized by British dictionaries, has stress on the first syllable like *cholera.* The newer and chiefly American variant has stress on the second syllable.

**clique** The pronunciation (klēk) appears to be the preferred pronunciation in English, but the less common Anglicized variant (klĭk) is also acceptable.

**clothes** The pronunciation (klōz) has been recorded in various dictionaries since the 1700s including Samuel Johnson's (1755) and Noah Webster's (1828). The pronunciation (klōthz), while not incorrect, is sometimes considered pedantic. Either pronunciation is acceptable, but (klōz) is much more common.

**colander** Traditionally the first vowel is pronounced as a short *u,* as in *cull,* but the pronunciation with a short *o,* (kŏl′ən-dər), is now more common.

**comptroller** This word is first recorded in the 15th century as an alternate spelling for *controller,* the first syllable of which had become associated with the etymologically unrelated word *count* and its variant *compt.* Although the historical pronunciation for this word would be the same as for *controller,* evidence indicates that the spelling pronunciations (kŏmp-trō′lər) and (kŏmp′trō′lər) are probably now used by a majority of speakers. In a recent ballot, 43 percent of the Usage Panel indicated that they pronounce *comptroller* like *controller,* while 57 percent pronounce it as it is spelled, with stress on either the first or second syllable. And of those who say they pronounce *comptroller* like *controller,* about half indicated that they also consider one or the other of the spelling pronunciations acceptable.
More at **spelling pronunciation.**

**conch** Strictly speaking the *ch* should be pronounced (k) as it is in *concha, conchoid,* and *conchology* (ultimately from Greek *konkhē,* "mussel"). However, many people, especially those not familiar with this mollusk as seafood, say (kŏnch) based on the spelling. Note that the same variant occurs in *conchfish.*
More at **Ch** and **spelling pronunciation.**

**coupon** This word, which was borrowed from French in the 19th century, was originally pronounced (kōō′pŏn′). The variant pronunciation (kyōō′pŏn′) developed in American English perhaps through association with words like *cube, cupid,* and *cute.* Both pronunciations are acceptable.

**covert** The traditional pronunciation of *covert,* which is related to *cover,* is (kŭv′ərt). In American English, however, a relatively new variant pronunciation with a long *o* in the first syllable has become the more common one. This is probably the result of the association of *covert* with its antonym *overt,* which is pronounced with a long *o.* Both pronunciations are acceptable.

**culinary** The pronunciation (kyōō′lə-nĕr′ē) is older, but (kŭl′ə-nĕr′ē) appears to be more common now in both American and British English. Either pronunciation is acceptable.

**dais** The one-syllable pronunciation (dās) is older, but the two-syllable pronunciation (dā′ĭs), or sometimes (dī′ĭs), is more common now.

**debacle** Although this borrowing from French has shed its accent marks and shifted its meaning since entering English nearly 200 years ago, it has managed for the most part to hang on to an original pronunciation. Most people continue to pronounce this word (dĭ-bä′kəl), or often (dā-bä′kəl), reflecting even more closely the French spelling *débâcle*. In American English the pronunciations (dĭ-băk′əl) and (dā-băk′əl) are also acceptable. Recent evidence suggests that the pronunciation (dĕb′ə-kəl), with stress on the first syllable, is becoming more common, but it is not yet widely accepted.

**deify / deity** Traditionally these are pronounced (dē′ə-fī′) and (dē′ĭ-tē), with a long *e* in the first syllable. Although the pronunciation with a long *a* (first syllable sounds like *day*) has become fairly common, some people still dislike it.

**demagogic / demagogy** Either (dĕm′ə-gŏg′ĭk) with a hard *g* or (dĕm′ə-gŏj′ĭk) with a soft *g* is acceptable, and the same thing applies to *demagogy*. More at **G**.

**despicable** Up until about the middle of this century most people pronounced this word with stress on the first syllable, and many deplored the pronunciation with stress on the second syllable. But times have changed, and now the pronunciation with stress on the second syllable is the usual one.

**desultory** This rather fancy and rarely heard word is pronounced with stress on the first and third syllables.

**diphtheria** This word is properly pronounced (dĭf-thîr′ē-ə), with the *ph* pronounced (f). Many people, however, say (dĭp-thîr′ē-ə), including medical professionals, and most dictionaries (of American English anyway) have included this variant pronunciation for the last thirty or forty years.

**diphthong** As is the case with *diphtheria*, the *ph* should properly be pronounced (f), not (p). Because so many people say (dĭp-), as opposed to (dĭf-), though, this variant has gradually become acceptable.

**disastrous** This word is properly pronounced (dĭ-zăs′trəs), or perhaps (dĭ-săs′trəs). Pronouncing the word (dĭ-zăs′tər-əs), as if it were spelled *disasterous*, could lead you to make that spelling error.

**disparate** The usual pronunciation is (dĭs′pər-ĭt), with stress on the first syllable. The pronunciation (dĭ-spăr′ĭt), with stress on the second syllable, is also acceptable, although less common.

**dissect** There are people who still object to the pronunciation (dī′sĕkt′), rhyming with *bisect*, although most dictionaries have listed it as an acceptable variant pronunciation for some decades. Those who dislike this pronunciation prefer the more established (dĭ-sĕkt′).

**dissimilation** *Dissimilation* is a phonological process that involves one of two similar or identical sounds within a word becoming less like the other or even disappearing entirely. Because *r*'s in successive syllables are particularly difficult to pronounce, they frequently dissimilate. One historical example of dissimilation is *marble,* from French *marbre.* In this case the second *r* has dissimilated to *l* in order to prevent a repetition of the *r* and ease articulation. Other contemporary examples of dissimilation include *enterprise, governor, impropriety, prerogative, surprise,* and *thermometer,* in which there is a tendency for the first *r* to drop out of the pronunciation resulting in (ĕn′tə-prīz′), (gŭv′ə-nər), (ĭm′pə-prī′ə-tē), (pə-rŏg′ə-tĭv), (sə-prīz′), and (thə-mŏm′ĭ-tər). None of these examples really receives any adverse criticism, but some instances of dissimilation may, as the pronunciation (lī′bĕr′ē) for *library.* Note that other consonants besides *r* may be altered or omitted as a result of dissimilation, such as *n* in *government* (gŭv′ər-mənt).

**doughty** Pronounce this (dou′tē), with the *ou* as in *doubt* or *pout.*

**dour** This word, which is etymologically related to *duress* and *endure,* traditionally rhymes with *tour.* Although some people might still scorn the variant pronunciation that rhymes with *sour,* it is, in fact, widely used and cannot be considered wrong.

**dwarf** The plural of this word is either *dwarfs* (dwôrfs) or *dwarves* (dwôrvz). The latter form is the older of the two, the change from *f* to *v* being the result of a phonological rule in Old English. Other words that follow this pattern are *thief/thieves, leaf/leaves,* and *wife/wives.* While many of the words that are in this category still have their traditional plurals, some have also adopted modern plurals ending in just *s,* as *dwarf* has. And some words of this type have lost the older plural almost completely, as has *roof,* whose only plural now is *roofs,* although you may still hear (roovz) or (roovz).
More at **roof.**

**ebullience / ebullient** Traditionally, these are pronounced (ĭ-bŭl′yəns) and (ĭ-bŭl′yənt), with a short *u* in the second syllable as in *gull.* This is apparently still the preferred pronunciation in British English. In American English, the variant pronunciations (ĭ-bool′-yəns) and (ĭ-bool′yənt), with the second syllable like *bull,* are now equally common.

**–ed** The suffix *-ed,* which is used to form the past tense and past participle of regular verbs, may be pronounced (t), (d), or (ĭd) depending on the phonological environment. That is, *-ed* is always pronounced (t) after the consonant sounds *p, f, s, ch, k;* (d) after vowels and the consonant sounds *b, m, n, v, l, z, j, r, g;* and (ĭd) after *t* and *d.* In a small group of adjectives including *aged, alleged, beloved, blessed, cursed, dogged,* and *learned, -ed* may also be pronounced (ĭd) following consonants other than *t* and *d.* This distinction between the pronunciation of the adjective form and the pronunciation of the past tense or past participle form is not always strictly preserved, though. We say *a learned* (lûr′nĭd) *professor* but *a beloved* (bĭ-lŭv′ĭd or bĭ-lŭvd′) *spouse.* There is some justification for retaining the pronunciation (ĭd) since it does signal a subtle shift in meaning.

**either** The usual pronunciation in American English is (ē′thər), with a long *e* sound. According to the *Dictionary of American Regional English,* the pronunciation (ī′thər), with a long *i,* is used mostly by well educated speakers in urban areas of the Northeast, and is often considered affected by others. Almost the opposite is true in British English, however, where (ī′thər) is more common. Both pronunciations have been recognized by English dictionaries since the 18th century. The same variation occurs in *neither.*

**envelope** A lot of people dislike the pronunciation (ŏn′və-lōp′) because, they argue, it is pseudo-French and superfluous since there exists a perfectly acceptable Anglicized pronunciation. As a recent ballot shows, however, the (ŏn′-) pronunciation is used by 30 percent of the Usage Panel and is recognized as an acceptable variant by about 20 percent of those panelists who normally use the (ĕn′-) pronunciation.

**environment** A careful pronunciation of this word is (ĕn-vī′rən-mənt), which closely reflects the spelling. In practice, this word is more often pronounced (ĕn-vī′ərn-mənt) or (ĕn-vī′ər-mənt) or (ĕn-vīr′mənt). All of these pronunciations are acceptable.

**epoch** In American English the usual pronunciation is (ĕp′ək) and less often (ē′pŏk′). In British English (ē′pŏk′) is usual.

**err** The pronunciation (ûr) is the older, traditional one, but in recent years the pronunciation (ĕr) has gained currency, perhaps as a result of association with *errant* and *error.* In a recent ballot, 56 percent of the Usage Panel preferred (ûr), 34 percent preferred (ĕr), and 10 percent accepted both pronunciations.

**escalator** The pronunciation (ĕs′kyə-lā′tər), which is generally not considered acceptable, is an example of *intrusion,* a phonological process that involves the addition or insertion of an extra sound. The usual pronunciation is (ĕs′kə-lā′tər).
More at **intrusion.**

**escape** The pronunciation (ĭk-skāp′) is considered nonstandard and is probably a result of confusion with words beginning with the prefix *ex-.*

**espresso / expresso** The Italian word is *espresso,* pronounced (ĭ-sprĕs′ō) or (ĕ-sprĕs′ō) in English. It is short for *caffè espresso,* or "coffee that has been pressed out." *Expresso,* pronounced (ĭk-sprĕs′ō), first occurred no doubt

through erroneous association with the word *express.* But now *expresso* is also common, even in edited prose.

**et cetera** This Latin phrase meaning "and the rest" is usually pronounced (ĕt sĕt′ər-ə) or (ĕt sĕt′rə). The pronunciation (ĕk sĕt′ər-ə), with a (k) substituted for the first *t,* is considered nonstandard.

**exquisite** The older pronunciation (and the one defended staunchly by usage writers for decades) has stress on the first syllable, rhyming with *requisite.* A newer pronunciation with stress on the second syllable, rhyming roughly with *exhibit,* is now fairly common, however. In a recent ballot, 55 percent of the Usage Panel indicated they prefer the first pronunciation, 35 percent indicated they prefer the second pronunciation, and a small percentage accepted both.

**February** The preferred pronunciation among usage writers is (fĕb′rōō-ĕr′ē), but in actual usage the pronunciation (fĕb′yōō-ĕr′ē) is more common and so cannot be considered incorrect. The loss of the first *r* in this pronunciation can be accounted for by the phonological process known as *dissimilation,* whereby one of two similar or identical sounds in a word is changed or dropped so that a repetition of that sound is avoided. In the case of *February,* the loss of the first *r* was also helped along by the influence of *January,* which has only one *r.*
More at **dissimilation.**

**flaccid** The older pronunciation is (flăk′sĭd), but the variant (flăs′ĭd) has been recorded in dictionaries since about the middle of the 20th century.

**forecastle** Pronounced (fōk′səl) by sailors, this word, like *boatswain,* has a pronunciation that is not easily predictable from the spelling. The variant spelling *fo'c'sle,* reflecting this pronunciation, has been around for well over 100 years. Note that it is also acceptable to pronounce *forecastle* (fôr′kăs′əl) or (fōr′kăs′əl). Other nautical words with tricky pronunciations include *bowline, gunwale, mainsail,* and *topgallant,* to name just a few.
More at **pronunciation spelling** and **spelling pronunciation.**

**formidable** Traditionally this word has been pronounced with stress on the first syllable, as (fôr′mĭ-də-bəl), but recently the pronunciation with stress on the second syllable, (fôr-mĭd′ə-bəl), which is a common variant in British English, appears to be on the increase in American English. The pronunciation with stress on the first syllable is apparently still preferred by a large majority of educated speakers, however. In a recent ballot, 80 percent of the Usage Panel said they pronounced the word with stress on the first syllable, 14 percent stress the second syllable, and a small percentage said they used both pronunciations.

**forte** This word, meaning "strong point," from French *fort,* meaning "strong," can be pronounced with one syllable, like the English word *fort,* or with two syllables. The two-syllable pronunciation, (fôr′tā′), is probably the most common in American English, but some people dislike it, arguing that it properly belongs to the music term *forte* from Italian.

**fulminant / fulminate** Traditionally, these are pronounced (fŭl′mə-nənt) and (fŭl′mə-nāt′), with a short *u* in the first syllable as in *gull*. This is apparently still the preferred pronunciation in British English. In American English, the variant pronunciations (fo͞ol′mə-nənt) and (fo͞ol′mə-nāt′), with the first syllable like *full*, are now slightly more common.

**fulsome** The older pronunciation is (fŭl′səm), which was still being recorded in dictionaries (increasingly as a less common variant) up to about the middle of the 20th century. *Fulsome* is now always pronounced (fo͞ol′səm), with the first syllable like *full*, in both British and American English.

**fungi** Although this word, the Latin plural of *fungus*, can be pronounced with a soft or hard *g*, as (fŭn′jī) or (fŭng′gī), the former is the most common pronunciation in medicine, as well as in American English in general. Note that *g* may also be soft or hard in *fungicide, fungiform, fungivorous*, and in other similar compounds.
More at **G.**

**G** The letter *G* was developed by the ancient Romans from the Roman letter *C*, which initially represented the sound (k) as well as (g). Eventually *C* came to be written *G* when used to represent (g), and *C* was then used exclusively for (k). In Latin and the Romance languages the pronunciation of (g) before *e, i,* and *y* gradually changed resulting in the "soft" *g* pronounced like (j). After the Norman Invasion of Britain in the 11th century, Middle English scribes continued the use of (soft) *g* before *e, i,* and y in words borrowed from French. (In Modern French, *g* before *e, i,* and *y* is now pronounced (zh).) Also with the influence of French the symbol *g* began to replace the symbol ʒ, which was the Irish form of Roman *g* that had been used to represent the hard *g* sound in Old English. In Modern English, words beginning with soft *g* before *e, i,* and *y* are generally of French or Latin origin, such as *gelid* and *giblet*, and words beginning with hard *g* before *e, i,* and *y* are generally of native English or Germanic origin, such as *gear* and *give*. Like *c, g* is generally hard before *a, o, u,* and consonants.

**genealogy** The effect of the influence of words ending in *-ology* is such that people now almost always say (jē′nē-ŏl′ə-jē), with a short *o*, and much less frequently (jē′nē-ăl′ə-jē), with a short *a*. Both pronunciations are acceptable, however.

**genuine** For a long time the two pronunciations of this word have clearly differentiated members of different social levels, especially in the southern and southwestern United States, with the pronunciation (jĕn′yo͞o-ĭn) usually occurring among well educated people and the pronunciation (jĕn′yōō-īn′) among the less well educated. There is now some evidence that the pronunciation with long *i* in the last syllable is becoming more widely used by people of all social levels, but the most widely accepted pronunciation is still (jĕn′yōō-ĭn). People who normally use the short *i* pronunciation often use the long *i* pronunciation jokingly.

**genus** Pronounce this word (jē′nəs), with a long *e* in the first syllable, but note that the Latin plural, *genera,* should be pronounced (jĕn′ər-ə), with a short *e* in the first syllable.

**gerrymander** Although Elbridge Gerry, who inspired this word, pronounced his name (gĕr′ē), with a hard *g, gerrymander* may be pronounced (jĕr′ē-măn′dər) or (gĕr′ē-măn′dər). Actually the pronunciation with a soft *g* is more common now.

**gibberish** A very small minority of people pronounces this word with a hard *g.* The overwhelming majority pronounces it (jĭb′ər-ĭsh).

**governor** Standard pronunciations for this word include (gŭv′ər-nər), (gŭv′ə-nər), and (gŭv′nər). The second of these has lost an *r* through *dissimilation,* a phonological process that involves the change or loss of one of two similar or identical sounds in a word in order to avoid a repetition of that sound.
More at **dissimilation.**

**grievous** The pronunciation (grē′vē-əs), which is considered nonstandard, is an example of *intrusion,* a phonological process that involves the addition or insertion of an extra sound. The usual pronunciation of *grievous* has only two syllables, (grē′vəs).
More at **intrusion.**

**gunwale** Like *boatswain* and *forecastle,* this nautical word has a pronunciation, (gŭn′əl), that is not easily predictable from the spelling. Note that although *gunwale* is the usual spelling, the word is always pronounced (gŭn′əl). The variant spelling *gunnel,* which reflects the pronunciation, has been used for several hundred years and is also acceptable. Other nautical words with tricky pronunciations include *bowline, mainsail,* and *topgallant,* to name just a few.
More at **pronunciation spelling** and **spelling pronunciation.**

**H** The letter *H* comes from the Roman alphabet. The (h) sound was eventually lost in Latin, and in the Romance languages, which are descended from Latin, *h* is not pronounced although it is retained in the spelling of some words. In both Old English and Middle English, *h* represented (h) at the beginning of words and before vowels, although in Middle English *h* "weakened" somewhat and was often silent before vowels in unstressed syllables. In

Modern English, *h* is usually pronounced in native English words such as *happy* and *hot* and, because of the influence of writing, in most words borrowed from French such as *haste* and *hostel*. In a few other words borrowed from French the *h* has remained silent, as in *honor, honest, hour,* and *heir.* And in another small group of French loan words, including *herb, humble, human,* and *humor,* the *h* may or may not be pronounced depending on the dialect of English.

**harass** The pronunciation with stress on the first syllable is the older, traditional pronunciation, and is the one still recommended by some, notably British, usage guides. The pronunciation with stress on the second syllable is a newer pronunciation that first occurred in American English and has gained in currency over the last half century or so. In a recent ballot, 50 percent of the Usage Panel preferred the pronunciation with stress on the first syllable, and 50 percent preferred stress on the second syllable.

**hegemony** Although this word may be pronounced (hĭ-jĕm′ə-nē), with stress on the second syllable, or (hĕj′ə-mō′nē), with stress on the first syllable, in a recent ballot a clear majority of the Usage Panel, 72 percent, preferred the first pronunciation.

**height** Although many people pronounce this word as if it were spelled *heightth,* the pronunciation (hīt) is still considered the only standard pronunciation by most dictionaries.

**heinous** For an overwhelming majority of the Usage Panel, the first syllable of this word rhymes with *mane,* and for a small minority it rhymes with *mean.*

**herb** In British English this word and its derivatives, such as *herbaceous, herbal, herbicide,* and *herbivore,* are pronounced with *h.* In American English the situation is not as simple. *Herb* and *herbal* are more often pronounced (ûrb) and (ûr′bəl) than (hûrb) and (hûr′bəl), and the opposite is true of *herbaceous, herbicide,* and *herbivore,* which are all more often pronounced with the *h.*
More at **H.**

**hoof** The plural of this word is either *hoofs,* (ho͝ofs) or (ho͞ofs), or *hooves,* (ho͝ovz) or (ho͞ovz). The latter spelling is the older of the two, the change from *f* to *v* being the result of a phonological rule in Old English. Other words that follow this pattern are *thief/thieves, leaf/leaves,* and *wife/wives.* While many of the words that are in this category still have their traditional plurals, some have also adopted modern plurals ending in just *s,* as *hoof* has. And some words of this type have lost the older plural almost completely, as has *roof,* whose only plural now is *roofs,* although you may still hear (ro͝ovz) or (ro͞ovz).
More at **roof.**

**hovel / hover** In American English these words are most commonly pronounced with a short *u* sound in the first syllable and less commonly with a short *o*.

**impious** The traditional pronunciation is (ĭm′pē-əs), with stress on the first syllable, but the pronunciation (ĭm-pī′əs), with stress on the second syllable, has been included in dictionaries since the middle of the 20th century.

**inherence / inherent** Traditionally, these are pronounced (ĭn-hîr′əns) and (ĭn-hîr′ənt), but the pronunciations with short *e*, (ĭn-hĕr′əns) and (ĭn-hĕr′ənt), are equally common now. The change is perhaps a result of association with *inherit.*

**integral** You can stress this word on the first or second syllable as (ĭn′tĭ-grəl) or (ĭn-tĕg′rəl), but take care to pronounce the one *r* in the proper syllable. Although many people say (ĭn′tər-grəl) or (ĭn′trə-gəl), these pronunciations are not considered standard.

**interest** This word is usually pronounced as if it were spelled *intrist* or *intrest,* with only two syllables, although the three-syllable pronunciation (ĭn′tər-ĭst) is also acceptable. Many people pronounce this word as if it were spelled *innerest,* without the *t* sound, but this pronunciation is considered nonstandard.

**intrusion** *Intrusion* is a type of phonological variation that involves the addition or insertion of a sound where there is no historical basis for it. The pronunciation (ə-krôst) for *across,* (fĭl′əm) for *film,* (grē′vē-əs) for *grievous,* (pûr′kyə-lāt′) for *percolate,* and (wôrsh) for *wash* are all examples of intrusion. Although these pronunciations may be pervasive, or even standard within a particular region, they are often stigmatized as regionalisms or viewed as a sign of ignorance as people sometimes conclude that the speaker does not know how to spell the word.

**inveigle** The pronunciation that rhymes with *beagle* is older, but the pronunciation that rhymes with *bagel* is predominant now in American English.

**jewelry** The standard pronunciation for this word is (jo͞o′əl-rē), which is admittedly somewhat difficult to say, and is why the word is often pronounced (jo͞ol′rē). The pronunciation (jo͞o′lə-rē) is considered nonstandard and may mislead you into wrongly spelling this word *jewelery.*

**junta** For a long time this 18th-century borrowing from Spanish was pronounced (jŭn′tə) by English speakers on both sides of the Atlantic. By the middle of the 20th century, however, the pronunciation (ho͞on′tə), an approximation to the Spanish pronunciation, had gained currency in the U.S. This word is now usually pronounced (ho͞on′tə) in American English, and (jŭn′tə) in British English.

**juvenilia** This word, which is related to *juvenile,* is properly pronounced (jo͞o′və-nĭl′ē-ə) or (jo͞o′və-nĭl′yə), with a short *i* in the third syllable. The misspelling *juvenalia* reflects the commonly heard pronunciation (jo͞o′və-nāl′yə), with a long *a* in the third syllable. This pronunciation arose probably by association with words such as *bacchanalia* and *paraphernalia,* or by confusion with *Juvenalian* (referring to the Roman satirist Juvenal), all of which are pronounced with a long *a.* Neither the spelling, *juvenalia,* nor the pronunciation with long *a* has yet to be included in any dictionary, however, and so cannot be considered standard.

**kerchief** The plural of this word is either *kerchiefs* (kûr′chĭfs) or (kûr′chēfs′) or *kerchieves* (kûr′chĭvz) or (kûr′chēvz′). The latter spelling is the older of the two, the change from *f* to *v* being the result of a phonological rule in Old English. Other words that follow this pattern are *thief/thieves, leaf/leaves,* and *wife/wives.* While many of the words that are in this category still have their traditional plurals, some have also adopted modern plurals ending in just *s,* as *kerchief* has. And some words of this type have lost the older plural almost completely, as has *roof,* whose only plural now is *roofs,* although you may still hear (ro͞ovz) or (ro͝ovz).
More at **dwarf, hoof,** and **roof.**

**kilometer** Many people insist that this word should have its primary stress on the first syllable so that it will conform to the same stress pattern in *millimeter* and *centimeter.* Language, however, does not always operate as regularly or logically as we might wish. Despite objections to the pronunciation with stress on the second syllable, which originally came about by false analogy with *barometer* and *thermometer,* it continues to thrive in American English. In a recent ballot, 69 percent of the Usage Panel preferred the pronunciation with stress on the second syllable, 29 percent preferred the pronunciation with stress on the first syllable, and 10 percent said they use both. Most dictionaries have given both pronunciations since the middle of the 19th century.

**kudos** Because of the *s* on the end, this word, which comes from Greek, is often treated as a plural form, when in fact it is etymologically singular. But even people who correctly treat the word syntactically as a singular often pronounce it as if it were a plural. So properly, we would expect the final syllable to rhyme with *loss,* but more often than not it is pronounced like *doze.* Both pronunciations are now considered standard.

**L** The letter *L* comes from the Roman alphabet and was used to represent the same sound in Old English as it did in Latin (and does now in Modern English). Although, generally speaking, the consonants have remained fairly stable throughout the history of recorded English, *l* is one exception, having been lost in Early Modern English in the pronunciation of many words such as *should, would, calf, half, talk, walk, folk, yolk, balm, calm,* and *palm.* But in recent years, this silent *l* has made something of a comeback in a number of

spelling pronunciations, as those for *almond, alms, balm, calm,* and *palm,* in which the *l* is now often pronounced.
More at **spelling pronunciation.**

**lasso** This 18th-century borrowing from Spanish is now usually pronounced (lăs′ō), and less commonly (lă-sōō′), which is the older pronunciation.

**leeward** This nautical word is usually pronounced (lōō′ərd), rhyming with *steward,* but the spelling pronunciation (lē′wərd) is also acceptable.
More at **spelling pronunciation.**

**leisure** In a recent ballot, 71 percent of the Usage Panel said they use the pronunciation that rhymes with *seizure,* and 29 percent said they use the pronunciation that rhymes with *pleasure.* The tendancy in British English is the reverse, with the pronunciation that rhymes with *pleasure* being the most common one.

**length** Just going by the spelling you would expect this word to be pronounced (lĕngth), but, in fact, it is probably more often pronounced (lĕngkth), with a (k) inserted between the (ng) and the (th). The (k) acts as a sort of anchor for the (ng), keeping it at the back of the mouth and preventing it from moving forward and becoming (n) before the (th), which is made at the front of the mouth. This last pronunciation, (lĕnth), which is made with (n) before (th), is often criticized adversely by usage writers and is not generally listed as a standard variant pronunciation in dictionaries despite the fact that many people pronounce the word this way. The same situation exists for the word *strength.*
More at **assimilation.**

**library** The most widely accepted pronunciation for this word is (lī′brĕr′ē), but the pronunciations (lī′brə-rē) and (lī′brē), which are probably more common in British English, are also considered acceptable. On the other hand many people from usage writers to school teachers deplore the pronunciation (lī′bĕr′ē), which is generally considered nonstandard. In this pronunciation the first *r* is lost by dissimilation.
More at **dissimilation.**

**lived** The pronunciation (līvd) in compounds such as *long-lived* and *short-lived* is historically correct since the compound is derived from the noun *life,* not from the verb *live.* The pronunciation (lĭvd), however, is so common now that it cannot be considered an error. In a recent ballot, 43 percent of the Usage Panel preferred the pronunciation with the short vowel, 39 percent preferred the one with the long vowel, and 18 percent accepted either pronunciation.

**lower / lour** The verb *lower,* also spelled *lour* and meaning "to frown," is properly pronounced (lou′ər) or (lour), to rhyme with *flower* or *flour.* The pronunciation (lō′ər) goes with *lower,* the comparative form of the adjective *low.*

**machinate** The older pronunciation of this word is (măk′ə-nāt′), with the *ch* pronounced like (k), as it is in other English words derived from Greek like *archetype, bronchus,* and *echo.* The pronunciation (măsh′ə-nāt′), with the *ch* pronounced like (sh), is a relatively new variant and has been given alongside the other pronunciation in most dictionaries since about the middle of the 20th century. Perhaps one reason for the change is the association of *machinate* with its etymological cousin *machine,* which derives from the same Greek ancestor, but came into English through the intermediary of French. More at **Ch.**

**mainsail** This nautical word is usually pronounced (mān′səl), but the spelling pronunciation (mān′sāl′) is also acceptable. More at **spelling pronunciation.**

**mauve** The pronunciation (mōv) is older and reflects the word's pronunciation in French. Also common now is the pronunciation (môv).

**mayoral** In a recent ballot approximately 70 percent of the Usage Panel said they pronounce this word with stress on the first syllable, and approximately 30 percent pronounce it with stress on the second syllable. Either pronunciation is acceptable.

**metathesis** *Metathesis* is a term used in linguistics to refer to the transposition of elements in a word or sentence. When the change occurs to two adjacent sounds in a word, it frequently involves the letters *l* or *r* and a vowel. Two historical examples of metathesis are Modern English *bird* and *horse* from Old English *brid* and *hros.* Over time the metathesized pronunciations became standard, and the spellings were changed to conform to the new pronunciations. A few examples from contemporary speech are the pronunciations (rē′lə-tər) instead of (rē′əl-tər) for *Realtor,* (jōō′lə-rē) instead of (jōō′əl-rē) or (jōōl′rē) for *jewelry,* and (pər-fûr′) instead of (prə-fûr′) for *prefer.* Although these pronunciations occur frequently, most dictionaries do not enter them as standard variants.

**millenary** The pronunciation with the main stress on the first syllable is the correct historical pronunciation, but the pronunciation with stress on the second syllable, which probably came about through association with *millennium,* is now equally common.

**mineralogy** Although this word has an *a* in the third syllable, such is the influence of words ending in *-ology* that it is most commonly pronounced (mĭn′ə-rŏl′ə-jē), as if it were spelled *minerology.* Note that a similar situation exists with the word *genealogy.*

**mischievous** The pronunciation (mĭs-chē′vē-əs), which is considered nonstandard, is an example of *intrusion,* a phonological process that involves the addition or insertion of an extra sound. The usual pronunciation of *mischievous* has only three syllables and is stressed on the first, (mĭs′chə-vəs). More at **intrusion.**

**moot** This word is properly pronounced (mo͞ot), never (myo͞ot), which goes with *mute.*

**mores** This word, which comes from Latin and means "customs" or "ways," has two syllables and may be pronounced with either a long *a* or a long *e* sound in the second syllable. The pronunciation with a long *a* sound, which is probably the more common one in contemporary English, is closer to a classical Latin pronunciation, while the pronunciation with a long *e* is an Anglicized Latin pronunciation.

**naphtha / naphthalene** As is the case with *diphtheria* and *diphthong,* the *ph* should properly be pronounced (f), not (p). Because so many people say (năp-), as opposed to (năf-), though, this variant has gradually become acceptable.

**neither** Most people pronounce this word (nē′*th*ər), with a long *e* sound, in American English, but the pronunciation (nī′*th*ər), with a long *i,* is also acceptable. More at **either.**

**niche** This 17th-century borrowing from French has traditionally been pronounced (nĭch), rhyming with *itch.* The pronunciation (nēsh), rhyming with *quiche,* is a 20th-century revival of the French pronunciation, which some people dislike because they think it seems affected. However, this pronunciation is now given by most dictionaries as a standard variant.

**nuclear** The pronunciation (no͞o′kyə-lər), which is strongly objected to by many usage writers and others of their ilk, is an example of how a familiar phonological pattern can influence an unfamiliar one. The usual pronunciation of the final two syllables of this word is (-klē-ər), but this sequence of sounds is rare in English. Much more common is the similar sequence (-kyə-lər), which occurs in words like *particular, circular, spectacular,* and in many scientific words like *molecular, ocular,* and *vascular.* You may want to avoid this pronunciation despite the fact that it has been used in the recent past by some prominent speakers including Presidents Eisenhower and Carter. Note that the stigmatized variant can also occur in the word *nucleus.*

**often** Simplification of consonant clusters has been an ongoing process in the history of English, but during the 15th century English experienced a widespread loss of consonants, as the *d* in *handsome* and *handkerchief,* the *p* in *consumption* and *raspberry,* and the *t* in *chestnut* and *often.* Because of the influence of spelling, however, there is sometimes a tendency to restore sounds that have become silent, as is the case with *often,* which is now commonly pronounced with the *t*. Curiously, in other words such as *soften* and *listen*, the *t* generally remains silent.

More at **spelling pronunciation.**

**ophthalmia** As is the case with *diphtheria, diphthong,* and *naphtha,* the *ph* should properly be pronounced (f), not (p). Because so many people say (ŏp-), as opposed to (ŏf-), though, this variant has gradually become acceptable.

**–or** This suffix often indicates a person or thing that performs a particular action determined by the root part of the word, as in *actor, governor, inventor, navigator,* and *spectator.* It is usually pronounced (ər), just like the suffix *-er*, although it may be pronounced (ôr) in cases where an emphasis is being placed on contrasting roles, as in *lessor/lessee.*

**panegyric** Traditionally this word has a soft *g* and rhymes with *lyric,* but the pronunciation of *gyr* with a long *i* sound, as in *gyre* and *gyrus,* is now also acceptable.

**penalize** The older pronunciation is (pē′nə-līz′), with a long *e* in the first syllable as in *penal.* A variant pronunciation with a short *e* in the first syllable is now common in American English, however, probably because of association with *penalty.*

**poinsettia** Although the pronunciation (poin-sĕt′ə) overlooks the fact that there is an *i* before the final *a,* so many people pronounce the word this way that it is now considered a standard variant by most dictionaries.

**portentous** The usual pronunciation of this word is (pôr-tĕn′təs). However, under the influence of words like *contentious, pretentious,* and *sententious, portentous* is sometimes pronounced (pôr-tĕn′shəs), as if it were spelled *portentious.* Neither the pronunciation ending in (shəs) nor the spelling ending in *tious* (which crops up occasionally in print) is considered standard.

**posthumous** In American English this word is most commonly pronounced (pŏs′chə-məs), with the stress on the first syllable and the *h* silent, which allows the *t* before *u* to assimilate to (ch), as it does in *culture* and *picture.*

**potpourri** The only pronunciation considered standard now in American English is (pō′pŏŏ-rē′), an approximation of the original pronunciation for this 17th-century borrowing from French. The pronunciation (pŏt-pŏŏr′ē) is an Anglicized variant that may be less rare in British English.

**primer** This word, meaning "a small textbook used to teach reading," is usually pronounced with a short *i,* rhyming with *dimmer,* in American English. A variant pronunciation with a long *i,* as in *prime,* occurs chiefly in British English.

**pronunciation spelling** A *pronunciation spelling* is a spelling that more closely reflects the pronunciation of a given word than the word's traditional spelling does. Over time the new spelling may become as acceptable as the original spelling, as is the case with the pronunciation spelling *bosun* for *boatswain*. Many writers use pronunciation spellings, as *wanna* for *want to* or *talkin'* for *talking*, to convey speech.
More at **spelling pronunciation.**

**prosody** This word, which is etymologically unrelated to the more common word *prose*, is normally pronounced (prŏs′ə-dē), with the first syllable rhyming with *cross*.

**pumpkin** The pronunciations (pŭmp′kĭn), (pŭm′kĭn), and (pŭng′kĭn) are all widespread and are all considered standard in American English. In the pronunciation (pŭm′kĭn), the (p) drops out so that the consonant cluster *mpk* becomes simplified, which also occurs in the words *assumption, bumpkin,* and *symptom.* In (pŭng′kĭn) the (p) has been lost and the (m) has assimilated to the (k), becoming (ng).
More at **assimilation.**

**quark** *Quark,* a term used to refer to a type of subatomic particle, is an invented word that is associated with the line "*Three quarks for Muster Mark!*" from James Joyce's novel *Finnegan's Wake.* Although Joyce clearly intended the word to rhyme with *mark*, physicists generally pronounce this word (kwôrk), with the same vowel as in *quart* and *quarter.* However, the pronunciation rhyming with *mark* is also considered acceptable.

**quasi** The pronunciation (kwä′sē) is Classical Latin and the pronunciation (kwā′sī) is Anglicized Latin. Note that in both of these the *s* is pronounced like *s.* In American English, speakers are more likely to pronounce the *s* like *z*, which is now also considered standard.

**quay** This word is an etymological cousin of the words *key* and *cay*, which both mean "a low offshore island or reef." *Quay* is traditionally pronounced like *key*, although the pronunciations (kā) and (kwā) are now also considered standard in American English.

**quixotic** This word, pronounced (kwĭk-sŏt′ĭk), derives from the English word *Quixote*, which in turn derives from the name of the hero of Cervantes's novel, *Don Quixote. Quixote* is generally pronounced (kwĭk′sət) in British English and (kē-hō′tē), an attempt at the Spanish pronunciation, in American English.

**ration** The older pronunciation rhymes with *nation.* The newer variant pronunciation, rhyming with *fashion*, has gained a lot of ground in the 20th century, however, and is now predominant in both American and British English.

**Realtor** The standard pronunciation for this word is (rē′əl-tər), which is admittedly difficult to say, which is why the word is more often pronounced (rēl′tər). Although the pronunciation (rē′lə-tər) is used by a lot of people, it is not generally given as standard by dictionaries.
More at **metathesis.**

**remonstrate** Traditionally this word has been pronounced (rĭ-mŏn′strāt′), with the main stress on the second syllable. During the last 30 years or so, however, the pronunciation (rĕm′ən-strāt′), with the main stress on the first syllable, has become more and more common. This shift in stress is normal, as it has occurred in many other verbs ending in -ate, such as *adumbrate, contemplate, demonstrate, enervate,* and *illustrate,* in some of which the process is complete and in others still in progress. One reason for the shift, no doubt, is the influence of the derived nouns ending in -tion, such as *contemplation* and *demonstration,* which are stressed on the first and third syllables. *Remonstrate* has perhaps lagged behind other verbs like it because *remonstration* is not very common.

**renaissance / Renaissance** This 19th-century borrowing from French, which literally means "rebirth," is usually stressed on the first and third syllables in American English. In British English the word is usually stressed on the second syllable, which is pronounced with a long *a* sound, as (rə-nā′səns). The American English pronunciation is an approximation to the French pronunciation, while the British English pronunciation reflects the typical English (Germanic) tendency to put the main stress on the root part of a word. Note that the word *renascence,* which also means "rebirth" or "revival," but which comes from Latin, is stressed on the second syllable.

**renege** The traditional pronunciation, and the one most common in British English, is (rĭ-nēg′), with a long *e* in the second syllable. In American English, however, this word is generally pronounced (rĭ-nĭg′) or (rĭ-nĕg′), with a short *i* or short *e* sound in the second syllable.

**renown** This word is properly pronounced (rĭ-noun′), rhyming with *noun,* never (rĭ-nōn′), rhyming with *own.*

**ribald** The traditional pronunciation of this word is (rĭb′əld). The spelling pronunciations (rī′bôld′) and (rī′bəld), which only began to appear in dictionaries in the second half of the 20th century, are now also considered to be standard.

**roof** The plural of this word is *roofs,* pronounced (ro͞ofs) or (roŏfs) or also sometimes (ro͞ovz) or (roŏvz). The latter pronunciations are actually older, the change from *f* to *v* being the result of a phonological rule in Old English. According to this rule, the consonants *f, th* as in *thin,* and *s* remained voiceless at the beginning and end of a word, but became voiced, that is, *v, th* as in *that,*

and *z,* when they occurred between vowels. In Middle English the word for "wife", for example, was spelled *wif* and pronounced (wēf), and its plural was spelled *wives* and pronounced (wē′vĭs), with two syllables. Some Modern English words in addition to *wife* that retain this pattern of sound alternation are *thief/thieves, leaf/leaves, calf/calves* and also *house/houses* and *mouth/mouths.* We think of these plural forms as irregular now, but they were actually once completely regular. Eventually, at the beginning of the Early Modern English period, the *e* in the ending *es* became silent or dropped out except after (ch), (j), (sh), (zh), (s), and (z), and we began forming plurals by adding just *s* in most cases instead of *es.* While many of the words that are in the *thief/thieves* category still have their traditional plurals, some have also adopted modern plurals ending in just *s,* as *dwarf* has. And some words of this type have lost the older plural almost completely, as has *roof,* whose plural is now only spelled *roofs,* although you may still hear the pronunciation (ro͞ovz) or (ro͝ovz).

**row** This word, meaning "brawl" or "uproar," normally rhymes with *cow* and *vow.* The pronunciation that rhymes with *flow* and *blow* belongs to the lookalikes *row,* "line" or "succession," and *row,* "to propel a boat with oars."

**sarcophagi** Although this word, the Latin plural of *sarcophagus,* can be pronounced with a soft or hard *g,* as (sär-kŏf′ə-jī) or (sär-kŏf′ə-gī), the former is the most common pronunciation.
More at **G.**

**scarify** Coming upon this word in print you might be tempted to pronounce it (skăr′ə-fī′), since at first glance it looks as if it were made up of the word *scar* + the verb suffix *-ify,* meaning "to cause to become." However, *scarify,* which is traditionally pronounced (skăr′ə-fī′), does not mean "to scar," but rather "to make scratches or shallow cuts" and by extension "to lacerate with criticism." Since scarification could cause scarring, though, it is easy to see how *to scar* and *to scarify* could be confused in both meaning and pronunciation.

**schism** This word, which was initially spelled *scisme* in English, is traditionally pronounced (sĭz′əm). The pronunciation (skĭz′əm) was long regarded as incorrect, but it became so common in both British and American English that it gained acceptability and is now entered as a standard variant in most dictionaries. In fact, in a recent ballot 58 percent of the Usage Panel indicated they use (skĭz′əm), while 36 percent said they use (sĭz′əm). The modern spelling with the *h* dates back to the 16th century when the word was respelled after its Latin and Greek ancestors.

**scone** This word is traditionally pronounced with a short *o,* rhyming with *gone,* though now it is more commonly pronounced with a long *o,* rhyming with *stone.*

**secretive** This adjective is derived from the verb *secrete,* meaning "to conceal in a hiding place," plus the adjectival suffix *-ive.* It makes sense, then, that the correct historical pronunciation is (sĭ-krē′tĭv). However, more often than not this word is pronounced (sē′krĭ-tĭv), as if it were derived from *secret* plus *-ive,* which is an association that is easy to make since someone who is secretive is likely to keep secrets. Note that when *secretive* is used to mean "secretory," it is always pronounced (sĭ-krē′tĭv), as in the phrase *secretive glands.*

**sheik** Recorded in English since the 16th century, this word is pronounced (shēk), rhyming with *cheek,* or (shāk), like *shake.* The former pronunciation is more usual in American English, while the latter is more usual in British English.

**shone** This past tense and past participle of *shine* is usually pronounced with a long *o,* rhyming with *stone,* in American English and with a short *o,* rhyming with *gone,* in British English.

**similar** The pronunciation (sĭm′yə-lər), which is generally not considered acceptable, is an example of *intrusion,* a phonological process that involves the addition or insertion of an extra sound. The usual pronunciation is (sĭm′ə-lər). More at **intrusion.**

**sloth** The traditional (and British English) pronunciation rhymes with *both,* although the word is now also commonly pronounced in American English so that it rhymes with *moth,* especially when used to refer to the sloth bear.

**sonorous** The older pronunciation is (sə-nôr′əs) or (sə-nōr′əs), with stress on the second syllable. As a recent usage ballot indicates, however, the variant pronunciation (sŏn′ər-əs), with stress on the first syllable, is now much more common in American English. In this ballot, 84 percent of the panelists gave the pronunciation with stress on the first syllable as their pronunciation, and only 16 percent gave the older pronunciation with stress on the second syllable as their pronunciation. Two of the panelists who are linguists noted that whereas they stress the first syllable, they pronounce it with a long *o,* as (sō′nər-əs).

**spelling pronunciation** A *spelling pronunciation* is simply a pronunciation that is based on the spelling of a word without regard to its historical or traditional pronunciation. A classic example of this is the modern spelling pronunciation (ôf′tən) or (ŏf′tən) for *often,* which for centuries has been pronounced (ô′fən) or (ŏf′ən), with the *t* silent. This particular example is so common today as to go practically unnoticed, although some people may still object to it as they feel it amounts to hypercorrection. Looking at it another way, though, you can argue that the modern spelling pronunciation merely represents a reversal of the historical process whereby the *t* had become silent.

Other words with commonly heard spelling pronunciations that are discussed in this chapter are *alms, boatswain, comptroller,* and *forecastle.*
More at **pronunciation spelling.**

**spontaneity** Traditionally this word has been pronounced (spŏn′tə-nē′ĭ-tē), with a long *e* in the third syllable. Although the pronunciation with a long *a* (third syllable sounds like *neigh*) has become fairly common and is given as a standard variant by most dictionaries, some people still dislike it.

**strength** Just going by the spelling you would expect this word to be pronounced (strĕngth), but, in fact, it is probably more often pronounced (strĕngkth), with a (k) inserted between the (ng) and the (th). The (k) acts as a sort of anchor for the (ng), keeping it at the back of the mouth and preventing it from moving forward and becoming (n) before the (th), which is made at the front of the mouth. This last pronunciation, (strĕnth), which is made with (n) before (th), is often criticized adversely by usage writers and is not generally listed as a standard variant pronunciation in dictionaries despite the fact that many people pronounce the word this way. The same situation exists for the word *length.*
More at **assimilation.**

**the** The pronunciation of this word changes according to the sound that immediately follows it. Generally, before a consonant, *the* is pronounced (thə), as in *the ball, the one, the school;* before a vowel, *the* is often pronounced (thē) or (thĭ), as in *the apple, the hour, the opening;* and when stressed for emphasis *the* is pronounced (thē), as in *This is the place to live.*

**tomato** The older pronunciation is (tə-mä′tō), with a broad *a,* which is the predominant pronunciation in British English. The more common pronunciation in American English is (tə-mā′tō), with a long *a.*

**topgallant / topmast / topsail** These nautical words are usually pronounced (tə-găl′ənt), (tŏp′məst), and (tŏp′səl), but the spelling pronunciations (tŏp′găl′ənt), (tŏp′măst′), and (tŏp′sāl′) are also acceptable.
More at **spelling pronunciation.**

**trauma** This word can be pronounced (trô′mə), with the first syllable rhyming with *law,* or (trou′mə), with the first syllable rhyming with *cow.* In a recent ballot, 56 percent of the Usage Panel preferred the former pronunciation, 41 percent preferred the latter, and a small percentage use both.

**troth** The traditional (and British English) pronunciation rhymes with *both,* although the word is now also commonly pronounced in American English so that it rhymes with *moth.*

**valet** This French loan word, which has been recorded in English since the 16th century, is traditionally pronounced (văl′ĭt), although the pseudo-French pronunciations (văl′ā) and (vă-lā′) are also common, especially in American English, as in the compound *valet parking.*

**vase** The usual pronunciation in American English is (vās) or (vāz), rhyming with *race* or *raise.* The pronunciation (väz) is British English.

**victual** The modern pronunciation (vĭt′l) represents an Anglicized pronunciation of the Old French form *vitaille,* which was borrowed into English in the early 14th century. The modern spelling is a result of the fact that in both French and English the word was sometimes spelled with a *c,* and later also with a *u,* under the influence of its Late Latin ancestor *victuālia,* meaning "provisions." The word is now usually spelled *victual,* or on occasion *vittle,* but the pronunciation has remained (vĭt′l).
More at **pronunciation spelling.**

**whilst** Traditionally, this word is pronounced with a long *i* as in *while.*

**wizen** The verb *wizen,* meaning "to shrivel up or wither," is pronounced with a short *i.*

**Xmas** The pronunciation (ĕks′məs) is the result of a misinterpretation of the abbreviation *Xmas,* where the *X* actually represents a Greek chi, the first letter of Χριστός, "Christ." It is generally only used jocularly or informally.

**zoo– / zo–** The first syllable of this prefix should properly be pronounced (zō), never (zoō): *zoogenic* (zō′ə-jĕn′ĭk), *zoology* (zō-ŏl′ə-jē), *zoon* (zō′ŏn′).

# Word Formation

## *Plurals, Possessives, Affixes, and Compounds*

This chapter tells you how to form the plural and possessive forms of nouns and how to style compound words. It also provides some basic rules that account for the spelling changes that occur when suffixes are added to a word. A final section lists and explains the most commonly used prefixes and suffixes.

### Guide to Forming Plurals

In this section we outline the rules for forming plurals in English.

The plural of most nouns is formed by adding *-s* to the singular: *apple, apples; bell, bells; epoch, epochs; grief, griefs; law, laws; month, months; pear, pears; shade, shades; George, Georges; the Walkers; the Romanos.*

Common nouns ending in *ch* (soft), *sh, s, ss, x, z* or *zz* usually form their plurals by adding *-es*: *church, churches; slash, slashes; gas, gases* or *gasses; class, classes; fox, foxes; quiz, quizzes; buzz, buzzes.*
   Proper nouns of this type always add *-es*: *Charles, Charleses; the Keaches; the Joneses; the Coxes.*

Common nouns ending in *y* preceded by a vowel usually form their plurals by adding *-s*: *bay, bays; guy, guys; key, keys; toy, toys.*
   Common nouns ending in *y* preceded by a consonant or by *qu* change the *y* to *i* and add *-es*: *baby, babies; city, cities; faculty, faculties; soliloquy, soliloquies.*
   Proper nouns ending in *y* form their plurals regularly, and do not change the *y* to *i* as common nouns do: *the two Kathys, the Connallys, the two Kansas*

*Citys*. There are a few well-known exceptions to this rule: *the Alleghenies, the Ptolemies, the Rockies, the Two Sicilies.*

Most nouns ending in *f, ff,* or *fe* form their plurals regularly by adding *-s* to the singular: *chief, chiefs; proof, proofs; roof, roofs; sheriff, sheriffs; fife, fifes.* However, some nouns ending in *f* or *fe* change the *f* or *fe* to *v* and add *-es: calf, calves; elf, elves; half, halves; knife, knives; life, lives; loaf, loaves; self, selves; shelf, shelves; thief, thieves; wife, wives; wolf, wolves.* A few nouns ending in *f* or *ff,* including *beef, dwarf, hoof, scarf, wharf,* and *staff* have two plural forms: *beefs* or *beeves; dwarfs* or *dwarves; hoofs* or *hooves; scarfs* or *scarves; wharfs* or *wharves; staffs* or *staves.* In this case, sometimes different forms have different meanings, as *beefs* (complaints) and *beeves* (animals) or *staffs* (people) and *staves* (long poles).

Nouns ending in *o* preceded by a vowel form their plurals by adding *-s* to the singular: *cameo, cameos; duo, duos; studio, studios; zoo, zoos.*

Most nouns ending in *o* preceded by a consonant also usually add *-s* to form the plural: *alto, altos; casino, casinos; ego, egos; Latino, Latinos; memo, memos; neutrino, neutrinos; poncho, ponchos; silo, silos.* However, some nouns ending in *o* preceded by a consonant add *-es: echo, echoes; hero, heroes; jingo, jingoes; no, noes; potato, potatoes; tomato, tomatoes.* Some nouns ending in *o* preceded by a consonant have two plural forms (the preferred form is given first): *buffaloes* or *buffalos; cargoes* or *cargos; desperadoes* or *desperados; halos* or *haloes; mosquitoes* or *mosquitos; zeros* or *zeroes.*

Most nouns ending in *i* form their plurals by adding *-s: alibi, alibis; khaki, khakis; rabbi, rabbis; ski, skis.* Three notable exceptions to this rule are *alkali, taxi,* and *chili: alkalis* or *alkalies; taxis* or *taxies; chilies.*

A few nouns undergo a vowel change in the stem: *foot, feet; goose, geese; louse, lice; man, men; mouse, mice; tooth, teeth; woman, women.* Usually compounds in which one of these nouns is the final element form their plurals in the same way: *webfoot, webfeet; gentleman, gentlemen; dormouse, dormice; Englishwoman, Englishwomen.* Note, however, that *mongoose* and many words ending in *man,* such as *German* and *human,* are not compounds. These words form their plurals by adding *-s: mongooses; Germans, humans.*

Three nouns have plurals ending in *en: ox, oxen; child, children; brother, brothers* (of the same parent) or *brethren* (a fellow member).

Compounds written as a single word form their plurals the same way that the final element of the compound does: *dishcloth, dishcloths; hairbrush, hairbrushes; midwife, midwives; anchorman, anchormen; businesswoman, businesswomen.*

In rare cases both parts of the compound are made plural: *manservant, menservants.*

Compounds ending in *-ful* normally form their plurals by adding *-s* at the end: *cupful, cupfuls; handful, handfuls; tablespoonful, tablespoonfuls.*

Compound words, written with or without a hyphen, that consist of a noun followed by an adjective or other qualifying expression form their plurals by making the same change in the noun that is made when the noun stands alone: *attorney-general, attorneys-general; daughter-in-law, daughters-in-law; man-of-war, men-of-war; heir apparent, heirs apparent; notary public, notaries public.*

Some nouns, mainly names of birds, fishes, and mammals, have the same form in the plural as in the singular: *bison, deer, moose, sheep, swine.* Some words that follow this pattern, such as *antelope, cod, crab, elk, fish, flounder, grouse, herring, quail, reindeer, salmon, shrimp,* and *trout,* also have regular plurals ending in *-s: antelope, antelopes; fish, fishes; salmon, salmons.* Normally in such cases the unchanged plural indicates that the animal in question is being considered collectively, while the plural ending in *-s* is used specifically to indicate different varieties or species or kinds: *We caught six fish* but *Half a dozen fishes inhabit the lake.* By far, however, most animal names take a regular plural: *dogs, cats, lions, monkeys, whales.*

Many words indicating nationality or place of origin have the same form in the plural as in the singular: *Japanese, Milanese, Swiss.*

Similarly a few names of tribes or peoples have the same form in the plural as in the singular: *Iroquois, Sioux.* Many other such names have both an unchanged plural form and a regular plural form ending in *-s: Apache* or *Apaches; Cherokee* or *Cherokees; Eskimo* or *Eskimos; Zulu* or *Zulus.*

Many nouns derived from a foreign language retain their foreign plurals: (from Latin) *alumna, alumnae; alumnus, alumni; bacillus, bacilli; genus, genera; series, series; species, species;* (from Greek) *analysis, analyses; basis, bases; crisis, crises; criterion, criteria* or *criterions; phenomenon, phenomena* or *phenomenons;* (from French) *adieu, adieux* or *adieus; beau, beaux* or *beaus; madame, mesdames;* (from Italian) *paparrazzo, papparazzi;* (from Hebrew) *cherub, cherubim* or *cherubs; kibbutz, kibbutzim.* As you can see, many words of this type also have a regular plural ending in *-s* or *-es,* in which case the English plural is usually the one used in everyday speech, and the foreign plural is reserved for a technical sense or for use by a specialist: *antennas* (TV or radio part) or *antennae* (physiological structure).

Usage with regard to forming the plurals of letters, numbers, and abbreviations varies somewhat. In some cases you have a choice between adding *-s* or *-'s,* although the trend is increasingly to add *-s* alone: *three As* or *three A's; the ABCs* or *the ABC's; the 1900s* or *the 1900's; PhDs* or *PhD's; several IOUs* or *several IOU's.* With lowercase letters, symbols, abbreviations with periods, and in cases where confusion might arise without an apostrophe, use *-'s* to form the plural: *p's and q's; +'s; -'s; M.A.'s; A's and I's; 2's.* Mainly your goal is to be as clear as possible and avoid confusion.

The plural of a word being used as a word is indicated by *-'s: underline all the but's.* Note that in typed or typeset copy, only the word *but* would appear in italics (the apostrophe and the *s* would be in regular type).

# Forming Possessives

In English the possessive case is used to show not only simple possession but also a variety of other relationships between the noun marked for possession and the noun that follows:

| | |
|---|---|
| *John's car, the senator's aide* | (possession or belonging) |
| *the tide's ebbing, Amy's presentation* | (subject of an action) |
| *the company's owners, the hero's betrayal* | (object of an action) |
| *learner's dictionary, a women's college* | (description or type) |
| *my father's gentleness, the character's greed* | (attribute) |
| *the bird's wing, the book's cover* | (a constituent part) |
| *Beethoven's symphonies, grandmother's letter* | (origin) |
| *a day's journey, an arm's length* | (measure or amount) |

Following are the few basic rules for forming the possessive case in English.

The possessive case of a singular noun is formed by adding -*'s*: *one's home, by day's end, our family's pet, the witness's testimony, a fox's habitat, the knife's edge.* Note that although some people use just the apostrophe after singular nouns ending in *s* (*the witness' testimony, Burns' poetry*), the -*'s* is generally preferred because it more accurately reflects the modern pronunciation of these forms. However, in a few cases where the -*'s* is not pronounced, it is usual to add just the apostrophe: *for righteousness' (appearance') sake.*

The possessive case of a plural noun ending in -*s* is formed by adding just an apostrophe: *the doctors' recommendations, the glasses' rims, the flies' buzzing noises.* However, when the plural noun does not end in -*s*, form the possessive by adding -*'s*: *children's clothes.*

The possessive case of most proper nouns is formed according to the rules for common nouns: (singular) *Eliot's novels, Yeats's poetry, Dostoyevsky's biography, Velázquez's paintings;* (plural) *the McCarthys' and the Williamses' parties, the Schwartzes' trip.* By convention, however, certain proper nouns ending in *s* form the possessive by adding just the apostrophe since adding -*'s* would make the pronunciation difficult or awkward: *Jesus' teachings, Moses' children, Achilles' heel, Hercules' strength, Ramses' reign, Xerxes' conquest.*

For compound names or titles that form short phrases, add the -*'s* or apostrophe to the final element: *the King of Belgium's birthday, Saint Francis of Assisi's life, the governor of New York's speech.* Long phrases such as *the man we met on the train's sister* should be avoided in writing. Reword them using *of: the sister of the man we met on the train.*

When two or more people or things possess something jointly, add the -*'s* or apostrophe to the last element only: *Martha and Dan's house.* However, when two or more people or things possess something separately, add the -*'s* or apostrophe to each element: *the Smiths' and the Joneses' houses are for sale.*

# Affixes

Lacking an exact correspondence between its sounds and its written symbols, English spelling can be frustratingly inconsistent and can pose problems for even the best spellers. Although it would be impossible to formulate a set of rules that would cover the spelling of all English words, many spelling difficulties arise in connection with suffixes, and the six basic rules given here for determining spelling changes in a word root when a suffix is added are intended as an aid in learning and understanding the correct spelling of a large number of English words. For a brief discussion of the development of Modern English spelling, see the introduction to *Pronunciation Challenges*.

## Adding a Suffix to a Word

**1.** Adding a suffix to a one-syllable word:

**a.** Words of one syllable that end in a single consonant preceded by a single vowel double the final consonant before a suffix beginning with a vowel: *bag, baggage; hop, hopper; hot, hottest; red, redder; run, running; stop, stopped.* There are two notable exceptions to this rule: *bus* (*buses* or *busses; busing* or *bussing*) and *gas* (*gasses* or *gases; gassing; gassy*).

**b.** If a word ends with two or more consonants or if it ends with one consonant preceded by two or more vowels instead of one, the final consonant is not doubled: *debt, debtor; lick, licking; mail, mailed; sweet, sweetest.*

**2.** Adding a suffix to a word with two or more syllables:

**a.** Words of two or more syllables that have the accent on the last syllable and end in a single consonant preceded by a single vowel double the final consonant before a suffix beginning with a vowel: *admit, admitted; confer, conferring; control, controller; regret, regrettable.* There are a few exceptions: *chagrin, chagrined; transfer, transferred, transferring* but *transferable, transference.*

**b.** When the accent shifts to the first syllable of the word after the suffix is added, the final consonant is not doubled: *prefer, preference; refer, reference.*

**c.** If the word ends with two consonants or if the final consonant is preceded by more than one vowel the final consonant is not doubled: *perform, performance; repeal, repealing.*

**d.** If the word is accented on any syllable except the last the final consonant is not usually doubled: *benefit, benefited; develop, developed; interpret, interpreted.* However, some words like *cobweb, handicap,* and *outfit* follow the models of *web, cap,* and *fit,* even though these words may not be true compounds. A few others ending in *g* double the final *g* so that it will not be pronounced like *j: zigzag, zigzagged.*

**3.** Adding a suffix beginning with a vowel to a word ending in a silent *e:*

Words ending with a silent *e* usually drop the *e* before a suffix beginning with a vowel: *force, forcible; route, routed; glide, gliding; operate, operator; tri-*

*fle, trifler*. However, there are many exceptions to this rule:

**a.** Many words of this type have alternative forms (the preferred form is given first): *blame, blamable* or *blameable; blue, bluish* or *blueish*. And in certain cases, alternative forms have different meanings: *linage* or *lineage* (number of lines) but *lineage* (ancestry).

**b.** Many words ending in *ce* or *ge* keep the *e* before the suffixes *-able* and *-ous: advantage, advantageous; change, changeable; trace, traceable*.

**c.** Words ending in a silent *e* keep the *e* if the word could be mistaken for another word: *dye, dyeing; singe, singeing*.

**d.** If the word ends in *ie*, the *e* is dropped and the *i* changed to *y* before the suffix *-ing*. A word ending in *i* remains unchanged before *-ing: die, dying; ski, skiing*.

**e.** *Mile* and *acre* do not drop the *e* before the suffix *-age: mileage, acreage*.

**4.** Adding a suffix beginning with a consonant to a word ending in a silent *e:*

Words ending with a silent *e* generally retain the *e* before a suffix that begins with a consonant: *plate, plateful; shoe, shoeless; arrange, arrangement; white, whiteness; awe, aweome; nice, nicety*. However, there are many exceptions to this rule. Some of the most common are *abridge, abridgment; acknowledge, acknowledgment; argue, argument; awe, awful; due, duly; judge, judgment; nine, ninth; true, truly; whole, wholly; wise, wisdom*.

**5.** Adding a suffix to a word ending in *y:*

**a.** Words ending in *y* preceded by a consonant generally change the *y* to *i* before the addition of a suffix, except when the suffix begins with an *i: accompany, accompaniment; beauty, beautiful; icy, icier, iciest, icily, iciness;* but *reply, replying*.

**b.** The *y* is retained in derivatives of *baby, city*, and *lady* and before the suffixes *-ship* and *-like: babyhood, cityscape, ladyship, ladylike*.

**c.** Adjectives of one syllable ending in *y* preceded by a consonant usually retain the *y* when a suffix beginning with a consonant is added: *shy, shyly, shyness; sly, slyly, slyness; wry, wryly, wryness;* but *dryly* or *drily, dryness*. These adjectives usually also retain the *y* when a suffix beginning with a vowel is added, although most have variants where the *y* has changed to *i: dry, drier* or *dryer, driest* or *dryest; shy, shier* or *shyer, shiest* or *shyest*.

**d.** Words ending in *y* preceded by a vowel usually retain the *y* before a suffix: *buy, buyer; key, keyless; coy, coyer, coyest; gay, gayer, gayest;* but *day, daily; gay, gaily* or *gayly*.

**e.** Some words drop the final *y* before the addition of the suffix *-eous: beauty, beauteous*.

**6.** Adding a suffix to a word ending in *c:*

Words ending in *c* almost always have the letter *k* inserted after the *c* when a suffix beginning with *e, i*, or *y* is added: *panic, panicky; picnic, picnicker*. This is done so that the letter *c* will not be pronounced like *s*.

## Affixes: What They Mean

**a–** The basic meaning of the prefix *a-* is "without." For example, *achromatic* means "without color." Before vowels and sometimes *h*, *a-* becomes *an-*: *anaerobic*. Many of the words beginning with this prefix are used in science, such as *aphasia, anoxia,* and *aseptic.* It is important not to confuse *a-* with other prefixes, such as *ad-*, that begin with the letter *a.*

**–able** The suffix *-able*, which forms adjectives, comes from the Latin suffix *-abilis*, meaning "capable or worthy of." Thus *a likable person* is one who is capable of or worthy of being liked. The suffix *-ible* is closely related to *-able* and has the same meaning, as in *flexible.* Since they sound exactly alike, it is important to consult your dictionary when spelling words that end in this suffix.

**ad–** The word element *ad-* is not an active prefix in English; that is, it is not used to create new words. It comes from the Latin preposition *ad*, meaning "to, toward, on top of." In Latin, this preposition became a prefix, and when it was followed by *c, f, g, l, n, r, s,* or *t,* it became *ac, af, ag, al, an, ar, as,* or *at,* respectively. Thus Latin *ad-* is easy to see in English words such as *adhere, admit,* and *adverse,* but it is not so obvious in words such as *affix, apply,* and *attend.*

**anti–** The prefix *anti-* goes back to Greek *anti*, meaning "against." *Anti-* is so recognizable and its meaning is so clear that it is frequently used to make up new words. For example, the meanings of words such as *anticrime* and *antipollution* are easy to guess. Sometimes, when followed by a vowel, *anti-* becomes *ant-*: *antacid.*

**–ation** The very common noun suffix *-ation* comes from a Latin suffix that is added to a verb and changes that verb to a noun. In English, the suffix *-ation* is used the same way. At first *-ation* was added especially to verbs that ended in *ate.* So, for example, we have the noun *creation*, formed from the verb *create.* But *-ation* has become so popular in English that it is used to form nouns from verbs that do not end in *ate*, such as *civilization* from the verb *civilize* and *starvation* from the verb *starve.*

**bio–** The prefix *bio-* comes from Greek *bios*, meaning "life." When used to form words in English, *bio-* generally refers to living organisms or to *biology*, the science of living organisms. Many of the words that begin with *bio-* have only come into being in the 20th century, as *bioethics* and *biotechnology.* Sometimes before an *o*, *bio-* becomes *bi-*: *biopsy.*

**co–** We can trace the prefix *co-* back to the Latin prefix *co-*, a form of *com-*, meaning "with." In English, the prefix *co-* means "together, joint, jointly." In words such as *coheir* and *coedit*, *co-* has simply been affixed to words that already existed to create new words whose meanings are easy to guess.

**com–** Like the element *ad-*, *com-* does not create new words in English, but it appears in many familiar words under a variety of spellings. The basic meaning of the prefix *com-* is "together, with." It comes from the Latin prefix *com-*. Before the consonants *l* and *r*, Latin *com-* became *col-* and *cor-*, respectively, as we see in our words *collaborate* and *correspond*. Before all other consonants except *p*, *b*, or *m*, *com-* became *con-*, as in *confirm, constitution*, and *contribute*.

**contra– / counter–** The prefixes *contra-* and *counter-* both derive from the Latin word *contra*, meaning "against." *Contra-* means primarily "against, opposite," and *counter-* means "contrary, opposite." Thus *contraposition* means "an opposite position," and *countercurrent* means "a current flowing in an opposite direction."

**de–** The prefix *de-* can be traced back through Middle English and Old French to Latin *de*, meaning "from, off, apart, away, down, out." In English, *de-* usually indicates reversal, removal, or reduction. Thus *deactivate* means "to make inactive," *decontaminate* means "to remove the contamination in," and *decompress* means "to remove or reduce pressure." *De-* is a prefix that occurs very frequently in English.

**dis–** The prefix *dis-* has several senses, but its basic meaning is "not, not any." Thus *disbelieve* means "to refuse to believe" and *discomfort* means "a lack of comfort." *Dis-* came into English from the Old French prefix *des-*, which in turn came from the Latin prefix *dis-*, which came from the adverb *dis-*, meaning "apart, asunder." *Dis-* is an important prefix that occurs very frequently in English in words such as *discredit, disrepair*, and *disrespect*.

**en–** There are two prefixes spelled *en-*. One comes from the Latin suffix *in-*, has as its basic meaning "into or onto," and chiefly forms verbs. Thus *encapsulate* means "to put into a capsule," and *enplane* means "to get on an airplane." This same *en-* also has the meanings "to cause to be," as in *endear*, and "to cover or provide with," as in *enrobe*. It sometimes has intensive force, as in *entangle*. *En-* has a variant spelling *in-*, which is why we have pairs like *enclose/inclose* and *enquire/inquire*.

The second *en-* goes back to Greek and means "in, into, within." It occurs chiefly in scientific terms like *enzootic*, which is used of diseases and means "affecting animals within a particular area."

Both suffixes change from *en-* to *em-* before *b* and *p: embroil, empathy*.

**–en** There are two suffixes spelled *-en* in English. The first has the basic meaning "to cause to be" or "to become." When added to nouns and adjectives, this *-en* forms verbs: *lengthen, soften*. The other suffix *-en*, meaning "made of, resembling," is an adjective suffix. That is, it changes nouns into adjectives: *wooden, golden*. The verb suffix *-en* comes from the Old English suffix *-nian*, and the adjective suffix *-en* is from Old English *-en*.

**equi–** The prefix *equi-* means "equal" or "equally." *Equi-* is from the Latin prefix *aequi-*, which came from Latin *aequus*, meaning "equal." Thus *equidistant* means "equally distant." *Equi-* often occurs in words with Latin elements. For example, *equinox* means "having the night equal (to the day)," from Latin *nox*, "night." *Equivalent* is from *valere*, "to be worth, amount to," and so is literally "amounting to the same thing."

**ex–** The prefix *ex-* comes from Latin *ex-, e-*, meaning "out of, from." It usually occurs with word roots that come from Latin verbs. Thus combining *ex-* with the Latin verb *tendere*, "to stretch," gives us *extend*, "to stretch out." Similarly, in *express*, *ex-* combines with the root *press*, which comes from the verb *premere*, "to squeeze." So when we express ourselves, we "squeeze out" our thoughts. When followed by *f*, *ex-* becomes *ef-*, as in *efface*. Sometimes *ex-* takes the form of *e-*, as in *emit* (from Latin *mittere*, "to send"). Today *ex-* only forms new words when it means "former," and it is always followed by a hyphen: *ex-President*.

**fore–** The prefix *fore-* means "before, in front." A *forerunner* is "one that goes before" and a *foreleg* is "a front leg of an animal." It is important not to confuse *fore-* with the prefix *for-* (sometimes spelled *fore-*), which appears in many English words but is no longer used to form words in English. This prefix bears the meaning of exclusion or rejection, and survives in words like *forbid* and *forswear*.

**–ful** The suffix *-ful* comes from the Old English adjective *full*, meaning "full." *Full* was commonly added to a noun in order to form adjectives meaning "full of, characterized by" whatever quality was denoted by the noun: *playful, careful*. The use of *-ful* to form nouns meaning "a quantity that would fill" a particular receptacle (*cupful, mouthful*) also goes back to Old English. In modern usage the correct way to form the plural of these nouns is to add an *s* to the end of the suffix: *cupfuls*.

**–fy** The verb suffix *-fy*, which means "to make or cause to become," derives from Latin *ficare* or *ficari*, from *facere*, meaning "to do or make." Thus *purify* means "to make pure, cleanse," (coming from Latin *purificare*, from *purus*, "clean," plus *ficare*). In English the suffix *-fy* now normally takes the form *-ify:*, *acidify, humidify, speechify*. Verbs ending in *-fy* often have related nouns that end in *-fication* or *-faction*: *magnify, magnification; satisfy, satisfaction*.

**geo–** The basic meaning of the prefix *geo-* is "country or land." It comes from the Greek prefix *geo-*, from the Greek word *ge*, meaning "earth" in the sense of "ground or land." Thus *geography* (from Greek *geo-* plus *graphia*, "writing") is "the study of Earth and its surface features." When used to form words in English, *geo-* can mean either "Earth" or "geography." For example, *geomagnetism* refers to the magnetism of Earth, and *geopolitics* refers to the relationship between politics and geography.

**hydro–** The prefix *hydro-* is from the Greek prefix *hudro-* or *hudr-*, which comes from the Greek noun *hudor*, meaning "water." Thus in the word *hydrophobia*, *hudro-* combines with the suffix *-phobia*, "fear," to mean "an abnormal fear of water." *Hydrophobia* is an example of a Greek word that was later adopted into Latin, then French, and then English. *Hydroelectric*, *hydroplane*, and *hydrosphere* are examples of words more recently formed in English. Before a vowel, *hydro-* sometimes becomes *hydr-*: *hydrate, hydrous.*

**hyper–** The basic meaning of the prefix *hyper-* is "excessive or excessively." For example, *hyperactive* means "highly or excessively active." *Hyper-* comes from the Greek prefix *huper-*, which comes from the preposition *huper*, meaning "over, beyond." *Hyper-* has been used actively in English since the 17th century and is now frequently used to make up new words, such as *hypercritical* and *hypersensitive*. In fact, most of the words in our language beginning with *hyper-* are relatively recent. Only a few, such as *hyperbole*, are of Greek origin.

**hypo–** The prefix *hypo-* means "beneath, below, or under." It can be traced back to the Greek prefix *hupo-*, from the word *hupo*, meaning "beneath, under." A few English words, such as *hypocrite, hypocrisy,* and *hypochondria*, come from Greek words using *hupo-*. But most English words beginning with *hypo-* have been made up by scientists and physicians. *Hypo-* either means "below or under," as in *hypodermic*, or "less than normal," as in *hypoglycemia.*

**in–** There are two prefixes spelled *in-*. Both come from Latin, but they are not related to each other. The basic meaning of one prefix is "not." Thus *inactive* means "not active." This *in-* is related to and sometimes confused with the prefix *un-* that means "not" (unfortunately, there are also two *un-*'s). In fact, sometimes *in-* is used interchangeably with *un-*, as when *incommunicative* is used instead of *uncommunicative*. Before the consonants *l* and *r*, *in-* becomes *il-* and *ir-* respectively: *illogical, irregular.* Before the consonants *b, m,* and *p*, *in-* becomes *im-*: *imbalanced, immeasureable, impossible.*

The second *in-* has for its basic meaning "in, within, or into." For example, *inlay* means "to set something in something else." *In-* is also a form of the prefix *en-*. And in pairs such as *enclose/inclose, enquire/inquire, ensure/insure,* the two prefixes can be used somewhat interchangeably. As with the other prefix *in-*, before the consonants *l* and *r*, *in-* becomes *il-* and *ir-*: *illuminate, irrigate.* Before the consonants *b, m,* and *p*, *in-* becomes *im-*: *imbibe, immigrate, implant.*

**inter–** The prefix *inter-* comes from the Latin prefix *inter-*, from the preposition *inter*, meaning "between, among." Thus the word *intercede*, in which *inter-* combines with the Latin verb *cedere*, "to go," means "to go between." Similarly, *interject*, which comes from Latin *iacere*, "to throw," means literally "to throw something between or among others." And *intervene*, coming from Latin *venire*, "to come," means "to come between people or things." In English, *inter-* is still producing new words, such as *interfaith, intertwine,* and *intercellular.*

**–ism** The suffix *-ism* is a noun suffix. That is, when added to words or word roots, *-ism* forms nouns. It comes from the Greek noun suffix *-ismos* and means roughly "the act, state, or theory of." Nouns that end in *-ism* often have related verbs that end in *-ize* (*criticism*/*criticize*), related agent nouns that end in *-ist* (*optimism*/*optimist*), and related adjectives that end in *-istic* (*optimistic*).

**–ist** The suffix *-ist*, which comes from the Greek suffix *-istes,* forms agent nouns, that is, nouns that denote someone who does something. Although *-ist* frequently forms agent nouns from verbs ending in *-ize* or nouns ending in *-ism*, it has also come to be combined with words that do not end in *-ize* or *-ism*. In fact in some cases *-ist* can be used much like the suffix *-er*. In pairs such as *conformer*/*conformist, copier*/*copyist,* and *cycler*/*cyclist, -ist* and *-er* may be used interchangeably.

**–ize** The suffix *-ize,* which comes from the Greek verb suffix *-izein,* has become very important in English as a means of turning nouns and adjectives into verbs. *Formalize, jeopardize, legalize,* and *modernize* are examples of words that were coined in English hundreds of years ago. Other words that were coined later, in the 19th and 20th centuries, such as *emphasize, hospitalize, industrialize,* and *computerize,* are now also well established. Words ending in *-ize* often have related nouns ending in *-ization: dramatize*/*dramatization.*

**–less** The suffix *-less* comes from the Old English suffix *-leas,* from the word *leas,* meaning "without." In Old English and Middle English, *-less* was often used to convey the negative or opposite of words ending in *-ful,* as in *careful*/ *careless* and *fearful*/*fearless.* But *-less* was also used to coin words that had no counterpart ending in *-ful: headless, loveless, motherless.* Although *-less* normally forms adjectives by attaching to nouns, sometimes it attaches to verbs, as in *tireless.*

**–ment** The suffix *-ment* forms nouns, chiefly by attaching to verbs. It can have several meanings, the most common being "an act or an instance of doing something" or "the state of being acted upon." Thus an *entertainment* can be "an act of entertaining" and *amazement* is "the state of being amazed." Sometimes *-ment* can mean "result of an action," as in *advancement.* The suffix *-ment* can be traced back to the Latin noun suffix *-mentum.* Although its use in English dates back to the 1300s, it wasn't until the 1500s and 1600s that a great number of words were coined with *-ment.*

**micro–** The basic meaning of the prefix *micro-* is "small." It comes from the Greek prefix *mikro-,* from *mikros,* meaning "small." In English *micro-* has been chiefly used since the 19th century to form science words. It is the counterpart for the prefix *macro-* ("large") in pairs such as *microcosm*/*macrocosm* and *micronucleus*/*macronucleus.* And *micro-* is also sometimes the counterpart for the prefix *mega-,* as in *microvolt* ("one millionth of a volt") and *megavolt* ("one million volts").

**mid–** The prefix *mid-*, which means "middle," combines primarily with nouns to form compounds, most of which represent a time (*midmorning, midsummer, midyear*) or place (*midbrain, midstream, midtown*). When *mid-* is affixed to a word beginning with a capital letter, it is always necessary to use a hyphen: *mid-November, mid-Atlantic states.* The prefix *mid-* can be traced back to the Old English adjective *midd*, meaning "middle."

**mis–** The basic meaning of the prefix *mis-* is "bad; badly; wrong; wrongly." Thus *misfortune* means "bad fortune" and *misbehave* means "to behave badly." Likewise, a *misdeed* is "a wrong deed" and *misdo* means "to do wrongly." *Mis-* forms compounds primarily by attaching to verbs: *mishear, misremember. Mis-* also frequently forms compounds by attaching to nouns that come from verbs: *miscalculation, mismanagement, mispronunciation.* The prefix *mis-* can be traced back to Old English. Another *mis-* is a variant of *miso-*, discussed below.

**miso–** The prefix *miso-* and its variant *mis-* come from Greek *misein* and *misos*, which mean "hatred." Thus, *misanthropy* (from *mis-* plus *anthropos*, "man") means "hatred or mistrust of humanity," and *misogyny* (from *miso-* plus *gune*, "woman") means "hatred or mistrust of women."

**neo–** The prefix *neo-*, which comes from Greek, means "new or recent." Thus our word *neophyte*, which means "a recent convert" or "a beginner," comes from Greek *neophutos*, which meant literally "newly planted," from *neo-* plus *phutos*, "planted." Many words beginning with *neo-* do not come from Greek but have been formed in English over the last 150 years. Many of these words refer to a new or a modern form of a movement or doctrine, such as *neoconservatism* or *neofascism.* Many other relatively recent formations are science words, such as *neodymium.*

**–ness** The suffix *-ness*, which goes back to Old English, continues to have a productive life. It commonly attaches to adjectives in order to form abstract nouns, such as *artfulness* and *destructiveness.* The suffix *-ness* also forms nouns from adjectives made of participles, such as *contentedness* and *willingness.* It can also form nouns from compound adjectives, such as *kindheartedness* and *straightforwardness.* The suffix *-ness* can even be used with phrases: *matter-of-factness.*

**non–** The prefix *non-*, which means "not," comes from Latin *non.* The prefix was used primarily in Roman law terms that were adopted into Old French, and then into English. By the 16th century, many compounds with *non*, mostly legal terms, were in use in English. But in the 17th century the prefix began to be used with many different kinds of words. Today *non-* can be added to almost any adjective. Some examples include *nonessential, nonmetallic,* and *nonproductive. Non-* also combines with many nouns, as in *nonentity, nonresident,* and *nonviolence.* Most recently *non-* is used in combination with some verbs to form adjectives, as in *nonskid* and *nonstop.*

**–oid** The basic meaning of the suffix *-oid* is "like" or "resembling." Words ending in *-oid* are generally adjectives but can also be nouns. Thus *humanoid* means "having human characteristics or form" (adjective sense) or "a being having human form" (noun sense). Nouns ending in *-oid* form adjectives by adding the suffix *-al: spheroid, spheroidal; trapezoid, trapezoidal.* The suffix *-oid* comes from the Greek suffix *-oeides,* from *eidos,* meaning "shape, form."

**omni–** The prefix *omni-* means "all." It comes from the Latin word *omnis,* also meaning "all." Because the meaning of *omni-* is so clear and easily recognizable, the prefix has long been used in English to make new words. For example, the meanings of words such as *omnipurpose* ("all-purpose") and *omnitolerant* ("tolerant of all things") are easy to guess, even without a definition. *Omni-* can be compared to the prefix *pan-,* which also means "all." *Pan-,* however, comes from Greek and is most commonly used in English in compounds with names of nationalities: *Pan-American.*

**–ous** The suffix *-ous,* which forms adjectives, has the basic meaning "having, full of, or characterized by." *Blusterous,* for example, means "full of or characterized by bluster." The suffix *-ous* can be traced back to the Latin adjective suffix *-osus.* Some English words ending in *-ous* that come from Latin adjectives ending in *-osus* are *copious, dolorous, famous, generous,* and *glorious.* Adjectives ending in *-ous* often have related nouns ending in *-ousness* or *-osity: copiousness, generosity.*

**out–** There are many words in English beginning with *out-.* In words such as *outbuilding, outcast, outpour,* and *outstanding, out-* has the same meaning as the adverb *out.* So an *outcast* is "one who is cast out," and one who is *outstanding* "stands out." But in other cases *out-* takes on the sense of doing better, being greater, or going beyond, as in *outdo, outnumber,* and *outrun.* Although *out-* can attach to nouns, adjectives, or verbs to form other nouns, adjectives, or verbs, it most frequently attaches to verbs: *outbowl, outcook, outride, outsing.*

**post–** The basic meaning of the prefix *post-* is "after." It comes from Latin *post,* meaning "behind, after." *Post-* is often used in opposition to the prefixes *ante-* and *pre-: antedate/postdate; prewar/postwar.* And *post-* occurs frequently in medical terminology. *Postnasal* and *postnatal* are two common examples, but there are many others, such as *postcranial* ("behind the cranium") and *postvertebral* ("behind the vertebrae").

**pre–** The basic meaning of the prefix *pre-* is "before." It comes from Latin *prae,* which means "before, in front." In fact, the word *prefix* comes from *prae* plus *fixus,* a form of the Latin verb *figere* ("to fasten"). *Pre-* often appears in combination with verbs of Latin origin. For example, as early as the 16th century we have *preconceive, preexist,* and *premeditate. Predispose* and *prepossess* came into use in the 17th century, and *prepay* came into use in the 19th century.

**pro–** *Pro-* is another prefix that exists in two forms. The first comes from Latin *pro*, meaning "for." In English, this *pro-* usually means "favoring" or "supporting," as when it is prefixed to names of nationalities: *pro-American*. In this sense, the opposite of *pro-* would be *anti: proslavery/antislavery*.

The other *pro-* comes from Greek *pro*, meaning "before, in front." The word *prologue* comes from Greek *prologos*, from *pro* plus *logos*, meaning "speech." In English, *pro-* often means "before" or "earlier" and is used mainly in science terms: *prophase*.

**re–** The primary meaning of the prefix *re-*, which comes from Latin, is "again." *Re-* combines chiefly with verbs, as in these examples: *rearrange, rebuild, recall, remake, rerun, rewrite*. The prefix has been used with this meaning extensively in English since the 1600s. Sometimes it is necessary to use a hyphen with *re-* to distinguish between pairs such as *recollect* (rĕk′ə-lĕkt′) and *re-collect* (rē′kə-lĕkt′) or *recreation* (rĕk′rē-ā′shən) and *re-creation* (rē′krē-ā′shən). A hyphen may also be used when *re-* precedes a word beginning with *e*, as in *re-enact* and *re-enter*.

**retro–** The prefix *retro-*, meaning "backward, back," comes from the Latin prefix *retro-*, meaning "backward, behind." The most common English words beginning with *retro-* are derived from Latin words or elements. *Retroactive* comes from Latin *retro-* and the verb *agere*, "to drive." *Retrograde* combines *retro-* with the verb *gradi*, "to walk." *Retrospect* adds *retro-* to the verb *specere*, "to look at." The 19th and 20th centuries have seen many scientific or technical terms coined with English *retro-*, such as *retrorocket*.

**self–** The prefix *self-* goes back to the Old English word *self*, meaning virtually the same thing it does today. In Old English there were about a dozen compounds with *self-* of which only one has remained common: *self-will*. In Modern English, however, the number of new compounds with *self-* has increased. *Self-* usually forms compounds with adjectives, as in *self-conscious, self-employed*, and *self-governing*, and nouns, as in *self-confidence, self-improvement*, and *self-satisfaction*, and indicates something about oneself.

**semi– / hemi– / demi–** The prefix *semi-* means "half" or "partially." In general it combines with adjectives: *semiattached, semidry, semisweet*. *Semi-* also combines, less commonly, with nouns: *semidarkness, semidesert, semidome*. *Semi-* can be compared with the prefixes *hemi-* and *demi-*. All three have basically the same meaning, but *semi-* comes from Latin *semi-*, meaning "half," and *hemi-* comes from Greek *hemi-*, meaning "half." *Demi-* comes from Latin *dimidius*, meaning "divided in half," from *dis*, "apart, asunder" plus *medius*, "half."

**–ship** The suffix *-ship* has a long history in English. It goes back to the Old English suffix *-scipe*, which was attached to adjectives and nouns to indicate a particular state or condition: *hardship, friendship*. In Modern English the suffix has been added only to nouns and usually indicates a state or condition (*authorship, kinship, partnership, relationship*), the qualities belonging to a class of human beings (*craftsmanship, horsemanship, sportsmanship*), or rank or office (*ambassadorship*).

**sub–** The prefix *sub-* can be traced back to the Latin preposition *sub*, meaning "under." Some words beginning with *sub-* that came into English from Latin include *submerge, suburb,* and *subvert*. When *sub-* is used to form words in English, it can mean "under" (*submarine, subsoil, subway*), "subordinate" (*subcommittee, subplot, subset*), or "less than completely" (*subhuman, substandard*). *Sub-* can form compounds by combining with verbs as well as with adjectives and nouns, as in *subdivide, sublease,* and *sublet*.

**thermo–** The prefix *thermo-* comes from Greek *thermos*, meaning "warm, hot." When used to form words in English, *thermo-* generally refers to heat, as in *thermodynamic*, or sometimes to thermoelectricity, as in *thermocouple*. Most of the words that begin with *thermo-*, such as *thermodynamics, thermoelectricity, thermostat,* and *thermosphere*, have only come into being in the 19th and 20th centuries. Sometimes before a vowel *thermo-* becomes *therm-*, as in *thermanesthesia*, which means "inability to feel hot or cold."

**trans–** The prefix *trans-* goes back to the Latin prefix *trans-*, from the Latin preposition *trans*, meaning "across, beyond, through." Many of the most common English words beginning with *trans-* are derived from Latin words or elements, as in *transfer, transfuse, translate, transmit, transpire,* and *transport*. Another large group of words has *trans-* in combination with English adjectives, as in *transatlantic, transcontinental, transoceanic, transpacific,* and *transpolar*, with the meaning "across" or "through" a particular geographic element.

**–ty** The suffix *-ty* forms nouns from adjectives. The word *subtlety*, for example, means "the quality or state of being subtle." *Subtlety* comes from the Latin noun *subtilitas*, from the adjective *subtilis* ("subtle") plus *-tas*, the ancestor of our suffixes *-ty* and *-ity*. Some other words that end in *-ty* are *certainty, cruelty, frailty, loyalty,* and *royalty*. In English the suffix *-ity* is now more common, as in *eccentricity, electricity, technicality, peculiarity,* and *similarity*. The suffixes *-ty* and *-ity* can be compared in meaning to the suffix *-ness*. Whereas *-ty* and *-ity* come from Latin, however, *-ness* comes from Old English.

**un–** There are two prefixes spelled *un-* in English. Both go back to Old English. One has the basic meaning "not." Thus *unhappy* means "not happy." This *un-* chiefly attaches to adjectives, as in *unable, unclean, unequal, uneven, unripe,* and *unsafe*. It also attaches to adjectives made of participles, as in *unfeeling, unflinching, unfinished,* and *unsaid*. Less frequently, this same prefix attaches to nouns: *unbelief, unconcern, unrest*.

The other *un-* is not related, despite its origin in Old English. It forms verbs and expresses removal, reversal, or deprivation: *undress, unravel, unnerve*.

**under–** The prefix *under-*, which can be traced back to Old English, has essentially the same meaning as the preposition *under*. For example, in words such as *underbelly, undercurrent, underlie,* and *undershirt, under-* denotes a position beneath or below. *Under-* also frequently conveys incompleteness or falling below a certain standard. Some examples are *undercharge, underdeveloped, underestimate,* and *underfeed*. Note that in this sense words beginning with *under* often have counterparts beginning with *over-: overcharge, overestimate*.

**uni–** The basic meaning of the prefix *uni-* is "one." It comes from the Latin prefix *uni-*, from the word *unus*, meaning "one." Many English words beginning with *uni-* were formed in Latin. The word *unicorn*, for example, comes from *uni-* plus *cornu*, meaning "horn" and refers to a one-horned animal. *Uniform* comes from *uni-* plus *forma*, "shape," and means "always the same" or literally "one shape." And *unison*, which comes from *uni-* plus *sonus*, "sound," means literally "one sound." The majority of new words with *uni-*, such as *unicellular, unicycle, unilateral,* and *univalent,* are from the 19th century. *Uni-* can be compared to the prefix *mono-*, which is from Greek.

**–ward** The basic meaning of the suffix *-ward* is "having a particular direction or location." Its use dates back to Old English. Thus *inward* means "directed or located inside." Other examples are *outward, forward, backward, upward, downward, earthward, homeward, northward, southward, eastward,* and *westward*. The suffix *-ward* forms adjectives and adverbs. Adverbs ending in *-ward* can also end in *-wards*. Thus *I stepped backward* and *I stepped backwards* are both correct. Only *backward* (and not *backwards*) is an adjective: *a backward glance*.

**–wise** The suffix *-wise* forms adverbs when it attaches to adjectives or nouns. It comes from an Old English suffix *-wise*, which meant "in a particular direction or manner." Thus *clockwise* means "in the direction that a clock goes," and *likewise* means "in like manner, similarly." For the last fifty years or so, *-wise* has also meant "with respect to," as in *saleswise*, meaning "with respect to sales," and *taxwise*, meaning "with respect to taxes." Many people consider this usage awkward, however, and you may want to avoid it, especially in formal settings.

**zoo–** The prefix *zoo-*, which is pronounced with two syllables, comes from Greek *zoion*, meaning "animal, living being." We know this prefix best from the one-syllable word *zoo*. *Zoo* is a popular shortening of the longer, more formal *zoological garden*, which was originally a park where wild animals were kept on display. *Zoological* is the adjective form of the noun *zoology*, which means "the study of animals." *Zoology* is thus part of *biology*, which means "the study of life."

# Word Compounding

A compound word is made up of two or more words that together express a single idea. There are three types of compounds. An *open compound* consists of

two or more words written separately, such as *salad dressing, Boston terrier*, or *April Fools' Day*. A *hyphenated compound* has words connected by a hyphen, such as *age-old, mother-in-law, force-feed*. A *solid compound* consists of two words that are written as one word, such as *keyboard* or *typewriter*. In addition, a compound may be classified as permanent or temporary. A *permanent compound* is fixed by common usage and can usually be found in the dictionary, whereas a *temporary compound* consists of two or more words joined by a hyphen as needed, usually to modify another word or to avoid ambiguity. In general, permanent compounds begin as temporary compounds that become used so frequently they become established as permanent compounds. Likewise many solid compounds begin as separate words, evolve into hyphenated compounds, and later become solid compounds. Although the dictionary is the first place to look when you are trying to determine the status of a particular compound, reference works do not always agree on the current evolutionary form of a compound, nor do they include temporary compounds. The following general rules apply to forming compounds. Keep in mind that words that are made up of a word root plus a prefix or a suffix are not normally considered compounds, strictly speaking. But for convenience we discuss them here since they are also sometimes hyphenated.

## Prefixes and Suffixes

Normally, prefixes and suffixes are joined with a second element without a hyphen, unless doing so would double a vowel or triple a consonant: *antianxiety, anticrime, antiwar* but *anti-intellectual; childlike, taillike* but *bell-like*. Even so, many common prefixes, such as *co-, de-, pre-, pro-*, and *re-*, are added without a hyphen although a double vowel is the result: *coordinate, preeminent, reenter*.

A hyphen is also used when the element following a prefix is capitalized or when the element preceding a suffix is a proper noun: *anti-American, America-like*.

The hyphen is usually retained in words that begin with *all-, ex-* (meaning "former"), *half-, quasi-* (in adjective constructions), and *self-: all-around; ex-governor; half-life* but *halfhearted, halfpenny, halftone, halfway; quasi-scientific* but *a quasi success; self-defense* but *selfhood, selfish, selfless, selfsame*.

Certain homographs require a hyphen to prevent mistakes in pronunciation and meaning: *recreation* (enjoyment), *re-creation* (new creation); *release* (to let go), *re-lease* (to rent again).

## When the Compound Is a Noun or Adjective

In order to avoid confusion, compound modifiers are generally hyphenated: *fine-wine tasting, high-school teacher, hot-water bottle, minimum-wage worker, rare-book store, real-life experiences.* If there is no possibility of confusion, or if the hyphen would look clumsy, omit the hyphen: *bubonic plague outbreak, chemical engineering degree, temp agency employee.*

When a noun that is an open compound is preceded by an adjective, the compound is often hyphenated to avoid confusion: *wine cellar, damp wine-cellar; broom closet, tiny broom-closet; house cat, old house-cat.*

Compound adjectives formed with *high-* or *low-* are generally hyphenated: *high-quality programming, low-budget films.*

Compound adjectives formed with an adverb plus an adjective or a participle are often hyphenated when they occur before the noun they modify: *a well-known actor, an ill-advised move, best-loved poems, a much-improved situation, the so-called cure.* However, when these compounds occur after the noun, or when they are modified, the hyphen is usually omitted: *the actor is well known; an extremely well known actor.*

If the adverb ends in *-ly* in an adverb-adjective compound, the hyphen is omitted: *a finely tuned mechanism, a carefully worked canvas.*

Compound adjectives formed with an adverb or a noun and a past participle are always hyphenated when they precede the noun they modify: *well-kept secret, above-mentioned reason, helium-filled balloons, snow-capped mountains.* Many compounds of this type have become permanent and are therefore hyphenated whether they precede or follow the noun they modify: *a well-worn shirt, his shirt was well-worn; the tongue-tied winner, she remained tongue-tied.*

Also hyphenate compound adjectives formed with an adjective and a noun to which *-d* or *-ed* has been added: *yellow-eyed cat, fine-grained wood, many-tiered cake, stout-limbed toddler.* Many of these compounds have become permanent hyphenated or solid compounds: *middle-aged, old-fashioned, lightheaded, kindhearted.*

Compound adjectives formed with a noun, adjective, or adverb and a present participle are hyphenated when the compound precedes the noun it modifies: *a bone-chilling tale, two good-looking sons, long-lasting friendship.* Many of these compounds have become permanent solid compounds: *earsplitting, farseeing.* Many other compounds have become permanent and are hyphenated whether they precede or follow the noun they modify: *far-reaching consequences; the consequences are far-reaching.*

Compound nouns formed with a noun and a gerund are generally open: *crime solving, house hunting, trout fishing.* Many of these compounds, however, have become permanent solid compounds: *faultfinding, housekeeping.*

Compound modifiers formed of capitalized words should not be hyphenated: *Old English poetry, Iron Age manufacture, New World plants.*

Usage is divided with regard to compounds that are proper names used to designate ethnic groups. Under normal circumstances such terms when used as nouns or adjectives should appear without a hyphen: *a group of African Americans, many Native Americans, French Canadians in Boston, a Jewish American organization, an Italian American neighborhood, Latin American countries.* However, many (but not all) compounds of this type are now frequently hyphenated: *African-Americans, Asian-American families, French-Canadian music* but *Native American myths.*

Nouns or adjectives consisting of a short verb combined with a preposition are either hyphenated or written solid depending on current usage. The same words used as a verb are written separately: *a breakup* but *break up a fight; a bang-up job* but *bang up the car.*

Two nouns of equal value are hyphenated when the person or thing is considered to have the characteristics of both nouns: *secretary-treasurer, city-state, time-motion study.*

Compound forms must reflect meaning. Consequently, some compounds may change in form depending on how they are used: *Anyone may go* but *Any one of these will do; Everyone is here* but *Every one of these is good.*

Scientific compounds are usually not hyphenated: *carbon monoxide poisoning, dichromic acid solution.*

## Phrases

Phrases used as modifiers are normally hyphenated: *a happy-go-lucky person, a here-today-gone-tomorrow attitude.*

A foreign phrase used as a modifier is not hyphenated: *a bona fide offer, a per diem allowance.*

## Numbers

Numbers from twenty-one to ninety-nine and adjective compounds with a numerical first element (whether spelled out or written in figures) are hyphenated: *twenty-one, thirty-first, second-rate movie, third-story window, three-dimensional figure, six-sided polygon, ten-thousand-year-old bones, 13-piece band, 19th-century novel, decades-old newspapers.*

Spelled-out numbers used with *-fold* are not hyphenated; figures and *-fold* are hyphenated: *tenfold, 20-fold.*

Compounds of a number and *-odd* are hyphenated: *four-odd, 60-odd.*

A modifying compound consisting of a number and a possessive noun is not hyphenated: *one week's pay, 35 hours' work.*

Fractions used as modifiers are hyphenated unless the numerator or denominator of the fraction contains a hyphen: *three-eighths inch, twenty-four hundredths part; The pie was one-half eaten.* Fractions used as nouns are usually not hyphenated: *He ate one half of the pie.*

## Color

Compound color adjectives are hyphenated: *a red-gold sunset, a cherry-red sweater.*

Color compounds whose first element ends in *-ish* are hyphenated when they precede the noun but should not be hyphenated when they follow the noun: *a darkish-blue color, a reddish-gold sunset; The sky is reddish gold.*

# E-mail

## *Conventions and Quirks*

In their book *Connections: New Ways of Working in the Networked Organization*, sociologists Lee Sproul and Sara Kiesler discuss experiments they designed to compare the efficiency and social dynamics of people making decisions in face-to-face meetings with those of people making decisions over a computer network. Sproul and Kiesler found that the groups making decisions electronically had far greater difficulty reaching consensus and ended up taking more extreme positions than the face-to-face groups did. Even more surprising, the on-line groups frequently got caught up in violent arguments, with members exchanging nearly ten times the number of rude remarks that their face-to-face counterparts did. The on-line behavior got so nasty that the researchers halted one of the studies; participants in one of the groups became so infuriated with one another that they had to be escorted out of the building.

Welcome to the brave new world of electronic mail, that exciting new medium that is supposed to make communication smoother. Most people who are "on" E-mail are dazzled by what they consider its advantages over other methods of communication but they remain oblivious to its shortcomings. It makes sense then for people who are "talking" on-line to be aware of the ups and downs of electronic communication.

## Advantages of E-mail

One of E-mail's chief virtues is that it is asynchronous—information can be exchanged without the participants having to interact at the same time. Eliminating the need to communicate in "real time" speeds up the flow of information by overcoming two of the drawbacks of the telephone: You never get a busy signal when you send an E-mail, and you never find yourself playing "telephone tag" with someone who happens to be out when you call.

A second advantage of E-mail is its speed. In seconds you can send messages, indeed entire documents, across time zones. You can respond to messages in seconds as well. The speed of E-mail allows people to work at great distances from each other and still communicate effectively. It lets people telecommute, giving them more flexibility in their schedules and sparing them the distractions that gobble up so much of the work day in an office.

Another benefit of communicating by computer is its variability. You can

communicate in a multitude of forms, from one-on-one personal communication to corporate memos and electronic distribution lists. Being able to contact large numbers of people with a single act represents an enormous increase in efficiency. You no longer have to print and photocopy a document and then see that it is hand-delivered to the individuals on a mailing list. Using E-mail, you can distribute a document to any number of people instantaneously with the click of a mouse.

Many people maintain that E-mail is a more democratic way of holding a discussion than the face-to-face meeting. Because E-mail eliminates the visual trappings of social status and position that are apparent to everyone in a face-to-face meeting, it allows people at various levels in an organization to participate as equals in a discussion. People at higher levels are less able to dominate a discussion. For this reason, ideas that are proposed on a computer network tend to be evaluated on their merits more than their origin. Moreover, because discussions tend to focus on the question at hand, there is less opportunity for social posturing and other forms of unproductive "talk" than in face-to-face meetings.

The final advantage of E-mail is psychological. It can nurture a sense of connectedness and commitment in people who see that they are actively involved in a discussion, whether with family members, friends, strangers who share certain interests, or coworkers.

Well, then, if E-mail is so wonderful, and people feel so connected, why do they get so angry with one another?

## Disadvantages of E-mail

Unfortunately, many of E-mail's virtues can also be drawbacks. While it is true that electronic communication has a wide variety of forms, each of these has its own requirements that the user must try to be aware of in order to avoid saying something inappropriate or incomprehensible. A variety of forms means a variety of audiences, some of which may include nonnative speakers of English, who may not understand American idioms or allusions to American culture.

E-mail discussions may be more democratic than face-to-face meetings, but equality of communication can increase the number of suggested solutions to a problem, making it more difficult for participants to reach a consensus. If disagreements arise, there is usually no one in charge to referee. Debate can degenerate into a verbal brawl.

Since the participants in an E-mail discussion can be neither seen nor heard, social cues are absent, making it easy for people to make injudicious remarks. It is hard to remember what sort of audience you are addressing when all you can see is text on a screen. There is no one sitting around a table. You cannot see people's clothes. You miss their facial expressions and cannot tell what tone of voice they are using.

Because it is so hard to size up the social situation, it is easy to say things that can have unwanted consequences, especially when people are responding spontaneously to a communication. Impulsive replies can be unduly harsh,

flippant, or defensive, and they often provoke other impulsive responses. The sending of an irate or rude message has been common enough to have been given its own name: *flaming.*

In fact, E-mail is little more than a ticker tape of words, and electronic messages are therefore subject to a variety of interpretations. Indications of interest or agreement, positive remarks, or even compliments that we easily interpret in face-to-face meetings can be construed as sarcasms when said in E-mail.

E-mail has other disadvantages. Among them is information overload. Many E-mail messages are irrelevant or redundant. Communicants often "copy" people that don't really need to be involved in the discussion. This practice tends to overburden people with messages and to retard the flow of productive information.

There is no easy solution to these problems. Restraining yourself from making an impulsive response is not always possible in a busy workday, nor is it always desirable to stifle the spontaneity of your remarks. But as an insurance policy against a potential disaster, it seems a good practice to consider whether you would utter your remarks in a face-to-face meeting, and if not, why not. You must always do your best to ascertain who your audience is and to anticipate how your remarks may be taken.

## Forms of E-mail

Audiences vary, of course. Electronic communication has a variety of forms, each with a different structure and different requirements.

**standard E-mail** In this format, a user can communicate with a single correspondent or with a group by exchanging messages across a computer network. Communication is asynchronous—each user has an electronic mailbox, either in a personal computer or in a central computer to which terminals are connected. Messages are stored in the mailbox until the user accesses them.

**bulletin boards** This E-mail format provides asynchronous forums for group discussions. Users can post messages, comments, questions, or responses that can be saved for or broadcast to participants. Many groups like to list *FAQ*'s (frequently asked questions) about the subject, along with responses, as an introduction to the group's interests.

**chat rooms** These are electronic meeting places where groups of people sharing a particular interest can hold a conversation. Chat rooms are not asynchronous—they take place in real time. As many as two dozen people can talk at the same time, with messages overlaying one another on the screen in a visual version of "room noise." Because the discussions can only take place sequentially, participants often find themselves lagging by several lines. They may respond to one remark only to find two or three other responses, or even entirely new topics, have appeared on the screen in the meantime. In this way, responses can appear without context and can get lost in the noise.

Because the immediacy of chat rooms resembles that of speech, they are the most informal of all modes of electronic communication. Because of their relative formlessness, chat rooms may be the least efficient way of using your computer to communicate.

## Informality

Because certain forms of E-mail are characterized by a rapid give-and-take that resembles conversation, they tend to be more informal in tone than conventional print writing and the more institutional forms of electronic messaging, such as corporate reports. In fact, these conversational E-mailers have developed a variety of practices to sustain an informal tone while at the same time saving keystrokes. E-mailers commonly use contractions and abbreviated expressions. They often omit pronoun subjects, as in *don't know* for *I don't know, depends* for *it depends,* and *glad you asked* for *I am glad that you asked.* Another common practice is the use of "eye dialect" spellings, as in *gonna* for *going to, gotta* for *have got to,* and *thru* for *through.* Many people use acronyms to stand for commonly used expressions or to indicate attitudes and emotional responses. These acronyms are usually capitalized. Here is a selection of commonly used E-mail acronyms:

| Acronym | Expression |
|---------|------------|
| BBL | Be Back Later |
| BFN | Bye For Now |
| BRB | Be Right Back |
| BTW | By The Way |
| FWIW | For What It's Worth |
| HSIK | How Should I Know |
| IAE | In Any Event |
| IMO | In My Opinion |
| IOW | In Other Words |
| JFYI | Just For Your Information |
| LOL | Laughing Out Loud |
| NBD | No Big Deal |
| NOYB | None Of Your Business |
| OIC | Oh, I See |
| OTL | Out To Lunch |
| OTOH | On The Other Hand |
| PMFJI | Pardon Me For Jumping In |
| ROTFL | Rolling On The Floor Laughing |
| TIC | Tongue In Cheek |
| TTFN | Ta Ta For Now |
| TTYL | Talk To You Later |
| WRT | With Respect To |
| WTG | Way To Go |

Other conventions add keystrokes in an attempt to capture some of the nonverbal clues and body language that allow speakers in a face-to-face conversation to recognize sarcasm, facetiousness, disbelief, dismay, and other attitudes. E-mailers have an affection for punctuation that would seem unorthodox in most print communication. E-mail tends to have more exclamations than the more deliberative printed letter and consequently the exclamation point crops up frequently, often in clusters to show astonishment or disbelief. Trailing dots are a favorite too, indicating incompleteness of thought, dissatisfaction with a train of thought, or an assumption that the reader can extrapolate what is implied. To give a message special emphasis, an E-mailer may write entirely in capital letters, a device E-mailers refer to as *screaming*. Some of these visual conventions have emerged as a way of getting around the constraints on data transmission that now limit many networks. Underlining, for example, does not travel over some networks, so E-mailers sometimes emphasize a word or phrase by enclosing it in asterisks.

Perhaps the most famous of all visual conventions are the "emoticons" or "smileys" that people use to summarize emotions. Here is a selection:

| Emoticon | Emotion |
| --- | --- |
| :-) | Happy |
| :-( | Sad |
| :-< | Very Sad or Upset |
| :-O | Shocked or Amazed |
| :-D | Laughing |
| ;-) | Winking |
| :-\| | Bored or Uninterested |
| 8-\| | What next! |
| 8-O | Extremely Shocked |
| :-] | Smirk, happy sarcasm |
| :-[ | Grimace, sad sarcasm |
| :-} | Grinning |
| :-\ | Undecided |
| :-# | Sealed Lips |
| :-& | Tongue Tied |
| :-I | Hmmm |

# Reader Expectations

Accompanying the general tendency of E-mailers to be informal is the tendency of readers to be more forgiving than readers of printed material. Since so much E-mail is a simple substitute for a routine telephone call, its quick brief messages are mostly ephemeral—there is no point in saving them, in styling them carefully, or in being concerned with the niceties of their grammar. Where a misspelling in a printed letter leaves many readers concluding that the writer is a slob or a dunce, the same misspelling in an E-mail message

hardly makes a difference to the readers. They assume that the writer must be too busy working or having fun in cyberspace to bother with spellcheckers and dictionaries.

These different expectations can liberate us from many of the more stodgy conventions that can make print communication slow, stuffy, and even tedious. But they can also lead us to inadvertent rudeness, levity that seems disrespectful, or the appearance of indifference to our readers.

It is too early to tell whether the informality of E-mail will begin to influence the way we write on paper. Certainly, bad spellers will hope that the more forgiving attitude of E-mail readers might spill over to print readers. It is more likely, however, that people will start clamoring for law and order on the wild frontier of E-mail and will insist upon incorporating in electronic English many of the conventions that regulate Standard English in print. Not to be tied down, many E-mailers will undoubtedly resist and become outlaws. The ephemerality of most electronic messages makes standardization irrelevant.

Still, it is important to remember in all of this talk about informality that E-mail is really a medium that can be used for a whole spectrum of rhetorical situations and not a brand of English that is noteworthy chiefly for a small set of hip stylistic conventions. It is easy to get entranced by the novelty and the speed of electronic communication and to think of it more as a playground than as a city full of varied neighborhoods. As a writer you must always keep your wits about you and be street smart.

It is also important to remember the virtues that traditional written communication has to offer: the opportunity to shape a piece of writing into something worth saving and the chance to move a reader by the careful arrangement of words for their cumulative effect. A formal occasion like an important business communication, a job application, or a serious personal letter has its own special writing requirements, whether you send it as a hard copy in the mail or as a series of blips over a cable. The informal chatter we like so much is not really suitable for every message we might send by E-mail. Everything has its limits. E-mail is no exception.

# A Grammar Toolkit

This section contains an alphabetical list of the important grammatical terms used in this book. Each term has one or more brief definitions. Many terms contain cross-references to the chapters where a discussion of the pertinent usage issues can be found.

**absolute construction** A construction that consists of a noun and a modifier and modifies the rest of the sentence, rather than a single element of the sentence. See *Grammar,* **absolute constructions.**

**active voice** A property of transitive verbs whereby the subject of the verb is the agent of the action. The verb *ate* in *Mike ate the watermelon* is in the active voice. See *Grammar,* **verbs, voice of.**

**adjective** A word that modifies a noun. Adjectives are distinguished chiefly by their suffixes, such as *-able, -ous,* and *-er,* or by their position directly preceding a noun or noun phrase.

**adverb** A word that modifies a verb, an adjective, or another adverb.

**affix** A word element, such as a prefix or suffix, that can only occur attached to a base form.

**agreement** Correspondence in gender, number, case, or person between words. See *Grammar,* **pronouns, agreement of** and **subject and verb agreement.**

**antecedent** The word, phrase, or clause to which a pronoun refers.

**appositive** A noun or noun phrase that is placed next to another to help explain it. *The composer* in *The composer Beethoven lived in Bonn* is an appositive.

**article** A word that indicates that the word which follows it is a noun and that specifies the noun's application. The indefinite articles are *a* and *an.* The definite article is *the.*

**aspect** A property of verbs that designates the relation of the action to the passage of time, especially in reference to completion, duration, or repetition.

**attributive** A word, such as an adjective or a noun, that is placed adjacent to the noun it modifies, as *city* in *the city streets.*

**auxiliary verb** A verb, such as *have, can,* or *will,* that accompanies the main verb in a clause and helps to make distinctions in mood, voice, aspect, and tense. See *Grammar,* **auxiliary and primary verbs.**

**base form** The form of a word to which affixes or other base forms can be added to make new words, as *mystify* in *mystifying, build* in *rebuild,* and *writing* in *skywriting.*

**case** The form of noun, pronoun, or modifier that indicates its grammatical relationship to other words in a clause or sentence. In English only pronouns are differentiated by case. English pronouns have three cases: Nominative or Subjective (*she*), Objective (*him*), and Possessive (*his*). See *Grammar,* **pronouns, personal.**

**clause** A group of words containing a subject and a predicate and forming part of a compound or complex sentence.

**collective noun** A noun, such as *flock* or *team* that refers to a collection of persons or things regarded as a unit. See *Grammar,* **collective nouns.**

**common noun** A noun, such as *book* or *dog,* that can be preceded by the definite article and that represents one or all of the members of a class.

**comparative degree** The intermediate degree of comparison of adjectives, as *better, sweeter,* or *more wonderful,* or adverbs, as *more softly.* See *Grammar,* **adjectives** and **adverbs, comparison of.**

**comparison** The modification or inflection of an adjective or adverb to indicate the positive, comparative, and superlative degrees. See *Grammar,* **adjectives** and **adverbs, comparison of.**

**complement** A word or group of words used after a verb to complete a predicate construction; for example, the phrase *to eat ice cream* in *We like to eat ice cream* is the complement.

**complex sentence** A sentence that consists of at least one independent clause and one dependent clause, such as *When I grow up, I want to be a doctor.*

**compound-complex sentence** A sentence consisting of at least two coordinate independent clauses and one or more dependent clauses, as *I wanted to go, but I decided not to when it started raining.*

**compound sentence** A sentence of two or more coordinate independent clauses, often joined by a conjunction, as *The problem was difficult, but I finally found the answer.*

**concord** Agreement.

**conditional** Of, relating to, or containing a clause that expresses a condition, that is, a circumstance that is necessary for something else to happen. Conditional clauses usually begin with *if, unless, provided that,* or a similar conjunction. Conditional sentences are sentences that contain conditional clauses: *If it starts to rain, we will have to leave. We cannot go to the beach unless he lends us his car.*

**conjunction** A word, such as *and, but, as,* and *because,* that connects words, phrases, or clauses.

**construction** A group of words arranged to form a meaningful phrase, clause, or sentence.

**coordinating conjunction** A conjunction, such as *and, but,* or *or,* that connects grammatical units that have the same function.

**correlative conjunction** Either of a pair of conjunctions, such as *either . . . or* or *both . . . and,* that connect two parts of a sentence and are not used adjacent to each other. The second of the pair is always a coordinate conjunction.

**count noun** A noun that can be referred to as a single entity, can occur in the plural, and can be used in a phrase with *a* or *an. Chair* and *experience* are count nouns. *Furniture* and *helium* are not.

**dangling participle** A participle with no clear grammatical relationship to the subject of the sentence. See *Grammar,* **dangling modifiers** and **participles.**

**definite article** A word that restricts or particularizes a noun. In English the definite article is *the.* It identifies a noun that has already been referred to (*I found the book under the chair*). It helps specify a particular thing (*I am reading about the development of the polio vaccine*). It also indicates a noun that stands as a typical example of its class (*The Golden Retriever is an ideal pet.*)

**degree** One of the forms used in the comparison of adjectives and adverbs. For example, *sweet* is the positive degree, *sweeter* the comparative degree, and *sweetest* the superlative degree of the adjective *sweet.*

**demonstrative** Specifying or singling out the person or thing referred to. The demonstrative adjectives are *this, these, that,* and *those.*

**dependent clause** A clause that cannot stand alone as a full sentence and functions as a noun, adjective, or adverb within a sentence.

**descriptive clause** A nonrestrictive clause.

**determiner** A word belonging to a group of noun modifiers (which include articles, demonstrative adjectives, possessive adjectives and words such as *any,* *both*, or *whose*) and occupying the first position in a noun phrase or the second or third position after another determiner.

**dialect** A variety of a language distinguished by pronunciation, grammar, or vocabulary and shared by a group that is set off from others geographically or socially. The term *dialect* is sometimes used to refer to a variety of language that differs from the standard literary language or speech pattern of the culture in which it exists.

**diminutive** A word, name, or suffix that indicates smallness, youth, familiarity, affection, or contempt. *Booklet, lambkin,* and *nymphet* are diminutives. The suffixes *-et, -let,* and *-kin* are diminutive suffixes.

**direct object** The noun, pronoun, or noun phrase referring to the person or thing that receives the action of a transitive verb. In *mail the letter* and *call him, letter* and *him* are the direct objects.

**disjunctive** Serving to establish a relationship of contrast or opposition. *But* in *sad but wiser* is disjunctive.

**double negative** A construction that employs two negatives, especially to express a single negation. See *Grammar,* **double negative.**

**elliptical** Characterized by the omission of a word or phrase that is necessary for a complete grammatical construction but is not necessary for understanding. In the sentence *While cleaning the desk, he found an old photograph,* the clause *while cleaning the desk* is elliptical in that it stands for *while he was cleaning the desk.*

**epicene pronoun** A pronoun that has one form for both masculine and feminine antecedents. See *Gender,* **epicene pronouns.**

**finite** Limited by person, number, tense, and mood. A finite verb can serve as the predicate of a sentence or as the initial verb in a verb phrase that is the predicate.

**function word** A word such as a preposition, conjunction, or article that has little meaning on its own and chiefly indicates a grammatical relationship.

**future perfect tense** The verb tense that expresses action completed by a specified time in the future and that is formed by combining *will have* or *shall have* with a past participle. See *Grammar,* **verbs, tenses of.**

**future tense** The verb tense that expresses action that has not yet occurred or a state that does not yet exist. See *Grammar,* **verbs, tenses of.**

**gender** 1. A category used in the selection or agreement of nouns, pronouns, and adjectives with modifiers, words being referred to, or grammatical forms. Grammatical gender may be arbitrary, or it may be based on characteristics such as sex or the quality of being animate. In English grammatical gender applies only to pronouns, which normally coincide with the sexual identity of their antecedents. In other languages, abstractions and inanimate objects may be grammatically masculine or feminine. In German, for example, the word for *fork* is feminine, the word for *spoon* is masculine, and the word for *knife* is neuter. 2. Sexual identity.

**gender-neutral** Free of explicit or implicit reference to biological gender or sexual identity, as the term *police officer* instead of *policeman*. See *Gender*, **epicene pronouns** and **he.**

**genitive case** The case that expresses possession, measurement, or source. See *Grammar*, **possessive constructions** and **pronouns, personal.**

**gerund** A noun derived from a verb and retaining certain features of verbs; in English gerunds end in *–ing*, as *singing* in *We admired the choir's singing.* See *Grammar*, **gerund.**

**grammar** 1. The system of inflections, word order, and word formation of a language. 2. The system of rules that allows the speakers of a language to create sentences. 3. A set of rules setting forth the current standard of usage in a language. 4. Writing or speech judged in relation to this set of rules.

**head** The word in a construction that has the same grammatical function as the construction as a whole and that determines relationships of agreement to other parts of the construction or sentence. The word *variety* is the head of the phrase *a wide variety of gardening tools* in the sentence *You can buy a wide variety of gardening tools at that store.*

**imperative** The verbal mood that expresses a command or request. *Stop* in *Stop running* and *Give* in *Give me a break* are in the imperative mood. See *Grammar*, **verbs, mood of.**

**imperfect tense** The tense of a verb that shows, usually in the past, an action or a condition as incomplete, continuous, or coincident with another action or condition.

**indefinite article** An article that does not fix the identity of the noun it modifies. In English the indefinite articles are *a* and *an.* They are typically used when the noun has not been mentioned before and so is unfamiliar: *A waiter appeared and asked to take our order.*

**indefinite pronoun** A pronoun such as *any* or *some* that does not specify the identity of its object.

**independent clause** A clause in a complex sentence that contains a subject and a verb and can stand alone as a complete sentence.

**indicative** The verbal mood used to make statements. See *Grammar*, **verbs, mood of.**

**indirect object** An object indirectly affected by the action of the verb, as *me* in *Sing me a song* and *the turtle* in *He feeds the turtle lettuce.*

**infinitive** A verb form that functions as a noun while retaining certain verbal characteristics, such as modification by adverbs. It is called the *infinitive* because the verb is not limited or "made finite" to indicate person, number, tense, or mood. In English the infinitive may be preceded by *to*, as in *We want him to work harder* and *To cooperate means to be willing to compromise*, or it may appear without *to*, as in *We may leave tomorrow* and *She had them read the letter.* The infinitive without *to* is called the *bare infinitive.*

**inflection** 1. A change in a word that expresses a grammatical relationship, such as case, gender, number, person, tense, or mood. 2. A word form or element that is involved in this change. In English most inflections are affixes, such as *-s*, which indicates the plural of many nouns (*dogs*), or *-ed*, which indicates past tense in many verbs (*relaxed*). Some English inflections involve a change in the base form of the word to indicate past tense or the past participle, as *spoke* and *spoken* from *speak.*

**intensive** Tending to emphasize or intensify, as the adverb *so* in *The music was so beautiful* or the pronoun *yourself* in *How can you ask me to help when you haven't done anything yourself?* See *Grammar*, **pronouns, reflexive and intensive**  and **so.**

**intransitive verb** A verb that does not require or cannot take a direct object, as *sleep* or *meditate.* See *Grammar*, **verbs, transitive and intransitive.**

**irregular** Departing from the usual pattern of inflection, derivation, or word formation, as the present forms of the verb *be* or the plural noun *children.* See *Grammar*, **verbs, principal parts of.**

**linking verb** A verb, such as a form of *be* or *seem*, that identifies the predicate of a sentence with the subject.

**main clause** An independent clause.

**main verb** A verb that expresses an action or a state. Main verbs can be inflected to show tense, number, person, and mood. They are distinguished from auxiliary verbs, which cannot be inflected. *Swim* is the main verb in the sentence *I could have swum a mile today.*

**mass noun** A noun, such as *sand* or *honesty,* that denotes a substance or concept that cannot be divided into countable units. Mass nouns are preceded in indefinite constructions by modifiers such as *some* or *much* rather than *a* or *one.*

**modifier** A word, phrase, or clause that limits or qualifies the sense of another word or word group.

**mood** A property of verbs that indicates the speaker's attitude toward the factuality or likelihood of the action or condition expressed. Mood determines whether a sentence is a statement, a command, or a conditional or hypothetical remark. English has three moods: indicative, imperative, and subjunctive. See *Grammar,* **verbs, mood of** and **subjunctive.**

**nominative case** The case of a pronoun used as the subject of a finite verb (as *I* in *I wrote the letter*) or as a predicate nominative (as *we* in *It is we who have made the mistake*).

**noncount noun** A mass noun.

**nonrestrictive clause** A dependent clause that describes but does not identify or restrict the meaning of the noun, phrase, or clause it modifies, as the clause *who live in a small house* in *The Smiths, who live in a small house, have ten cats.* Nonrestrictive clauses are normally set off by commas. See *Grammar,* **that.**

**noun** A word that is used to name a person, place, thing, quality, or action and can function as the subject or object of a verb, as the object of a preposition, or as an appositive.

**number** The indication of whether a word is singular or plural. Number in English nouns is usually indicated by inflection, that is, by the presence or absence of the suffix *-s* or *-es.*

**object** A noun or word acting like a noun that receives or is affected by the action of a verb or that follows and is governed by a preposition.

**objective case** The case of a pronoun used as the object of a verb or preposition. The pronoun *him* is in the objective case.

**objective complement** A noun, pronoun, or adjective serving as complement to a verb and qualifying its direct object, as *governor* in *They elected him governor.*

**parallelism** The use of identical or equivalent syntactic structures in corresponding clauses or phrases. See *Style,* **parallelism.**

**participle** A form of the verb that can serve as an adjective or is used with an auxiliary verb to indicate tense, aspect, or voice. In English the present participle ends in *-ing*, and the past participle ends in *-ed* or is an altered base form, as *ridden* from *ride* or *spoken* from *speak*. See *Grammar,* **participles** and **verbs, principal parts of.**

**passive voice** A property of verbs whereby the subject receives the action or effect of the verb. In the sentence *The house was built in a month,* the verb *build* is in the passive voice. See *Grammar,* **verbs, voice of.**

**past participle** A verb form indicating past or completed action or time that is used as an adjective and is used with auxiliary verbs to form the passive voice or the perfect and pluperfect tenses. In English the past participle is formed by the addition of the suffix *-ed* or by altering the base form of the verb, as *spoken* from *speak.* See *Grammar,* **participles** and **verbs, principal parts of.**

**past perfect tense** The pluperfect tense.

**past tense** The verb tense used to express an action or a condition prior to the time it is expressed.

**perfect tense** A verb tense expressing action completed prior to a fixed point of reference in time. English has two perfect tenses: the present perfect and the past perfect, or pluperfect. See *Grammar,* **verbs, tenses of.**

**person** Any of the pronoun forms or verb inflections that distinguish the speaker (first person), the individual addressed (second person), and the individual or thing spoken about (third person). See *Grammar,* **pronouns, agreement of; pronouns, personal;** and **pronouns, reflexive and intensive.**

**personal pronoun** A pronoun designating the person speaking (*I, me, we, us*), the person spoken to (*you*), or the person or thing spoken of (*he, she, it, they, him, her, them*). See *Grammar,* **pronouns, personal.**

**phrase** Two or more words occurring in sequence that form a grammatical unit that is less than a complete sentence.

**pluperfect tense** A verb tense used to express action completed before a stated or implied past time. In English the pluperfect tense is formed with the past participle of a verb and the auxiliary verb *had,* as *had learned* in *He had learned to skate before his fourth birthday.* See *Grammar,* **verbs, tenses of.**

**plural** 1. A grammatical form that designates more than one of the things specified. In English most plurals are formed by adding *-s* or *-es* to nouns. Some words, like *sheep* and *deer,* can have plural meaning but have no plural form: *The deer are in the field again.* A few words form their plurals by the addition of *-en: children; oxen.* 2. A verb form that expresses the action of a plural subject.

**positive degree** The simple, uncompared degree of an adjective or adverb. See *Grammar,* **adjectives, comparison of** and **adverbs, comparison of.**

**possessive** A form of a noun or pronoun that indicates possession. In English the possessive of singular nouns is usually formed by the addition of an apostrophe and *s.* See *Word Formation,* **possessives** and *Grammar,* **possessive constructions,** and **pronouns, personal.**

**possessive case** The case of a pronoun that indicates possession. The pronoun *my* is in the possessive case. Pronouns in the possessive case are often considered adjectives. See *Grammar,* **pronouns, personal.**

**predicate** One of the two main parts of a sentence containing the verb, objects, or phrases governed by the verb, as *opened the door* in *Jane opened the door* or *is very sleepy* in *The child is very sleepy.*

**predicate adjective** An adjective that follows a linking verb and modifies the subject, as *hot* in *The sun is hot.*

**predicate nominative** A noun or pronoun that follows a linking verb and refers to the same person or thing as the subject, as *firefighter* in *Jim was a firefighter.*

**prefix** An affix put before a word to alter its meaning. The element *dis-* in *disbelieve* is a prefix.

**preposition** A word, such as *in* or *to,* or a group of words, such as *in regard to,* that is placed before a noun or pronoun and indicates a grammatical relation to a verb, adjective, or another noun or pronoun.

**prepositional phrase** A phrase that consists of a preposition and its object and functions as an adjective or an adverb.

**present participle** A participle expressing present action, formed by adding the suffix *-ing* to verbs and used as an adjective and with the auxiliary verb *be* to make progressive tenses. See *Grammar,* **participles** and **verbs, tenses of.**

**present perfect tense** A verb tense expressing action completed at the present time, formed by combining the present tense of *have* with a past participle, as in *He has spoken.* See *Grammar,* **verbs, tenses of.**

**present tense** The verb tense expressing action in the present time, as in *She writes* and *She is writing.* See *Grammar,* **verbs, tenses of.**

**principal parts** The forms of a verb that are necessary to derive other forms. In English these are the infinitive, the past tense, the past participle, and the present participle. See *Grammar,* **verbs, principal parts of.**

**progressive** A verb form that expresses an action or condition in progress. In English progressive verb forms employ a form of the verb *be* and a present participle of the main verb, as in *He is walking, He has been walking, He had been walking.* See *Grammar,* **verbs, tenses of.**

**pronoun** A word that functions as a substitute for a noun or noun phrase.

**proper noun** A noun used as a name for a specific individual, event, or place and usually having few possibilities for modification.

**reflexive pronoun** A pronoun used as the direct object of a reflexive verb. Reflexive pronouns end in *-self* or *-selves.*

**reflexive verb** A verb whose subject is identical with its object, as *dressed* in *She dressed herself.*

**regular** Conforming to the usual pattern of inflection, derivation, or word formation. A plural ending in *-s* is a regular plural.

**relative clause** A dependent clause introduced by a relative pronoun, as *which is downstairs* in *The stereo, which is downstairs, has four speakers.*

**relative pronoun** A pronoun that introduces a relative clause and refers to an antecedent. *Who, whom, whose, which,* and *that* the relative pronouns. See *Grammar,* **that, who,** and **which.**

**restrictive clause** A dependent clause that identifies the noun, phrase, or clause it modifies and limits or restricts its meaning, as the clause *who live in glass houses* in *People who live in glass houses should not throw stones.*

**singular** 1. A grammatical form that designates a single person or thing or a group of things considered as a single unit. 2. A verb form that expresses the action or state of a grammatically singular subject.

**split infinitive** An infinitive with an element, usually an adverb, interposed between *to* and the verb, as *to boldly go.* See *Grammar,* **split infinitive.**

**strong verb** A verb such as *drink, ride,* or *speak,* that forms its past tense by a change in the vowel of the base form and that forms its past participle by a change in vowel and sometimes by adding *-n* or *-en.* See *Grammar,* **verbs, principal parts of.**

**subject** The noun, noun phrase, or pronoun in a sentence or clause that denotes the doer of the action or what is described by the predicate. In some sentences the subject is not a doer but is acted upon. This is true for sentences with verbs in the passive voice and for verbs with a passive meaning, such as *undergo* in *She underwent surgery to repair her shoulder.*

**subjunctive** The verbal mood that expresses the speaker's attitude about the likelihood or factuality of the situation and is also used in conditional clauses, in *that*-clauses making a command or expressing an intention, and in other clauses. See *Grammar*, **verbs, mood of** and **subjunctive.**

**subordinate clause** A dependent clause.

**subordinate conjunction** A conjunction, such as *after, because, if,* and *where,* that introduces a dependent clause.

**substantive** A word or group of words functioning as a noun, as *wealthy* in *Only the wealthy can afford to belong to that club.*

**suffix** An affix added to the end of a word, forming a new word or serving as an inflectional ending, as *-ness* in *gentleness, -ing* in *walking,* or *-s* in *sits.*

**superlative degree** The extreme degree of comparison of an adjective or adverb, as *best* and *brightest.*

**syntax** 1. The system of rules whereby words are combined to form grammatical phrases and sentences. 2. The pattern of word arrangement in a given phrase or sentence.

**tense** A set of verb forms that indicates the time (as past, present, or future) and the continuance or completion of the action or state. See *Grammar*, **verbs, tenses of.**

**transitive verb** A verb that requires a direct object to complete its meaning, carrying the action of the verb from the subject to the object. In the sentence *She played the waltz, play* is a transitive verb. In the sentence *She plays beautifully, play* is not transitive. See *Grammar*, **verbs, transitive and intransitive.**

**verb** A word that expresses existence, action, or occurrence.

**voice** A property of verbs that indicates the relationship between the subject and the action of the verb. See *Grammar*, **verbs, transitive and intransitive** and **verbs, voice of.**

**weak verb** A verb that forms its past tense and past participle by adding a suffix that ends in *-d, -ed,* or *-t,* as *start, have,* and *send.* See *Grammar*, **verbs, principal parts of.**

# Word Index

awaken, 141
awhile, 75

# B

backward, 75
backwards, 75
bad, 75
badly, 75
baited, 76
baleful, 76
balm, 228
banal, 215
baneful, 76
barbarism, 76
barbarity, 76
barbiturate, 215
barely, 15
bated, 76
be, 8, 29
because, 9, 63
behalf, 107
beloved, 220
beside, 76
besides, 76
best, 9, 76
better, 9, 18, 76
between, 30, 77
bimonthly, 77
bio- (prefix), 244
bit, 116
biweekly, 77
black, 190
blackguard, 215
blatant, 77
blessed, 220
blind, 191
blond, 171
boast, 78
boatswain, 215
bogey, 216
bogeyman, 216
bogy, 216
bogyman, 216
boogarman, 216

boogerman, 216
boogeyman, 216
boogieman, 216
boogyman, 216
born, 78
borne, 78
bos'n, 216
bo's'n, 216
bosun, 216
both, 26, 54, 60, 78
bouquet, 216
bowline, 216
breeches, 216
bring, 78
brooch, 216
brown, 191
brunet, 171
brung, 79
buggerman, 216
bulimia, 216
buoy, 216
burgeon, 79
but, 9, 10, 29, 60, 91
but also, 56

# C

cabal, 217
cache, 217
cachet, 217
cadre, 217
callous, 79
callus, 79
calm, 228
can, 8, 10, 104
cannot, 10
capital, 79
capitol, 79
careen, 79
career, 79
caring, 79
catacomb, 217
Caucasian, 191
Caucasoid, 191
celebrant, 80

celebrator, 80
Celt, 217
Celtic, 217
centenary, 217
center, 80
centi- (prefix), 153
cerebral, 217
certain, 80
challenged, 192
Chicana, 192, 200, 201
Chicano, 192, 200
chief, 1
choleric, 217
chord, 80
circular, 1
civilization, 76
claustrophobic, 81
clergy, 11
clique, 217
close, 3
close proximity, 60
clothes, 218
co- (prefix), 244, 254
coauthor, 75
cohort, 81
cohost, 105
colander, 218
color, 193
colored, 193
com- (prefix), 245
commentate, 82
committee, 11
companion, 172
compare, 82
complacent, 82
complaisant, 82
complement, 82
complete, 1, 82
compliment, 82
compose, 82
comprise, 82
comptroller, 218
concerning, 13, 25
conch, 218
conflicted, 83
connote, 88

only, 4, 23, 56
onto, 122
ophthalmia, 231
or, 16, 21, 22, 23, 55
-or (suffix), 231
oral, 74, 141
Oriental, 205
-osity (suffix), 250
ought, 24
-ous (suffix), 250
out- (prefix), 250
over- (prefix), 253

## P

Pacific Islanders, 189
pair, 122
palm, 228
pan- (prefix), 250
panegyric, 231
paradigm, 122
parallel, 1, 123
parameter, 123
parent, 183
parenting, 183
partner, 172
pass, 124
past, 124
pathogen, 160
penalize, 231
people, 124
percent, 124
percentage, 125
perfect, 1, 125
perimeter, 124
periodic, 125
perpendicular, 1
person of color, 205
personality, 125
persons, 124
persuade, 84
pert, 184
peruse, 126
phase, 96
phenomenon, 86, 126

physically challenged, 192
plead, 126
plus, 25
poinsettia, 231
politics, 126
pore, 126
portentous, 231
possessed, 126
POSSLQ, 172
post- (prefix), 250
posthumous, 231
potpourri, 231
pour, 126
practicable, 127
practical, 127
practically, 127
pre- (prefix), 250, 254
precipitate, 127
precipitous, 127
prefer, 229
premier, 127
prerogative, 220
prescribe, 128
presently, 128
prim, 184
prime, 1
primer, 231
principal, 128
principle, 128
prioritize, 128
pro- (prefix), 251, 254
proponent, 129
proscribe, 128
prosody, 232
protagonist, 128
prove, 129
proved, 129
proven, 129
provided, 129
providing, 129
pumpkin, 232

## Q

quark, 232
quarter, 129
quasi, 232
quasi- (prefix), 254
quay, 232
quite, 47
quixotic, 232
quote, 129

## R

race, 205
rack, 130
rarely, 19, 63
rather, 32, 56
ration, 232
re- (prefix), 251, 254
Realtor, 233
reason, 63
red, 206
redskin, 206
refer, 63, 71
reference, 71
regard, 130
remonstrate, 233
renaissance, 233
Renaissance, 233
renascence, 233
renege, 233
renown, 233
repel, 130
repulse, 130
research, 131
resemble, 60
respect, 130
responsible, 131
restaurateur, 172
restive, 131
restless, 131
retro- (prefix), 251
revert, 63
rhetoric, 61
ribald, 233

roof, 233
row, 234

# S

sacrilegious, 131
said, 131
same, 132
same-sex, 184
sarcophagi, 234
sassy, 184
SAT, 64
saucy, 184
savings, 132
scarcely, 15, 18, 32
scarify, 234
schism, 234
scone, 234
Scotch, 207
Scots, 207
Scottish, 207
sculptress, 174
seasonable, 132
seasonal, 132
secretive, 235
seem, 11
seldom, 63
self- (prefix), 251, 254
self-styled, 135
semi- (prefix), 251
semimonthly, 77
semiweekly, 77
senior, 207
senior citizen, 207
sensual, 132
sensuous, 132
series, 132
serve, 132
service, 132
set, 133
sex, 176
shall, 8, 32
shambles, 133
she, 177, 184
sheik, 235

-ship (suffix), 251
shone, 235
short-lived, 228
should, 8, 32, 33
showcase, 134
significant other, 172
similar, 235
sit, 133
sloth, 235
slow, 134
sneak, 134
snuck, 135
so, 7, 34
so-called, 135
so that, 34
some, 17
someday, 135
someplace, 94
sometime, 135
sonorous, 235
sooner, 56, 121, 135
specious, 136
spontaneity, 236
spouse-equivalent, 172
stamp, 136
stanch, 136
staunch, 136
stewardess, 174
stomp, 136
stratum, 136
strength, 236
suave, 184
sub- (prefix), 252
suffer, 136
suffragette, 175
surprise, 220
surveil, 136

# T

take, 78
teach, 136
team, 11
telepathy, 62
than, 7, 28, 30, 54, 56

that, 7, 34, 39, 40, 41, 70, 90
the, 236
their, 17
thence, 62
there, 40
thermo- (prefix), 252
thermometer, 220
they, 178
this, 41
though, 72
thusly, 136
tight, 137
tightly, 137
till, 137
tomato, 236
too, 137
topgallant, 236
topmast, 236
topsail, 236
tortuous, 138
torturous, 138
toward, 138
tragedy, 138
tragic, 138
trans- (prefix), 252
transpire, 138
trauma, 236
-trix (suffix), 175
troth, 236
try, 139
tsar, 86
-ty (suffix), 252

# U

un- (prefix), 252
-un (suffix), 247
unanticipated, 73
unaware, 139
unawares, 139
under- (prefix), 253
unexceptionable, 139
unexceptional, 139
uni- (prefix), 253

unique, 1, 139
until, 137
urbane, 184
used, 41
utilize, 140

# V

valet, 236
various, 140
vase, 237
VAT, 63
verbal, 140
very, 47
victual, 237
visually impaired, 199
vittle, 237
vivacious, 184

# W

wait on, 141
wait upon, 141
waitress, 174
wake, 141
waken, 141
want, 75, 141, 143
-ward (suffix), 253
-wards (suffix), 253

was, 38
way, 141
ways, 142
weaned, 142
well, 100, 142
wellness, 142
welsh, 207
were, 38
what, 47, 48
whatever, 48
when, 49
whence, 62
whenever, 48
where, 49
wherever, 48
whether, 90, 106
which, 39, 49
whichever, 48
while, 75
whilst, 237
white, 190, 208
who, 7, 40, 49
whoever, 48
whom, 49
whose, 27
why, 63
will, 8, 32
-wise (suffix), 143, 253
wish, 38, 143
wizen, 237
woke, 141

wonder, 38
won't, 4
world-class, 143
would, 8, 32, 33
wrack, 130
wreak, 143
wreck, 143
wrought, 143

# X

Xmas, 237

# Y

yellow, 208
yet, 144

# Z

zo- (prefix), 237
zoo- (prefix), 237, 253
zoonotic, 157

# Subject Index

## A

Abbreviations
  E-mail, 261, 262
  forming plurals, 240
Absolute construction
  defined, 264
  participles and, 24
  use of, 1
Absolute terms, 1-2
Active voice
  avoiding wordiness
    with, 64
  defined, 264
  use of, 46-47, 57, 58-
    59
Adjectives
  adverbial forms, 3
  comparison of, 2-3
  compounds, forming,
    254-256
  defined, 264
  participles as, 25
Adverbs
  *any* as an, 6
  comparison of, 3-4
  compounds, forming,
    255
  defined, 264
  double negative and, 15
  position of, 4
  *scarcely* as negative, 32
  split infinitives and, 34-
    35
Affixes
  defined, 264
  meanings of, alphabeti-
    cal listing, 244-253
  spelling changes, rules
    for, 242-243

Agreement
  defined, 264
  *either. . . or* and, 16
  pronouns, 27-28
  subject/verb, 35-37
Antecedent, defined, 264
Apostrophes, possessive
  constructions, 25-27
Appositive, defined, 264
Articles
  defined, 264
  indefinite, 66
  instead of personal pro-
    nouns, 178
Aspect, defined, 264
Assimilation, 214
Attributive, defined, 264
Auxiliary verbs
  *dare* as, 13
  defined, 265
  *must* as, 20
  *need* as, 20
  *ought* as, 23
  use of, 8

## B

Base form, defined, 265
Bulletin boards, E-mail,
  260

## C

Calculations, use in writing. See Scientific
  writing
Capitalization
  of *black*, 190
  compounds, forming,
    255

Case, defined, 265
Chat rooms, E-mail, 260
Clauses
  defined, 265
  elliptical, 12, 267
  *if* clauses, use of, 38
  *plus* as connector, 25
  restrictive/nonrestric-
    tive, 39, 50
  *scarcely* with, 32
  *should* in conditional,
    33
  *so/so that* in, 34
  subject of, 47-48
  *which* referring to, 49
Collective nouns, 11, 265
Color, compound adjec-
  tives, 257
Commas, use with
  adverbs, 4
  *but*, 10
  *whatever*, 48
Common nouns, defined,
  265
Comparative degree
  adjectives, 3
  adverbs, 3-4
  *better/best*, 9
  defined, 265
Comparisons
  absolute terms, 1-2
  defined, 265
Complement, defined,
  265
Complex sentence,
  defined, 265
Compound-complex sen-
  tence, defined, 265
Compound sentence,
  defined, 265

# O

Object
  defined, 270
  direct, 267
  indirect, 269
  transitive/intransitive
    verbs and, 45-46
Objective case
  defined, 270
  personal pronouns, 31
Objective complement,
    defined, 270
One-syllable words
  adding suffixes to, 242
  adjectives, adverbial
    forms, 3
  adjectives, compared, 2
Open compound word,
    253

# P

Parallelism
  *as* in, 7
  compound verbs, 55
  construction guidelines,
    51, 52-54
  constructions, 54-56
  defined, 270
  *either . . . or* and, 16
Participles. *See also*
    Dangling participles/
    modifiers
  absolute constructions, 1
  adjectives, use as, 25
  defined, 270
  fused (gerund and pos-
    sessives), 17
  past, 47
  prepositions, use as, 13,
    24, 27
  use of, 24
Passive voice
  abuses of, 59
  construction guidelines,
    56-57

  defined, 271
  double passive, 15
  past participles, 25
  use of, 46-47, 57-59
Past participles
  defined, 271
  use of, 25
  *very* and, 47
Past perfect tense, defined,
    271
Past tense
  defined, 271
  use of, 42
Past (were) subjunctive
    mood, 37
Perfect tense
  defined, 271
  use of, 42, 43
Permanent compound
    word, 254
Person
  defined, 271
  pronouns, agreement
    of, 27-28
  subject/verb agreement,
    35-36
Personal pronouns
  after *as*, 28-29
  after *but*, 29
  after *except*, 29-30
  after forms of *be*, 29
  after *than*, 30
  defined, 271
  objective case as sub-
    ject, 31
  *between you and I*, 30
Phrases
  defined, 271
  *had better*, as idiomatic
    verb phrase, 18
  hyphenating, 256
  modifying, 12
  prepositional, forming
    possessives, 26
Pluperfect tense, defined,
    271

Plurals
  collective nouns, 11
  defined, 271
  forming, 238-240
  *neither* and, 21
  pronouns, *any/anyone*
    with, 6
  subject/verb agreement,
    35-37
  verbs with *each*, 15-16
  verbs with *either*, 16
Positive degree, defined,
    272
Possessive case, defined,
    272
Possessives
  construction guidelines,
    26-27
  defined, 272
  forming, 241
  gerund and (fused par-
    ticiple), 17
  group, 26
Predicate, defined, 48, 272
Predicate adjective,
    defined, 272
Predicate nominative,
    defined, 272
Prefixes
  defined, 272
  formation, 254
Prepositional phrases
  dangling modifiers, 12
  defined, 272
  indicate possession, 26
Prepositions
  defined, 272
  ending a sentence, 27
  participles as, 13, 24, 27
Present participle, defined,
    272
Present perfect tense,
    defined, 272
Present tense
  defined, 272
  use of, 42